B형: 고1, 2

유형편

고득점 수능듣기

Listening Power Is in You

RHK
알엔비컨텐츠

집필진

이은지

현) 경기 성사중학교 교사
전) 경기 현산중학교 교사
San Diego State University TEFL/TESL Certificate 취득
한국외국어대학교 교육대학원 영어교육학과
한국외국어대학교 영어전공

박명재

현) 메가스터디 외국어 듣기 전문강사
현) 경선식 에듀 듣기 대표강사
전) EBS 듣기 대표강사
전) 비타에듀 외국어 듣기 대표강사
전) 강남 영독학원 외국어 듣기 대표강사
전) 청평 비타 외국어 듣기 대표강사

감수

변성우

현) 인천고등학교 교사
전) 인천공항중학교 교사
숙명여자대학교 SMU-TESOL Diploma
인하대학교 영어영문학과

Robert St. Claire

B형: 고1, 2 유형편

Listening Power Is in You

1판 1쇄 **인쇄** 2013년 3월 22일
1판 1쇄 **발행** 2013년 3월 29일

지은이 이은지 · 박명재

발행인 양원석
총편집인 이헌상
편집장 오수민
책임편집 유정윤
디자인 황선재
전산편집 함동춘
삽화 김태복
해외저작권 황지현, 지소연
제작 문태일, 김수진
영업마케팅 김경만, 임충진, 곽희은, 주상우, 장현기, 임우열, 정미진, 송기현, 우지연, 윤선미

펴낸 곳 ㈜알에이치코리아
주소 서울시 금천구 가산동 345-90 한라시그마밸리 20층
편집문의 02-6443-8800 **구입문의** 02-6443-8838
홈페이지 www.dobedobe.com
등록 2004년 1월 15일 제2-3726호

© 2013 이은지

ISBN 978-89-255-5015-2 (53740)

※ 두앤비컨텐츠는 ㈜알에이치코리아의 어학 전문 브랜드입니다.
※ 이 책은 ㈜알에이치코리아가 저작권자와의 계약에 따라 발행한 것이므로
   본사의 서면 허락 없이는 어떠한 형태와 수단으로도 이 책의 내용을 이용하지 못합니다.
※ 잘못된 책은 구입하신 서점에서 바꾸어 드립니다.
※ 책값은 뒤표지에 있습니다.

RHK 는 랜덤하우스코리아의 새 이름입니다.

Contents

이 책의 구성

신유형 전략법과 예시 문항 파악

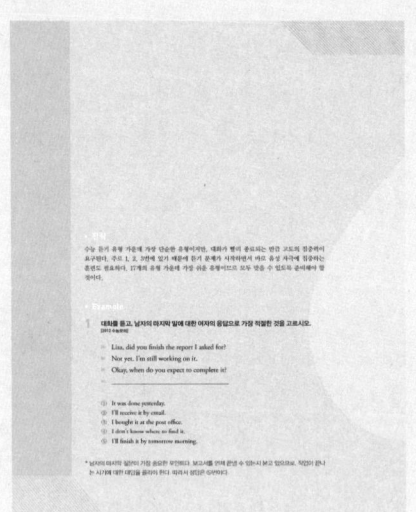

새로 등장한 수능 문제 유형을 해부해 봅니다. 신유형 문제의 특징이 무엇인지, 어떻게 접근해야 하는지, 어떤 전략을 써야 하는지를 간단하게 소개합니다. 그리고 답을 바로 찾는 고득점 수능 듣기 비법의 실마리를 제시합니다.

실전 연습 문제를 풀어봅니다. 16개의 유형에 맞춰 구성한 이 문제들은 수년간 입시 지도를 하고 계신 선생님들의 집필과 검수를 통해 엄선된 양질의 문제로 구성되어 있습니다. 따라서 시간 낭비할 필요 없이 수능에 나올 수밖에 없는 수능 듣기 모의고사를 알차게 풀어 볼 수 있습니다.

이 책의 구성

수능 듣기 유형 공부, 리스닝 웹(Listening Web)이 정답이다!

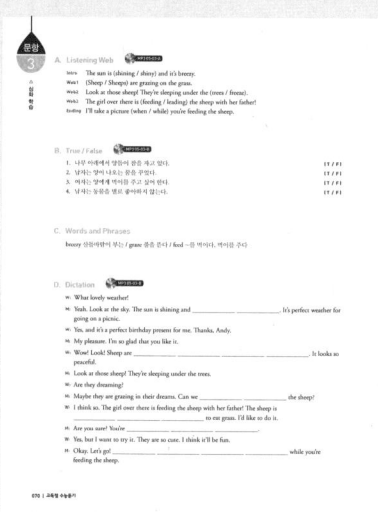

각각의 문제를 **Introduction-Web 1-Web 2-Web 3-Ending** 단계로 분석하여 영어식 사고의 틀에 맞춰 리스닝을 하는 것이 바로 '리스닝 웹'입니다. 한 방향으로 흘러가는 영어 문단 흐름 특성상 혼란스러울 수밖에 없는 지문을 하나의 큰 개념으로 이해할 수 있게 해주는 리스닝 웹. 이 리스닝 웹은 여러분이 여유를 갖고 머릿속에서 web을 그리며 수능 듣기를 할 수 있게 해 줍니다. 듣기에만 급급하고 성적 안 오르는 수능 듣기는 이제 안녕~

True or False로 듣기 대화문이나 담화문에서 내가 놓친 부분이 어디인지 좀 더 세밀하고 심층 있게 다룹니다. 한 지문으로 두세 문제를 푸는 효과가 있어 같은 시간에 남들보다 배로 공부하는 효과를 누릴 수 있습니다.

Words and Phrases로 주요 수능 어휘를 차근차근 정리할 수 있습니다. 앞에서 배운 지문에 쏙쏙 들어간 핵심 어휘가 집약적으로 들어 있어 어휘 학습이 보다 쉽습니다.

Dictation으로 지문을 완벽하게 정리할 수 있습니다. 받아쓰기(Dictation)는 듣기 실력 향상에 가장 기본적이면서 효과적인 방법입니다. 받아쓰기 동안의 반복 청취는 청취력 향상은 물론 어휘력 향상에도 큰 도움이 됩니다. 처음에는 단어, 구 단위로 받아쓰다가 점차로 문장 단위로 기억하며 받아 써 보세요. 그리고 들리지 않는 부분은 반복해서 듣다 보면 어느 순간 다음 지문 내용이 쉽게 느껴지게 됩니다.

수능 듣기 유형 가운데 가장 단순한 유형이지만, 대화가 빨리 종료되는 만큼 고도의 집중력이 요구된다. 주로 1, 2, 3번에 있기 때문에 듣기 문제가 시작하면서 바로 음성 자극에 집중하는 훈련도 필요하다. 17개의 유형 가운데 가장 쉬운 유형이므로 모두 맞을 수 있도록 준비해야 할 것이다.

Example

1 대화를 듣고, 남자의 마지막 말에 대한 여자의 응답으로 가장 적절한 것을 고르시오.
[2012 수능모의]

M: Lisa, did you finish the report I asked for?

W: Not yet. I'm still working on it.

M: Okay, when do you expect to complete it?

W: _____

① It was done yesterday.
② I'll receive it by email.
③ I bought it at the post office.
④ I don't know where to find it.
⑤ I'll finish it by tomorrow morning.

* 남자의 마지막 질문이 가장 중요한 포인트다. 보고서를 언제 끝낼 수 있는지 묻고 있으므로, 작업이 끝나는 시기에 대한 대답을 골라야 한다. 따라서 정답은 ⑤번이다.

유형 1

짧은 대화
응답 찾기

짧은 대화 응답 찾기

1 대화를 듣고, 남자의 마지막 말에 대한 여자의 응답으로 가장 적절한 것을 고르시오.

① Sorry, we don't carry milk.
② Do it as quickly as you can.
③ I don't take milk in my coffee.
④ Now it's cool enough for you to drink.
⑤ Okay. Two cups of coffee with milk, please.

2 대화를 듣고, 남자의 마지막 말에 대한 여자의 응답으로 가장 적절한 것을 고르시오.

① It's bittersweet.
② You're pretty good at P.E.
③ The speech practice really worked!
④ This is not the occasion for laughing!
⑤ Yeah, walking always makes you feel good.

3 대화를 듣고, 남자의 마지막 말에 대한 여자의 응답으로 가장 적절한 것을 고르시오.

① Now I'm in my 30s.
② You haven't changed a bit.
③ Have you been out of Korea?
④ I've been out of town on business.
⑤ I'm Cindy from New York. Do you remember me?

4 대화를 듣고, 여자의 마지막 말에 대한 남자의 응답으로 가장 적절한 것을 고르시오.

① Why not?
② It won't happen again.
③ You can say that again.
④ I totally agree with you.
⑤ Thank you for your support.

5 대화를 듣고, 남자의 마지막 말에 대한 여자의 응답으로 가장 적절한 것을 고르시오.

① Where did you put the glasses?
② I saw a glass of milk in the fridge.
③ Are these what you are looking for?
④ I've already put the glass on the desk.
⑤ I saw a glass of water in the bathroom.

6 대화를 듣고, 여자의 마지막 말에 대한 남자의 응답으로 가장 적절한 것을 고르시오.

① No, I can't tonight. Thanks anyway.
② Yes, I want to be introduced to Melissa.
③ Of course I really want to go to England.
④ Oh, thank you. How nice of you to ask me.
⑤ Melissa will come to the party this weekend.

7 대화를 듣고, 남자의 마지막 말에 대한 여자의 응답으로 가장 적절한 것을 고르시오.

① I can do that for you.
② I want to make up with you.
③ Things will get better. Cheer up!
④ Don't worry about it. I can get over it.
⑤ Why don't you write a letter to your friend first?

8 대화를 듣고, 여자의 마지막 말에 대한 남자의 응답으로 가장 적절한 것을 고르시오.

① Just open the window.
② When will it be ready?
③ I'd like a 6:30 wake-up call.
④ We'll send someone up in a minute.
⑤ If you need anything, please call me.

9 대화를 듣고, 여자의 마지막 말에 대한 남자의 응답으로 가장 적절한 것을 고르시오.

① We're not free until after lunch.
② Sorry, but I don't have a watch.
③ I'm sorry, but we can't make a guarantee.
④ We'll come to your office at six o'clock.
⑤ It's ten o'clock.

10 대화를 듣고, 여자의 마지막 말에 대한 남자의 응답으로 가장 적절한 것을 고르시오.

① Okay, I'll study first.
② I had a pop quiz today.
③ Yes, he always makes excuses.
④ I'll not break the rules. Don't worry.
⑤ Thanks, Mom. I'll be back in an hour.

해답/해설 240p

A. Listening Web  MP3 01-01-A

Intro Hurry up and finish your coffee. We'll be (laid / late)!

Web1 I can't. This coffee is too hot for me to (bring / drink).

Ending Why don't you put some (cold / cool) milk in it?

B. True / False  MP3 01-01-B

1. 두 사람은 시간이 넉넉하지 않은 상황이다.   (T / F)
2. 남자는 여자에게 커피를 빨리 마시길 권한다.   (T / F)
3. 여자는 아이스커피를 마시고 있다.   (T / F)
4. 남자는 여자에게 커피에 따뜻한 우유를 넣을 것을 권한다.   (T / F)

C. Words and Phrases

hurry up 서두르다

D. Dictation  MP3 01-01-B

M: Hurry up and _____ _____ _____. We'll be late!

W: I can't. This coffee is too hot _____ _____ _____ _____.

M: Why don't you put some cold _____ _____ _____?

A. Listening Web  MP3 01-02-A

Intro   Sally, I'm (walking / working) on air now.

Web1   Oh! What (happen / happened) to you?

Ending My (debate / donate) team has gone into the semi-final.

B. True / False  MP3 01-02-B

1. 두 사람은 지금 산책 중이다.   (T / F)
2. 남자는 기분이 좋다.   (T / F)
3. 여자는 토론대회 준비를 했다.   (T / F)
4. 남자는 토론대회에서 준결승에 진출했다.   (T / F)

C. Words and Phrases

walk on air 들뜨다 / debate 토론 / semi-final 준결승

D. Dictation  MP3 01-02-B

M: Sally, I'm _____ _____ _____ now.

W: Oh! What happened to you?

M: _____ _____ _____ has gone into the semi-final.

문항
3

△
심화
학습

A. Listening Web  MP3 01-03-A

Intro   I (have / haven't) seen you for ages.

Web1   It's been a (wrong / long) time, hasn't it?

Ending   Where have you (be / been)?

B. True / False  MP3 01-03-B

1. 남자와 여자는 한동안 만나지 못했다.   (T / F)
2. 남자는 여자를 알아보지 못했다.   (T / F)
3. 여자는 남자를 만나 반갑다.   (T / F)
4. 남자는 그동안 잘 지내지 못했다.   (T / F)

C. Words and Phrases

for ages 오랫동안

D. Dictation  MP3 01-03-B

M: Look who's here! I haven't seen you _____ _____.

W: I should say so. It's been a long time, _____ _____? How have you been?

M: Quite well. _____ _____ _____ _____?

A. Listening Web

Intro (Cooperation / Congratulations) on your graduation!
Web1 Mom, it's no big (bill / deal).
Ending You (deserve / reserve) it.

B. True / False

1. 여자는 남자에게 못마땅하다.   (T / F)
2. 남자는 졸업을 했다.   (T / F)
3. 남자는 직장에 다닌다.   (T / F)
4. 남자는 누구나 졸업을 하는 것이 아니라고 생각한다.   (T / F)

C. Words and Phrases

no big deal 별 일 아니다, 대수롭지 않다 / deserve ~을 받을 만 하다

D. Dictation

W: Congratulations on your graduations! I'm so _____ _____ _____.

M: Mom, it's no big deal. It happens to everyone.

W: No, you did a good job. You _____ _____.

A. Listening Web  MP3 01-05-A

Intro   Do you mind helping me find my (glass / glasses)?

Web1   Have you looked in the (bedroom / bathroom)?

Ending   I put them on the desk as far as I know, but I (can / can't) find them anywhere.

B. True / False  MP3 01-05-B

1. 남자는 안경을 찾는 중이다.   (T / F)
2. 여자는 남자가 책상을 고르는 것을 봐주고 있다.   (T / F)
3. 남자는 책상에 안경을 두고 왔다.   (T / F)
4. 여자는 남자의 부탁을 응해주고 있다.   (T / F)

C. Words and Phrases

glasses 안경 / as far as 내가 아는 한, 내가 기억하기로는

D. Dictation  MP3 01-05-B

M: Do you mind helping me _____ _____ _____?

W: Have you looked in the bathroom?

M: Yes, I have, but they weren't there. I put them on the desk _____ _____
_____ I know, but I can't find them anywhere.

A. Listening Web  MP3 01-06-A

Intro   What are you (do in / doing) this weekend?

Web1   We're having a (fair and / farewell) party for Melissa.

Web2   Right. She will (leave / live) for England soon.

Ending   I'd love to have you (join / joy and) us. Will you come?

B. True / False  MP3 01-06-B

1. 이번 주말 Melissa의 생일 파티가 열릴 것이다.   (T / F)
2. 여자는 주말에 영국에 갈 예정이다.   (T / F)
3. 여자는 남자가 파티에 오기를 바란다.   (T / F)
4. 남자는 여자의 제안에 반가워한다.   (T / F)

C. Words and Phrases

farewell party 환송회 / leave for ～로 떠나다

D. Dictation  MP3 01-06-B

M: What are you doing this weekend?

W: We're having a _____ _____ for Melissa.

M: Right. She will _____ _____ England soon.

W: I'd love to _____ _____ _____ _____. Will you come?

A. Listening Web  MP3 01-07-A

Intro   Why are you (pooling / pulling) the long (face / fence)?
Web1   I had a (terrible / trouble) argument with my friend.
Ending   Is there (anything / everything) I can do for you?

B. True / False  MP3 01-07-B

1. 여자는 얼굴이 긴 스타일이다.   (T / F)
2. 남자는 여자와 싸웠다.   (T / F)
3. 여자는 난처한 사항에 처해있다.   (T / F)
4. 남자는 여자에게 미안해하고 있다.   (T / F)

C. Words and Phrases

pull a long face 우울한 얼굴을 하다 / argument 논쟁, 말싸움 / get over (힘든 일을)잊고 극복하다

D. Dictation  MP3 01-07-B

M: Why are you _____ _____ _____ _____?

W: I had a _____ _____ with my friend. She never wants to talk to me again.

M: I'm sorry to hear that. Is there anything I can do for you?

A. Listening Web  MP3 01-08-A

Intro   The air conditioner is never turned (on / off).

Web1   We'll take care (about / of) it right away.

Ending   I'm staying in room (613 / 630).

B. True / False  MP3 01-08-B

1. 여자가 머무르는 방의 에어컨이 작동하지 않는다.   (T / F)
2. 여자는 수리공을 불렀다.   (T / F)
3. 여자는 613호에 머무르고 있다.   (T / F)
4. 남자는 여자의 문제를 해결해주려고 한다.   (T / F)

C. Words and Phrases

air conditioner 에어컨 / turn on 켜다 / right away 즉시, 곧바로

D. Dictation  MP3 01-08-B

W: Excuse me. The air conditioner is never _____ _____.

M: I'm really sorry. We'll _____ _____ _____ _____ right away. What's your room number?

W: I'm staying in room _____.

문항
9

△
심화
학습

A. Listening Web

Intro   I'd like (the better / a bottle of) ice water, please.

Web1   Cold items are not (available / valid) right now.

Ending   What time are you going to be (heady / ready) again?

B. True / False

1. 여자는 얼음물을 마시고 싶다.   (T / F)
2. 남자는 감기에 걸렸다.   (T / F)
3. 여자는 현재 시간이 궁금하다.   (T / F)
4. 남자는 지금 찬물을 제공할 수 없다.   (T / F)

C. Words and Phrases

power 전기 / fridge 냉장고 / available 구할 수 있는

D. Dictation

W: I'd like a bottle of ice water, please.

M: I'm sorry. The _____ _____ _____ now and the fridge isn't working. Cold items are not _____ right now.

W: What time are you _____ _____ _____ _____ again?

A. Listening Web

Intro   Have you already finished (study / studying)?

Web1   I need a (brave / break).

Ending   Daniel, you're constantly (make an excuse / making excuses).

B. True / False

1. 여자는 남자가 공부하기를 바란다.   (T / F)
2. 남자는 공부를 끝냈다.   (T / F)
3. 여자는 남자의 행동이 못마땅하다.   (T / F)
4. 남자는 여자의 아들이다.   (T / F)

C. Words and Phrases

break 휴식 / constantly 계속해서 / excuse 핑계

D. Dictation

W: Where are you going? Have you already finished studying?

M: Mom, I promise I'll be back ＿＿＿＿＿ ＿＿＿＿＿ ＿＿＿＿＿ and prepare for the exam. ＿＿＿＿＿ ＿＿＿＿＿ ＿＿＿＿＿ ＿＿＿＿＿.

W: Daniel, you're constantly ＿＿＿＿＿ ＿＿＿＿＿.

적절한 의견 찾기 유형은 행간의 의미를 파악하는 것이 관건이다. 화자가 자신의 의견을 명확히 드러내지 않을 수도 있다. 따라서 대화의 흐름을 이해하고, 화자가 그 발언을 통해 진정 말하고자 하는 것이 무엇인지를 파악해야 한다.

• Example

1 대화를 듣고, 여자의 의견으로 가장 적절한 것을 고르시오. [2012 수능모의]

M: Emily, it's my first time flying. What time should we meet at the airport tomorrow?

W: Well, our flight leaves at 9, so around 6.

M: So early? Do we need to be at the airport for three hours?

W: Sure. It'll take a long time to get boarding passes and pass through security.

M: Does it really take that long?

W: Yeah. And since you're planning on checking in your bags, you need enough time for that as well.

M: Ah, I understand. I also want to get a digital camera in duty-free.

W: Cool, then you'll want to leave time for that.

M: All right then. See you early at 6 tomorrow!

① 여권 만기일을 확인해야 한다.
② 보안 검색 절차를 따라야 한다.
③ 항공권은 미리 예약하는 것이 좋다.
④ 공항에 여유 있게 일찍 도착해야 한다.
⑤ 세관 신고 물품을 확인할 필요가 있다.

* 보딩 패스를 받고 보안 검색을 통과하는데 시간이 오래 걸리므로 결론적으로 여자는 공항에 일찍 도착해야 한다는 말을 한 것이다. 따라서 정답은 ④번이다.

유형 2

적절한
의견 찾기

Unit 02 적절한 의견 찾기

유형 2

1 대화를 듣고, 여자의 의견으로 가장 적절한 것을 고르시오.

① 후진국은 환경 오염과 관련이 없다.
② 사람들의 난개발이 환경 오염을 부추겼다.
③ 우리 모두 환경 오염의 심각성을 인지해야 한다.
④ 선진국이 환경 오염에 더 큰 책임감을 가져야 한다.
⑤ 환경 오염에 대한 각국 정부의 엄격한 조치가 필요하다.

2 대화를 듣고, 여자의 의견으로 가장 적절한 것을 고르시오.

① 유학 중 친척에게 신세를 지는 것은 좋지 않다.
② 영어 공부를 위해 굳이 미국에 갈 필요는 없다.
③ 유학 문제는 부모님과 상의하여 결정해야 한다.
④ 기숙사 생활은 영어를 연습하는 데 도움이 된다.
⑤ 친구를 너무 많이 사귀는 것은 유학 생활에 도움이 되지 않는다.

3 대화를 듣고, 남자의 의견으로 가장 적절한 것을 고르시오.

① 산장에 울타리를 쳐야 한다.
② 국립 공원의 자연을 보호해야 한다.
③ 야간 운전은 위험하니 삼가야 한다.
④ 야생동물을 만나면 죽은 척해야 한다.
⑤ 야생동물 보호 규정을 만들어야 한다.

4 대화를 듣고, 여자의 의견으로 가장 적절한 것을 고르시오.

① 친구의 대학 합격에는 중대한 문제가 있다.
② 대학별 입시 전략을 세우는 것이 중요하다.
③ 대학의 합격 기준이 모호해서 이해할 수 없다.
④ 포트폴리오 구성에 여름 캠프 참가는 필수적이다.
⑤ 성적은 대학 입시에서 사실상 결정적인 부분을 차지한다.

5 대화를 듣고, 남자의 의견으로 가장 적절한 것을 고르시오.

① 새벽에는 밥을 먹고 싶지 않다.
② 내일 새벽 일찍 출발해야 한다.
③ 아이들은 7시 이후에 깨워야 한다.
④ 내일은 차 안에서 도시락을 먹어야 한다.
⑤ 휴가철에 휴가를 떠나는 것은 매우 지치는 일이다.

6 대화를 듣고, 남자의 의견으로 가장 적절한 것을 고르시오.

① 뱃삯을 깎아보자.
② 일단 비를 피하자.
③ 두 곳에 모두 가자.
④ 여행은 다음번에 가자.
⑤ 세 시간 후에 표를 사자.

7 대화를 듣고, 여자의 의견으로 가장 적절한 것을 고르시오.

① 차려놓은 음식은 다 먹어야 한다.
② 45분 뒤에 요리를 시작해야 한다.
③ 남자가 가게에 다녀오는 것이 좋겠다.
④ 감자튀김을 패스트푸드점에서 사 먹는 것이 좋겠다.
⑤ 여자가 직접 마음에 드는 샐러드 드레싱을 고를 것이다.

8 대화를 듣고, 여자의 의견으로 가장 적절한 것을 고르시오.

① 왔던 길로 되돌아가야 한다.
② 택시를 타고 이동해야 한다.
③ 주차장 표지판을 따라가야 한다.
④ 나무가 우거진 길로 가는 것이 좋다.
⑤ 각자 가고 싶은 길로 가는 것이 좋다.

9 대화를 듣고, 여자의 의견으로 가장 적절한 것을 고르시오.

① 소설 위대한 유산은 꼭 읽어봐야 한다.
② 찰스 디킨스는 독자들을 배려한 훌륭한 작가이다.
③ 인기 있는 드라마는 결말을 연장하지 말아야 한다.
④ TV를 함께 볼 때는 상대방을 배려할 줄 알아야 한다.
⑤ 인기 있는 드라마는 시청자의 의견을 받아들여야 한다.

10 대화를 듣고, 여자의 의견으로 가장 적절한 것을 고르시오.

① 동물 보호 협회에 가입할 것이다.
② 프리덤 푸드 소비를 막아야 한다.
③ 동물들도 자유로운 환경에서 길러져야 한다.
④ 더 많은 동물 보호 운동가들의 활동이 필요하다.
⑤ 부드러운 고기를 얻기 위해서 동물들을 가둘 수 있다.

해답/해설 242p

A. Listening Web

Intro   There are a lot of cars on the street, fuming out (exhaust / just) gas.

Web1   The government should take some strong actions (again / against) those kinds of car owners.

Web2   Now that the developed (countries / counties) face some serious environmental problems, they want to share the responsibility with underdeveloped countries.

Ending I think it's (fair / unfair) to share the same amount of responsibility with them.

B. True / False

1. 남자는 매연으로 숨을 쉴 수가 없다.   (T / F)
2. 남자는 환경 문제 중 대기오염이 가장 심각하다고 생각한다.   (T / F)
3. 여자는 환경 오염의 심각성을 잘 인지하지 못하고 있다.   (T / F)
4. 남자는 모두가 환경 보호에 힘써야 한다고 생각한다.   (T / F)

C. Words and Phrases

fume out exhaust gas 배기가스를 내뿜다 / take actions 조치를 취하다 / developed country 선진국 / underdeveloped country 후진국

D. Dictation

M: I can't breathe. There are a lot of cars on the street, fuming out exhaust gas.

W: The government should _____ _____ _____ _____ against those kinds of car owners. They're polluting the air, causing a lot of environmental problems…

M: You're right.

W: But _____ _____ _____ _____ has responsibility for these environmental problems like air pollution?

M: What do you mean?

W: Who spoiled the earth? Now that the _____ _____ face some serious environmental problems, they want to share the responsibility with _____ _____.

M: Well, we have only one earth and limited natural resources. We all should protect the environment.

W: Yes. But I think _____ _____ to share the same _____ _____ responsibility with them.

A. Listening Web  MP3 02-02-A

Intro I'm (planting / planning) to go to America to study English.

Web1 My uncle lives there. Maybe I'll stay there and (coming to / commute to) school.

Web2 Why don't you (live in / living) a dorm?

Web3 Making foreign friends, speaking in English all the time, and experiencing American students' lives, will all help you to improve your English.

Ending I'll (discuss / discuss on) it with my parents again.

B. True / False  MP3 02-02-B

1. 남자는 여름 방학에 미국에 갈 것이다.   (T / F)
2. 여자는 여름 방학 동안 영어 공부를 할 계획이다.   (T / F)
3. 남자는 기숙사 생활을 좋아하지 않는다.   (T / F)
4. 남자의 부모님은 기숙사 생활을 반대하신다.   (T / F)

C. Words and Phrases

commute 통근하다 / strict 엄격한 / improve 개선시키다

D. Dictation  MP3 02-02-B

W: What are you going to do this summer vacation?

M: I'm planning to go to America to study English.

W: Where are you going in America?

M: L.A. My uncle lives there. Maybe I'll stay there and _____ _____ _____.

W: Why don't you _____ _____ _____ _____?

M: It's expensive, and maybe there are _____ _____...

W: But you'll speak only Korean when you're home. You need to _____ _____ every day for 24 hours, don't you?

M: Yes, but I don't want to share a room with somebody _____ _____ _____.

W: Make friends with them. Making foreign friends, speaking in English all the time, and experiencing American students' lives, will all _____ _____ _____ _____ your English.

M: Well, I think you're right. I'll _____ _____ with my parents again.

A. Listening Web

Intro	I was kind of scared because it's so dark and I almost (hit / kick) an animal.
Web1	I only saw a (dead / that) animal body.
Web2	I think it's very (danger / dangerous) to let wild animals live that way.
Web3	The National Park (authorities / authority) need to make regulations to protect them.
Ending	We must not (hurl / hurt) them.

B. True / False

1. 여자는 세 시간 동안 차를 타고 왔다.   (T / F)
2. 여자는 오는 길에 야생동물과 마주쳤다.   (T / F)
3. 남자는 살아있는 야생동물을 차로 치었다.   (T / F)
4. 국립 공원 당국은 야생동물을 위한 전용 길을 설치 중이다.   (T / F)

C. Words and Phrases

authorities 당국, 관계자 / fence 울타리 치다 / trail 산길 / regulation 규정 / encounter 마주치다

D. Dictation

W: Is everybody here? Am I the last?

M: No. David is still coming.

W: It took about three hours. It was a long journey. I was _____ _____ _____ because it's so dark and I almost _____ _____ _____.

M: You have to be careful. There are some wild animals around here.

W: Did you also _____ _____ _____ _____ on the way?

M: Yes, but I only saw a dead animal body.

W: No way. I think it's very dangerous to _____ _____ _____ _____ that way. They are always injured _____ _____.

M: I think the National Park authorities need to _____ _____ to protect them.

W: Like fencing or a trail for the wild animals.

M: Yes, we must not hurt them.

W: Oh! Here comes David! Hi, David!

A. Listening Web  MP3 02-04-A

Intro   Eunice, did you hear the news?

Web1   Steve got (accepted / upset) to Blooming University. It doesn't make sense!

Web2   He has been (anger / eager) to make his own portfolio. He was enthusiastically (involved in / involving) a lot of activities.

Web3   Brian, grades are not everything. Maybe Blooming University wants more (acting / active) students, and Steve had an excellent strategy.

Ending   You're a smart student, Brian. Some other good universities will want you to (calm / come).

B. True / False  MP3 02-04-B

1. 남자는 원했던 대학으로부터 입학허가를 받지 못했다.   (T / F)
2. Steve는 Brian보다 성적이 우수하지 않았다.   (T / F)
3. Brian은 마지막 학기에 전 과목 A를 받았다.   (T / F)
4. Steve는 3년 내내 우등상을 받았다.   (T / F)

C. Words and Phrases

make sense 뜻을 이루다, 이치에 맞다 / eager to ~를 열렬히 하고 싶어하다 / enthusiastically 열정적으로 / strategy 전략

D. Dictation  MP3 02-04-B

M: Eunice, did you hear the news?

W: What?

M: Steve _____ _____ _____ Blooming University. It doesn't _____ _____!

W: _____ _____ _____. What's the matter?

M: He didn't do well in school. I got _____ A's last semester, but I failed to get accepted. And he's a Blooming student now.

W: Calm down. Steve is worth it. He has been _____ _____ _____ his own portfolio. Do you remember that he was the leader of our summer camp last year? He was enthusiastically _____ _____ a lot of activities.

M: You know _____ _____ _____ through all three years.

W: Brian, grades are not everything. Maybe Blooming University wants more active students, and Steve had an _____ _____.

M: I cannot _____ this situation.

W: You're a smart student, Brian. Some other good universities will want you to come.

A. Listening Web    MP3 02-05-A

Intro   What time are we (leaving / living) tomorrow?

Web1   Five in the morning. The holiday (season / seas) started yesterday, so I think there is a lot of (traffic / terrific).

Web2   But it's hard for the kids to get up before five.

Ending   But if we (don't / won't) leave at five, it'll take more than five hours. It'll make all of us tired before we get there.

B. True / False    MP3 02-05-B

1. 두 사람은 내일 아이들과 휴가를 떠날 계획이다.   (T / F)
2. 남자는 내일 길이 많이 막힐 것이라고 예상한다.   (T / F)
3. 여자는 도착하기 전에 지칠까 봐 걱정하고 있다.   (T / F)
4. 남자는 집에서 아침 식사를 하자고 제안한다.   (T / F)

C. Words and Phrases

be stuck in the traffic 교통체증에 막히다 / highway service area 고속도로 휴게소

D. Dictation    MP3 02-05-B

W: What time are we leaving tomorrow?

M: Five in the morning.

W: That's too early. I'm not sure I can get up so early.

M: The holiday season started yesterday, so I think there is _____ _____ _____ _____.

W: But it's hard for the kids to get up before five.

M: If we leave after seven, we'll be _____ _____ _____.

W: But we need to have breakfast before leaving.

M: What about eating at a highway service area or carrying a breakfast box?

W: I don't think we'll have _____ _____ _____ _____ a breakfast box tomorrow morning.

M: But if we don't leave at five, it'll take more than five hours. It'll make _____ _____ _____ _____ way before we get there.

A. Listening Web

Intro There's no (ticket / tickets) to only Springville.

Web1 The board says the ship goes to both Springville and Summerfield on Sunday. There's (no / none) ship that goes to only one of them.

Web2 But Summerfield (was / wasn't) on our itinerary.

Ending It's (across / close) to our town, and we can come again any time. Let's take a rain check.

B. True / False

1. 여자는 Summerfield에 가고 싶어 한다.   (T / F)
2. 남자는 Springville에만 가고 싶어 한다.   (T / F)
3. Summerfield는 오렌지로 유명하다.   (T / F)
4. Summerfield에 가는 데 일인당 50달러이다.   (T / F)

C. Words and Phrases

board 게시판 / itinery 여행 일정 / take a rain check 다음 기회로 미루다

D. Dictation

M: How much is the ticket to Springville?

W: There's no ticket to only Springville.

M: What do you mean?

W: _____ _____ _____ the ship goes to both Springville and Summerfield on Sunday. There's no ship that goes to only _____ _____ _____.

M: But Summerfield wasn't on our itinerary.

W: But it's not bad to travel to both. It takes only two more hours and Summerfield is very _____ _____ its beautiful buildings with orange roofs.

M: How much is the _____ _____ both of them?

W: $25. Transportation and admission _____ _____.

M: Then we need to spend $50 for both of us. It's too expensive. I'm not _____ _____ _____ _____ Summerfield.

W: We didn't plan to go to Summerfield this time, but I want to go there someday. I think this is the chance.

M: It's close to our town, and we can come again any time. Let's take _____ _____ _____.

W: Okay.

문항 7

△
심화
학습

A. Listening Web

MP3 02-07-A

Intro   What about having some (fried / frying) potatoes?

Web1   Well, let's (fly / fry) them at home. Your fried potatoes are more delicious.

Web2   But we don't have any (potato / potatoes). Will you go to the mart and buy some potatoes?

Web3   How about going to the mart and (get in / getting) some milk and potatoes, and a salad dressing you'd like?

Ending   You want me to run an errand.

B. True / False

MP3 02-07-B

1. 남자는 지금 배가 고프다.   (T / F)
2. 지금 감자가 다 떨어졌다.   (T / F)
3. 남자는 집에 있는 우유와 샐러드를 먹기로 했다.   (T / F)
4. 여자는 시장에 갈 것이다.   (T / F)

C. Words and Phrases

do an errand 심부름하다

D. Dictation

MP3 02-07-B

M: I'm feeling a little hungry, Mom. What about having some fried potatoes?

W: Do you ＿＿＿＿＿＿ ＿＿＿＿＿＿ ＿＿＿＿＿＿ ＿＿＿＿＿＿ potatoes or to go buy fried potatoes?

M: Well, let's fry them at home. Your fried potatoes are more delicious.

W: But we don't have any potatoes. Will you go to the mart and buy some potatoes?

M: Then it'll take a lot of time. It'll take about 30 minutes to buy potatoes and about 15 more ＿＿＿＿＿＿ to cook them.

W: Yes, maybe the fried potatoes would be ready ＿＿＿＿＿＿ ＿＿＿＿＿＿ 45 minutes.

M: Mom, I think it's better to buy fried potatoes at a fast food restaurant.

W: But we need milk and salad dressing. How about going to the mart and getting some milk and potatoes, and a salad dressing ＿＿＿＿＿＿ ＿＿＿＿＿＿?

M: Mom, you want me to ＿＿＿＿＿＿ ＿＿＿＿＿＿ ＿＿＿＿＿＿.

W: Brian, it's all for you anyway.

M: Okay, Mom.

A. Listening Web  MP3 02-08-A

Intro   Now let's move (in / on) to the next destination.

Web1   There are two (paths / pats) to go down.

Web2   Yes, but (we came up / we kind of) that way.

Web3   But we can make a (detour / the tour) (around / ground) the mountain, or what if the parking lot
        isn't the very parking lot where we parked?

Ending   But if I'm right, we'll spend a lot (of / on) riding a taxi.

B. True / False  MP3 02-08-B

1. 두 사람은 지금 산에 올라와 있다.   (T / F)
2. 산에서 내려가는 길이 두 갈래로 갈라져 있다.   (T / F)
3. 표지판에 따르면, 나무가 우거진 길이 주차장으로 가는 길이다.   (T / F)
4. 여자는 새로운 길로 내려가기를 원한다.   (T / F)

C. Words and Phrases

scenery 경치 / detour 우회로 / tree-shaded 나무가 우거진, 나무 그늘이 있는

D. Dictation  MP3 02-08-B

M: Wow! The view is really fantastic!

W: Yeah, this is the most beautiful scenery _____ _____ _____.

M: Now let's _____ _____ _____ the next destination.

W: Okay. Let's go down to the parking lot. Andy, Look! There are two paths to go down.

M: The sign says _____ _____ _____ for the parking lot.

W: Yes, but we came up that way.

M: I think we need to follow the sign to the mountain.

W: But we can _____ _____ _____ around the mountain, or what if the
   parking lot isn't the very parking lot where we parked?

M: No way.

W: But if I'm right, we'll spend a lot on riding a taxi.

M: _____ _____ _____ the case! Don't worry. This way is tree-shaded, and
   it looks much better. Follow me.

W: Oh, Andy please.

A. Listening Web

Intro The soap opera you like (has / have) just started.

Web1 See any other program you'd like to see. Once the soap operas become popular, they're always (extended / extend it).

Web2 Because people keep asking (for / four) extensions on the website.

Ending I know. But it's not right. It almost got close to the ending, but it seemed to develop another topic. Now it's a quite different story.

B. True / False

1. 여자가 좋아하던 드라마가 끝났다.   (T / F)
2. 남자는 웹사이트에 드라마를 연장해 달라고 부탁할 예정이다.   (T / F)
3. 여자는 소설 위대한 유산의 결말이 두 개인 것을 모르고 있었다.   (T / F)
4. 여자는 드라마의 결말 연장에 긍정적인 입장이다.   (T / F)

C. Words and Phrases

soap opera 드라마 / extend 연장시키다 / cannot help ~ing ~하는 것을 피할 수 없다, 하지 않을 수 없다

D. Dictation

M: The soap opera you like has just started. Come on!

W: No. See any other program you'd like to see.

M: Why? Isn't it interesting anymore?

W: No.

M: What happened?

W: Once the soap operas become popular, they're _____ _____.

M: Because people keep asking for extensions on the website.

W: I know. But it's not right. It almost got close _____ _____ _____, but it seemed to _____ _____ _____. Now it's a quite different story.

M: It happens _____ _____ _____. Do you know that Charles Dickens' "Great Expectations" has _____ _____ _____?

W: No, I didn't know that.

M: The novel was so popular and people back then asked for a happy ending. So the author _____ _____ _____ it. And he wrote the original ending and also a more _____ _____.

W: That's interesting. But that extended soap opera isn't interesting.

A. Listening Web

Intro   'Freedom food'? What is that?

Web1   A lot of animals are (an ethically / unethically) raised. For example, calves are locked up in a small box and can't move. Because a lack of physical activity makes tender meat.

Web2   So 'freedom food' means that this food is from animals raised on a large (farm / palm).

Ending I think we need to (consume / subsume) this kind of food and encourage the ethical farmers.

B. True / False

1. 남자가 먹고 있는 스테이크는 프리덤 푸드이다.   (T / F)
2. 여자는 동물 윤리보다 소비자의 입맛에 부응하는 것이 더 중요하다고 생각한다.   (T / F)
3. 남자는 동물 보호 운동가이다.   (T / F)
4. 윤리적인 농부들은 동물들을 좁은 곳에서 키운다.   (T / F)

C. Words and Phrases

unethically 비윤리적으로 / calf 송아지 (복수: calves) / tender 부드러운, 씹기 쉬운 /
animal rights activist 동물 보호 운동가

D. Dictation

W: How is the steak?

M: Very delicious. Is it different from _____ _____ _____ _____ eat?

W: Yes, it's 'freedom food.'

M: 'Freedom food'? What is that?

W: A lot of animals are _____ _____. For example, calves are _____ _____ in a small box and can't move.

M: Why is that?

W: Because a lack of _____ _____ makes tender meat.

M: The farmers take the freedom away from the animals to make money.

W: That's right.

M: So 'freedom food' means that this food is from animals _____ _____ a large farm.

W: Exactly. I think we need to consume this kind of food and encourage the ethical farmers.

M: Wow. You're like an _____ _____ _____.

담화의 주제와 목적은 수능에 반드시 출제되는 유형이다. 담화의 요지를 찾는 것은 듣기 이해에 핵심이 되는 인지 활동인 만큼 잘 연습해 둘 필요가 있다. 담화의 큰 그림을 파악하면 사소한 부분을 놓치더라도 정답을 고르는데 크게 어려움이 있지는 않지만, 크게 들리는 몇 가지 세부 사항만으로 섣불리 정답을 고르는 것은 오답의 대표적인 사례가 된다. 따라서 세부 사항에 지나치게 집중하지 말고, 호흡을 길게 전체적인 내용을 파악할 수 있도록 연습하는 것이 중요하다. 단독 문제로 출제될 뿐만 아니라, 세트형 문제에서 첫 번째 문제로도 등장하는 유형이므로 절대 놓치지 말자.

• Example

1 다음을 듣고, 남자가 하는 말의 주제로 가장 적절한 것을 고르시오. [2011 수능기출]

M: Last class, we talked about the possible link between blood type and personality. Today, we have another very interesting topic to discuss. Do you have a favorite position that you go to sleep in? Well, a British study has shown that there may be a relationship between sleeping position and personality. For example, if you like to curl up on your side, you're often shy and sensitive. If you lie straight on your side like a "log," that means you're generally easygoing and social. A person who lies on his back with his arms stuck to his side like a soldier is usually quite reserved. Which one are you?

① 나이에 따른 성격의 변화
② 나쁜 잠버릇을 고치는 방법
③ 타고난 기질이 안 바뀌는 이유
④ 수면 자세와 성격 간의 관련성
⑤ 혈액형과 성격 간의 연관 가능성

* 혈액형과 성격과의 관계는 지난 시간의 주제였고, 오늘의 주제는 수면 자세와 성격과의 관계이다. 따라서 답은 ④번이다.

유형 3

주제 및
목적 찾기

주제 및 목적 찾기

1 다음을 듣고, 여자가 하는 말의 목적으로 가장 적절한 것을 고르시오.

① 새로 생긴 공원을 홍보하려고
② 여름휴가 장소를 권유하려고
③ 공원 내 자연보호 규정을 강조하려고
④ 공원 내 텐트 철거를 안내하려고
⑤ 방문객들에게 감사의 인사를 전하려고

2 다음을 듣고, 남자가 하는 말의 목적으로 가장 적절한 것을 고르시오.

① 반바지 교복을 건의하기 위해
② 에어컨 설치를 요청하기 위해
③ 방송국에 감사의 인사를 전하기 위해
④ 전기 수요 급증 사태를 경고하기 위해
⑤ 전기 절약 방법에 대한 조언을 구하기 위해

3 다음을 듣고, 여자가 하는 말의 목적으로 가장 적절한 것을 고르시오.

① 연회에 초대하기 위해
② 할인 행사를 홍보하기 위해
③ 호텔의 특징을 설명하기 위해
④ 호텔 이용 후기를 남기기 위해
⑤ 호텔 서비스에 감사를 표하기 위해

4 다음을 듣고, 남자가 하는 말의 목적으로 가장 적절한 것을 고르시오.

① 세 가지 R의 의미를 설명하기 위해
② 재활용의 중요성을 알리기 위해
③ 쓰레기를 줄이는 방법을 알리기 위해
④ 쓰레기 분리수거 방법을 알리기 위해
⑤ 쓰레기가 지구에 미치는 영향을 설명하기 위해

5 다음을 듣고, 여자가 하는 말의 주제로 가장 적절한 것을 고르시오.

① 독서의 일반적 목적
② 지나친 독서의 역기능
③ 독서를 통한 발전 가능성
④ 책에 대한 객관적 태도의 중요성
⑤ 나와 타인을 대하는 객관적 태도의 필요성

6 다음을 듣고, 남자가 하는 말의 주제로 가장 적절한 것을 고르시오.

① 현재 멸종 위기에 처한 동식물의 종류
② 멸종 위기의 동식물 보호구역의 필요성
③ 해안에 서식하는 동식물들의 멸종 과정
④ 멸종 위기의 동식물을 보호해야 하는 이유
⑤ 멸종 위기의 동식물 보호에 대한 정부 정책

7 다음을 듣고, 여자가 하는 말의 주제로 가장 적절한 것을 고르시오.

① 수화의 과학적 근거
② 수화의 다양한 표현력
③ 동물의 언어 습득 능력
④ 동물의 다양한 의사소통 방식
⑤ 동물에 따른 언어 습득 능력의 차이

8 다음을 듣고 남자가 하는 말의 요지로 가장 적절한 것을 고르시오.

① 미래 광고 시장의 전망
② 청소년 광고 출현의 문제점
③ 광고가 청소년에 미치는 부정적 영향
④ 광고가 상품의 이미지 형성에 미치는 영향
⑤ 전체 광고 시장에서 TV 광고의 지배적인 영향력

9 대화를 듣고, 두 사람의 대화의 주제로 가장 적절한 것을 고르시오.

① 장애인 가족의 애환
② 맹인 안내견 훈련 방법
③ 장애인을 돕는 애완동물
④ 원숭이와 강아지의 좋은 점
⑤ 장애인 삶의 질을 향상시키는 방법

10 대화를 듣고, 두 사람의 대화의 주제로 가장 적절한 것을 고르시오.

① 회사의 복지제도
② 직장생활의 고충
③ 상사의 다양한 유형
④ 직장에서 감정 조절하는 법
⑤ 성공적인 직장생활에 대한 지침

해답/해설 247p

A. Listening Web  MP3 03-01-A

Intro Good evening, visitors. This is Green Park's main office.

Web1 So please strike your tents before 9 p.m. for your (safely / safety).

Web2 We are temporarily allowing you to set up tents or awnings during the daytime since there are (a few / few) trees and (a little / little) shade.

Web3 But if you leave your tent up in the dark, it can stand (another's / in others') way.

Ending Thank you in advance for your (cooperation / corporation).

B. True / False  MP3 03-01-B

1. 공원 이용의 불편함 때문에 방문객들의 불만이 많다.　　　　　　　　　　(T / F)
2. 규정상 공원 내에서는 야간에 불을 켤 수 없다.　　　　　　　　　　　　(T / F)
3. 낮에는 텐트와 차양 사용이 허용된다.　　　　　　　　　　　　　　　　(T / F)
4. 밤 9시 이후에 텐트를 사용하려면 요금을 내야 한다.　　　　　　　　　　(T / F)

C. Words and Phrases

strike the tent 텐트를 걷다 / temporarily 일시적으로 / stand in one's way 길을 막다 / in advance 미리

D. Dictation  MP3 03-01-B

W: Good evening, visitors. This is Green Park's main office. We hope you're enjoying summer with your family or friends at Green Park. Our staff is always doing its best for you to have a great time at Green Park. Also we're always ready to help you ＿＿＿＿＿ ＿＿＿＿＿ ＿＿＿＿＿ and to listen to your opinion. According to the Nature Protection Regulations, we cannot ＿＿＿＿＿ ＿＿＿＿＿ the lamps at night in the park. So please ＿＿＿＿＿ ＿＿＿＿＿ ＿＿＿＿＿ before 9 p.m. for your ＿＿＿＿＿. We are temporarily allowing you to ＿＿＿＿＿ ＿＿＿＿＿ ＿＿＿＿＿ or awnings during the daytime since there are few trees and little shade. But if you ＿＿＿＿＿ ＿＿＿＿＿ ＿＿＿＿＿ ＿＿＿＿＿ in the dark, it can stand in others' way. Thank you ＿＿＿＿＿ ＿＿＿＿＿ for your cooperation.

A. Listening Web  MP3 03-02-A

Intro I'd like to thank Hankuk High School Broadcast Studio for giving me this opportunity to give a guest announcement.

Web1 But there is only one air (conditioner / conditioning) for over 30 students in a classroom.

Web2 I heard the (demand / demands) for electricity soars during daytime these days because of this awfully hot weather.

Web3 I just want our summer uniforms to be (shirt / short) pants.

Ending I think it is the best way to save (elasticity / electricity).

B. True / False  MP3 03-02-B

1. 남자는 교실에 에어컨이 더 많이 있어야 한다고 주장한다.　　　　　　　　　(T / F)
2. 남자는 교실 실내 온도를 더욱 낮춰야 한다고 주장한다.　　　　　　　　　(T / F)
3. 남자는 교실에서 자유롭게 에어컨 온도를 조절할 수 있기를 바란다.　　(T / F)
4. 남자는 반바지 교복이 전기를 절약하는 방법이리고 생각한다.　　　　　(T / F)

C. Words and Phrases

beneficial 이로운 / demand 수요 / supply 공급 / soar 치솟다 / meet 충족시키다

D. Dictation  MP3 03-02-B

M: Good afternoon. I'm Jacob Smith, a 3rd grader. First of all, I'd like to thank Hankuk High School Broadcast Studio for giving me this opportunity to give a guest announcement. I have only three minutes, so I'll just _____ _____ _____ _____. Now it's summer, and it's so _____ _____ _____. But there is only one air conditioner for over 30 students in a classroom. Unfortunately it is not _____ to everybody. Some of the students sitting at the corner never enjoy air conditioning all day long. Furthermore, we cannot _____ _____ _____. However, I heard the _____ _____ electricity soars during daytime these days because of this awfully hot weather. So the electricity supply cannot _____ _____ _____. So I'll not say we need more air conditioning. I just want our summer uniforms to be short pants. I think it is the best way to save electricity.

A. Listening Web  MP3 03-03-A

Intro Summerfield Hotel will be (open / opened) next month.
Web1 It will be the symbol of a cozy and (relaxed / relaxing) atmosphere.
Web2 Summerfield Hotel invites you to its Grand Opening Banquet on September 1st.
Web3 Please come and see our beautiful interior and (modern / mother) amenities.
Ending Everybody who will (join / join in) our banquet will be given a 50% discount coupon for a poolside BBQ valid until the end of this year.

B. True / False  MP3 03-03-B

1. 호텔은 도심에 있다.   (T / F)
2. 호텔에는 중식과 일식의 퓨전 레스토랑이 있다.   (T / F)
3. 9월 1일에 오픈 행사가 있다.   (T / F)
4. 올해 말까지 식대를 50% 할인해 준다.   (T / F)

C. Words and Phrases

authentic 진짜의 / access 접근 / equipped with ~을 갖춘 / amenities 생활 편의시설 / banquet 연회 / valid 유효한

D. Dictation  MP3 03-03-B

W: The best choice for your trip! Summerfield Hotel will be open next month. It will be the symbol of a cozy and relaxing atmosphere. _____ _____ _____ _____ of downtown, it is complete with guest rooms, authentic Chinese and Japanese restaurants, and a fitness center. All the guests can enjoy _____ _____ _____ with wifi in the rooms. They are fully _____ _____ individual air-conditioning and heating system controls, and 100 channels with English, Japanese, and Chinese. Summerfield Hotel _____ _____ _____ its Grand Opening Banquet on September 1st. Please come and see our beautiful interior and modern amenities, and have a wonderful night with a lot of celebrities. Everybody who will join our banquet will be given a 50% discount coupon for a poolside BBQ _____ _____ the end of this year.

A. Listening Web

Intro   Waste is a big problem for our (planet / plant).

Web1   We need to find ways to throw less waste away. These are (known / none) as the three Rs.

Web2   The first R is for reduce, which means (cut it / cutting) down on the things we buy so that we have to throw less away.

Web3   The second R is for reuse, which means using (all / old) things again instead of throwing them away.

Ending   The third R is for recycle, which means making new things out of old.

B. True / False

1. 쓰레기는 태워버려야 한다.   (T / F)
2. 쓰레기를 줄이려면 적게 사는 것이 좋다.   (T / F)
3. reuse는 물건을 다시 사는 것이다.   (T / F)
4. recycle은 옛 물건을 새로운 물건으로 변형시킬 수 있다.   (T / F)

C. Words and Phrases

precious 소중한 / material 재료, 소재 / cut down 줄이다

D. Dictation

M: Waste is a big problem for our planet. We have to find places to put all the waste _____ _____ _____, and we are running out of space. Besides, every time we throw something away, we waste precious materials. We need to find ways to throw less waste away. There are three ways to do this. These are known as the three Rs. The first R is _____ _____, which means cutting down on the things we buy so that we have to throw less away. The second R is _____ _____, which means using old things again _____ _____ throwing them away. The third R is _____ _____, which means making new things _____ _____ _____. Things should only be thrown away when we cannot reuse or recycle them.

문항 5

△ 심화 학습

A. Listening Web  MP3 03-05-A

Intro   There is a saying that too much is as bad as too little.

Web1   If you are (indulged in / indulging) reading to excess, it can be a vice.

Web2   One of the main (objective / objectives) of reading, generally, is to have an ability to observe yourself and other people candidly.

Web3   Therefore, to anyone who is already able to do so, (excessive / obsessive) reading is only a waste of time and energy.

Ending   Sometimes it can (destruct / distract) their (attention / tension) from reality.

B. True / False 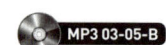 MP3 03-05-B

1. 독서는 언제나 좋은 것이다.   (T / F)
2. 독서가 해악으로 간주되기도 한다.   (T / F)
3. 나와 타인을 있는 그대로 바라보는 능력을 키우는 것은 독서의 중요한 목적이다.   (T / F)
4. 능력을 갖춘 사람들은 과한 독서라도 에너지를 얻을 수 있다.   (T / F)

C. Words and Phrases

indulged in ~에 몰두하다 / to excess 과도하게 / vice 해악 / candidly 솔직하게, 숨김없이

D. Dictation  MP3 03-05-B

W: There is a saying that too much is _____ _____ _____ too little. As with all other things, Aldous Huxley said, reading is not always good. That is, if you are _____ _____ reading to excess, it can be a vice. Reading is not usually _____ _____ _____ a vice, so excessive reading can be more dangerous because you don't recognize that it's dangerous. One of the main objectives of reading, generally, is to have an _____ _____ _____ yourself and other people candidly. Therefore, to anyone who is already able to do so, excessive reading is only a waste of time and energy. Sometimes it can _____ _____ _____ from reality.

A. Listening Web  MP3 03-06-A

Intro (In dangered / Endangered) species are in serious trouble.

Web1 Then the wildlife that already lived there has no (place / places) to live.

Web2 The animals living on the shore cannot (move inland / moving land), so finally they may become extinct.

Web3 If they become extinct, it may cause the loss of the (all / whole) ecosystem.

Ending That's why scientists and governments get (involve / involved) with protecting endangered species.

B. True / False  MP3 03-06-B

1. 해안가에 서식하던 동물은 삶의 터전에 위협을 받으면 생존을 위해 내륙으로 이동하는 경향이 있다. (T / F)

2. 사람들이 다양한 개발을 통해 지구 상의 많은 부분을 차지하게 됨에 따라 야생 동식물들과 공생 관계가 되었다. (T / F)

3. 연구에 따르면, 생태계의 한 부분이 멸종되면 다른 종이 그 부분을 대신하는 것으로 나타났다. (T / F)

4. 멸종 위기의 동식물을 구하기 위해 과학자와 정부는 모두 노력하고 있다. (T / F)

C. Words and Phrases

endangered 멸종 위기에 처한 / what if ~라면 어떻게 될까? / extinct (동식물이) 멸종된 / get involved 몰두, 관여하다

D. Dictation  MP3 03-06-B

M: Many living things on the earth are disappearing now. Endangered species are in serious trouble. Think about this situation. People _____ _____ _____ more and more areas of the earth. Then the wildlife _____ _____ _____ _____ has no place to live, and they have to move to find another place to live. But _____ _____ people keep building their houses along the beach? The animals living on the shore cannot move inland, so finally they may _____ _____. Every species plays a _____ _____ in the ecosystem. For example, plants usually provide food for animals. If they become extinct, it may _____ _____ _____ of the whole ecosystem. That's why scientists and governments get involved with protecting endangered species.

7

△
심화
학습

A. Listening Web

Intro Very often, you may think your dog understands you, and scientists say it's true.
Web1 New (research / researcher) shows that dogs can learn new words the same way children do.
Web2 It was (taught / thought) that gorillas, chimpanzees, and other primates can't speak.
Web3 A researcher in the U.S. (talk / taught) American Sign Language to a baby gorilla, and finally she was able to communicate with her hands.
Ending Animals can learn languages.

B. True / False

1. 과거의 과학자들은 동물도 언어를 배울 수 있다고 믿었었다.   (T / F)
2. 미국에서 고릴라에게 수화를 가르치는 데 성공한 적이 있다.   (T / F)
3. 동물과 인간의 언어 학습 성취에는 차이가 있다.   (T / F)
4. 개와 인간은 동일한 언어 능력을 지니고 있었다.   (T / F)

C. Words and Phrases

used to 과거에(한 때는) ~하곤 했다 / primate 영장류 / sign language 수화

D. Dictation

W: Very often, you may think your dog understands you, and scientists say it's true. Moreover, new research shows that dogs can learn new words _____ _____ _____ children do. Scientists used to believe only humans learn and this makes us different from other animals, but now it is proved _____ _____ _____. It was thought that gorillas, chimpanzees, and other primates can't speak. However, a researcher in the U.S. taught American Sign Language to a baby gorilla, and finally she was able to _____ _____ _____ _____. Surprisingly, she could use _____ _____ 1,000 signs. Animals can learn languages. In other words, they have the same _____ _____ _____ languages. The only difference is its degree.

A. Listening Web

Intro Advertising today is an over $100 billion a year industry and affects all of us throughout our (life / lives).

Web1 But the ads sell more than products.

Web2 And usually adolescents are the prime (target / targets).

Web3 Adolescents are particularly vulnerable to ads because they are new and (inexperienced / inexperience) consumers.

Ending Most teenagers are (sensible / sensitive) to peer pressure and find it difficult to (exist / resist) or even question the dominant cultural message communicated by the ads.

B. True / False

1. 평균적으로 성인은 평생 1년 반 동안 TV 광고를 보는 셈이다. (T / F)
2. 광고는 우리에게 성공의 개념을 주입하기도 한다. (T / F)
3. 청소년들은 광고주들에게 주요 목표 계층이 되곤 한다. (T / F)
4. 사실 청소년들은 광고의 지배적 문화 메시지를 잘 받아들이지 않는다. (T / F)

C. Words and Phrases

billion 10억 / vulnerable 상처받기 쉬운, 저항력이 없는 / self-concept 자아개념 / dominant 지배적인, 가장 유력한, 우세한

D. Dictation

M: Advertising today is an over $100 billion a year industry and affects all of us throughout our lives. The average adult will spend _____ _____ _____ _____ years of their life watching TV commercials. But the ads sell more than products. They sell values, images, concept of success, and so on. And usually adolescents are the prime target. However, adolescents are particularly _____ _____ _____ because they are new and inexperienced consumers. They are in the _____ _____ _____ their values and developing their self-concepts. Most teenagers are sensitive to _____ _____ and find it difficult to resist or even question the dominant cultural message communicated by the ads.

문항 9

△ 심화 학습

A. Listening Web

Intro   It's a seeing eye dog.

Web1   The dog is (trade / trained) to help the owner. It guides the owner on the street.

Web2   And some dogs let the owner know when the telephone or doorbell rings. They are for the (deaf / death).

Web3   Many disabled people depend on their pets to improve the (quality / quantity) of their lives.

Ending   Some monkeys help people who cannot move by themselves. They are very helpful.

B. True / False

1. 남자는 강아지를 쓰다듬어 주었다.   (T / F)
2. 전화벨이 울리는 것을 주인에게 알려주는 개가 있다.   (T / F)
3. 스스로 움직이지 못하는 사람들을 도와주는 개가 있다.   (T / F)
4. 여자는 많은 장애인들의 삶의 질 향상을 위해 식물을 키운다.   (T / F)

C. Words and Phrases

seeing eye dog 맹인안내견 / bother 괴롭히다 / deaf 귀가 먹은, 청각장애의 / disabled 장애를 가진

D. Dictation

M: Mom, look at the dog. He's really cute. I want to go to _____ _____.

W: No. It's a seeing eye dog.

M: Seeing eye dog?

W: Yes, it's for blind people. The dog is _____ _____ _____ the owner. It guides the owner on the street. If you touch the dog, it'll _____ _____ _____.

M: I see. Look! The dog stopped its owner in front of the crosswalk.

W: Of course. And some dogs let the owner know when the telephone or doorbell rings. They are _____ _____ _____.

M: Sometimes dogs are like family.

W: Yes. Many _____ people _____ _____ their pets to improve the _____ _____ _____ _____. Some monkeys help people who cannot move _____ _____. They are very helpful.

A. Listening Web  MP3 03-10-A

Intro I'm thinking about (kidding / quitting) my job. My boss always irritates me.

Web1 He sends me on his personal errands.

Web2 In addition, he always gives me a lot of work at once and then asks me if it's finished at (early / hourly) intervals.

Web3 Why aren't all bosses (considerable / considerate)?

Ending These days I wonder how my parents have (endured / enjoyed) their burdens for decades.

B. True / False  MP3 03-10-B

1. 여자는 직장을 그만둘까 생각 중이다.   **(T / F)**
2. 여자는 자신의 책을 반납하러 도서관에 갔다.   **(T / F)**
3. 남자의 상사는 개인적인 심부름을 시키지 않는다.   **(T / F)**
4. 두 사람은 같은 사무실에서 일한다.   **(T / F)**

C. Words and Phrases

interval 간격 / considerate 배려 깊은 / endure burden 부담을 견디다

D. Dictation  MP3 03-10-B

M: You look so tired. What _____ _____ _____?

W: I'm thinking about quitting my job. My boss always irritates me.

M: Come on. It is a job. What do you expect?

W: He sends me on his _____ _____. Today I went to the library to return his books.

M: My boss has had me pick up his son at school.

W: What? So you did it?

M: In addition, he always gives me a lot of work at once and then asks me if it's finished at _____ _____.

W: Oh, he must make you crazy. Why aren't all bosses considerate?

M: They _____ _____ _____ considerate when they were clerks. They just forgot as time went on.

W: Nothing is easy. These days I wonder how my parents _____ _____ their burdens _____ _____.

대화가 일어나는 장소, 화자의 직업이나 화자 간의 관계를 파악하는 것은 담화의 맥락을 파악하는 중요한 요소이다. 주의할 점은 단순히 표면적으로 들리는 단어에만 집중하지 말고, 담화의 전반적인 흐름을 파악함과 동시에 정답의 단서가 되는 주요한 표현들을 놓치지 않는 것이 중요하다. 전체적으로 내용 파악이 잘 안 되는 가운데 너무 집중적으로 들리는 단어가 있다면 이는 오답을 유도할 수 있으므로 주의하도록 한다.

• Example

1 대화를 듣고, 두 사람의 관계로 가장 적절한 것을 고르시오. [2012 수능기출]

W: Good morning. What can I do for you?

M: I'm looking for a book about traveling in South America, but I don't remember the title.

W: Do you know the writer's name, then?

M: It was written by a woman who traveled to South America.

W: Well, I'm not sure which book you mean. Let me ask another clerk.

M: Ah, I remember! She's from Canada and is famous for her breathtaking pictures taken during her trips.

W: Now I see. It's "Walking Through South America" by Alice Kingston.

M: Yeah, that's it! Do you have a copy here now?

W: Let me check. *[Typing sound]* I'm sorry, but it's sold out. Do you want to place an order for it?

M: Yes, please. When will it be available?

W: Probably by tomorrow afternoon. But you can use the delivery service.

M: No, thanks. I'll come back tomorrow.

① 신문기자 – 소설가
② 서점 직원 – 고객
③ 도서관 사서 – 학생
④ 택배기사 – 경비원
⑤ 여행사 직원 – 손님

* 전체적으로 책을 찾고 있는 대화임을 쉽게 알 수 있다. 단순하게 생각하면 도서관 사서와 학생의 대화처럼 들릴 수 있으나, librarian (사서)이 아닌, clerk (직원)이라는 단어가 사용되었고, 결정적으로 여자가 "it's sold out. Do you want to place an order for it? (품절되었습니다. 주문하시겠어요?)"라고 물은 것을 보면, 대화가 이루어지는 장소가 도서관이 아닌 서점임을 알 수 있다. 따라서 정답은 ②번이다.

유형 4

장소 · 관계
추론하기

장소 · 관계 추론하기

1 대화를 듣고, 두 사람이 대화하고 있는 장소로 가장 적절한 곳을 고르시오.

① gallery
② laundry
③ clothing store
④ stationery store
⑤ convenient store

2 대화를 듣고, 두 사람이 대화하고 있는 장소로 가장 적절한 곳을 고르시오.

① farm
② grocery
③ souvenir shop
④ fortune teller's tent
⑤ the Canadian Embassy

3 대화를 듣고, 두 사람이 대화하고 있는 장소로 가장 적절한 곳을 고르시오.

① ski slopes
② parking lot
③ indoor ice-rink
④ sportswear shop
⑤ swimming pool

4 대화를 듣고, 두 사람이 대화하고 있는 장소로 가장 적절한 곳을 고르시오.

① atelier
② restaurant
③ coffee shop
④ photo studio
⑤ hairdresser's

5 대화를 듣고, 두 사람이 대화하고 있는 장소로 가장 적절한 곳을 고르시오.

① plane
② cafeteria
③ bus terminal
④ broadcasting studio
⑤ travel agency office

6 대화를 듣고, 두 사람의 관계로 가장 적절한 것을 고르시오.

① artist – model
② architect – client
③ repairman – boss
④ real estate agent – tenant
⑤ photographer – house owner

7 대화를 듣고, 두 사람의 관계로 가장 적절한 것을 고르시오.

① trader – buyer
② banker – client
③ accountant – CEO
④ cashier – customer
⑤ travel agent – insurance broker

8 대화를 듣고, 두 사람의 관계로 가장 적절한 것을 고르시오.

① taxi driver – customer
② travel agent – traveler
③ police officer – tourist
④ rescue worker – climber
⑤ hotel receptionist – guest

9 대화를 듣고, 두 사람의 관계로 가장 적절한 것을 고르시오.

① doctor – patient
② trainer – customer
③ P.E. teacher – student
④ photographer – model
⑤ yoga instructor – student

10 대화를 듣고, 두 사람의 관계로 가장 적절한 것을 고르시오.

① mechanic – driver
② car dealer – customer
③ police officer – driver
④ insurance agent – client
⑤ engineering professor – student

A. Listening Web

Intro	I'd like to pick up my pants.
Web1	These (have / haven't) been (iron / ironed) well, and the stain here didn't come out.
Web2	We don't sell any detergents. There is a big (mark at / market) just around the corner.
Web3	(Then / When) will my pants be ready? Can I pick them up tomorrow?
Ending	I will. Thank you.

심화 학습

B. True / False

1. 옷 다림질이 제대로 되어 있지 않았다.   (T / F)
2. 여자는 남자로부터 세제를 샀다.   (T / F)
3. 남자는 너무 바빠서 여자의 요청을 거절하였다.   (T / F)
4. 바지는 내일 다시 찾을 수 있다.   (T / F)

C. Words and Phrases

stain 얼룩, 때 / oil paint 유화물감 / the day after tomorrow 모레

D. Dictation

W: I'd like to _____ _____ my pants.

M: What's your name?

W: Jessica Adams.

M: Here you are.

W: Oh, these haven't been ironed well, and the stain here didn't come out.

M: Let me see. I'm sorry. I tried to _____ _____ _____ _____, but I couldn't.

W: Could you try to remove the stain _____ _____?

M: Okay, I will.

W: Can I buy a strong detergent here? There is a lot of oil paint on my clothes because I study oil painting.

M: Sorry, we don't sell any detergents. There is a big market _____ _____ _____ _____. You may find what you want there.

W: I see. Thanks. When will my pants be ready? Can I pick them up tomorrow?

M: We're very busy these days, so why don't you call me _____ _____ _____ _____?

W: I will. Thank you.

A. Listening Web  MP3 04-02-A

Intro Now we are at our (last / rest) destination in Canada. What would you like to buy?
Web1 Anything to remind me of this (trick / trip).
Web2 I want something (unique / unit), and something (ascetically / authentically) Canadian.
Web3 Then let's buy some maple syrup for you. And I'd like these (fridge / frizzer) magnets.
Ending I'll be able to think of Canada (whenever / wherever) I see them.

심화 학습

B. True / False  MP3 04-02-B

1. 두 사람은 캐나다 여행 중이다.   (T / F)
2. 두 사람은 먹을 것을 고르는 중이다.   (T / F)
3. 여자는 메이플 시럽을 사지 않을 것이다.   (T / F)
4. 남자는 사진이 들어간 자석이 실용적이라고 생각한다.   (T / F)

C. Words and Phrases

authentically 진정으로, 진짜로 / magnet 자석 / tourist spot 관광지

D. Dictation  MP3 04-02-B

M: Now we are at our last destination in Canada. What would you like to buy?

W: Anything to _____ _____ _____ this trip.

M: What about maple syrup? It was so delicious and you liked it.

W: That's good, but we can get it in Korea, too. I want something unique, and something authentically Canadian.

M: Yes, that's why you should buy maple syrup. This is _____ _____ Canada, and _____ _____ Canada, and you buy it in Canada. And above all, it is the symbol of Canada.

W: You mean you want to buy it?

M: You're _____ _____ _____.

W: Then let's buy some maple syrup for you. And I'd like these fridge magnets.

M: That's good, too. They're quite practical.

W: Yes, and they have beautiful pictures of _____ _____ in Canada. I'll be able to think of Canada whenever I see them.

Unit 04 | 053

A. Listening Web

Intro	How long is the (land / lane)?
Web1	It's 50 meters.
Web2	It's for the Olympics, so it's even longer than the other (pools / pulls) that you've been to.
Web3	Where are the (kickboards / quick boards)?
Ending	Okay, don't forget to put on the (cab / cap) in your hand.

B. True / False

1. 레인은 50 미터이다.   (T / F)
2. 남자와 여자가 말하고 있는 수영장은 다른 수영장에 비해 크다.   (T / F)
3. 여자는 이미 수영모자를 착용하고 있다.   (T / F)
4. 지금 날씨가 매우 춥다.   (T / F)

C. Words and Phrases

spacious 넓은 / bump into ~에 부딪히다 / kickboard 수영 연습용 널빤지

D. Dictation

M: Don't run! It's dangerous.

W: But it's really spacious.

M: The floor is slippery, and there are many people. Watch out all the time _____ _____ _____ _____ others.

W: Don't worry, Dad. I'll be careful.

M: Good.

W: How long is the lane?

M: It's 50 meters. It's for the Olympics, so it's even longer than the other pools that _____ _____ _____.

W: I see. Where are the kickboards?

M: Over there. Oh, it's too small.

W: That's for kids. I think this one _____ _____ _____.

M: Good. Now we need to _____ _____ first. Remember that it's very cold in there and it can be dangerous if you just go in without exercise.

W: Dad, I know. I'm not a baby. It's getting chilly. We need to exercise right away.

M: Okay, don't forget to _____ _____ _____ _____ in your hand. Now let's go! Practice makes perfect! Just follow the line. Come on.

A. Listening Web

Intro   I have (an / on) appointment at 3.

Web1   I'd like to (change / exchange) my hair style.

Web2   How about the style on this (model / moral)?

Web3   It costs $(15 / 50) because your hair is long.

Ending   But it (collaborates / coordinates) with your dress now.

B. True / False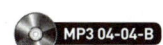

1. 여자는 예약을 하지 않고 왔다.   (T / F)
2. 여자는 스타일을 어떻게 바꿀지 미리 생각해왔다.   (T / F)
3. 여자는 오늘 사진 찍으러 갈 것이다.   (T / F)
4. 여자는 가격이 비싸다고 생각한다.   (T / F)

C. Words and Phrases

elegant 우아한 / coordinate (옷차림, 가구 등이) 잘 어울리다 / reasonable 타당한, 합리적인

D. Dictation

W: Hello, I have an appointment at 3.

M: Oh, you're Ms. Green! Right this way and have a seat, please. What would you like? Do you have anything _____ _____ _____?

W: Well, I'd like to change my hair style. What style do you think _____ _____ _____ for me?

M: It's always a difficult question. These pictures will help you to _____ _____ _____. It seems you have an important promise.

W: Not really. I'll have _____ _____ _____ today.

M: How about the style on this model?

W: She looks very elegant. How much will it cost?

M: It costs $50 because your hair is long. But it _____ _____ your dress now.

W: That's reasonable, I think. How long will it take?

M: About _____ _____ _____ _____ hours. Would you like to have some tea?

W: Yes, please. I'd like to have some hot tea. Thank you.

A. Listening Web

△ 심화 학습

Intro   I didn't understand the announcement.

Web1   Another (plan / plane) for Europe has just departed, so we need to keep some (distance / distant) from it.

Web2   When are we going to take (off / up)?

Web3   But I'll transfer at Prague for a (flight / fly) to Rome.

Ending   We'll be in Prague (in / on) time.

B. True / False

1. 남자의 최종 목적지는 로마이다.   (T / F)
2. 비행기는 도착지에 예정보다 50분 늦게 도착할 것이다.   (T / F)
3. 남자는 프라하에서 환승할 계획이다.   (T / F)
4. 남자는 지금 쌀쌀하다고 느낀다.   (T / F)

C. Words and Phrases

transfer 환승하다 / behind the schedule 예정보다 늦게 / chilly 쌀쌀한

D. Dictation

M: Excuse me, I didn't understand the announcement. Why _____ _____ _____ _____?

W: Another plane for Europe has just departed, so we need to _____ _____ _____ from it.

M: When are we going to take off?

W: In 50 minutes.

M: But I'll transfer at Prague for a flight to Rome. What if we're _____ _____?

W: We'll be in Prague in time. Don't worry. Would you like some snacks or drinks?

M: What kind of tea do you have?

W: We have green tea and black tea. We can _____ _____ _____ _____ if you want.

M: I'd like hot green tea, please.

W: And what else do you need?

M: Can I get a blanket? It's _____ _____ _____.

W: Of course. I'll bring them right away.

W: Thank you very much.

A. Listening Web

Intro   How many (bathrooms / bedrooms) do you want in your house?

Web1   You're thinking of a two-(stories / story) house.

Web2   Look at (these pictures / this picture). Which house would you like the most?

Web3   Do you want a garden to be on the list?

Ending   I'll have finished the blueprint by next Friday, and we'll (discuss / discuss on) more (detail / details) then.

B. True / False

1. 여자는 화장실이 세 개 있는 집을 원한다.   (T / F)
2. 여자는 집 두 채를 원한다.   (T / F)
3. 여자는 거실과 부엌 사이에 복도가 있기를 원한다.   (T / F)
4. 여자는 정원이 있는 집을 원한다.   (T / F)

C. Words and Phrases

aisle 복도 / attic 다락방 / blueprint 설계도 / detail 세부 사항

D. Dictation

M: How many bedrooms do you want in your house?

W: Three. And I _____ _____ _____ _____ two bathrooms. One on the 1st floor, and the other on the 2nd floor.

M: Oh, you're thinking of _____ _____ _____.

W: Yes. I want the living room and the kitchen to be _____ _____ _____ _____.

M: Look at these pictures. Which house would you like the most?

W: I like this one. I like this garden.

M: Do you want a garden to be on the list?

W: Yes. I want _____ _____ _____ a very big window around here, so I can see the garden while sitting in the living room.

M: Anything else? An attic or…

W: No. I just want the walls to be white and the roof to be blue.

M: Okay. _____ _____ _____ the blueprint by next Friday, and we'll discuss more details then.

W: Thanks a lot.

문항 7

△ 심화 학습

A. Listening Web

Intro   I'd like to remit some money to a travel (agency / agent) in Australia.
Web1   If you have an (account / count), you can save the remittance charge.
Web2   How much would you like to (remit / limit)?
Web3   I have an account with your bank in Australia.
Ending   I can arrange it for you.

B. True / False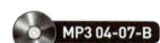

1. 여자는 송금하려고 한다.   (T / F)
2. 여자는 계좌를 새로 개설할 것이다.   (T / F)
3. 남자는 송금 수수료를 절약할 수 있는 방법을 안내하고 있다.   (T / F)
4. 남자는 처음에 여자의 전화번호를 잘못 이해했다.   (T / F)

C. Words and Phrases

remit 송금하다 / account 계좌 / remittance charge 송금 수수료 / arrange 처리하다

D. Dictation

M: May I help you?

W: Yes, I'd like to remit some money to a travel agency in Australia.

M: First you'll have to _____ _____ _____ _____. Could I have your name and phone number, please?

W: Jennifer Lauren. And here's my phone number.

M: If you _____ _____ _____, you can save the remittance charge.

W: How much is the remittance charge?

M: _____ _____. How much would you like to remit?

W: $500.

M: It's 30,000 won.

W: I have an account _____ _____ _____ in Australia. I've just moved to Seoul…

M: Then I don't think you need another account. I can arrange it for you. Please _____ _____ that your phone number is correct on this form. It _____ _____ an error message.

W: Oh, this is a four, not a nine.

M: Thank you very much. Please be seated here for a second.

A. Listening Web  MP3 04-08-A

Intro Are you Erin Baker who (stay / stayed) at the Grand Hill Inn?

Web1 After you checked out, we (found / found out) your passport in your room.

Web2 I remember your face because I was at the front (deck / desk) when you checked out.

Web3 I hope you'll (enjoy / joy) the journey home.

Ending Thank you very much.

B. True / False  MP3 04-08-B

1. 남자는 여자와 함께 비행기를 탈 것이다. (T / F)
2. 여자는 여권을 호텔에 두고 나왔다. (T / F)
3. 여권은 여자의 가방 안에 있었다. (T / F)
4. 남자는 여자의 짐을 부치는 곳까지 들어주었다. (T / F)

C. Words and Phrases

check out (호텔 등에서 비용을 지불하고) 나가다 / luggage 수화물 / check in (투숙 또는 탑승) 수속을 밟다

D. Dictation  MP3 04-08-B

M: Excuse me.

W: Yes?

M: Are you Erin Baker who stayed at the Grand Hill Inn?

W: Yes. I'm sorry, but who are you?

M: I'm Ted Johnson from the Grand Hill Inn. After you checked out, we found your passport in your room. It's yours, right?

W: I think so, but I have _____ _____ _____ _____ here…
Oh, no! You've saved my life!

M: I remember your face because I was at the front desk when you checked out. That's why _____ _____ _____ by taxi.

W: I'd have wasted a lot of time _____ _____ _____ _____ at this airport. I really appreciate it.

M: My pleasure. I'll carry your luggage to the _____ _____.

W: Thanks, but that's okay. The counter _____ _____ _____ _____.

M: I hope you'll _____ _____ _____ _____.

W: Thank you very much.

A. Listening Web

Intro   And lift up your head, and lift up your chest slowly. Now hold. One, two, three. Okay. Now (low / lower) your chest.

Web1   The surgery was a success. Now all you have to do is to (strengthen / strength) the muscle around the waist.

Web2   So if it gets stronger, the pain will be (relieved / believed) much more.

Web3   Then you should come again and get an (injection / rejection) to relax the muscle.

Ending   I see. I think I need to exercise every day. Thanks.

B. True / False

1. 여자는 허리가 아프다.   (T / F)
2. 여자는 바닥에 엎드려서 가슴을 들어 올리는 동작을 배우고 있다.   (T / F)
3. 여자의 통증은 운동을 하면 완전히 사라질 것이다.   (T / F)
4. 여자는 허리가 아프면 다시 수술을 해야 한다.   (T / F)

C. Words and Phrases

surgery 수술 / muscle 근육 / stiffen 뻣뻣해지다 / injection 주사

D. Dictation

M: Lie down _____ _____ _____ _____.

W: Like this?

M: Yes. And _____ _____ _____ _____, and lift up your chest slowly. Now hold. One, two, three. Okay. Now lower your chest. Good.

W: It takes _____ _____ _____ _____ in the waist.

M: Yes. The surgery was a success. Now all you have to do is to strengthen the muscle around the waist. Do this exercise ten or fifteen times a day.

W: Then will the pain disappear forever?

M: The pain occurs simply because the muscle around your waist is too weak. Even though you work only a little, the muscle _____ _____ _____. So if it gets stronger, the pain _____ _____ _____ much more. But I cannot guarantee you'll never get hurt again.

W: I understand. What if my waist is painful again?

M: Then you should come again and _____ _____ _____ to relax the muscle.

W: I see. I think I need to exercise every day. Thanks.

A. Listening Web

Intro   What (bought / brought) you here again?
Web1   There seems to be a problem with the steering (heel / wheel).
Web2   Whenever I (steer / stir) to the right, I hear a strange sound.
Web3   I need to inspect all the (suspected / suspecting) parts.
Ending Would you mind coming with me to test-drive the car? I need to hear the sound.

B. True / False

1. 여자는 며칠 전에 이미 이곳에 방문했었다.   (T / F)
2. 예전부터 핸들에서 소리가 났다.   (T / F)
3. 남자는 이 차를 살 계획이다.   (T / F)
4. 여자는 작은 차 사고가 났다.   (T / F)

C. Words and Phrases

steering wheel (자동차의) 핸들 / suspected 의심되는, 미심쩍은 / insurance agent 보험 중개인, 보험 대리점 /
test-drive a car 시 운전하다

D. Dictation

W: Good afternoon.

M: Good afternoon. _____ _____ _____ here again?

W: There seems to be a problem with the steering wheel.

M: I didn't notice any problem the other day.

W: No, but from this morning, whenever I steer to the right, I hear a strange sound.

M: _____ _____ _____ _____ have an accident again?
    Even a small accident, like you bumped into a pole at the parking lot or…

W: No, never. I _____ _____ _____ the car until yesterday since I picked it
    up last week.

M: It can't be a problem with the steering wheel. I need to _____ all the _____
    _____.

W: I _____ _____ the insurance will cover this kind of thing.

M: It depends. You need to contact your insurance agent about it.

W: I see.

M: Would you mind coming with me _____ _____ the car? I need to hear the sound.

W: Of course not.

이번에 새로 추가된 그림 유형은 기존의 그림 유형에서 다소 변형된 유형으로, 기존 수능의 1번 유형 (대화를 듣고 옳은 그림 찾기)과 13번 유형 (그림 상황과 어울리는 대화 찾기)이 복합적으로 응축된 형태라고 생각하면 될 것이다. 우선 대화가 시작되기 전에 그림이 어떤 상황인지 파악하고, 대화를 들으면서 그림의 내용과 맞는 부분, 맞지 않는 부분을 가려나가야 한다. 실제 일상생활에서 듣기는 음성 자극만 있는 것이 아니라 시각적인 자극도 함께 있기 마련이다. 이런 점에서 이 그림 문제는 실제적인 듣기 능력을 시험하고자 하는 것이다.

● Example

1 대화를 듣고, 그림에서 대화의 내용과 일치하지 <u>않는</u> 것을 고르시오. [2012 수능모의 변형]

W: Hi, This is your niece, Jenny.

M: Hi, Jenny! How is the preparation for your cousin's party going?

W: It's going well. I put up a banner saying "Happy 5th Birthday!" on the wall as you asked.

M: Great! Did you get heart-shaped balloons?

W: Yes, I attached them to the wall. You'll like them.

M: Did you prepare a round table instead of a square one?

W: Of course!

M: What about the birthday cake?

W: I bought a two-layer birthday cake. Anything else, Uncle Paul?

M: Well… Did you find a birthday hat with a cat on it? You know how much she likes cats.

W: Yes, I did. I placed the cake and the hat on the table.

* 여자가 사각 테이블 대신 둥근 테이블을 준비했다고 했으므로 정답은 ③번이다. "instead of" 구문을 잘 듣고 의미를 파악하는 것이 이 문제를 해결하는 포인트이다.

유형 5

그림과 일치하지 않는 내용 찾기

그림과 일치하지 않는 내용 찾기

1 대화를 듣고, 그림에서 대화의 내용과 일치하지 <u>않는</u> 것을 고르시오.

2 대화를 듣고, 대화가 이루어지고 있는 현재의 상황과 일치하지 <u>않는</u> 것을 고르시오.

3 대화를 듣고, 그림에서 대화의 내용과 일치하지 <u>않는</u> 것을 고르시오.

4 대화를 듣고, 그림에서 대화의 내용과 일치하지 <u>않는</u> 것을 고르시오.

5 다음 대화를 듣고, 남자가 핼러윈에 입을 복장과 일치하지 <u>않는</u> 것을 고르시오.

6 대화를 듣고, 그림에서 대화의 내용과 일치하지 <u>않는</u> 것을 고르시오.

7 대화를 듣고, 그림에서 대화의 내용과 일치하지 <u>않는</u> 것을 고르시오.

8 대화를 듣고, 그림에서 대화의 내용과 일치하지 <u>않는</u> 것을 고르시오.

9 대화를 듣고, 그림에서 대화의 내용과 일치하지 <u>않는</u> 것을 고르시오.

10 대화를 듣고, 그림에서 대화의 내용과 일치하지 <u>않는</u> 것을 고르시오.

A. Listening Web  MP3 05-01-A

Intro   There's a big window. I put my (bat / bed) right under the window.

Web1   I put the computer (next / next to) the bed.

Web2   Did you (draw / throw) away your table when you moved?

Web3   My brother (fits / fixed) it. And now it's in the middle of my room.

Ending   I made a really big (bookshelf / bookshelves) on the wall, but it's only half full with books.

B. True / False  MP3 05-01-B

1. 여자는 살던 집의 방을 새롭게 꾸몄다.   (T / F)

2. 남자는 여자의 방 꾸미는 것을 도와주고 있다.   (T / F)

3. 탁자는 다리가 부러져서 버렸다.   (T / F)

4. 책장을 크게 만들었는데도 책이 많아서 다 채워졌다.   (T / F)

C. Words and Phrases

bookshelf 책장 / attach ~을 붙이다

D. Dictation  MP3 05-01-B

M: How's ＿＿＿＿＿ ＿＿＿＿＿ ＿＿＿＿＿?

W: I love it! There's a big window. I put my bed ＿＿＿＿＿ ＿＿＿＿＿ ＿＿＿＿＿
＿＿＿＿＿, so that I can get up in the morning in the beautiful sunshine.

M: Wow! Beautiful!

W: And I put the computer ＿＿＿＿＿ ＿＿＿＿＿ ＿＿＿＿＿ ＿＿＿＿＿,
so that I can go to bed quickly after work.

M: You're so funny. By the way, did you throw away your table ＿＿＿＿＿ ＿＿＿＿＿
＿＿＿＿＿? I remember you told me that the legs were broken.

W: My brother fixed it. And now it's ＿＿＿＿＿ ＿＿＿＿＿ ＿＿＿＿＿ ＿＿＿＿＿
my room.

M: Where are your books? Did you bring all the books? You had a lot of books.

W: I made a really big bookshelf on the wall, but it's only ＿＿＿＿＿ ＿＿＿＿＿ ＿＿＿＿＿
books.

M: Did you also bring your old TV?

W: No, I bought a new one. I ＿＿＿＿＿ ＿＿＿＿＿ ＿＿＿＿＿ the wall.

A. Listening Web

Intro   It's not easy at all to (set / set up) the tent.
Web1   Here's the (burner / earner), and dinner will be ready soon.
Web2   Where is the radio? I want to hear the sound of civilization.
Web3   It's (on / over) the table.
Web4   Take a rest in the hammock. You look so (tire / tired).
Ending   I think we have to have a quick dinner and make a (big fire / bonfire).

B. True / False

1. 여자는 텐트 설치를 어려워한다.   (T / F)
2. 여자는 텐트를 처음 설치해 보았다.   (T / F)
3. 텐트를 다 설치하니 해가 저물기 시작했다.   (T / F)
4. 저녁을 준비하기 전에 모닥불부터 피울 것이다.   (T / F)

C. Words and Phrases

be (all) done (일을) 다 끝내다 / set up 설치하다 / civilization 문명 / hammock 해먹

D. Dictation

M: Now _____ _____ _____.

W: It's not easy at all to set up the tent. I don't think I'll go camping again.

M: Don't worry. It's your first time.

W: I'm hungry anyway. Let's have dinner.

M: Okay, wait a second. I'll prepare dinner for you. Here's the burner, and dinner will be ready soon.

W: _____ _____ _____ _____ trees, it's like a primitive life. Where is the radio? I want to hear the sound of civilization.

M: It's on the table. Take a rest in the hammock. You look so tired.

W: Where is the lamp? It's only 6:30 p.m., but it's getting dark. We need light.

M: Oh, my God! I _____ _____ _____ _____.

W: Oh, no. I think we have to have a quick dinner and make a bonfire. _____ _____ _____. You go get some firewood now.

M: This is not _____ _____ _____. Sorry about it.

A. Listening Web

Intro   The sun is (shining / shiny) and it's breezy.
Web1   (Sheep / Sheeps) are grazing on the grass.
Web2   Look at those sheep! They're sleeping under the (trees / freeze).
Web3   The girl over there is (feeding / leading) the sheep with her father!
Ending I'll take a picture (when / while) you're feeding the sheep.

B. True / False

1. 나무 아래에서 양들이 잠을 자고 있다.   (T / F)
2. 남자는 양이 나오는 꿈을 꾸었다.   (T / F)
3. 여자는 양에게 먹이를 주고 싶어 한다.   (T / F)
4. 남자는 동물을 별로 좋아하지 않는다.   (T / F)

C. Words and Phrases

breezy 산들바람이 부는 / graze 풀을 뜯다 / feed ~를 먹이다, 먹이를 주다

D. Dictation

W: What lovely weather!

M: Yeah. Look at the sky. The sun is shining and _____ _____. It's perfect weather for going on a picnic.

W: Yes, and it's a perfect birthday present for me. Thanks, Andy.

M: My pleasure. I'm so glad that you like it.

W: Wow! Look! Sheep are _____ _____ _____ _____. It looks so peaceful.

M: Look at those sheep! They're sleeping under the trees.

W: Are they dreaming?

M: Maybe they are grazing in their dreams. Can we _____ _____ the sheep?

W: I think so. The girl over there is feeding the sheep with her father! The sheep is _____ _____ _____ to eat grass. I'd like to do it.

M: Are you sure? You're _____ _____ _____.

W: Yes, but I want to try it. They are so cute. I think it'll be fun.

M: Okay. Let's go! _____ _____ _____ _____ while you're feeding the sheep.

A. Listening Web

Intro Did you (decorate / renovate) the tree by yourself?

Web1 Are these presents in front of the fireplace for your nephews?

Web2 That's why they put their socks (on / over) the fireplace.

Web3 Now I see the Christmas (lease / wreath) on the door.

Ending Is that turkey on the table (that / what) your mother made?

B. True / False

1. 여자는 조카에게 줄 선물을 준비했다.   (T / F)
2. 남자는 지팡이를 사용한다.   (T / F)
3. 여자는 크리스마스 이브에 양말을 침대에 걸어두곤 했었다.   (T / F)
4. 칠면조는 남자와 어머니가 함께 준비했다.   (T / F)

C. Words and Phrases

nephew 조카 / decorate 장식하다, 꾸미다 / Christmas wreath 크리스마스 때 장식으로 문에 거는 화환

D. Dictation

W: Did you decorate the tree by yourself?

M: With my nephews. They love to do it.

W: Yeah, children always _____ _____ Christmas trees. The candy canes on the tree are cute.

M: Have a seat in front of the fireplace. I'll get some tea.

W: Thanks. Are these presents in front of the fireplace _____ _____ _____?

M: Yes. They believe that Santa Claus will put the presents in their socks while they're sleeping. That's why they put their socks over the fireplace.

W: I _____ _____ Santa Claus, too. I always put my socks _____ _____ _____ on Christmas Eve. Oh! Now I see the Christmas wreath on the door. That's beautiful.

M: My mother makes it every year.

W: Is that turkey on the table what your mother made?

M: I cooked it with her. I learned _____ _____ _____ _____.

W: I wish _____ _____ _____ early so we can taste that turkey!

A. Listening Web  MP3 05-05-A

Intro	I saw Brian's Batman costume and I want to wear a (long / wrong) cape.
Web1	Then you need gloves with long and (shark / sharp) nails.
Web2	I want to carry the jack-o'-lantern.
Web3	Dracula never wears a hat. His hair stands out like (corns / horns).
Ending	I'll wear the shoes, but I (want to / won't) wear the hat.

B. True / False  MP3 05-05-B

1. 남자는 드라큘라 복장을 하고 싶어한다.   (T / F)
2. 남자는 Brian의 복장을 보고 호박 등을 만들기로 했다.   (T / F)
3. 여자는 남자가 드라큘라와 똑같은 복장을 하기를 원한다.   (T / F)
4. 남자는 작년에 신었던 신발을 신을 것이다.   (T / F)

C. Words and Phrases

costume 복장 / cape 망토 / jack-o'-lantern 도깨비 등, 호박 초롱

D. Dictation  MP3 05-05-B

W: Jack, _____ _____ _____ costume do you want for Halloween Night?

M: I'm thinking of Dracula. I saw Brian's Batman costume and I want to _____ _____ _____ _____.

W: Okay. Then you need gloves with long and sharp nails.

M: Yes, and I want to carry the jack-o'-lantern.

W: What about a hat? You have a wizard hat, like Harry Potter's.

M: Mom, Dracula never wears a hat. His hair _____ _____ _____ _____.

W: Right, but you don't need to be _____ _____ _____ the real Dracula. Make _____ _____ _____. And if you wear your black shoes, it'll be cute.

M: You mean the wizard shoes _____ _____ _____ _____?
Mom, I think you want me to reuse last year's costume. I'll wear the shoes, but I won't wear the hat. That's not Dracula.

W: Okay, Jack. Let's go get your Dracula costume.

A. Listening Web  MP3 05-06-A

Intro The road has (diverged / diverse) into three. Where should we go?

Web1 Do you have a (map / net)? No, but I have a compass.

Web2 It's 12 p.m. now, and that's why the sun is over the road on the very (light / right).

Web3 If I (didn't / don't) wear a hat, I would melt.

Ending The sun is too hot, and the (bag pack / backpack) is too heavy.

B. True / False  MP3 05-06-B

1. 두 사람은 남쪽으로 갈 것이다.   (T / F)
2. 두 사람은 지도를 가져왔다.   (T / F)
3. 여자는 모자를 쓰지 않은 것을 후회하고 있다.   (T / F)
4. 남자는 물과 과일을 챙겨왔다.   (T / F)

C. Words and Phrases

diverge (다른 방향으로) 갈라지다 / compass 나침반 / backpack 배낭 / shade 그늘 / cucumber 오이

D. Dictation  MP3 05-06-B

W: I think we're _____ _____. The road has _____ _____ three. Where should we go?

M: We just need to go south.

W: Do you have a map?

M: No, but I have a compass. Look at this. It will show us where south is.

W: Is the road _____ _____ _____ _____ heading south?

M: Yes. That's right. It's 12 p.m. now, and that's why the sun is over the road _____ _____ _____ _____. By the way, it's very hot and humid.

W: If I didn't wear a hat, _____ _____ _____.

M: Yeah, the sun is too hot, and the backpack is too heavy. I want to take a rest in the shade for a second.

W: Cool. What's in your bag?

M: Water, cucumber, and some fruit. I thought we _____ _____ _____.

문항 7
△ 심화 학습

A. Listening Web MP3 05-07-A

Intro   A lot of (cards / cars) are parked along the street.
Web1   Yeah, there's (no / one) police officer.
Web2   Tom, don't walk under the (ladder / letter).
Web3   There are so many trees (across / cross) the street that we cannot see what there is on the opposite side.
Ending   There's (a crosswalk / across walk) over there.

B. True / False  MP3 05-07-B

1. 두 사람은 자동차 경주 중이다.   (T / F)
2. 오늘은 일요일이다.   (T / F)
3. 여자는 사다리 아래로 지나가는 것을 꺼린다.   (T / F)
4. 두 사람은 육교를 건널 것이다.   (T / F)

C. Words and Phrases

under construction 공사 중인 / ladder 사다리 / taboo 터부, 금기 / superstition 미신

D. Dictation  MP3 05-07-B

M: This street is too messy. A lot of cars are parked along the street.

W: Yeah, there's no police officer. Maybe _____ _____ _____ because it's Sunday.

M: But it looks dangerous. The building is _____ _____.

W: Tom, don't walk under the ladder. Come this way.

M: What's the problem?

W: It's a taboo. Americans think _____ _____ _____ if you walk under the ladder.

M: It's just a superstition! I _____ _____ _____ we're close to the hospital or not.

W: There are so many trees across the street that we cannot see what there is _____ _____ _____ _____.

M: There's a crosswalk over there. Let's cross the street.

W: That's a good idea. Oh! It turned green. Run!

A. Listening Web

Intro You're a (chef / shelf), who comes from the bakery on the top.
Web1 You have to carry the cake to the (prince / princess) at the bottom safely.
Web2 If you fall on them, the ghost will (catch up / ketchup) with you.
Web3 If you jump (on / up) to a diamond, you'll get another chance.
Ending The diamonds (of / on) the top show you how many chances you have.

B. True / False

1. 남자는 새로운 게임에 도전하는 중이다. (T / F)
2. 여자는 새로운 게임에 큰 흥미를 보이지 않는다. (T / F)
3. 게임의 내용은 요리사가 케이크를 전달하는 것이다. (T / F)
4. 게임에서 다이아몬드의 개수는 기회의 개수를 나타낸다. (T / F)

C. Words and Phrases

catch up 따라잡다

D. Dictation

W: What are you doing?

M: Yesterday I saw my friend playing this game, and now I'm trying it.

W: It looks interesting. Will you show me how to do it?

M: Sure. _____ _____ _____, who comes from the bakery on the top. You have to carry the cake to the princess _____ _____ _____ safely.

W: That's quite simple.

M: Yes, but you need to _____ _____ these rocks. If you fall on them, the ghost will _____ _____ _____ you. The ghost keeps following you, and you'll lose a chance if you're caught by him.

W: What are these diamonds _____ _____ _____ _____?

M: If you jump up to a diamond, you'll get another chance.

W: How can I know how many chances are left?

M: The diamonds on the top show you how many chances you have.

W: So, the number of diamonds is _____ _____ _____ my lives.

M: That's right.

A. Listening Web

Intro The big lamp was still on beside the desk, and lots of books were still (stacked / stepped) up on the desk.

Web1 Oh, you (said / sat at) the piano.

Web2 I remember Sarah (feet / picked) a flower on the street and put it in the vase under the window.

Web3 This is a real flower.

Web4 But where is the cat on the (log / rug)?

Ending It's impossible to make (a live / alive) cat stay still.

B. True / False

1. 여자는 남자가 어제 다녀온 곳에 가본 적이 있다.　(T / F)
2. 남자는 방문한 곳에서 피아노를 연주해 보았다.　(T / F)
3. 남자는 길에서 꽃을 꺾어서 방문한 곳의 꽃병에 꽂아 두었다.　(T / F)
4. 방에는 양탄자가 깔려 있다.　(T / F)

C. Words and Phrases

stack up 쌓다 / rub 문지르다 / petal 꽃잎

D. Dictation

M: Guess what?

W: What?

M: Look at this picture. I went there yesterday.

W: It's Sarah's room in the film "Sad Genius." I've always wanted to go there. How was it?

M: You should go. The big lamp was _____ _____ beside the desk, and lots of books were still stacked up on the desk.

W: Oh, you sat at the piano. Did you try playing it?

M: No, you are _____ _____ _____ touch it.

W: I remember Sarah picked a flower on the street and _____ _____ in the vase under the window. She stood in front of the window _____ _____ _____.

M: This is a real flower. It's not artificial.

W: Really? Everything's _____ _____ _____ _____ in the movie. But where is the cat on the rug?

M: She was always there in the movie, but you know, it's impossible to make a live cat stay still.

A. Listening Web  MP3 05-10-A

Intro The couple at the bottom is my (creation / translation).

Web1 Was the window on the 2nd floor originally open?

Web2 I'd like to sit at one of these (around / round) tables.

Web3 That's why there are stars in the sky.

Ending I was going to draw a lamp on the wall last. But when I was about to paint it, the time was (off / up).

B. True / False  MP3 05-10-B

1. 여자의 그림은 원작과 똑같다.   (T / F)
2. 여자는 이 그림을 집에서 그렸다.   (T / F)
3. 여자는 그림에 있는 카페에 가 본 적이 없다.   (T / F)
4. 여자는 낮의 풍경을 그렸다.   (T / F)

C. Words and Phrases

exist 존재하다 / the time is up 시간이 다 됐다, 시간이 끝났다

D. Dictation  MP3 05-10-B

M: _____ _____ _____! Do you really paint it yourself?

W: Thanks. It's just _____ _____ _____ _____ in art class.
It's not the same as the original work. The couple at the bottom is my creation.

M: Was the window on the 2nd floor originally open?

W: Yes, _____ _____ is almost the same.

M: This café _____ _____. Have you ever been there?

W: No, but I'd like to sit at one of these round tables and have dinner on a summer night, like in this picture.

M: Night? Ah-ha, that's why there are stars in the sky. At first I thought you _____ _____ because it's so bright.

W: It's because I was going to draw a lamp on the wall last. But when I was about to paint it, _____ _____ _____ _____.

여기에서는 대본에서 언급되는 거의 모든 내용이 그대로 매력적인 오답으로 나와 있음에 주의 해야 한다. 따라서 부분적으로만 내용을 이해하는 수준이라면 틀리기 십상이다. 전체적으로 모든 내용을 정확히 파악하고 결정적인 단서가 되는 부분을 잡아낼 수 있어야 한다. 또한 선택지가 영어로 출제될 수 있으므로 이럴 때에는 대화가 시작되기 전 빠르게 선택지 내용을 파악해 두는 것도 잊지 말아야 한다.

• Example

1 **대화를 듣고, 남자가 여자를 위해 할 일로 가장 적절한 것을 고르시오.** [2011 수능기출]

W: Excuse me. Is this the SCA Express office?

M: Yes. What can I do for you?

W: I took a bus from Busan and I left my cell phone on the bus.

M: Okay. What time did your bus depart from Busan?

W: My bus left at four-twenty p.m.

M: Let's see. No one has turned in anything yet.

W: I really need to find my phone because all my contacts are stored in it.

M: Well, since your bus arrived half an hour ago, it should be on its way to the car wash.

W: Is there any chance that the bus driver is still around?

M: He may be at the drivers' lounge. Let me give him a call.

W: Thank you. I hope he didn't go anywhere too far.

① 세차 도와주기
② 버스 기사에게 전화하기
③ 휴대폰 수리 맡기기
④ 터미널 휴게실 청소하기
⑤ 차량 운행 시간 알려 주기

* 남자의 마지막 발언 중 "Let me give him a call."이 정답을 고르는 결정적인 단서가 된다. 여자가 휴대폰을 잃어버렸고, 버스가 세차장으로 가는 중이고, 버스 기사가 기사 라운지에 있다는 내용이 언급되었지만, 이와 비슷한 내용의 선택지들과 정답을 혼동하는 일이 없도록 한다. 정답은 ②번이다.

유형 6

부탁 및
할 일 추론하기

부탁 및 할 일 추론하기

1 대화를 듣고, 여자가 남자를 위해 할 일로 가장 적절한 것을 고르시오.

① 여성용 티셔츠를 보여준다.
② 양말과 넥타이를 보여준다.
③ 티셔츠의 치수를 줄여준다.
④ 정장 셔츠를 여성용 티셔츠로 바꿔준다.
⑤ 정장 셔츠를 분홍색 티셔츠로 교환해준다.

2 대화를 듣고, 남자가 **퇴근 후에** 할 일로 가장 적절한 것을 고르시오.

① 계약서를 수정한다.
② 전화해서 모임을 취소한다.
③ 아이를 유치원에서 데려온다.
④ 친구들과의 약속에 간다.
⑤ 유치원 학부모 모임에 참석한다.

3 대화를 듣고, 남자가 여자를 위해서 할 일로 가장 적절한 것을 고르시오.

① 손을 내민다.
② 공원을 산책한다.
③ 함께 떡을 먹는다.
④ 케이크를 사다 준다.
⑤ 전구를 교환해 준다.

4 대화를 듣고, 여자가 취할 행동으로 가장 적절한 것을 고르시오.

① 911에 전화한다.
② 혼자 병원으로 간다.
③ 가까운 병원을 검색한다.
④ 부축해 줄 사람을 찾는다.
⑤ 현재 장소에서 남자를 기다린다.

5 대화를 듣고, 여자가 Career Expo에서 어떤 직업에 관한 강의를 듣게 될지 고르시오.

① diplomat
② food stylist
③ photographer
④ fashion designer
⑤ She hasn't decided yet.

6 대화를 듣고, 남자가 여자에게 부탁한 일로 가장 적절한 것을 고르시오.

① to buy a sketchbook
② to give the money back
③ to lend him some money
④ to negotiate their meeting time
⑤ to drop by the convenience store

7 대화를 듣고, 여자가 취할 행동으로 가장 적절한 것을 고르시오.

① to fix the printer
② to refill the ink
③ to call David
④ to find the pictures
⑤ to email her homework to him

8 대화를 듣고, 여자가 취할 행동으로 가장 적절한 것을 고르시오.

① to borrow his raincoat
② to lend him an umbrella
③ to wait for the rain to stop
④ to go on a trip to another place
⑤ to call her roommate to pick her up

9 대화를 듣고, 여자가 취할 행동으로 가장 적절한 것을 고르시오.

① to go to a bookstore
② to go to Africa with the man
③ to buy the book from the man
④ to borrow the book at the library
⑤ to take pictures of African students

10 대화를 듣고, 남자가 여자에게 부탁한 일로 가장 적절한 것을 고르시오.

① to buy the score
② to lend the score
③ to introduce Tom to him
④ to join Tom's clarinet club
⑤ to play clarinet with him at the music test

해답/해설 261p

A. Listening Web

Intro Can I (change / exchange) this dress shirt?
Web1 Do you have this in a (major / larger) size?
Web2 Please show me (another / other) one in a larger size, then.
Web3 It's cheaper than that dress shirt. Do you need anything else?
Ending I want to see a (woman's / women's) T-shirt in the same design for my girlfriend.

B. True / False

1. 남자는 정장 셔츠를 선물 받았었다.   (T / F)
2. 남자는 원래 정장 셔츠를 환불받으려 했다.   (T / F)
3. 양말과 넥타이가 할인 중이다.   (T / F)
4. 티셔츠가 정장 셔츠보다 비싸다.   (T / F)

C. Words and Phrases

dress shirt 정장 셔츠, 와이셔츠 / on sale 할인 중

D. Dictation

M: Excuse me. Can I exchange this dress shirt?

W: Yes, of course. What seems to be the _____ _____ _____?

M: It was my birthday gift, but it's not _____ _____. Do you have this in a larger size?

W: I'm sorry. We don't.

M: Please show me another one in a larger size, then.

W: This way, please. How would you like this blue T-shirt?

M: That looks good, but do you have this _____ _____ _____?

W: How about this pink one?

M: That's _____ _____. I'll take the blue one _____.

W: No problem. It's cheaper than that dress shirt. Do you need anything else? Socks and neckties are _____ _____.

M: Those are good, but I want to see a women's T-shirt in the same design for my girlfriend.

W: Okay.

A. Listening Web

Intro I'm really sorry, but I'll be (late / rate).

Web1 It's your turn to pick up Amy at kindergarten.

Web2 But I have (an expected / an unexpected) meeting at 5 p.m. with an important buyer.

Web3 I told you I have an appointment (for / to) dinner with my friends.

Ending I'll go to the kindergarten right after work.

B. True / False

1. 여자는 오늘 늦게 퇴근하게 될지도 모른다.   (T / F)
2. 오늘은 원래 여자가 유치원에서 딸을 데려오는 날이다.   (T / F)
3. 여자는 회의 도중에 남자에게 전화했다.   (T / F)
4. 남자는 오늘 저녁 식사를 마치는 대로 유치원으로 갈 것이다.   (T / F)

C. Words and Phrases

unexpected 예상치 못한 / casual (관계가) 가벼운 / contract 계약(서) / priority 우선 사항

D. Dictation

M: Hello?

W: Honey, it's me.

M: What's up?

W: I'm really sorry, but _____ _____ _____.

M: No! It's your turn to pick up Amy at kindergarten.

W: I know. But I have an unexpected meeting at 5 p.m. with an important buyer.

M: Just tell them you _____ _____ _____ _____!

W: This is not a casual thing. There seems to be something wrong _____ _____ _____, and it will be a long conversation.

M: But… but I told you I have an appointment for dinner with my friends. I haven't seen them for years. I invited them to dinner. I cannot cancel it.

W: I know. But _____ _____ _____, your daughter or dinner with friends?

M: Don't be upset. I'll go to the kindergarten right after work. But please call me if the meeting cancels.

A. Listening Web  MP3 06-03-A

Intro   Jack, will you give me a hand, please?

Web1   I'm trying to change the (bulb / herb), but I can't reach it.

Web2   That's a (walk / work) in the park.

Web3   I mean it's easy for me to do it. It's the same expression as 'a (peace / piece) of cake.'

Ending   Now help me with this.

B. True / False  MP3 06-03-B

1. 여자는 전구에 손이 닿지 않는다.   (T / F)
2. 남자는 공원을 산책하려던 참이었다.   (T / F)
3. 남자는 누워서 떡을 먹어본 적이 있다.   (T / F)
4. 남자는 여자를 도울 수가 없다.   (T / F)

C. Words and Phrases

bulb 전구 / walk in the park 쉬운 일 / choked 목 막히는

D. Dictation  MP3 06-03-B

W: Jack, will you _____ _____ _____ _____, please?

M: Sure, what do you want me to do?

W: I'm trying to change the bulb, but I can't reach it.

M: That's a _____ _____ _____ _____.

W: What do you mean by that?

M: I mean it's easy for me to do it. It's the same expression as 'a piece of cake.'

W: I've heard of the expression. We have a similar expression in Korean. Have you ever heard of 'eating rice cake while _____ _____'?

M: Yeah, that's interesting. But actually eating rice cake while lying down is not a piece of cake. I've tried to, but I choked and I almost died.

W: Haha. I know what you mean.

M: I don't understand where that expression came from.

W: I _____ _____ _____, Jack. Now help me with this.

A. Listening Web

Intro   I just now fell down the stairs, and I think I (sprained / spring) my ankle.

Web1   I didn't try walking yet, but it's getting (swollen / swallow).

Web2   Christine, the hospital is just (around / round) the corner.

Web3   How about calling 911?

Ending   Well, that's okay. I can walk slowly (by myself / myself).

B. True / False

1. 여자는 지금 혼자 있다.   (T / F)
2. 남자는 여자를 만나러 갈 것이다.   (T / F)
3. 여자는 집 근처에 있다.   (T / F)
4. 여자가 있는 곳 가까이에 병원이 없다.   (T / F)

C. Words and Phrases

fall down the stairs 계단에서 굴러떨어지다 / sprain one's ankle 발목을 삐다 / swollen 부어오른

D. Dictation

M: Hello?

W: Brad, I just now fell down the stairs, and I think I _____ _____ _____.

M: Where are you now?

W: I'm in the Twinkle Tower in Summerfield town.

M: Can you walk? Or do you want me to go there?

W: It's kind of _____ _____ _____ _____. It'll take a lot. I didn't try walking yet, but it's getting swollen.

M: Wait. I'll search where the _____ _____ is. Christine, the hospital is just around the corner. Can you drive?

W: No, I can't.

M: Is there anybody who can help you?

W: Unfortunately no. I'll _____ _____. Ouch!

M: Don't do that! How about calling 911?

W: Well, that's okay. I can walk slowly by myself.

M: I'll _____ _____ _____ _____ right away. See you there.

A. Listening Web  MP3 06-05-A

Intro   Have you decided which class you (will / would) go to at Career Expo?

Web1   I'm thinking of the food stylist and the fashion designer (course / courses).

Web2   I heard a famous photographer will come, and the student (response / respond) to him was very good last year.

Web3   I'm interested in taking (features / pictures), too.

Web4   Now you've (change / changed) your mind?

Ending   Yes, I think so.

B. True / False  MP3 06-05-B

1. 남자는 어려서부터 외교관을 꿈꿔왔다.   (T / F)
2. 여자는 초등학교 때부터 미술에 관심이 많았다.   (T / F)
3. 여자는 사진 찍기를 좋아한다.   (T / F)
4. 작년에 사진작가의 강의가 인기 있었다.   (T / F)

C. Words and Phrases

Expo(=exposition) 박람회 / diplomat 외교관 / global 세계적인, 지구의 / response 반응

D. Dictation  MP3 06-05-B

W: Have you decided which class you would go to at Career Expo?

M: I'm thinking of the _____ _____.

W: I remember you told me that you're _____ _____ learning foreign languages.

M: Yes, and I want to live in a foreign country.

W: That'll be interesting. Do you want to be a diplomat or are you just interested in _____ _____?

M: I have wanted to be a diplomat since I was in elementary school. I think I can get some useful information. What about you?

W: I'm thinking of the food stylist and the fashion designer courses.

M: You like art. I heard a famous _____ will come, and the student response to him was very good last year.

W: Really? I'm interested in taking pictures, too.

M: Now you've changed _____ _____?

W: Yes, I think so.

A. Listening Web

Intro See you at 7:(14 / 40) in front of the convenience store.

Web1 I'll leave for school (earlier / early) today to buy a sketchbook.

Web2 I'm really sorry, but will you please buy one for me?

Web3 But what if there is a wide range in (quality / quantity)?

Ending Then please get me one the same (as / with) yours.

B. True / False

1. 남자는 항상 학교 가는 길에 편의점에 들른다. (T / F)
2. 여자는 오늘 아침 일찍 집을 나설 것이다. (T / F)
3. 여자는 남자와 함께 등교하는 것을 좋아하지 않는다. (T / F)
4. 여자는 오늘 아침 스케치북을 두 권 사야 한다. (T / F)

C. Words and Phrases

convenience store 편의점 / stationery store 문구점 / range 다양성, 범위

D. Dictation

W: Hello?

M: Hi, Emily. Let's go to school together. See you at 7:40 in front of the convenience store.

W: I'll leave for school early today to buy a sketchbook. We need it in _____ _____ today. Did you buy one?

M: Oh, I forgot to.

W: Buy one _____ _____ _____ _____ school. I'll leave home at 7:20 a.m.

M: Where is the nearest stationery store?

W: Across _____ _____ _____.

M: It's too far away from my house. How much is it?

W: Around $5? I'm not sure, _____.

M: I'm really sorry, but will you please buy one for me? I'll give you the money at school.

W: Okay. But what if there is a wide range _____ _____?

M: Then please get me one the same as yours.

W: I see.

문항 7

△ 심화 학습

A. Listening Web  MP3 06-07-A

Intro   Have you (vanished / finished) the history homework?

Web1   I'm still working on it. Did you find (all / out) the pictures Mr. Green mentioned?

Web2   Yes, (I'm ready to / I've already) put them in. I found seven pictures.

Web3   By the way, will you please print my report? My printer is (outer / out of) ink.

Web4   I'm really sorry, but my printer doesn't work. I (fix / fixed) it yesterday, but it's out of order again. Why don't you call David?

Ending   I see. I'd better hurry. I hope he's not in bed yet.

B. True / False 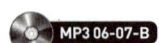 MP3 06-07-B

1. 남자는 숙제를 다 끝내지 못했다.   (T / F)
2. 여자는 역사를 전공하고 있다.   (T / F)
3. 남자의 프린터는 고장 났다.   (T / F)
4. 여자는 남자에게 이메일을 보낼 것이다.   (T / F)

C. Words and Phrases

in the early 1900s 1900년대 초기 / major 전공하는 학생 / be out of 다 떨어지다 / out of order 고장 난

D. Dictation  MP3 06-07-B

M: Hello?

W: Hi, this is Chloe. Have you finished the history homework?

M: I'm still _____ _____ _____. Did you find all the pictures Mr. Green mentioned? Did he say that we should include at least five pictures?

W: Yes, I've already _____ _____ _____. I found seven pictures.

M: Where did you get them?

W: At www.photophoto.com. You can find many pictures of New York _____ _____ _____ _____ at the site.

M: I see. Thank you. How did you know about this site?

W: My sister is a _____ _____. By the way, will you please print my report? My printer is out of ink. I'll email it to you.

M: I'm really sorry, but my printer doesn't work. I fixed it yesterday, but it's _____ _____ _____ _____. Why don't you call David?

W: I see. I'd better hurry. I hope he's not in bed yet.

A. Listening Web  MP3 06-08-A

Intro It's (pouring / pulling).
Web1 (Lend / Let) me your umbrella and you wear my coat.
Web2 I'll call my roommate and ask if she can pick me up.
Web3 But I can't give you (back / bag) your raincoat tomorrow because I'll be on a business trip for a week from tomorrow.
Ending Then I'll (stand / stay) with you here until your roommate comes.

△
심
화
학
습

B. True / False  MP3 06-08-B

1. 여자는 우산이 없다.   (T / F)
2. 남자는 여자에게 비옷을 빌려주려 한다.   (T / F)
3. 여자는 내일 출장을 떠난다.   (T / F)
4. 남자는 이미 비에 옷이 다 젖었다.   (T / F)

C. Words and Phrases

rain cats and dogs 비가 거세게 오다 / soak 담그다 / grateful 고마워하는

D. Dictation  MP3 06-08-B

M: _____ _____. Do you have an umbrella?

W: Yes, I have one. But it's raining _____ _____ _____. I can't walk home.

M: Your home is far away from here. Will you wear my raincoat?

W: Then what are you going to wear?

M: Lend me your umbrella and you wear my raincoat. It takes only two or three minutes to my house. But you'll be _____ with only this umbrella.

W: How nice of you. But you'll be soaked, too. I'll call my roommate ask if she can pick me up.

M: Then you'll have to wait for her for a long time here alone.

W: But I can't give you back your raincoat tomorrow because I'll be _____ _____ _____ _____ for a week from tomorrow. So I'm very grateful, but I don't think it's a good idea.

M: Then I'll stay with you here until _____ _____ _____.

W: Thank you.

A. Listening Web    MP3 06-09-A

Intro   I've always been dreaming of international voluntary service. I applied for it last semester, (and fortunately / unfortunately) I'm in.

Web1   That's why these days I'm reading a book about Brundi.

Web2   It is about the students in Brundi who take pictures of their daily (life / lives) with (disposable / this posable) cameras and present their dreams in the pictures.

Web3   I heard all the profits from the books are (donated / donating) to the schools in Africa.

Ending   Wow, then I'm willing to buy one right now.

B. True / False    MP3 06-09-B

1. 남자는 방학 동안 아프리카에 갈 계획이다.   (T / F)
2. 여자는 해외 봉사활동에 관심이 많다.   (T / F)
3. 남자가 읽고 있는 아프리카 관련 서적은 도서관에서 빌린 것이다.   (T / F)
4. 여자는 남자에게 책을 빌려 볼 것이다.   (T / F)

C. Words and Phrases

voluntary service 자원봉사활동 / disposable 일회용의 / present 보여주다, 나타내다 / donate 기증하다

D. Dictation    MP3 06-09-B

W: Kevin, I heard you have an awesome plan during this summer vacation.

M: Yeah. I've always been dreaming of international _____ service. I applied for it last semester, and fortunately _____ _____.

W: But aren't you afraid of going to Africa? We don't have lots of information about it.

M: That's why these days I'm reading a book about Brundi.

W: Brundi? What is it?

M: It's a country in Africa.

W: I see. What's the title?

M: "Dreaming with a Camera." It is about the students in Brundi who take pictures of their daily lives with _____ _____ and present their dreams in the pictures.

W: Interesting. I'd like to read the book. Could you lend me the book after _____ _____ _____?

M: I'm sorry. I borrowed it from my friend. I heard all the profits from the books are donated to the schools in Africa.

W: Wow, then I'm _____ _____ _____ _____ right now.

A. Listening Web

Intro I'm on the way to the bookstore.
Web1 I promised to play "Nella Fantasia" to my girlfriend (in / on) her birthday, so I'm going to the bookstore to buy the score.
Web2 By the way, you know my brother, Tom. He also plays the clarinet, and he has the (score / store).
Web3 Can you lend it to me, please?
Ending No problem.

B. True / False

1. 두 사람은 서점으로 가는 길이다.   (T / F)
2. 여자는 서점에 악보를 사러 간다.   (T / F)
3. 여자의 남동생은 클라리넷을 연주한다.   (T / F)
4. 여자는 음악 수행평가를 준비 중이다.   (T / F)

C. Words and Phrases

score 악보 / musical instrument 악기 / clarinet 클라리넷

D. Dictation

W: What's up?

M: Hi, Irene. I'm on the way _____ _____ _____.

W: Really? Me, too. Let's go together. What are you looking for?

M: A score.

W: Score? Do you play a _____ _____?

M: I play clarinet. I promised to play "Nella Fantasia" to my girlfriend on her birthday, so I'm going to the bookstore to buy the score.

W: How sweet of you. By the way, you know my brother, Tom. He also plays the clarinet, and he has the score.

M: Are you sure?

W: Yes, I heard him practice it a week ago. Maybe he practiced it for the _____ _____ _____.

M: Can you lend it to me, please?

W: No problem. I think Tom wants to be friends with you. He is trying to make a club for _____ _____.

M: Wow, I'm interested in the club.

대본에서 정답의 단서는 대체로 대화의 중간이나 마지막에 언급된다. 따라서 초반에는 대화의 주제가 무엇인지 파악하고, 중반 이후부터는 세밀한 내용을 모두 파악해야 한다. 이유를 명확하게 말하기도 하지만, 정황을 이해해야 하는 경우도 있으므로 행간의 의미도 파악할 수 있는 능력을 기르도록 연습해야 한다.

● **Example**

1 **대화를 듣고, 남자가 늦게 귀가하는 이유를 고르시오.** [2012 수능모의]

M: Hey, what's up, Mom?

W: Paul, when are you coming home?

M: I haven't even left the computer lab.

W: You're later than usual. Is there anything wrong?

M: Yeah, I need to hand in an assignment by tomorrow but the computer froze. All the work I have done is gone.

W: Oh, my goodness. You must be upset.

M: Don't worry. I have everything about the assignment in my memory. It'll just take a little more time to retype it.

W: That's my boy. Dinner is almost ready. Are you going to eat at home?

M: Go ahead and eat first. It'll take two more hours or so.

W: Okay. I hope it all works out well.

① 빙판길 때문에
② 시험공부 때문에
③ 과제물 재작성 때문에
④ 컴퓨터실 청소 때문에
⑤ 저녁 식사 약속 때문에

* 남자는 과제물을 다시 작성하기 위해 컴퓨터실에 늦게까지 남아있는 상황이다. 남자의 말 중 "It'll just take a little more time to retype it"이 정답을 고르는 결정적인 단서가 된다. 저녁 식사, 컴퓨터실, 컴퓨터 멈춤(froze) 등의 발언에 유혹되지 않도록 주의한다. 정답은 ③번이다.

유형 7

이유 문제

이유 문제

1 대화를 듣고, 남자가 과속을 한 이유를 고르시오.

① 아기가 아팠기 때문에
② 아내가 출산했기 때문에
③ 운전이 서툴렀기 때문에
④ 눈길에 미끄러졌기 때문에
⑤ 예매 시간이 촉박했기 때문에

2 대화를 듣고, 여자가 래프팅에 갈 수 없는 이유를 고르시오.

① 허리가 아프기 때문에
② 물을 무서워하기 때문에
③ 비가 올 것으로 예상되기 때문에
④ 사촌의 결혼식에 참석해야 하기 때문에
⑤ 이번 주말에 친구와 쇼핑 약속이 있기 때문에

3 대화를 듣고, 남자가 Buddy Book을 자주 하지 않는 이유를 고르시오.

① 게으르기 때문에
② ID가 없기 때문에
③ 남자애들이나 하는 거라는 생각 때문에
④ 주변 친구들이 Buddy Book을 안 하기 때문에
⑤ 모르는 사람들에게 사생활이 노출되는 것이 싫기 때문에

4 대화를 듣고, 남자가 한국 대중가요를 좋아하는 이유를 고르시오.

① 주변 친구들이 좋아하기 때문에
② 가수들의 외모가 뛰어나기 때문에
③ 플래시 몹 공연을 하기 쉽기 때문에
④ 한국 드라마 내용과 연관이 있기 때문에
⑤ 리듬이 단순해서 따라 부르기 쉽기 때문에

5 다음을 듣고, 여자가 걱정하는 이유를 고르시오.

① 다음 주에 비가 그친다는 예보 때문에
② 남자가 실내 활동만을 원하기 때문에
③ 비 때문에 휴가를 망칠 것 같기 때문에
④ 가뭄이 농가에 피해를 심하게 끼쳤기 때문에
⑤ 비가 너무 많이 와서 농작물에 피해가 가기 때문에

6 다음을 듣고, 남자가 19세기 미 소설 강의를 수강할 수 없는 이유를 고르시오.

① 학점이 부족하기 때문에
② 영어 전공자가 아니기 때문에
③ 지난해에 이미 수강했기 때문에
④ 아르바이트를 해야 하기 때문에
⑤ 영어 회화 수업을 들어야 하기 때문에

7 다음을 듣고, 남자가 피곤한 이유를 고르시오.

① 집에 불이 났기 때문에
② 식구들이 사고를 당했기 때문에
③ 화재경보기가 잘못 울렸기 때문에
④ 지난밤에 역사 공부를 했기 때문에
⑤ 지난밤에 숙제를 늦게까지 했기 때문에

8 다음을 듣고, 남자가 방학 중 학교에 가야 하는 이유를 고르시오.

① 상을 받아야 하기 때문에
② 지휘를 연습해야 하기 때문에
③ 뮤지컬을 연습해야 하기 때문에
④ 피아노를 연주해야 하기 때문에
⑤ 여름 보충 수업을 들어야 하기 때문에

9 대화를 듣고, 남자가 연수에 참여할 수 없는 이유를 고르시오.

① 교회에 가야 하기 때문에
② 태국 여행 홍보 준비 때문에
③ 수련회에 참가해야 하기 때문에
④ 외국여행을 갈 예정이기 때문에
⑤ 친구가 가지 않는다고 했기 때문에

10 대화를 듣고, 여자가 점심을 먹지 않은 이유를 고르시오.

① 낮잠을 잤기 때문에
② 운동을 했기 때문에
③ 식사 조절 중이기 때문에
④ 치과 치료를 받았기 때문에
⑤ 남자와 전화를 했기 때문에

해답/해설 266p

A. Listening Web  MP3 07-01-A

Intro Springville District Police. May I help you?

Web1 I got a ticket for (speeding / speedy).

Web2 My wife was giving birth (through / to) a baby, and I was on the way to the hospital.

Web3 Then you need to (hand in / handle) the proof of birth at the police office.

Ending And from now on don't forget that speeding is very dangerous, especially in winter. The streets are very (snowing / snowy) and slippery.

B. True / False  MP3 07-01-B

1. 남자는 영화 표에 대해 문의하고 있다. (T / F)
2. 벌금 납부 기한은 이틀이다. (T / F)
3. 남자가 과속 벌금을 내지 않기 위해서는 경찰서에 서류를 제출해야 한다. (T / F)
4. 남자는 과속으로 교통 사고가 났다. (T / F)

C. Words and Phrases

a ticket for speeding 과속딱지 / fine 벌금 / give birth 출산하다 / proof of birth 출생증명서

D. Dictation  MP3 07-01-B

W: Springville District Police. May I help you?

M: Hi, I'm calling to see if I can _____ _____ _____ .

W: What's the problem?

M: I got a ticket for speeding.

W: Then you have to pay the fine _____ _____ _____ at the nearest police office.

M: I know, but I _____ _____ _____ at the time.

W: What happened?

M: My wife was giving birth to a baby, and I was on the way to the hospital.

W: Oh, congratulations. Then you need to hand in the proof of birth at the police office.

M: Then can I simply get the fine cancelled?

W: Yes. And _____ _____ _____ don't forget that speeding is very dangerous, especially in winter. The streets are very snowy and slippery.

M: Of course. I'm always _____ _____ _____ . Thanks.

W: You're welcome.

A. Listening Web

Intro I called you to go to a movie, but you didn't get the phone.

Web1 I recognized that I'd missed your calls too late, so I couldn't give you a (return / turn) call.

Web2 I was going to ask you if you can go rafting (next / text) Friday.

Web3 I do love (left / rafting). But actually I have a backache.

Ending Yes, the doctor said I need to (avoid / void) active exercise for a while.

B. True / False

1. 여자는 사촌 결혼식에 다녀왔다.   (T / F)
2. 여자는 비를 맞으며 쇼핑을 했다.   (T / F)
3. 남자는 래프팅을 가려고 한다.   (T / F)
4. 여자는 래프팅을 원래 좋아하지 않는다.   (T / F)

C. Words and Phrases

hang around 돌아다니다 / for a while 한동안

D. Dictation

W: What did you do last weekend? I called you to go to a movie, but you didn't _____ _____ _____.

M: I'm sorry. I went to _____ _____ _____ on Sunday. I recognized that _____ _____ _____ _____ too late, so I couldn't give you a return call.

W: That's okay. I _____ _____ with my friends during the weekend.

M: But it was rainy a lot!

W: Yeah. That's why I spent _____ _____ _____ _____ at the shopping mall, and I got rain boots.

M: I see. I was going to ask you if you can go rafting next Friday.

W: I'd love to, but…

M: Are you _____ _____ water?

W: No way. I do love rafting. But actually I have a backache.

M: Did you go to the hospital?

W: Yes, the doctor said I need to _____ _____ _____ for a while.

M: I see. I hope you'll get better soon.

A. Listening Web  MP3 07-03-A

Intro	Do you also have your own Buddy Book?
Web1	I just (search / surf) my friends' Buddy Books.
Web2	I don't want somebody I don't know to know about my (privacy / private) life. What about you?
Web3	You're not (interested in / interesting) this kind of thing. I thought it was kind of girlish.
Ending	I think I'm just too lazy to visit my friends' Buddy Books and put (off / up) some comments.

B. True / False  MP3 07-03-B

1. 여자는 자신의 Buddy Book 사이트를 운영 중이다.   (T / F)
2. 여자는 지금 자신의 Buddy Book 사이트를 보고 있다.   (T / F)
3. 여자는 한 달에 두세 번 정도 Buddy Book 사이트를 방문한다.   (T / F)
4. 남자는 친구들의 Buddy Book 사이트를 방문만 한다.   (T / F)

C. Words and Phrases

upload 업로드하다 / surf 인터넷 서핑(검색)하다 / private 사적인, 개인 소유의 / girlish 여자아이 같은

D. Dictation  MP3 07-03-B

W: Paul, what are you doing?

M: I'm looking at my friend's Buddy Book. She uploads _____ _____ _____ _____ and comments every day.

W: Do you also have your own Buddy Book?

M: I don't have my own. I just surf my friends' Buddy Books.

W: Why don't you have one?

M: Well, it's very interesting, but I think it's _____ _____ _____. I don't want somebody I don't know to know about my private life. What about you?

W: I just _____ _____ my friends', like you.

M: How often do you visit the Buddy Book site?

W: Only two or three times a month.

M: You're not interested in this kind of thing. I thought it was _____ _____ _____.

W: Well, some of my male friends like Buddy Book. I think I'm just _____ _____ _____ _____ my friends' Buddy Books and put up some comments.

A. Listening Web

Intro   This is the performance of a K-pop star. I'm practicing this (top / type) of dance these days.

Web1   What makes you like K-pop?

Web2   The rhythm is so simple that anybody can sing (alone / along).

Web3   And the Korean pop singers are also professional when it comes to dancing, so their performances are not (bored / boring) at all.

Ending   I'm planning a (flash / fresh) mob dance with a Korean pop song. Will you join?

B. True / False

1. 여자는 한국 대중가요를 들어본 적이 없다.   (T / F)
2. 남자는 한국 드라마를 통해 한국 대중가요를 좋아하게 되었다.   (T / F)
3. 남자는 한국 대중가요의 리듬이 단순하고 박자가 빠르지 않아 좋아한다.   (T / F)
4. 여자는 플래시 몹에 참여할 것이다.   (T / F)

C. Words and Phrases

soap opera 드라마 / flash mob 플래시 몹 (미리 정한 장소에 모여 아주 짧은 시간 동안 약속한 행동을 한 후, 바로 흩어지는 불특정 다수의 군중 행위)

D. Dictation

W: What are you looking at?

M: This is the performance of a K-pop star. I'm practicing this type of dance these days.

W: I didn't know that you like dancing.

M: I became _____ _____ Korean pop songs after I saw some Korean _____ _____. Do you like K-pop?

W: Well, I've heard only a few songs. What makes you like K-pop?

M: The rhythm is _____ simple _____ anybody can sing along.

W: But if the rhythm is simple, I don't think it's interesting.

M: The songs have a quick tempo. And the Korean pop singers are also professional _____ _____ _____ _____ dancing, so their performances are not boring at all.

W: Really? I can't imagine. Can you let me listen to a Korean pop song?

M: Sure, why not? Oh! I'm planning a flash mob dance with a Korean pop song. Will you join?

W: No, Jack. I'm really _____ _____ _____.

A. Listening Web  MP3 07-05-A

Intro   It's raining (heavenly / heavily).

Web1   But we haven't had rain for a long time, so the current drought has been extremely (harder / hard on) farmers.

Web2   Farmers are glad to have rain, but I'm (worried / worry) because of this rain.

Web3   I'm going to take (a / up) few days off next week. The weather forecast says that it will last for about five days from now.

Ending   I was going to go hiking.

B. True / False  MP3 07-05-B

1. 지금 비가 너무 많이 와서 홍수가 날 것 같다.   (T / F)
2. 한동안 비가 안 왔었다.   (T / F)
3. 남자는 비 오는 것을 좋아한다.   (T / F)
4. 여자는 다음 주에 설악산에 갈 예정이다.   (T / F)

C. Words and Phrases

current 현재의, 지금의 / drought 가뭄 / suffer from ~으로 고통받다 / take a (few) day(s) off 휴가 내다

D. Dictation  MP3 07-05-B

W: It's raining heavily.

M: You don't like rain, do you?

W: No. It's _____ _____ _____ all day long.

M: I don't like rain, either. But we haven't had rain for a long time, so the current drought has been extremely hard on farmers.

W: I've heard the news that farmers have _____ _____ drought damage.

M: Maybe this rain will be helpful. I think we need more rain. This is _____ _____.

W: You're right. Farmers are glad to have rain, but I'm worried _____ _____ _____ _____.

M: Why?

W: I'm going to take _____ _____ _____ _____ next week. The weather forecast says that it will last for about five days from now.

M: Uh-oh. I'm sorry to hear that. You can _____ _____ _____, like swimming in an indoor swimming pool.

W: I've already reserved a hotel room near Sorak Mountain. I was going to go hiking.

A. Listening Web

Intro   I'm thinking of changing one (of / or) my classes next semester.

Web1   I'll take (19 / 19th) century American literature instead of English Conversation.

Web2   Will you sign (on / up) for this course with me?

Web3   Sorry, I have a part-time job then. Mina is an English major, too. Why don't you call her?

Ending She (taught / took) this course last semester.

B. True / False

1. 여자는 영어 전공이다.   (T / F)
2. 여자는 영어 회화 수업을 듣지 않을 것이다.   (T / F)
3. 남자는 월요일에 아르바이트를 한다.   (T / F)
4. 여자는 미나에게 전화할 것이다.   (T / F)

C. Words and Phrases

requirement 필수과목 / demanding 부담이 큰, 힘든 / elective 선택과목 / credit 학점

D. Dictation

W: Yoon, will you _____ _____ _____ English Conversation next semester?

M: Sure. It's a requirement _____ _____ _____ I know.

W: Not really. I'm thinking of changing one of my classes next semester.

M: What's _____ _____ _____?

W: I'll take 19th century American literature instead of English Conversation.

M: I heard it's _____ _____.

W: I know, but it's not an elective for English majors.

M: Who's going to teach it next semester?

W: Ms. Quinn. Will you sign up for this course with me? Why don't we help each other next semester? You told me that you need _____ _____ _____ for graduation.

M: What time is the class?

W: _____ _____ _____ Wednesday from 10 a.m. to 12 p.m.

M: Sorry, I have a part-time job then. Mina is an English major, too. Why don't you call her?

W: She _____ _____ _____ last semester.

A. Listening Web    MP3 07-07-A

Intro   Hi, Chelsea. You look (tire / tired).

Web1   Because I had to cover the (entire / attire) Middle Ages, I slept for only four hours.

Web2   The fire alarm went off at (middle night / midnight) in my apartment.

Web3   But the firefighters and the police officers (investigated / invigorated) what the problem was, so I couldn't come back home until 6 a.m.

Ending   But the problem is that I was going to do my homework this morning, and I (could do / couldn't) after all.

B. True / False    MP3 07-07-B

1. 두 사람 다 지난밤에 잠을 제대로 자지 못했다.   (T / F)
2. 여자는 지난밤에 역사 시험공부를 했다.   (T / F)
3. 남자는 어제 화재 대피 훈련을 했다.   (T / F)
4. 남자는 숙제를 하지 못했다.   (T / F)

C. Words and Phrases

the Middle Ages 중세 시대 / cram for ~공부를 벼락치기 하다 / exhausted 기진맥진 한 / fire alarm 화재경보기

D. Dictation    MP3 07-07-B

M: Hi, Chelsea. You look tired.

W: I have a history test today, so I _____ _____ _____ _____ last night. Because I had to cover the entire Middle Ages, I slept for only four hours.

M: You don't review _____ _____ _____ every day?

W: No. Do you?

M: _____ _____.

W: Do you also have a test today? You look exhausted, too.

M: No, the _____ _____ _____ _____ at midnight in my apartment. All of my family escaped from the house.

W: Was the fire in your house?

M: Fortunately, no. It was an accident. But the firefighters and the police officers investigated what the problem was, so I couldn't come back home until 6 a.m.

W: _____ _____ _____ that everything was okay, _____.

M: Yes. But the problem is that I was going to do my homework this morning, and I couldn't after all.

A. Listening Web

Intro I'm going to school.

Web1 I have to prepare for (Daniel's / the annual) school festival.

Web2 Your piano (recycle / recital) last year was really excellent, too.

Web3 But I'm (conducting / constructing) the school orchestra this year.

Ending I promise to go see the orchestra.

B. True / False

1. 남자는 학교에 가는 길이다.   (T / F)
2. 여자는 작년에 학교 축제에서 뮤지컬을 했었다.   (T / F)
3. 남자는 작년에 학교 축제에서 피아노 독주를 했었다.   (T / F)
4. 남자는 올해 학교 축제의 오케스트라에서 연주할 계획이다.   (T / F)

C. Words and Phrases

grand prize 최우수상, 그랑프리 / enthusiastically 열광적으로 / piano recital 피아노 독주 / conduct 지휘하다

D. Dictation

W: Where are you going?

M: I'm going to school.

W: During vacation? Do you attend summer school?

M: No. I have to prepare for the _____ _____ _____.

W: Oh, I remember last year's festival. The musical was enthusiastically supported by the audience.

M: _____ _____ the grand prize. It was really impressive.

W: What will you do to at the festival? Will you play the piano again? Your piano recital last year was really excellent, too.

M: Thank you. But I'm _____ the school _____ this year.

W: Good for you! That's what _____ _____ _____ _____!
Now you're a maestro.

M: Not really. I'm just practicing.

W: I _____ _____ _____ _____ the orchestra.

문항 9 △ 심화 학습

A. Listening Web  MP3 07-09-A

Intro I heard you've been chosen to take (part in / party in) a training program as the representative of our school.

Web1 I was going to participate in the global leadership (trainee / training) program, but I gave up.

Web2 Brian was to (attend / tend to) the program at first, but he gave up because he had to go on a (retreat / treat).

Web3 So I was going to (append / attend) it instead of him, but I'll be traveling to Phuket.

Ending Have a nice vacation.

B. True / False  MP3 07-09-B

1. 연수에 참여하고 싶어하는 학생이 많았다.   (T / F)
2. 연수는 원래 여자가 가기로 되어 있었다.   (T / F)
3. Brian은 교회에 다닌다.   (T / F)
4. 남자의 아버지는 푸껫에서 근무하신다.   (T / F)

C. Words and Phrases

go on a retreat 수련회에 가다 / devout 독실한 / churchgoer 교회 다니는 사람 / get a promotion 승진하다

D. Dictation  MP3 07-09-B

W: I heard you've been chosen to take part in a training program as the _____ _____ our school. Buy the way, what is it?

M: Well, I was going to participate in the global leadership training program, but _____ _____ _____.

W: What happened? There were so many applicants that it was very _____, as far as I know.

M: Actually, Brian _____ _____ _____ the program at first, but he gave up because he had to go on a retreat.

W: Yeah, he is a _____ _____.

M: So I was going to attend it instead of him, but I'll be traveling to Phuket.

W: Phuket? In Thailand?

M: Yes. My father _____ _____ _____, and he got flight tickets to Phuket.

W: Wow! Congratulations! Have a nice vacation.

M: Thanks. You, too.

A. Listening Web

Intro   You're the only person (I see / I've seen) today.

Web1   I'm starving. I (keep / skipped) lunch.

Web2   I had a (late / lot) breakfast. I ate salad.

Web3   I went to the gym to exercise, but it's (close / closed) today.

Ending   And I lay down on the sofa (shopping / surfing) TV channels. And then maybe I fell asleep.

B. True / False

1. 여자는 온종일 집에 있었다.   **(T / F)**
2. 여자는 다음 주에 치과에 갈 것이다.   **(T / F)**
3. 여자는 요즘 식사를 조절하고 있다.   **(T / F)**
4. 남자는 점심 식사를 걸렀다.   **(T / F)**

C. Words and Phrases

skip 거르다

D. Dictation

W: You're the only person I've seen today.

M: You told me on the phone _____ _____ _____ _____ a dentist this afternoon.

W: I called the dentist's and found out that I had to wait for over an hour. So I _____ _____ _____ for next week.

M: I see. Where do you want to go for dinner?

W: Let's go to the nearest restaurant. I'm starving. _____ _____ _____.

M: Do not skip three meals even if you're on a diet.

W: I had _____ _____ _____. I ate salad.

M: What did you do after that?

W: I went to the gym to exercise, but it's closed today.

M: So you came home?

W: Yes. And I _____ _____ on the sofa surfing TV channels. And then maybe I fell asleep. Your call an hour ago _____ _____ _____.

M: That's why you skipped lunch.

W: That's right.

• 전략

세부 사항 일치 여부를 묻는 유형과 비슷한 인지 과정을 요구하는 유형이다. 그러나 선택지의 일치 여부를 판단하기보다는 선택지의 내용에 관한 언급 자체가 있었는지 그 여부를 묻는 유형이므로, 일치 여부를 묻는 유형보다는 더 쉽게 느껴질 수도 있다. 단, 선택지의 내용이 언급되더라도 문제에서 요구하는 조건 (예컨대, 남자가 갈 곳으로 언급되지 않은 것 혹은 여자가 먹으려고 하는 음식으로 언급되지 않은 것 등)에 들어맞지 않는다면 정답에서 제외될 수 있음을 유의한다.

• Example

1 다음 대화를 듣고, 댐에 관해 두 사람이 언급하지 <u>않은</u> 것을 고르시오. [2012 수능모의]

W: Hi, I'm Nicole from WEO Newspaper.

M: Nice to meet you. I'll be your guide for today.

W: Thank you. What an amazing place! I've never seen a huge wall like this.

M: It's the largest dam in the world, containing billions of tons of water.

W: Wow, how much electricity does this facility generate, anyway?

M: Once we open the floodgates, it generates 84 billion kilowatts per year.

W: That's incredible. I heard the income from tourism is large as well.

M: That's right. Tourism provides enormous economic benefits for the local community.

W: One more thing, I also heard there're environmental problems with water storage.

M: As you can see in the upper region of the dam, water pollution is present.

W: I see. Thank you for answering my questions.

M: My pleasure.

① 저수량
② 준공 시기
③ 관광 수익
④ 환경 문제
⑤ 전력 생산량

* 저수량 (containing billions of tons of water), 관광 수익 (Tourism provides enormous economic benefits), 환경 문제 (water pollution is present), 전력 생산량 (it generates 84 billion kilowatts per year)에 대해서는 언급하고 있으나, 댐의 준공 시기에 대한 언급은 없다. 따라서 정답은 ②번이다.

유형 8

내용 중
언급되지 않은
내용 찾기

내용 중 언급되지 않은 내용 찾기

1 대화를 듣고, 남자의 항공 예약에 관해 두 사람이 언급하지 <u>않은</u> 것을 고르시오.

① 행선지
② 떠나는 날짜
③ 좌석 등급
④ 항공료
⑤ 돌아오는 날짜

2 다음 살구파이를 만드는 방법에 관한 대화를 듣고, 두 사람이 언급하지 <u>않은</u> 것을 고르시오.

① 살구 잼을 휘젓는 이유
② 반죽에 필요한 재료
③ 오븐의 온도
④ 살구파이 굽는 시간
⑤ 좋은 살구 잼의 색깔

3 대화를 듣고, 두 사람이 먹고 있는 음식에 관하여 언급하지 <u>않은</u> 것을 고르시오.

① 음식의 이름
② 음식을 먹는 순서
③ 음식을 만든 사람
④ 음식을 만드는 방법
⑤ 곁들여 먹는 음식

4 대화를 듣고, 이스터 아일랜드에 관해 언급하지 <u>않은</u> 것을 고르시오.

① 이름의 유래
② 섬의 위치
③ 섬의 크기
④ 섬의 모양
⑤ 섬의 주민

5 대화를 듣고, 남자가 여행할 곳으로 언급하지 <u>않은</u> 것을 고르시오.

① 경복궁
② 남산
③ 창덕궁
④ 남대문 시장
⑤ 제주도

6 대화를 듣고, 한국의 전통 가옥과 관련하여 언급되지 <u>않은</u> 것을 고르시오.

① 한국식 정원
② 부잣집의 방 개수
③ 화장실 위치
④ 주방 위치
⑤ 난방 시설

7 대화를 듣고, 놀이공원에 가는 방법과 관련하여 언급되지 <u>않은</u> 것을 고르시오.

① 남은 지하철 역 개수
② 지하철 탑승 시간
③ 하차할 지하철 역 이름
④ 역과 역 사이 이동 시간
⑤ 셔틀버스 운행 시간 간격

8 대화를 듣고, 인도 영화에 관해 두 사람이 언급하지 <u>않은</u> 것을 고르시오.

① 영화의 특징
② 연간 관객 수
③ 영화 포스터 제작의 목적
④ 영화 포스터의 특징
⑤ 연간 제작되는 영화 편수

9 대화를 듣고, 개념 미술에 관해 두 사람이 언급하지 <u>않은</u> 것을 고르시오.

① 개념 미술의 등장 배경
② 개념 미술 작가
③ 개념 미술의 철학
④ 개념 미술 감상법
⑤ 개념 미술의 기법

10 대화를 듣고, 셰르파에 관해 언급하지 <u>않은</u> 것을 고르시오.

① 셰르파가 하는 일
② 유명한 셰르파의 이름
③ 셰르파의 보수
④ 셰르파가 사는 곳
⑤ 셰르파 명칭의 유래

해답/해설 271p

A. Listening Web  MP3 08-01-A

Intro   I'd like to make a (reservation / reserve) for a flight to Paris next Tuesday morning.

Web1   Good. I'll take it. What's the (fair / fare)?

Web2   Which class would you like?

Web3   First class, please.

Web4   All right. When will you return here?

Ending   December (13th / 30th).

B. True / False  MP3 08-01-B

1. 남자는 다음 주 목요일 파리로 떠날 것이다.   (T / F)
2. 남자는 돌아오는 항공편까지 예약했다.   (T / F)
3. 남자는 비행기 좌석 등급을 결정하지 못했다.   (T / F)
4. 여자는 남자의 여권 번호를 요구하였다.   (T / F)

C. Words and Phrases

round-trip 왕복 / one-way 편도 / fare 요금 / first class 일등석

D. Dictation  MP3 08-01-B

W: Good evening. What can I do for you?

M: I'd like to make a reservation for a flight to Paris next Tuesday morning.

W: Would it be a _____ ticket or one-way?

M: Round-trip, please.

W: Hold on, please. I'll check to _____ _____ there's room. We have a 10 a.m. flight on Tuesday morning.

M: Good. I'll take it. What's _____ _____?

W: Which class would you like?

M: First class, please.

W: It's $200. If you have a Summer Sky membership, you can _____ _____ 5% _____.

M: No, thanks.

W: All right. When will you return here?

M: December 30th.

W: I'll _____ _____ _____ for your return. Would 3 p.m. that day be okay?

M: Perfect. Thank you.

W: May I have your name and phone number, please?

M: Scott Hue. 013-4236-9395.

A. Listening Web  MP3 08-02-A

Intro　I tried to make an (African / apricot) pie, but I couldn't.

Web1　First of all, you need to beat the apricot jam, so that its (text / texture) becomes smooth.

Web2　Butter, sugar, egg, and (floor / flour).

Web3　Preheat it to 180°C.

Ending　Bake it for about 20 to 25 minutes until it becomes (gold / golden).

B. True / False  MP3 08-02-B

1. 살구파이 반죽에는 살구를 갈아 넣는다.　　　　　　　　　　　　　　(T / F)
2. 살구 잼을 휘젓는 이유는 질감을 부드럽게 하기 위해서이다.　　　　　(T / F)
3. 살구파이를 굽는 적당한 온도는 섭씨 180도이다.　　　　　　　　　　(T / F)
4. 살구파이를 굽는 데 걸리는 시간은 최대 25분이다.　　　　　　　　　(T / F)

C. Words and Phrases

mess 혼잡, 뒤죽박죽 / apricot 살구 / beat 휘젓다

D. Dictation  MP3 08-02-B

W:　_____ _____ _____! What are you doing?

M:　I tried to make an apricot pie, but I couldn't.

W:　Do you want me to help you?

M:　Yes, please.

W:　Okay, let's get started! First of all, you need to beat the apricot jam, _____ _____ its texture becomes smooth.

M:　I see. Like this?

W:　Good. I'll make the dough while you're doing it.

M:　Okay. _____ _____ _____?

W:　Butter, sugar, egg, and flour. You need to beat them for about 2 to 3 minutes until the dough _____ _____ _____.

M:　Oh! We forgot _____ _____ _____ _____!

W:　You're right. Preheat it to 180°C. When the dough is ready, put the apricot jam on the dough and bake it for about 20 to 25 minutes until it becomes golden. It's quite easy, isn't it?

M:　Yes. Thank you. I think you're _____ _____ _____.

A. Listening Web  MP3 08-03-A

Intro   I can't wait to try some of the foods you (talk / told) me about.

Web1   Try these shish kebabs.

Web2   My dad cooked (them / then).

Web3   Grill the meat first, and then just wrap the grilled meat and (a salted / assorted) vegetables with (Turkish / Turkey) bread.

Ending   It's the yoghurt sauce. You can (deep / dip) the kebabs in the sauce.

B. True / False  MP3 08-03-B

1. 여자는 시시케밥을 지금 처음 먹어본다.   (T / F)
2. 시시케밥에는 고기나 채소 중 한 가지씩만 들어간다.   (T / F)
3. 여자는 시시케밥을 한번 만들어볼 생각이 있다.   (T / F)
4. 여자는 요거트 소스 맛을 별로 좋아하지 않는다.   (T / F)

C. Words and Phrases

feast 연회, 잔치, 축제 / assorted 여러 가지의 / dip ~을 (액체에) 살짝 담그다, 적시다

D. Dictation  MP3 08-03-B

M: I'm so glad that you could come to our family feast!

W: Thanks for _____ _____. I can't wait to try some of the foods you told me about.

M: Right! I'm hungry, too. Let's eat!

W: Great! You've _____ _____ _____ _____, so I don't know what to try.

M: Try these shish kebabs. I'm sure you'll love them. My dad cooked them.

W: I've never had it before. What's in it?

M: Meat and vegetables. Grill the meat first, and then just _____ the grilled meat and _____ vegetables with Turkish bread.

W: It's very easy to make. I'll try to make one at home.

M: You should. And don't forget to invite me then.

W: Sure. What is this _____ _____?

M: It's the yoghurt sauce. You can _____ the kebabs in the sauce.

W: Mmm, that's so good!

A. Listening Web  MP3 08-04-A

Intro   What's this in the pictures? Oh, it's Easter Island!

Web1   Because it was discovered (in / on) Easter Sunday.

Web2   It's in the middle of the Pacific Ocean, and the (near east / nearest) land is another small island more than 1,000 miles west.

Web3   This island is (shaped / sharp) like a triangle.

Ending   They are farming a few crops like bananas or sugar (can / cane).

B. True / False  MP3 08-04-B

1. 이스터 아일랜드는 독일의 탐험가에 의해 발견되었다.   (T / F)
2. 이스터 아일랜드 주민들은 기독교인들이다.   (T / F)
3. 이스터 아일랜드의 해변은 서쪽으로 1,000마일이나 뻗어있다.   (T / F)
4. 이스터 아일랜드에 있는 화산은 다시는 폭발하지 않는다.   (T / F)

C. Words and Phrases

Easter 부활절 / Dutch 네덜란드의 / extinct volcano 사(死)화산 / sugar cane 사탕수수

D. Dictation  MP3 08-04-B

W: What's this in the pictures? Oh, it's Easter Island!

M: Do you know this island?

W: I've read about this island. It's _____ _____ _____ _____ mysteries.

M: Right. Look at these statues.

W: So unbelievable, isn't it? Do you know _____ _____ _____ _____ Easter Island?

M: Why?

W: Because it was discovered on Easter Sunday.

M: The discoverer _____ _____ _____ a Christian.

W: Maybe. He was a Dutch explorer. It's in the middle of the Pacific Ocean, and _____ _____ _____ is another small island more than 1,000 miles west.

M: It must be _____ _____ _____ _____ in the world. Look! This island is shaped like a triangle.

W: Yes, and do you see these volcanoes? It has _____ _____ _____ in each corner.

M: Are people living on this island?

W: Sure. They are farming a few crops like bananas or sugar cane.

M: Interesting. I wish I could go there someday.

△
심화 학습

A. Listening Web

Intro   First of all, I'll go to Gyongbok Palace and Namsan tomorrow.
Web1   You should also go to Changduk Palace.
Web2   Really? I (don't / won't) miss it. And I'll go to Namdaemun Market.
Web3   Why don't you go to Jeju Island?
Ending   I've been thinking of it, but I'll (stay / staying) for only three days in Seoul.

B. True / False

1. 남자는 지금 한국에 도착했다.   (T / F)
2. 여자는 남자를 호텔까지 데려다 주고 있다.   (T / F)
3. 여자는 남자에게 남대문 시장을 안내해주려고 한다.   (T / F)
4. 여자는 남대문 시장에서 식사를 하려고 한다.   (T / F)

C. Words and Phrases

be designated as a UNESCO World Heritage 유네스코 세계문화유산으로 등재되다 /
give a ride (탈것에) 태워주다

D. Dictation

W: Welcome! How was your flight?

M: It was a long flight. But the weather here in Korea is fantastic, and I'm sure the long and boring
_____ _____ _____ _____.

W: Where do you plan to go?

M: First of all, I'll go to Gyongbok Palace and Namsan tomorrow. I heard I can see _____
_____ _____ Seoul from the top of Namsan.

W: You should also go to Changduk Palace. It's _____ _____ a UNESCO World
Heritage site.

M: Really? I won't miss it. And I'll go to Namdaemun Market.

W: I know some delicious restaurants in Namdaemun Market. I can _____ _____ if
you want.

M: Thank you very much.

W: Why don't you go to Jeju Island?

M: I've been _____ _____ _____, but I'll stay for only three days in Seoul.

W: You don't have enough time. You should go to Jeju another time. Now we've arrived at your hotel.

M: Thanks for _____ _____ _____ _____.

W: My pleasure.

A. Listening Web

Intro Now we're in Namsan Hanok Village.

Web1 This is the richest house. This kind of house has a Korean traditional garden. It looks quite different from (west / western) style houses, doesn't it?

Web2 It is said that the richest house has (19 / 99) rooms. And look at this. This is the toilet.

Web3 It's outside of the house. It's separate (for / from) the main building.

Ending I heard that "ondol" is a scientific heating system. I've always wondered how it (walks / works).

B. True / False

1. 한옥마을의 입장료는 비싸다.   (T / F)
2. 남자는 한국식 정원이 서양의 것과 크게 다르지 않다고 생각한다.   (T / F)
3. 남자는 한국식 화장실이 위생적이지 않다고 생각한다.   (T / F)
4. 남자와 여자는 온돌을 체험해 보고 싶어한다.   (T / F)

C. Words and Phrases

authentic 진짜의 / admission 입장료 / exotic 이국적인 / hygiene 위생

D. Dictation

M: Wow! Now we're in Namsan Hanok Village.

W: This is authentic Korea! How much is the admission?

M: It's free! Let's go. This is the richest house. This kind of house has a Korean traditional garden. It looks _____ _____ _____ western style houses, doesn't it?

W: Yes, it's very _____ and really beautiful. How many rooms does it have?

M: It is said that the richest house has 99 rooms. And look at this. This is the toilet.

W: It's _____ _____ _____ _____. It's separate from the main building.

M: Yes, it reflects that Korean people had _____ _____ _____ _____ hygiene. And this is the kitchen. That is a kind of heating system. Have you ever heard of "ondol"?

W: Yes, I heard that "ondol" is a scientific _____ _____. I've always wondered how it works.

M: Would you like to _____ _____?

W: Sure. Let's go inside.

문항 7

△ 심화 학습

A. Listening Web  MP3 08-07-A

Intro	We still have (19 / 90) stations to go.
Web1	Will we get off at the Wonderland Park Station?
Web2	I think it'll take (about / around) an hour in total from now.
Web3	There are free shuttles to commute from the subway station (direct / directly) to the amusement park every 10 minutes as far as I know.
Ending	Oh, it's Wonderland Park! Let's get off.

B. True / False  MP3 08-07-B

1. 두 사람은 현재 지하철을 타고 있다.   (T / F)
2. 두 사람은 지하철을 무료로 탔다.   (T / F)
3. 두 사람은 지하철을 타고 목적지까지 한 번에 갈 것이다.   (T / F)
4. 최종 목적지는 놀이공원이다.   (T / F)

C. Words and Phrases

on average 평균적으로 / transfer 환승하다 / in total 전부, 통틀어 / commute 통근하다

D. Dictation  MP3 08-07-B

M: How many stations are left?

W: We still have 19 stations to go. It takes two minutes _____ _____ to go to the next station.

M: Then 38 minutes exactly for the subway only. Will we _____ _____ _____ the Wonderland Park Station?

W: That's right. We have to take a bus to _____ _____ _____.

M: I see. Have you ever been there?

W: Yes, I have. I think it'll take about an hour _____ _____ _____ _____.

M: Are there a lot of buses that go to the amusement park at the Wonderland Park station?

W: There are free shuttles to commute from the subway station directly to the amusement park _____ _____ _____ as far as I know.

M: Oh, it's Wonderland Park! Let's get off.

A. Listening Web  MP3 08-08-A

Intro I heard Indian films are so (fascinated / fascinating).

Web1 Most Indian films are thrillers or romantic movies, action-(package / packed), with extravagant sets and plenty of singing and dancing.

Web2 They also make really fantastic posters to (attract / trap) people.

Web3 Their colors are manipulated and the eyes are (exaggerated / exaggerating).

Ending You should. India makes about 850 films a year. That's 300 more than Hollywood.

B. True / False  MP3 08-08-B

1. 여자는 인도 영화를 본 적이 없다.   (T / F)
2. 남자가 본 인도 영화는 액션 영화이다.   (T / F)
3. 인도 영화에는 노래와 춤이 많이 나온다.   (T / F)
4. 인도 영화사는 관객을 끌기 위해 포스터를 사실적으로 만든다.   (T / F)

C. Words and Phrases

extravagant 낭비하는, 사치하는 / manipulate ~을 잘 다루다, 조작하다 /
exaggerate ~을 지나치게 강조하다, 두드러지게 하다

D. Dictation  MP3 08-08-B

M: Hey! I saw _____ _____ _____.

W: I've never seen Indian movies before. What was it?

M: The title is "The Robot." It was a _____ _____, and also it was comic and adventurous.

W: Wow! I heard Indian films are so fascinating.

M: Yeah. Most Indian films are _____ or romantic movies, action-packed, with _____ _____ and plenty of singing and dancing.

W: Maybe that's because the film companies want to gather a lot of audience.

M: Yes, and they also make really fantastic posters _____ _____ _____.
The posters are not based on reality. Their colors are manipulated and the eyes are _____.

W: Hmm, I'm getting interested in Indian films. I want to see one some time.

M: You should. India makes about 850 films a year. That's 300 more than Hollywood.

W: I've heard of "Bollywood." It means Mumbai has become the center of the film industry, right?

M: You're right.

A. Listening Web  MP3 08-09-A

Intro I went to an (all / art) museum last weekend.

Web1 Joseph Beuys, the (leading / reading) conceptual artist.

Web2 Conceptual artists tried to convey meaning by showing something in a new and interesting way, without long (explanations / explains).

Web3 So you need to think about the concept that (led / let) the artist to choose and present the works in that way.

Ending To show the concept effectively, they used various kinds of techniques like performance, video, or (escalation / installation).

B. True / False  MP3 08-09-B

1. 남자는 지난 주말 미술관에 갔었다.   (T / F)
2. Joseph Beuys는 개념 미술의 선두주자이다.   (T / F)
3. 개념 예술가들은 긴 설명으로 작품을 보여준다.   (T / F)
4. 개념 미술에는 행위 예술, 설치 기술 등이 포함된다.   (T / F)

C. Words and Phrases

Superrealism 수퍼리얼리즘 (극사실주의), 실제와 꼭 같은 기법 / well-versed in ~에 조예가 깊은 / convey 전달하다 / installation 설치 / shelter 은신처

D. Dictation  MP3 08-09-B

W: I went to an _____ _____ last weekend.

M: Cool! How was it?

W: Honestly, it was so difficult that I couldn't understand. Superrealism, Conceptual art…

M: Joseph Beuys, the _____ conceptual artist.

W: Oh, I didn't know that you're well-versed in art!

M: I'm just interested in art. Conceptual artists tried to _____ _____ by showing something in a new and interesting way, without long explanations. So you need to think about the concept that led the artist to choose and present the works in that way.

W: It's still hard.

M: Yes, it's not easy at all. To show the concept effectively, they used _____ _____ _____ techniques like performance, video, or installation.

W: Oh, yes. I remember an artist, Nam June Paik. He made a robot with _____ _____. I felt it was like a _____ _____.

M: Wow. You're a fast learner. That's the right way to enjoy the conceptual art!

A. Listening Web

Intro A (document / documentary) about Edmund Hillary is on TV.

Web1 The Sherpas lay the (trail / tray) and carry supplies with the climbers.

Web2 You know Norgay? He was Edmund Hillary's Sherpa when he (climbed / climbed to) Mount Everest.

Web3 The Sherpas are a group of people who have always lived in the Himalayas.

Ending It is originally from a Tibetan word which means "(East / Eastern) People."

B. True / False

1. Edmund Hillary는 셰르파의 도움 없이 혼자 에베레스트를 등반한 최초의 인물이다. **(T / F)**
2. 셰르파는 원래 히말라야 지역에서 도로를 닦고 생필품을 운반하는 일을 하는 사람들이다. **(T / F)**
3. 셰르파는 등반가의 일을 도와주는 대가로 수백 달러를 받는다. **(T / F)**
4. 셰르파라는 이름은 티베트 어에서 유래되었다. **(T / F)**

C. Words and Phrases

lay 놓다, 설치하다 / trail 산길 / supply 보급품 / Tibetan 티베트의

D. Dictation

M: A documentary about Edmund Hillary is on TV. He was the first to get to the top of Mount Everest. _____ _____ he was one of the greatest men in the world.

W: But do you know that Edmund Hillary was _____ _____ when he was climbing?

M: What do you mean?

W: The Sherpas _____ _____ _____ and carry supplies with the climbers. You know Norgay? He was Edmund Hillary's Sherpa when he climbed Mount Everest. He is a very famous Sherpa.

M: By the way, how much are they _____ _____ that tough work? I think it should be more than _____ _____ _____ _____ of labor. Think about carrying that heavy stuff up to the mountain.

W: I'm not sure about it. But "Sherpa" itself is not a job, actually. The Sherpas are a group of people _____ _____ _____ _____ in the Himalayas. It is originally from a Tibetan word which means "East People."

M: That's interesting.

수치 문제를 잘 맞추기 위해서는 먼저 숫자를 잘 듣고 바로 이해하는 연습을 해야 한다. 어느 물건이 얼마인지 간단하게 표를 만들면서 듣는 것이 요령이다. 표를 만들면서 구매 여부를 구별하고, 화자가 낸 돈과, 거스름돈을 적으면서 빠른 속도로 계산해야 한다. 계산 자체는 단순하거나 암산으로도 충분한 수준이나, 화자가 선택한 아이템을 분명하게 구별하는 것이 포인트이다. 또한 할인이나 멤버십 카드 적용으로 이전 계산을 모두 버리고 다시 계산해야 하는 경우도 있으니 지문이 끝날 때까지 긴장을 풀지 말아야 한다.

● Example

1 대화를 듣고, 남자가 주문한 물건값으로 한 달에 지불할 금액을 고르시오. [2011년 수능기출]

[Telephone rings.]

W: Hello, Roger's Office Supplies. Would you like to place an order?

M: Yes. I'd like to order a fax machine.

W: May I have the model number, please?

M: It's FX-1000.

W: All right. That model is $150. Which color would you like?

M: I'd like a black one, please. And I'd also like to order a scanner. The model number is SCN-2000.

W: That's $250. Would you like to order anything else?

M: No. That's all for today.

W: Then your total comes to $400. Do you have any discount coupons?

M: Yes. I have a special 10% discount coupon.

W: Okay. We'll apply that to your order. Would you like to take advantage of our three-month or six-month installment plan? It's interest-free.

M: I'll pay using the three-month installment plan.

① $60
② $120
③ $250
④ $360
⑤ $400

* 주문한 총 금액 400달러에서 10%를 할인 받았으므로, 남자가 지불해야 할 총 금액은 360달러가 된다. 여기에 3개월 할부를 신청했으므로, 한 달에 남자가 지불해야 할 금액은 120달러가 된다. 따라서 정답은 ②번이다.

수치 문제

수치 문제

1 대화를 듣고, 여자가 지불할 금액을 고르시오.

① $70
② $75
③ $100
④ $105
⑤ $150

2 대화를 듣고, 남자가 지불할 금액을 고르시오.

① $5
② $13
③ $15
④ $45
⑤ $62

3 대화를 듣고, 여자가 지불할 금액을 고르시오.

① $240
② $255
③ $270
④ $285
⑤ $295

4 대화를 듣고, 남자가 받을 거스름돈을 고르시오.

① $40
② $50
③ $60
④ $70
⑤ $80

5 대화를 듣고, 남자가 지불할 금액을 고르시오.

① $12
② $13
③ $14
④ $15
⑤ $16

6 대화를 듣고, 남자와 여자가 각각 수영 강습비로 지불할 금액을 고르시오.

	남자	여자
①	$70	$100
②	$100	$70
③	$100	$100
④	$120	$100
⑤	$120	$120

7 대화를 듣고, 두 사람이 지불해야 할 금액을 고르시오.

① $80
② $95
③ $100
④ $110
⑤ $120

8 대화를 듣고, 남자가 지불해야 할 금액을 고르시오.

① $36
② $50
③ $70
④ $74
⑤ $90

9 다음 표를 보면서 대화를 듣고, 여자가 지불할 금액을 고르시오.

	Johnson		Starworld	
Memory	32GB	64GB	32GB	64GB
WiFi	① $800	② $900	③ $600	$700
3G+WiFi	④ $900	$1000	⑤ $700	$800

10 대화를 듣고, 여자가 받을 거스름돈을 고르시오.

① $1
② $2
③ $2.5
④ $3
⑤ $5.5

해답/해설 276p

A. Listening Web

Intro I'm looking for something for my son.

Web1 How about this jacket? It comes (in / with) several colors.

Web2 It costs more than I thought.

Web3 They are $70, but they are season-off items. So if you buy one pair, you'll get another for (15 / 50)% off.

Ending I'll take two pairs of jeans.

B. True / False

1. 재킷의 가격은 여자가 예상했던 것보다 저렴하다. (T / F)
2. 여자는 원래 100달러 정도 쓰려고 생각하고 있었다. (T / F)
3. 신발과 재킷은 원래 같은 가격이다. (T / F)
4. 여자가 최종적으로 사기로 한 물건은 신발이다. (T / F)

C. Words and Phrases

recommend ~을 추천하다, 권하다 / budget 예산, 경비

D. Dictation

W: Excuse me. I'm looking for something for my son.

M: Okay. What kind of thing are you looking for?

W: Well, he's ten years old. What would you recommend for him?

M: How about this jacket? It _____ _____ _____ _____.

W: How much is it?

M: It is $150.

W: It costs more than I thought.

M: _____ _____ _____?

W: About $100 or so.

M: Then, what about these shoes? Actually, they cost the same as the jacket, but I can give you _____ _____ _____.

W: They are good, but my son may want clothes more. How much are these jeans?

M: They are $70, but they are _____ _____. So if you buy one pair, you'll get another _____ _____ _____.

W: That's good. I'll take two pairs of jeans.

A. Listening Web

Intro   I'd like to send this package to Korea.

Web1   The cost depends on the (weigh / **weight**) and size. Let me weigh it. It's $4.

Web2   You have to pay $1 for the insurance.

Web3   Three times as much as regular. There's (**no** / none) additional (change / **charge**) for the insurance.

Ending   Yes, please.

B. True / False

1. 소포를 보험에 가입하기 위해서는 50달러를 더 내야 한다.	(T / F)
2. 항공 운임은 소포의 크기와 무게에 따라 다르다.	(T / F)
3. 소포가 특급으로 배달되는 데는 일주일 이상 걸린다.	(T / F)
4. 특급 운임은 일반 운임보다 3달러 비싸다.	(T / F)

C. Words and Phrases

postage 우편요금 / insure 보험을 들다 / fill out ~에 기입하다 / express 속달우편

D. Dictation

M: Excuse me. I'd like to send this package to Korea.

W: Do you want to send it by ship or by airmail?

M: By airmail. What's the postage?

W: _____ _____ _____ _____ the weight and size. Let me weigh it. It's $4.

M: And I'd like to _____ _____ _____ _____ $50.

W: Then you need to fill out this form first. You have to pay $1 for the insurance.

M: How long will it take for the package _____ _____?

W: Fifteen days.

M: I'm sorry, but how much does it cost to send it by express? I want it to arrive in a week.

W: Three times _____ _____ _____ _____. There's no additional charge for the insurance. Would you like to send it by express?

M: Yes, please.

문항
3

△
심화
학습

A. Listening Web  MP3 09-03-A

Intro	What is the (price / prize) of the tour?
Web1	It's $100 for an adult, (included / including) lunch.
Web2	You'll get 20% off for under fifteen, and 30% off for under ten. How old is the child?
Web3	She's nine. I'll take the tour. Two adults and one child, please.
Web4	If you pay $(15 / 50) more, you'll get 10% off for all our tour packages for the next year. Do you want it?
Ending	Well, that's a good deal. But no, thanks.

B. True / False  MP3 09-03-B

1. 여행 비용에는 점심값이 포함되어 있다. (T / F)
2. 여자가 신청한 여행자 수는 총 3명이다. (T / F)
3. 일행 중 아이가 있으면 총 여행 비용의 20%를 할인받을 수 있다. (T / F)
4. 15달러를 더 내면 다음 여행에서 한 사람당 10달러씩 할인받을 수 있다. (T / F)

C. Words and Phrases

including ~를 포함하여 / resident 거주자

D. Dictation  MP3 09-03-B

M: Hello. California Tour Company. May I help you?

W: Yes. Do you have _____ _____ _____ on the Dreaming Los Angeles tour tomorrow?

M: Yes, there are several seats left.

W: What is the price of the tour?

M: It's $100 _____ _____ _____, including lunch.

W: How much is it for a kid?

M: It depends. You'll get 20% off _____ _____ _____, and 30% off for under ten. How old is the child?

W: She's nine. I'll take the tour. Two adults and one child, please.

M: If you are _____ of California, you can get $10 off for each person.

W: We live _____ _____ _____ _____.

M: Okay. If you pay $15 more, you'll get 10% off for all our tour packages for the next year. Do you want it?

W: Well, _____ _____ _____ _____. But no, thanks.

A. Listening Web

Intro   All the carry-overs are (15 / 50)% off.

Web1   What about those brown ones?

Web2   And they cost $(12 / 20) originally.

Web3   I love this (black / brown) color, though. I'll take two pairs.

Ending   I'll pay (in / with) cash. Here's $100.

B. True / False

1. 대화가 이루어지는 시점은 여름이다.   (T / F)
2. 모든 겨울 상품이 50달러에 팔리고 있다.   (T / F)
3. 남자는 여자가 권하는 상품을 사기로 했다.   (T / F)
4. 남자는 현금으로 계산했다.   (T / F)

C. Words and Phrases

now is the time 지금이 적기이다 / carry-over 이월 상품

D. Dictation

M: Hi. Do you have _____?

W: Sure. Come in.

M: I was worried I couldn't _____ _____ because it's summer.

W: _____ _____ _____ _____ if you want to buy some winter items! All the carry-overs are 50% off.

M: Really? Which ones were the best-seller?

W: These black ones were very popular last winter. They're very light, and the color _____ _____ _____ _____.

M: How much are they?

W: They were originally $30.

M: What about those brown ones?

W: They were popular, too. And they cost $20 originally. But I recommend the black ones.

M: Hmm. I love this brown color, though. I'll take two pairs.

W: Okay. _____ _____ _____?

M: I'll pay _____ _____. Here's $100.

A. Listening Web    MP3 09-05-A

Intro   Chocolate cake is popular among kids. Our chocolate is so (deep / rich) that kids love it.

Web1   The chocolate cake in regular size is $(12 / 20), and the size bigger costs two more dollars.

Web2   Then I'll take the chocolate cake in (family / party) size, please.

Web3   Do you have a Cake Lovers' membership card? You can (get / take) a $1 discount for each cake with the membership.

Ending   Yes, I have the card. Here you are.

B. True / False    MP3 09-05-B

1. 남자는 딸의 생일 케이크를 고르는 중이다.   (T / F)
2. 여자는 딸기 케이크를 남자에게 권하고 있다.   (T / F)
3. 남자가 사려는 케이크는 같은 크기의 딸기 케이크보다 비싸다.   (T / F)
4. 회원카드가 있으면 10% 할인된다.   (T / F)

C. Words and Phrases

regular (크기가) 표준의, 보통의 (주로 가장 작은 크기) / rich (맛이) 기름진, 유지방이 많이 들어간

D. Dictation    MP3 09-05-B

W: May I help you?

M: I'm looking for a birthday cake for my little daughter.

W: Chocolate cake is popular among kids. Our chocolate is _____ rich _____ kids love it.

M: How much is it?

W: We have three sizes: _____, family size, and party size. Which one would you like?

M: Is party size the biggest?

W: That's right. The chocolate cake _____ _____ _____ is $12, and the size bigger costs _____ _____ _____.

M: I see. What about the strawberry cake?

W: It's more expensive. The regular one is $13, and the family size is $16. Strawberry cake has only two sizes.

M: Okay. Then I'll take the chocolate cake in family size, please.

W: Do you have a Cake Lovers' membership card? You can get a $1 _____ _____ _____ _____ with the membership.

M: Yes, I have the card. Here you are.

W: Thank you very much!

A. Listening Web

 MP3 09-06-A

Intro An (ad / aid) for a swimming pool.

Web1 It's $100 a month, and three days of lessons a week. Or $70 a month, and two days of lessons a week.

Web2 You can choose any (5 / 15) days for a month and it costs only $(112 / 120). It's not a lesson, but a free swimming class after nine.

Web3 I want to take the (three / two) days of lessons.

Ending I think free swimming is better for me.

B. True / False

 MP3 09-06-B

1. 여자는 수영을 좋아한다.   (T / F)
2. 여자는 운동 삼아 수영을 할 계획이다.   (T / F)
3. 여자와 남자는 서로 다른 수영 프로그램을 신청할 것이다.   (T / F)
4. 여자는 이미 접영을 배웠다.   (T / F)

C. Words and Phrases

renovate 개조하다, 보수하다 / facilities 시설 / butterfly 접영

D. Dictation

 MP3 09-06-B

M: What are you looking at?

W: _____ _____ _____ a swimming pool. It says they've _____ the old swimming pool. I think it's clean and the _____ are good. It will open on December 1st.

M: Do you like swimming?

W: Yes. I'm thinking of swimming for exercise. They're _____ _____ for the renewal event.

M: Let me see. It's $100 a month, and three days of lessons a week. Or $70 a month, and two days of lessons a week. That's quite _____.

W: You can choose _____ _____ _____ for a month and it costs only $120. It's not a lesson, but a free swimming class after nine.

M: That's better. You've already learned _____ _____ _____.

W: Yes, but I haven't learned the butterfly. Shall we go swimming together? I want to take the three days of lessons.

M: I think free swimming is better for me.

W: That's a good idea!

문항 7

△ 심화 학습

A. Listening Web  MP3 09-07-A

Intro Wow! I'm always (excited / exciting) when I come to ski.

Web1 Then you need to (lend / rent) them. How much is the rental fee?

Web2 Look, it costs $(12 / 20) for the ski full set.

Web3 It's $(14 / 40) for under 18. It's still expensive, though.

Ending Anyway, we need to rent the ski full set for you, and buy the lift admission for us, right?

B. True / False MP3 09-07-B

1. 남자는 스노보드를 탈 것이다.   (T / F)
2. 여자는 본인의 스키와 스키복을 가져왔다.   (T / F)
3. 스노보드 풀 세트 대여료는 15달러이다.   (T / F)
4. 리프트 요금은 나이에 따라 다르다.   (T / F)

C. Words and Phrases

ski-suit 스키복 / rental fee 대여료 / admission 입장료

D. Dictation  MP3 09-07-B

W: Wow! I'm always excited _____ _____ _____ _____ ski.

M: Did you bring your skis and ski-suit?

W: No. Guess what? I lost my ski-suit, and my skis were broken last winter.

M: Then you need to rent them. How much is the rental fee?

W: It says $15 for the full set, _____ _____ the suit and skis.

M: No, that's for snowboards. Look, it costs $20 for the ski full set.

W: You're right. And we need the lift admission. It's $45. It seems more expensive _____ _____ _____.

M: Jessica, it seems you're really excited. Calm down. The $45 is _____ _____. We're under 18.

W: Oops! Sorry. It's $40 for under 18. It's still expensive, though.

M: Yes, I think so. Anyway, we _____ _____ _____ the ski full set for you, and buy the lift admission for us, right?

W: Yes, that's right. Let's go!

A. Listening Web  MP3 09-08-A

Intro   I came here to buy detergent. I became (depend on / independent) of my parents last month.

Web1   I need a (softener / softer), too. Where is it?

Web2   Here you are. It's $10.

Web3   Then the (natural / neutral) detergent for general washers is $(13 / 30).

Ending   I'll take two boxes of detergent and a softener.

△
심화
학습

B. True / False  MP3 09-08-B

1. 남자는 부모님과 함께 살고 있다.   (T / F)
2. 합성세제는 중성세제보다 비싸다.   (T / F)
3. 남자의 집에는 드럼세탁기가 없다.   (T / F)
4. 남자는 세제와 섬유유연제를 한 상자씩 살 것이다.   (T / F)

C. Words and Phrases

synthetic detergent 합성세제 / neutral 중성의 / drum washer 드럼세탁기 / softener 섬유유연제

D. Dictation  MP3 09-08-B

W: What are you doing here?

M: I came here to buy detergent. I _____ _____ _____ my parents last month. Ever since I started _____ _____ _____ _____, I have so much to do.

W: Now you're grown up. Do you want me to help you?

M: Yes, please. What about the synthetic detergent?

W: It's not _____ _____ _____ _____, and it's expensive. Look. It's $40. I think it is better to buy neutral detergent. It's only $32.

M: I need a softener, too. Where is it?

W: Here you are. It's $10.

M: Look, the detergent you told me to get is _____ _____ _____.

W: Oh, you don't use a drum washer?

M: No.

W: Then the neutral detergent for general washers is $30.

M: I'll take _____ _____ _____ _____ and a _____.

A. Listening Web  MP3 09-09-A

Intro   I'd like to buy a tablet PC.

Web1   One is "3G+WiFi," (in / with) which you can use the Internet everywhere. And the other is "WiFi," (in / with) which you can use the Internet only in a WiFi zone.

Web2   I'd like to take the (form / former) one.

Web3   You mean I don't need 64GB? Does the price (differ / different) depending on the (manufacture / manufacturer)?

Web4   Johnson's design is (definite / definitely) superior (than / to) Starworld's.

Ending   Design is (an / not) important factor to me.

B. True / False  MP3 09-09-B

1. 여자는 IT 제품에 대해 잘 모른다.   (T / F)
2. 남자는 메모리 용량이 큰 제품을 추천한다.   (T / F)
3. 여자는 인터넷을 자유롭게 사용할 수 있는 제품을 선호한다.   (T / F)
4. Johnson 사의 제품이 디자인 면에서 더 우수하다.   (T / F)

C. Words and Phrases

unfamiliar with ~에 익숙하지 않은 / communication method 통신 방식 / manufacturer 제조사 / superior to ~보다 뛰어난

D. Dictation  MP3 09-09-B

W: I'd like to buy a tablet PC.

M: Do you have anything in mind?

W: No, actually I'm _____ _____ IT items.

M: I see. You need to consider the amount of memory available and the _____ _____.

W: What kind of communication methods are there?

M: One is "3G+WiFi," with which you can use the Internet everywhere. And the other is "WiFi," with which you can use the Internet only in a WiFi zone.

W: I'd like to take _____ _____ _____. How much memory is usually good?

M: We have 32GB and 64GB. But "3G+WiFi" allows you to use the Internet everywhere, so you don't need to _____ _____ _____ in the tablet PC.

W: You mean I don't need 64GB? Does the price differ _____ _____ _____ _____?

M: Not very much. But Johnson's design is definitely _____ _____ Starworld's.

W: Design is an important factor to me.

A. Listening Web  MP3 09-10-A

Intro I'd like to have two cheeseburgers, two (backs / bags) of potato chips, one iced tea and one Coke.

Web1 Why don't you order a cheeseburger set? It's $(8.50 / 85). If you order a cheeseburger, potato chips and iced tea (separable / separately), it costs $10.

Web2 Then that would be $17. You have to choose between soda and iced tea. Or you can change the drink to a milkshake for only one more dollar.

Ending Okay. Then I'll take two cheeseburger sets with one iced tea and one milkshake. Here's $20.

B. True / False  MP3 09-10-B

1. 맨 처음 여자가 주문한 총 금액은 19달러이다. (T / F)
2. 버거와 칩, 음료를 따로 주문하는 것과 세트 가격은 같다. (T / F)
3. 치즈버거 세트 가격은 8.5달러이다. (T / F)
4. 밀크셰이크는 탄산음료 보다 비싸다. (T / F)

C. Words and Phrases

soda 탄산음료 / separately 따로따로, 별도로

D. Dictation  MP3 09-10-B

M: Good morning. May I help you?

W: I'd like to have two cheeseburgers, two bags of potato chips, one iced tea and one Coke.

M: _____ _____ _____ _____ a cheeseburger set? It's $8.50. If you order a cheeseburger, potato chips and iced tea _____, it costs $10.

W: Okay, then I'll take two cheeseburger sets.

M: Then that would be $17. You have to _____ _____ soda _____ iced tea. Or you can change the drink to a milkshake for only one more dollar.

W: How much is a milkshake?

M: It's $2, and iced tea is $1.

W: Okay. Then I'll take two cheeseburger sets with one iced tea and one milkshake. Here's $20.

일치하지 않는 내용 찾기 유형을 정복하기 위해서는 세부 사항을 파악하는 능력을 키워야 한다. 대본과 선택지의 순서가 일치하므로, 들으면서 동시에 선택지 하나씩 일치 여부를 파악해 가는 것이 이 유형의 문제를 푸는 요령이다. 문제 유형의 특성상 모든 세부 사항에 주의를 기울여야 한다. 따라서 시작부터 끝까지 집중력이 흐트러지지 않도록 주의한다.

● Example

1 다음을 듣고, Chicago Student Exchange Program에 관한 내용과 일치하지 <u>않는</u> 것을 고르시오. [2012년 수능기출]

M: Hello, students! Our university is offering the Chicago Student Exchange Program. The students who join this program will be staying in Chicago for six months from March 1st to August 31st. Students have classes from 9 a.m. to 4 p.m. Lunch meals and transportation to and from school are provided by the school. On weekends, students can enjoy a variety of outdoor activities. The participants are selected through an interview. For more information, please visit our website. We hope many of you will apply for this program. Thank you.

① 참가 학생들은 6개월 동안 Chicago에 머무르게 된다.
② 수업 시간은 오전 9시부터 오후 4시까지이다.
③ 학교에서 교통편은 제공하지만, 점심을 제공하지 않는다.
④ 주말에 학생들은 다양한 야외 활동을 즐길 수 있다.
⑤ 학생 선발은 면접을 통해 이루어진다.

* 내용을 들으면서 선택지의 내용과 일치 여부를 차근차근 따져보면 알 수 있다. 학교에서 lunch meals (점심 식사)와 transportation (교통편)을 제공한다고 말하고 있다. 따라서 정답은 ③번이다.

일치하지 않는
내용 찾기

일치하지 않는 내용찾기

1 Mr. Johnson의 내일 진료에 관한 다음 내용을 듣고, 일치하지 <u>않는</u> 것을 고르시오.

① 오전 7시까지 병원에 도착해야 한다.
② 채혈을 하게 된다.
③ 내일은 병원에 두 번 내원해야 한다.
④ 혈압을 체크한 후 의사의 진료를 받을 것이다.
⑤ 오늘 진료비는 내일 한 번에 지불하면 된다.

2 아마존에 관한 다음 내용을 듣고, 일치하지 <u>않는</u> 것을 고르시오.

① 현재 많은 브라질 사람들은 해변에 살고 있다.
② 브라질 정부는 아마존 지역으로의 이사를 장려했다.
③ 원래 아마존 지역의 토양은 비옥했다.
④ 아마존 지역에 정착한 사람들은 그곳의 나무를 태워서 없앴다.
⑤ 아마존 지역에서의 농사는 성공적이었다.

3 영어 말하기 대회에 대한 다음 내용을 듣고, 일치하지 <u>않는</u> 것을 고르시오.

① 영어 말하기 대회는 9월 1일에 열린다.
② 참가 희망자는 7월 29일까지 대본을 제출해야 한다.
③ 개인이나 그룹으로 참여할 수 있다.
④ 20명의 참가자가 선발될 것이다.
⑤ 우승자는 학교 대표로 시 대회에 참가하게 된다.

4 학생회장 후보자 등록에 관한 다음 내용을 듣고, 일치하지 <u>않는</u> 것을 고르시오.

① 성적이 낮아도 B⁺는 되어야 한다.
② 30명 이상의 학생들로부터 추천을 받아야 한다.
③ 2명의 부회장 후보와 함께 출마해야 한다.
④ 회장과 부회장은 서로 다른 성별이어야 한다.
⑤ 등록에 필요한 양식은 학교 홈페이지에 있다.

5 미술관에 관한 다음 내용을 듣고, 일치하지 <u>않는</u> 것을 고르시오.

① 미술관은 원래 개인 주택이었다.
② 미술관 건물은 15세기에 건축되었다.
③ 유럽과 동양의 예술품들이 소장되어 있다.
④ 2003년 이후로 새로운 소장품이 들어오지 않았다.
⑤ 전 세계의 미술 교사는 무료로 입장할 수 있다.

6 Botanic Garden Island에 관한 다음 내용을 듣고, 일치하지 <u>않는</u> 것을 고르시오.

① 이 섬은 세 개의 섬으로 구성되어 있다.
② 이 섬에는 800개가 넘는 열대 품종이 자생하고 있다.
③ 이 섬은 작은 하와이라는 별명을 갖고 있다.
④ 이 섬은 원래 사유지이었다가 지역 사회 소유로 편입되었다.
⑤ 섬 주인이 TV에 나오면서 이 섬이 유명해졌다.

7 강사 소개에 관한 다음 내용을 듣고, 일치하지 <u>않는</u> 것을 고르시오.

① 강사를 소개하고 있는 사람은 워크숍 관리자이다.
② 강사는 현재 대학교수이다.
③ 강사는 5년 동안 상담가로 활동하였다.
④ 강사의 저서는 3년 전에 출간되었다.
⑤ 청중은 현직 상담가들이다.

8 콜로세움에 대한 다음 내용을 듣고, 일치하지 <u>않는</u> 것을 고르시오.

① 귀족뿐만 아니라 여성과 노예에게도 개방되어 있었다.
② 동물 운반용 엘리베이터와 차양이 설치되어 있었다.
③ 사람 80여 명이 한 번에 빠져나갈 수 있는 아치형 문이 하나 있다.
④ 경기가 끝난 뒤 15분 안에 관람객들이 모두 밖으로 나갈 수 있다.
⑤ 폐허가 된 3분의 2는 오늘날 관람할 수 없다.

9 노예들의 노래에 대한 다음 내용을 듣고, 일치하지 <u>않는</u> 것을 고르시오.

① 노예들은 주인들 앞에서 노래를 부를 수 있었다.
② 당시 많은 노예들이 기독교로 종교를 바꾸도록 장려되었다.
③ 노예들이 부르던 노래에는 종교적 의미가 포함되어 있었다.
④ 노예들은 종교에 의지하여 행복을 느낄 때 주로 노래를 불렀다.
⑤ 노예들이 탈출할 때 물 주변에 머물러야 하는 이유는 음식을 얻기 위해서이다.

10 음식에 관한 다음 강의를 듣고, 일치하지 <u>않는</u> 것을 고르시오.

① 식사는 사교적 의미가 있기도 한다.
② 식습관에 큰 영향을 미치는 것은 문화이다.
③ 좋은 식습관은 적절한 음식 선택에서 비롯된다.
④ 그리스나 이탈리아 음식에는 기름이 많이 함유되어 있다.
⑤ 기름기 많은 음식은 심장병 발병 위험을 높인다.

해답/해설 281p

A. Listening Web

Intro   You have to come to the hospital at 7 a.m.

Web1   When you come to the hospital, you'll have your blood (take / taken) first.

Web2   After breakfast, come back to the hospital by 9:30 a.m.

Web3   We'll (check / take) your blood pressure, and you'll see the doctor.

Ending   You don't need to pay for the medical service tomorrow because everything is included in today's (bill / deal).

B. True / False

1. 내일 병원에 오자마자 채혈을 해야 한다.   (T / F)
2. 아침 식사 후 혈압을 잴 것이다.   (T / F)
3. 내일 수납을 한 후 처방전을 받을 것이다.   (T / F)
4. 약국은 병원 건너편에 있다.   (T / F)

C. Words and Phrases

blood pressure 혈압 / prescription 처방전 / drug store 약국(=pharmacy)

D. Dictation

W: Mr. Johnson. I'll tell you what you'll do tomorrow. You have to come to the hospital at 7 a.m. Be aware you _____ _____ _____ _____. When you come to the hospital, you'll _____ _____ _____ _____ first. And then you can have breakfast. After breakfast, come back to the hospital by 9:30 a.m. We'll check your blood pressure, and you'll see the doctor. You don't need to pay for the _____ _____ tomorrow because everything _____ _____ _____ today's bill. Just get the prescription and go to the pharmacy. There are three drug stores across the street. Any questions?

A. Listening Web  MP3 10-02-A

Intro In Brazil, most people live in the cities along the coast.

Web1 In the 1960s, the government (encouraged / courage) people to move inland to the Amazon (reason / region).

Web2 The Amazon rain forest was so (lush / rush) that the soil was very rich.

Web3 And the people wanted to farm there when they settled down, so they started to (burn / earn) the trees to clear the woods.

Ending Any crops could not be grown well there.

B. True / False  MP3 10-02-B

1. 1960년대 많은 브라질 사람들이 내륙으로 이사했다.　　　　　　　　　　　　　　(T / F)
2. 아마존 지역으로 이사한 사람들은 그곳에서 농사를 지으려고 했다.　　　　　　　(T / F)
3. 아마존 지역의 토양은 생각보다 비옥하지 않았다.　　　　　　　　　　　　　　(T / F)
4. 이주민들의 노력으로 아마존 지역에 도시가 형성되어 번창하게 되었다.　　　　　(T / F)

C. Words and Phrases

inland 내륙으로 / settle down 정착하다 / lush (초목이) 무성한, 비옥한 / sweep 쓸어가다, 날려버리다

D. Dictation  MP3 10-02-B

M: In Brazil, most people live in the cities _____ _____ _____. In the 1960s, the government encouraged people to move _____ to the Amazon region. The Amazon rain forest was so lush that the soil was very rich. And the people wanted to farm there when _____ _____ _____, so they started to burn the trees to clear the woods. However, after they _____ _____ _____ the trees, the soil got poor. Any crops could not be grown well there. Moreover, whenever it rained, almost everything _____ _____ _____. Finally, a lot of people _____ _____ living in the Amazon region, and returned to the cities.

A. Listening Web

Intro Our school will hold an English Speech Contest on September 1st.

Web1 Any student who wants to participate in this contest should (hand / hold) in a script to your English teacher by July 29th.

Web2 This contest will be an individual contest and groups are not (allow / allowed).

Web3 Twenty speech contest participants will be (selected / selecting) based on the scripts first.

Ending And the student who wins the first prize will participate on behalf (for / of) our school in the High School Student English Speech Contest (held / hold) by Summerfield City on September 30th.

B. True / False

1. 영어 말하기 대회 참가 신청을 원하는 학생은 대본을 담임 선생님께 미리 제출해야 한다.　(T / F)
2. 영어 말하기 대회는 개인적으로 출전할 수 있다.　(T / F)
3. 영어 말하기 대회에서 1등을 하면 상품을 준다.　(T / F)
4. 영어 말하기 대회 관련 질문은 영어 교실 게시판을 활용한다.　(T / F)

C. Words and Phrases

hold (회의, 시합 등을) 열다, 개최하다 / participate in ~에 참가하다 / individual 개인의 / participant 참가자 / on behalf of ~를 대표하여

D. Dictation

W: Attention, please! Our school _____ _____ an English Speech Contest on September 1st. Any student who wants to _____ _____ this contest should hand in a script to your English teacher by _____ _____. This contest will be an _____ _____ and groups are not allowed. Twenty speech contest participants will be selected based on the scripts first. And the student who wins the first prize will participate _____ _____ _____ our school in the High School Student English Speech Contest held by Summerfield City on September 30th. If you have any questions about this contest, please _____ _____ _____ _____.

A. Listening Web

Intro   Anybody who meets the (qualification / qualifications) can come (for / forward) to be a candidate.

Web1   And he or she should be (recommended / recommending) by more than three teachers and also more than thirty students.

Web2   They should choose two other running mates.

Web3   The (both presidential / vice-presidential) candidates should be different genders from each other.

Ending   If you're (interested / interesting), contact the current student president to get the forms you need, or you can download them from our school homepage.

B. True / False

1. 선생님 세 명 이상, 또는 학생 30명 이상의 추천을 받아야 한다.   (T / F)
2. 자격 조건에 맞으면 혼자서도 출마할 수 있다.   (T / F)
3. 등록에 필요한 양식은 교장 선생님으로부터 받을 수 있다.   (T / F)
4. 서류는 학교 홈페이지에서 다운로드 할 수 있다.   (T / F)

C. Words and Phrases

candidate 후보자 / running mate 러닝메이트(부통령 후보, 동반 출마자) / vice-president 부회장 / current 현재의

D. Dictation

M: Student President Election time _____ _____. Anybody who meets the _____ can come forward to be a candidate. Their average grade for the last year should be better than a B⁺. And he or she _____ _____ _____ _____ more than three teachers and also more than thirty students. The candidates for the president should be second-year students, and they should choose _____ _____ _____ _____. The vice-presidential candidates should be different genders from each other. If you're interested, contact the _____ _____ _____ to get the forms you need, or you can download them from our school homepage.

A. Listening Web  MP3 10-05-A

Intro Garden Art Museum was originally Mrs. Garden's home.
Web1 It was built in the (15 / 15th) century Gothic style.
Web2 When she was (alive / live), she collected drawings, ceramics, and traditional clothing from all over Europe.
Web3 She had an excellent (eye / eyes) for oriental art, so her collection has virtually a wide (variety / various).
Web4 Since she (passed / past) away in 2003, there has been no more new collecting.
Ending Art teachers all over the world can enter for free.

B. True / False  MP3 10-05-B

1. 미술관은 건물이 아름다운 것으로 유명하다.   (T / F)
2. Mrs. Garden은 동양적인 눈매를 가졌다.   (T / F)
3. Mrs. Garden은 2003년에 세상을 떠났다.   (T / F)
4. 입장료는 20달러이다.   (T / F)

C. Words and Phrases

ceramic 도자기 / have an eye for something 보는 눈이 있다 / virtually 실제로 / in accordance with ~에 따라

D. Dictation  MP3 10-05-B

W: Garden Art Museum was originally Mrs. Garden's home. It was built ＿＿＿＿＿＿ ＿＿＿＿＿＿ ＿＿＿＿＿＿ ＿＿＿＿＿＿ Gothic style, and it is famous for being a beautiful building. This museum is full of Mrs. Garden's ＿＿＿＿＿＿ ＿＿＿＿＿＿. When she was alive, she collected drawings, ceramics, and traditional clothing from ＿＿＿＿＿＿ ＿＿＿＿＿＿ ＿＿＿＿＿＿. In addition, she had an excellent eye for oriental art, so her collection has virtually ＿＿＿＿＿＿ ＿＿＿＿＿＿ ＿＿＿＿＿＿. Since she passed away in 2003, there has been no more new collecting, ＿＿＿＿＿＿ ＿＿＿＿＿＿ ＿＿＿＿＿＿ her wishes. The admission is $2, and art teachers all over the world can enter for free.

A. Listening Web  MP3 10-06-A

Intro This Botanic Garden Island consists (of / with) a big main island, which you're standing on, and two smaller rocky islands.

Web1 It has over 800 tropical (space / species) and evergreen plants.

Web2 This Botanic Garden Island is (called / cold) "Mini Hawaii."

Web3 Actually this island is a private island.

Ending He was on TV several years ago, and this island became very famous and now is one of the best tourist (attraction / attractions).

B. True / False  MP3 10-06-B

1. 이 섬에는 두 개의 작은 바위섬이 있다. (T / F)
2. 섬 주인은 이 섬을 꾸미기 위해 하와이에서 식물 품종을 가져왔다. (T / F)
3. 이 섬은 처음에 황량했다. (T / F)
4. 이 섬은 몇 년 전 TV에서 가장 멋진 관광 명소 중 하나로 선정되었다. (T / F)

C. Words and Phrases

botanic 식물의 / evergreen 상록수 / exclusive 배타적인, 독점적인 / deserted 사람이 없는

D. Dictation 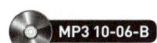 MP3 10-06-B

M: This Botanic Garden Island consists of a big main island, which you're standing on, and two smaller rocky islands. It has over 800 tropical species and evergreen plants. Because of these _____ _____ gardens and the ocean _____ this island, this Botanic Garden Island is called "Mini Hawaii." Actually this island is a private island. At first, it was _____ _____, but Mr. Green, the owner of this island made _____ _____ _____ _____ to make it like this. He was on TV several years ago, and this island became very famous and now is one of the best tourist attractions.

문항 7

△ 심화 학습

A. Listening Web  MP3 10-07-A

Intro I'm Jenny Kim, the (supervise / supervisor) of this workshop.
Web1 Mr. Lee is a professor in the (apartment / department) of Psychology at Hankuk University.
Web2 Also, he has worked as a (counseling / counselor) for five years.
Web3 It's been a steady seller for the last three years since it was (publish / published).
Ending This will be useful and helpful to all of you, the would-be counselors.

B. True / False  MP3 10-07-B

1. Jenny Kim은 심리학과 교수이다.   (T / F)
2. 강사는 5년간 대학에서 심리학을 가르쳤다.   (T / F)
3. 오늘 강연의 주제는 'Relationship and Leadership'이다.   (T / F)
4. 강연을 듣는 사람들은 상담가 지망생들이다.   (T / F)

C. Words and Phrases

supervisor 관리자, 감독 / lecture 강의 / would-be ~이 되려고 하는, 지망하는 / give a big hand 손뼉 치다

D. Dictation  MP3 10-07-B

W: I'm Jenny Kim, the _____ _____ _____ _____, and I'm so glad to meet you all. I'm here _____ _____ the first lecturer of this workshop. Mr. Lee is a professor in the department of Psychology at Hankuk University. Also, he has worked _____ _____ _____ for five years. I think all of you've heard of the famous book "Relationship and Leadership." He is the author, and it's been a steady seller for the last three years _____ _____ _____ _____. Today he's going to give us a good lecture about "Here and Now." This will be useful and helpful to all of you, the would-be counselors. Please give him _____ _____ _____!

A. Listening Web    MP3 10-08-A

Intro Now we're moving on to go to the Colosseum.

Web1 It was (accessible / addressable) to all the people, like the emperor, the nobility, women, and even slaves.

Web2 It has elevators to move animals, and (awnings / earnings).

Web3 It also has 80 (arched / arching) doors to get all the people out of the stadium within (15 / 50) minutes after the show.

Ending Today only one-third of the stadium remains, so we cannot see the (all / whole) Colosseum.

B. True / False    MP3 10-08-B

1. 콜로세움은 오직 검투사의 경기장으로만 쓰였다.   (T / F)
2. 현재 콜로세움의 3분의 2가 손상되었다.   (T / F)
3. 콜로세움은 모든 경기는 15분 안에 종료되었다.   (T / F)
4. 콜로세움은 15명씩 입장이 가능하다.   (T / F)

C. Words and Phrases

gladiatorial combat 검투사 경기 / accessible to ~에게 접근할 수 있는 / the nobility 귀족 / arched 아치 모양의 / awning 차양

D. Dictation    MP3 10-08-B

M: Now we're moving on to go to the Colosseum. The Colosseum was mainly used for gladiatorial combat, but also for circuses or plays. And it was _____ _____ all the people, like the _____, the _____, women, and even _____. It has such wonderful facilities that we cannot believe it was built in the 1st century. It has elevators to move animals, and awings. It also has 80 arched doors to get all the people out of the stadium within 15 minutes after the show. Unfortunately, today only _____ _____ _____ _____ remains, so we cannot see the whole Colosseum. We're almost there. You can see the Colosseum on your right side.

△ 심화 학습

A. Listening Web  MP3 10-09-A

Intro Sometimes the slaves could sing songs while their masters were listening to them.

Web1 In fact, a lot of African Americans were encouraged to take (off / up) Christianity as their religion.

Web2 And apparently some of the songs were about God or going to heaven.

Web3 So the masters believed that the slaves were very happy with the (religion / reason) when they were singing.

Ending It was not only (because / because of) they needed water to drink but also because they might be able to catch fish during their escape.

B. True / False  MP3 10-09-B

1. 노예들의 노래는 기독교를 비판하는 내용이었다. (T / F)
2. 주인들은 노예들이 노래로 종교적 위안을 받는다고 믿었다. (T / F)
3. 노예들의 노래는 노예가 도망가지 않고 주인 곁에 머무르도록 유도했다. (T / F)
4. 노예들은 탈출 시, 식량을 얻기 위해 물가에 있을 필요가 있었다. (T / F)

C. Words and Phrases

Christianity 기독교 / religion 종교 / apparently 겉으로 보기에는, 외관상으로는 /
escape 달아나다, 탈출하다, 도망, 탈출

D. Dictation  MP3 10-09-B

W: Sometimes the slaves could sing songs while their masters were listening to them. In fact, a lot of African Americans were _____ _____ _____ _____ Christianity as their religion. And apparently some of the songs were about God or going to heaven. So the masters believed that the slaves were very _____ _____ _____ _____ when they were singing. However, some songs were very practical to the slaves as well. For example, the song, "Wade in the Water" let the African Americans remember that they had to stay near water. It was not only _____ _____ _____ water to drink, but also because they might be able to catch fish during _____ _____.

A. Listening Web

Intro We eat for (pleasure / treasure) or as a part of social situations!

Web1 So culture has the (stronger / strongest) influence on eating habits.

Web2 Any (kind / type) of diet can be healthy as long as proper food choices are made.

Web3 In Greece or Italy, people enjoy a so-called Mediterranean diet, which includes a lot of olive oil.

Ending Studies have shown that a diet rich in olive oil is associated with a (low / lower) risk of heart disease.

B. True / False

1. 음식은 영양분 공급 이상의 의미가 있다.   (T / F)
2. 음식에 대한 개인적 취향이 식습관에 큰 영향을 미친다.   (T / F)
3. 그리스, 이탈리아에서는 지중해식 식단이 유명하다.   (T / F)
4. 심장병을 예방하는데 올리브유가 가장 효과적인 것으로 밝혀졌다.   (T / F)

C. Words and Phrases

nutrient 영양분 / aspect 면, 측 / Mediterranean 지중해의 / associated with ~와 관련된

D. Dictation

M: Food means a lot for people. That is, food is not only a way of providing _____. We eat for pleasure or as a part of _____ _____! So culture has the strongest _____ _____ eating habits. There are positive and negative aspects to all kinds of food habits, and any type of diet can be healthy as long as _____ _____ _____ are made. For example, in Greece or Italy, people enjoy a so-called Mediterranean diet, which includes a lot of olive oil. Studies have shown that a diet rich in olive oil is _____ _____ a lower risk of heart disease. It means the Mediterranean diet is considered to be a heart-healthy diet.

일치하는 내용을 찾는 것은 일치하지 않는 내용을 찾는 것과 사실상 같은 인지 과정을 요구한다. 그러나 수험생에게는 일치하지 않는 내용을 찾기보다 약간 어렵게 느껴질 수 있다. 왜냐하면 대개 대화가 시작되기 전에 선택지를 미리 보면서 대화의 내용을 대충 짐작하게 되는데, 본 유형은 하나를 제외한 나머지 네 개의 선택지가 모두 잘못된 내용이므로 이것이 오히려 듣기를 하는데 방해 요소로 작용할 수 있다. 그러나 앞서 밝힌 바와 같이 두 유형을 해결하는 원리는 같으므로, 침착하게 풀어간다면 어렵지 않다. 이 유형도 마찬가지로 선택지의 순서는 대본의 순서가 같으므로, 들으면서 순서대로 진위를 가리면 된다.

● **Example**

1   **Bonobos에 관한 다음 내용을 듣고, 일치하는 것을 고르시오.** [2012 수능모의]

W: Have you ever heard of bonobos? The bonobo is a type of African ape. It lives in the forests of the Democratic Republic of the Congo. Compared to its close relatives, the bonobo is more slender and has a smaller head. It often walks upright instead of on all fours. If it hunts, it usually hunts alone. Interestingly, female bonobos are sometimes the hunters. Bonobos don't use tools to hunt or get food, but for other purposes. For example, the bonobo uses a leaf as a rain hat or a stick to indicate direction. Strangely, they often share food with each other. Sound interesting? How about visiting one at your local zoo today?

① 콩고의 숲에 무리 지어 서식한다.
② 종종 서서 걷는다.
③ 혼자 사냥하지 않는다.
④ 사냥할 때 도구를 사용한다.
⑤ 비가 오면 방향 감각을 상실한다.

* "It often walks upright instead of on all fours." 라고 했으므로, 네 다리로 서는 대신 두 다리로 직립 보행할 때가 종종 있음을 알 수 있다. 따라서 정답은 ②번이다.

유형 11

일치하는
내용 찾기

Unit 11

유형 11

일치하는 내용 찾기

1 다음을 듣고, 일치하는 것을 고르시오.

① 토마토케첩이 처음 만들어진 곳은 멕시코이다.
② 아즈텍족이 먹던 토마토는 지금의 토마토보다 더 동그랗고 작았다.
③ 스페인이 멕시코를 점령하러 떠날 때 토마토를 멕시코로 가져갔다.
④ 스페인 사람들은 토마토를 관상용으로 키웠다.
⑤ 스페인에서 자라는 토마토에는 독이 있어서 먹을 수가 없었다.

2 오케스트라 단원 모집에 관한 다음 내용을 듣고, 일치하는 것을 고르시오.

① 대인 관계 기술이 뛰어나야 한다.
② 모든 현악기 연주자를 선발한다.
③ 아마추어 오케스트라 경력이 있는 경우 반드시 선발된다.
④ 오디션은 앞으로 일주일 뒤에 열린다.
⑤ 합격자는 교내 식당 앞에서 방송으로 공지할 것이다.

3 다음을 듣고, 일치하는 것을 고르시오.

① 7시 30분에 착륙할 것이다.
② 기내의 시계는 현지 시각을 표시하고 있지 않다.
③ 서울 날씨는 흐리고 약하게 바람이 불고 있다.
④ 서울 기온은 영하이다.
⑤ 착륙한 뒤에도 잠시 의자에서 대기해야 한다.

4 가면올빼미에 관한 다음 내용을 듣고, 일치하는 것을 고르시오.

① 날개의 길이는 최소한 116센티미터가 넘는다.
② 암컷이 수컷보다 작다.
③ 나무 꼭대기에 둥지를 튼다.
④ 남극에는 서식하지 않는다.
⑤ 한국에서는 2003년에 멸종되었다.

5 가상현실 공간에서의 외국어 학습에 관한 다음 내용을 듣고, 일치하는 것을 고르시오.

① 아직 학습자들의 관심을 끌지 못하고 있다.
② 부끄럼이 많은 학습자도 많은 이야기를 할 수 있다.
③ 건전한 의사소통을 위해 익명성은 제한된다.
④ 수업 콘텐츠는 게임으로 이루어져 있다.
⑤ 강제성이 낮아 학습을 중단하기 쉬운 단점이 있다.

6 주말농장에 관한 다음 내용을 듣고, 일치하는 것을 고르시오.

① 개인당 경작 구역의 크기는 정해져 있다.
② 농장은 도심에서 두 시간 거리에 있다.
③ 무료로 농기구 대여가 가능하다.
④ 희귀 품종 종자 구매 대행이 가능하다.
⑤ 어린이 교육 프로그램은 12명 이하로 운영된다.

7 자전거 회사에 관한 다음 내용을 듣고, 일치하는 것을 고르시오.

① 자전거는 빌린 곳에 반납해야 한다.
② 정류장은 한적한 곳에 있다.
③ 출퇴근용으로 이용하는 사람들이 많다.
④ 연간 회원권을 구매하면 하루 무료 이용이 가능하다.
⑤ 친환경 기업으로 선정되었다.

8 호박에 관한 다음 내용을 듣고, 일치하는 것을 고르시오.

① 아랍권에서 먼저 사용되기 시작했다.
② 원시시대에는 장신구로 사용되지 않았다.
③ 동식물이 들어있는가에 따라 가치가 달라진다.
④ 치료제로써의 효능이 과학적으로 입증되었다.
⑤ 1990년대 초반에 과학적 연구 가치를 인정받게 되었다.

9 다음을 듣고, 일치하는 것을 고르시오.

① 1920년대 총 5,000명의 사람들이 미국으로 이민해 왔다.
② 엘리스 섬에서 이민 심사가 이루어졌다.
③ 2차 대전 끝 무렵 170만 명의 사람들이 미국으로 이민해 왔다.
④ 1950년대 유럽인의 미국 이민은 더욱 활성화되었다.
⑤ 오늘날에도 여전히 엘리스 섬은 미국 이민자들로 붐빈다.

10 박람회에 관한 다음 내용을 듣고, 일치하는 것을 고르시오.

① 총 50개의 주제로 이루어진 프로그램이 준비되어 있다.
② 70일간 지속될 예정이다.
③ 3,500명의 관람객이 모여들 것으로 예상한다.
④ 대규모 이벤트와 소규모 이벤트는 서로 다른 날 열린다.
⑤ 안전을 위해 공연장 내에서 지정석에 앉아야 한다.

해답/해설 284p

A. Listening Web

Intro   When you are (pouring / pulling) tomato ketchup on your burger or potato chips, do you think of Mexico?

Web1   That's where the tomato was (developed / developing).

Web2   They were (small / smaller) and not as round.

Web3   The Spanish took tomato plants back to Europe.

Web4   But they were grown as (decorating / decorative) plants.

Ending They were also afraid that tomatoes might be poisonous.

B. True / False

1. 아즈텍족이 먹던 토마토는 한 가지 종류가 아니었다.   (T / F)

2. 스페인 사람들이 침략했을 때 멕시코에서는 이미 토마토를 먹고 있었다.   (T / F)

3. 초기 토마토는 지금의 것과 모양이 달랐다.   (T / F)

4. 스페인 사람들은 멕시코에서 토마토 요리법을 배웠다.   (T / F)

C. Words and Phrases

pour 붓다 / invader 침략군 / decorative 장식용의 / poisonous 유독한, 독성이 있는

D. Dictation

M: When you are pouring tomato ketchup on your burger or potato chips, do you think of Mexico? That's where the tomato ＿＿＿＿＿＿ ＿＿＿＿＿＿. When Spanish invaders moved into Mexico in 1519, the Aztec people were eating ＿＿＿＿＿ ＿＿＿＿＿ ＿＿＿＿＿ ＿＿＿＿＿. These early tomatoes looked different. They were not as big, shiny, red as we eat today. They were smaller and ＿＿＿＿＿ ＿＿＿＿＿ ＿＿＿＿＿. The Spanish took tomato plants back to Europe. But they were ＿＿＿＿＿ ＿＿＿＿＿ ＿＿＿＿＿ ＿＿＿＿＿. Because the Europeans had never seen anything like them before, no one knew ＿＿＿＿＿ ＿＿＿＿＿ ＿＿＿＿＿ ＿＿＿＿＿. They were also afraid that tomatoes ＿＿＿＿＿ ＿＿＿＿＿ ＿＿＿＿＿.

A. Listening Web  MP3 11-02-A

Intro Applicants should possess strong (communicating / communication) and interpersonal skills as well as musical skills because you'll be working in a team environment.

Web1 Only string players are (wanted / wanting) at this time, but we don't have an opening for contrabassists.

Web2 You don't have to have had a career in any amateur orchestra, but if you have, it can be (beneficial / benefit) for you to be chosen.

Web3 The audition will be on the 1st of November in the music room.

Ending A week later, we'll announce the applicants who have passed the audition (at / on) the main bulletin board in front of the cafeteria.

B. True / False  MP3 11-02-B

1. 오케스트라 단원을 급하게 모집하고 있다. (T / F)
2. 연주 실력뿐 아니라 대인 관계 기술도 좋아야 한다. (T / F)
3. 콘트라베이스 연주자는 선발하시 않는다. (T / F)
4. 오디션 결과는 오디션 후 일주일 뒤에 발표된다. (T / F)

C. Words and Phrases

possess 소유하다 / interpersonal 대인 관계에 관련된 / contrabassist 콘트라베이스 연주자 / bulletin board 게시판

D. Dictation  MP3 11-02-B

W: This is an announcement for _____ _____ _____ _____ student musicians of our school orchestra. Applicants should _____ _____ communication and interpersonal skills as well as musical skills because you'll be working _____ _____ _____ _____. Only string players are wanted at this time: two violinists, one cellist, and one violist, but we don't have an opening for contrabassists. You don't have to have had _____ _____ _____ any amateur orchestra, but if you have, it can be beneficial for you _____ _____ _____. The audition will be on the 1st of November in the music room. A week later after that, we'll announce the applicants _____ _____ _____ the audition on the main bulletin board in front of the cafeteria.

A. Listening Web  MP3 11-03-A

Intro   We'll begin descending for Incheon International Airport in (thirteen / thirty) minutes.
Web1   The current time is 7:30 a.m.
Web2   Please set your watch forward if you have not done so.
Web3   The weather in Seoul is cloudy with a (strong / strongly) wind.
Web4   The temperature is 2 degrees Celsius.
Ending   We have an emergency patient on board, so after we land, passengers please be seated and wait so that the patient can be (taken / taking) out of the cabin first.

B. True / False  MP3 11-03-B

1. 방송을 하는 사람은 기장이다.   (T / F)
2. 눈 때문에 비행기 착륙이 지연되었다.   (T / F)
3. 지금 곧 비행기는 착륙을 시작할 것이다.   (T / F)
4. 기내에는 응급환자가 있다.   (T / F)

C. Words and Phrases

descend 하강하다 / land 착륙하다 / cabin (배의) 객실, (항공기) 선실 / flight deck (비행기) 조종실 /
cabin crew 승무원

D. Dictation  MP3 11-03-B

M: Ladies and Gentlemen, this is your captain speaking. We'll _____ _____ _____ Incheon International Airport in thirty minutes. Landing is being postponed because it's snowing suddenly. _____ _____ _____ is 7:30 a.m. Please _____ _____ _____ _____ if you have not done so. The weather in Seoul is cloudy with a strong wind. The temperature is 2 degrees Celsius, which is 35.6 degrees Fahrenheit. And we have an emergency patient _____ _____, so after we land, passengers please be seated and wait _____ _____ the patient can be taken _____ _____ _____ _____ first. I hope you enjoyed the flight, and on behalf of the flight deck and cabin crew, I'd like to thank you for choosing Summer Sky Airways today. Welcome to Korea.

A. Listening Web  MP3 11-04-A

Intro   This is the barn owl, a type of nocturnal bird.
Web1   Its wings are 116cm at (least / most).
Web2   And the (male / man) barn owl is a little bit smaller than the female.
Web3   It hunts small rats, and builds a nest in a (hollow / hollowed) tree or on the tops of buildings.
Web4   It lives everywhere (exact / except) the Antarctic.
Ending   In Korea, one was first (found / founded) near the west coast in 2003.

B. True / False  MP3 11-04-B

1. 야행성 조류이다.   (T / F)
2. 올빼미 종류 중 가장 작다.   (T / F)
3. 몸의 크기에 비해 다리가 긴 편이다.   (T / F)
4. 위험한 동물로 인식되고 있다.   (T / F)

C. Words and Phrases

nocturnal 야행성 / at most 기껏해야, 최대한으로 잡아서 / hollow 속이 빈 / the Antarctic 남극

D. Dictation  MP3 11-04-B

W: Look at the picture on the screen. This is the barn owl, a type of _____ _____.

It's smaller than any other type of owl. It is only 30 to 40cm tall and its wings are 116cm at most.

And the male barn owl is a little bit smaller than the female. Although its body is small, it has long

legs _____ _____ the size of body. It hunts small rats, and _____

_____ _____ in a hollow tree or on the tops of buildings. It lives _____

_____ the Antarctic. In Korea, one was _____ _____ _____

the west coast in 2003. Now it is listed as an endangered species.

A. Listening Web  MP3 11-05-A

Intro   Attention is (drawing / drawn) to learning a foreign language in a virtual reality space among foreign language learners.

Web1   Even though you're a shy or (lizard / reserved) person, you can talk a lot.

Web2   Anonymity is (guaranteed / guarani) in the virtual reality space.

Web3   In addition, lessons in a virtual reality space are considered a game.

Ending   (A few / Few) learners will quit studying a foreign language.

B. True / False  MP3 11-05-B

1. 가상현실 공간은 오직 외국어 학습만을 위한 곳이다.   (T / F)
2. 가상현실 공간은 익명성이 보장된다.   (T / F)
3. 가상현실 공간 학습장에서는 다양한 게임 콘텐츠들이 개발되어 있다.   (T / F)
4. 가상현실 공간에서는 자유롭게 의견을 낼 수 있다.   (T / F)

C. Words and Phrases

virtual reality space 가상현실 공간 / stranger 낯선 사람, 모르는 사람 / reserved 내성적인, 소극적인 /
anonymity 익명성

D. Dictation  MP3 11-05-B

M: _____ _____ _____ _____ learning a foreign language in a virtual reality space among foreign language learners. A virtual reality space allows a lot of _____ _____ _____ each other and communicate in a foreign language. Even though you're a shy or reserved person, you can talk a lot. Because _____ _____ _____ in the virtual reality space, everybody can express their thoughts and emotions freely. So you'll have a lot more chances to practice a foreign language in this space than in reality. In addition, lessons in a virtual reality space are considered a game. That's why it can _____ _____ _____ and few learners will _____ _____ a foreign language.

A. Listening Web  MP3 11-06-A

Intro   The size of the plot is your (choice / choose).

Web1   The location is so great that it takes only two hours from Mr. Kevin's Farm to the (inner / in the) city and back.

Web2   We also provide wonderful service such as (lending / renting) farming tools for a small charge.

Web3   You have to buy (seats / seeds) yourselves, but if it's a rare species, we can buy them for you.

Ending   And if you have children (over / under) 12, they can take (part / parts) in the free farming education program.

B. True / False  MP3 11-06-B

1. Mr. Kevin은 주말농장을 꿈꾸고 있다.   (T / F)
2. Mr. Kevin은 도시에 살고 있다.   (T / F)
3. Mr. Kevin의 농장은 아주 넓어서 양 끝을 왕복하는 데 두 시간 걸린다.   (T / F)
4. 9세 어린이는 무료로 교육 프로그램에 참여할 수 있다.   (T / F)

C. Words and Phrases

city dweller 도시 주민 / plot 작은 구획의 땅 / for rent 임대 / for a small charge 소액으로 / rare species 희귀 품종

D. Dictation  MP3 11-06-B

W: Are you dreaming of weekend farming? Mr. Kevin's Farm provides _____ _____ with the whole new experience of growing their own vegetables and fruits _____ _____ _____ _____. You can come here once a week or more often and grow carrots, pumpkins or tomatoes in plots for rent. The size of the plot is your choice. The location is so great that it takes only two hours from Mr. Kevin's Farm to the inner city _____ _____. We also provide wonderful service such as lending farming tools _____ _____ _____ _____. You have to buy seeds yourselves, but if it's a _____ _____, we can buy them for you. And if you have children _____ _____, they can take part in the free farming education program.

A. Listening Web  MP3 11-07-A

Intro East Bike has (hundred / hundreds) of stations where people rent bicycles and return them near subway stations or at places where a lot of people pass by.

Web1 You can rent a bike in a station and return it to (another / other) station which is near your destination. So it is very convenient to use.

Web2 That's why many people use these bicycles when they (coming / commute) to work.

Web3 An annual membership costs only $100, and you can enjoy a one-day (free / full) experience before you register.

Ending Above all, riding a bike is eco-friendly.

B. True / False  MP3 11-07-B

1. 이 회사는 자전거 판매와 대여를 함께하는 회사이다.　　　　　　(T / F)
2. 이 회사는 수백 개의 자전거 정류장을 갖고 있다.　　　　　　　(T / F)
3. 이용 요금은 택시보다는 싸고, 버스나 지하철과 비슷한 수준이다.　(T / F)
4. 가입 후 하루 무료 이용혜택이 있다.　　　　　　　　　　　　(T / F)

C. Words and Phrases

pass by 지나가다 / commute 통근하다 / way 훨씬 / eco-friendly 친환경적인

D. Dictation  MP3 11-07-B

M: East Bike is not a company that sells bicycles. It is a bike rental company. East Bike has hundreds of stations where people rent bicycles and return them near subway stations or at places where a lot of people _____ _____. You can rent a bike in a station and return it to another station which is _____ _____ _____. So it is very convenient to use. That's why many people use these bicycles when they _____ _____ _____. In addition, it's _____ _____ than a taxi, of course - even a bus or subway. An _____ _____ costs only $100, and you can enjoy a one-day free experience before you register. Above all, riding a bike is _____. Why don't you join East Bike?

A. Listening Web  MP3 11-08-A

Intro Actually the English name amber (derives / drives) from the Arabic (word / world).

Web1 It has been (appreciated / appreciating) for its golden brown color and natural beauty since primitive ages.

Web2 If it contains animals or plants in it, it goes up in value.

Web3 And it has been used as an ingredient in perfume, and even a healing (agent / engine) in folk medicine as well.

Ending You may remember that this was a motive in a sci-fi movie in the early 1990s.

B. True / False  MP3 11-08-B

1. 호박이라는 단어는 원래 고체 밀랍 물질이라는 뜻이다.　　　　　　　　(T / F)
2. 호박은 부드럽고 점성이 있는 액체 물질이다.　　　　　　　　　　　　(T / F)
3. 동식물이 들어있는 호박은 보석으로서의 가치가 없다.　　　　　　　　(T / F)
4. 호박에서 착안하여 영화가 만들어지기도 했다.　　　　　　　　　　　(T / F)

C. Words and Phrases

amber 호박 / derive (다른 것에서) 끌어내다 / refer to 언급하다, 말하다 / substance 물질 / fossilized 화석화된 / resin 송진 / appreciate 진가를 알아보다, 인정하다

D. Dictation  MP3 11-08-B

W: This is called "amber." Actually the English name amber ＿＿＿＿＿＿ ＿＿＿＿＿＿ an Arabic word. The word originally ＿＿＿＿＿＿ ＿＿＿＿＿＿ a solid waxy substance. Amber is ＿＿＿＿＿ resin, which is the soft and gummy liquid from pine trees. It has been ＿＿＿＿＿ ＿＿＿＿＿ its golden brown color and natural beauty since primitive ages. That's why amber has been widely used for decorative objects like jewelry. If it contains animals or plants in it, it ＿＿＿＿＿ ＿＿＿＿＿ ＿＿＿＿＿ ＿＿＿＿＿. And it has been used as an ingredient in perfume, and even a healing agent ＿＿＿＿＿ ＿＿＿＿＿ ＿＿＿＿＿ as well. These days, scientists use it to study animals and plants that lived in the past. You may remember that this was a motive in a sci-fi movie in the early 1990s.

A. Listening Web  MP3 11-09-A

Intro Through the late 1920s, 5,000 people a day were (heard / herded) in and processed in Ellis Island's Great Hall.

Web1 It was at Ellis Island where it was (decide / decided) if you could stay in America.

Web2 By the end of the 2nd World War in 1945, 17 (million / millions) people would sail through this New York gateway to America.

Web3 By the 1950s, the great (age / wave) of European immigration to America had subsided.

Ending It's still the symbol of new hope today.

B. True / False  MP3 11-09-B

1. 엘리스 섬에 이민국이 처음 생긴 것은 1900년대이다. (T / F)
2. 2차 대전 후 미국으로 이민 오는 사람들은 대부분 유럽인이었다. (T / F)
3. 엘리스 섬은 오늘날 새로운 희망의 상징으로 남아있다. (T / F)
4. 엘리스 섬은 여전히 입국 심사장으로 사용되고 있다. (T / F)

C. Words and Phrases

immigration 이민 / herd (특정 방향으로) 이동하게 하다 / process 처리하다 / oppression 억압, 심한 차별 / subside 가라앉다, 진정되다

D. Dictation  MP3 11-09-B

M: It was in 1892 when the Great Immigration Hall at Ellis Island first opened. It was in the port of New York. Through the late 1920s, 5,000 people a day were _____ _____ and _____ in Ellis Island's Great Hall. It was at Ellis Island _____ _____ _____ _____ if you could stay in America. By the end of the 2nd World War in 1945, 17 million people would sail through this New York gateway to America. They came mostly from Europe. They came to escape _____ _____ _____ at home. By the 1950s, the great wave of European immigration to America _____ _____, and Ellis Island was closed. People were coming here looking for new opportunity, and it's still _____ _____ _____ new hope today.

A. Listening Web  MP3 11-10-A

Intro The Expo is full of (culture / cultural) programs with 50 performances and events.

Web1 They will take (place / plus) every day for the entire 70 days.

Web2 That is 3,500 in total.

Web3 More (frequent / frequently) and smaller-scale events such as street performances will also be offered.

Ending So we offer a lot of audience (participant / participation) programs.

B. True / False 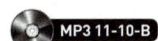 MP3 11-10-B

1. 매일 50개의 공연과 이벤트가 열린다. (T / F)
2. 세계 곳곳에서 온 가수들의 공연을 볼 수 있다. (T / F)
3. 소규모 길거리 공연이 자주 열린다. (T / F)
4. 관람객이 참여할 수 있는 프로그램도 있다. (T / F)

C. Words and Phrases

state-of-the-art 최신식의 / world-class 세계 최상급의 / onlooker 구경꾼 / to the fullest 최대한으로, 완전하게

D. Dictation  MP3 11-10-B

W: The Expo is full of cultural programs with 50 performances and events. They will take place every day for the entire 70 days. That is 3,500 in total. It _____ large-scale events such as the state-of-the-art Multi Media Show, world-class performances, and concerts of popular singers from all around the world. _____ _____ and smaller-scale events such as street performances will also be offered. Today's exposition-goers _____ _____ _____ _____ simply remaining an onlooker. They are _____ _____ _____ _____ become part of the exposition. So we offer a lot of audience participation programs. The Expo will promote _____ _____ and enable visitors to enjoy themselves to the fullest.

도표는 나와 있는 모든 내용에 대해서 언급하지 않을 수도 있으므로, 언급되지 않은 것이 있다고 하여 당황하거나 헷갈려 하는 일이 없도록 한다. 언급되지 않은 부분은 과감하게 무시하면 된다. 대화를 들으면서 언급되는 내용 중 조건에 맞지 않는 것은 ×표, 맞는 것은 ○표를 하면서 들으면 비교적 쉽게 정답을 가려낼 수 있을 것이다.

• **Example**

1   **다음 표를 보면서 대화를 듣고, 두 사람이 방문할 박물관을 고르시오.** [2011 수능기출]

W: John, you know we're supposed to visit a museum this week, right?

M: Yeah. We have to write a report about it. So, I've narrowed the choices down to these five museums.

W: Let's see… They all seem interesting. I want to go to all of them.

M: Well, we can only choose one for the report. How about this museum?

W: Don't you remember our teacher told us to put photographs in the report? We need to go somewhere photography is allowed.

M: Oh, yeah. Then, what about this one? Cars are fun.

W: But, I don't want to spend more than $10 for admission.

M: Okay. That leaves us with these two.

W: Let's go to the museum with do-it-yourself activities.

M: I'm not so sure. Aren't those activities just for children?

W: Of course not. They're fun for people of all ages.

M: Fine. Then let's go to that museum.

		Photography Permitted	Do-It-Yourself Activities	Admission Floor
①	Natural History Museum	○	○	$15
②	Robot Museum	○	×	$5
③	Modern Art Museum	×	○	$9
④	Dinosaur Museum	○	○	$8
⑤	Automobile Museum	○	○	$13

* 입장료가 10달러가 넘으면 안 되고, 사진을 찍을 수 있어야 하며, do-it-yourself 활동을 하는 곳이다. 이 모든 조건을 충족시키는 것은 ④번이다.

유형 12

도표 문제

도표 문제

1 다음 표를 보면서 대화를 듣고, 남자가 주문하려는 음료를 고르시오.

Menu for Beverage

	Flavor	Ice	Syrup
①	Lemon	Cubed	○
②	Cherry	Cubed	×
③	Cherry	Crushed	○
④	Mint	Cubed	×
⑤	Mint	Crushed	×

2 다음 표를 보면서 대화를 듣고, 남자가 진료받게 될 의사 선생님을 고르시오.

Doctors' Schedule

	Mon	Tue	Wed	Thu	Fri	Sat & Sun
Neck	Dr. Kim	Dr. Son	Dr. Kim	Dr. Son	Dr. Son	Closed
Arms & Legs	Dr. Han	Dr. Lee		Dr. Lee	Dr. Lee	Closed
Knees & Legs		Dr. Park	Dr. Park		Dr. Park	Closed

① Dr. Kim
② Dr. Son
③ Dr. Lee
④ Dr. Han
⑤ Dr. Park

3 다음 표를 보면서 대화를 듣고, 두 사람이 주문한 메뉴의 개수가 바르게 표시된 것을 고르시오.

Check List for Lunch

Sandwich	Club Sandwich	Turkey Sandwich	Ham & Egg Sandwich
	① 1	② 1	③ 1
Salad	Green	Caesar	Mango
	④ 2	⑤ 1	0

4 대화를 듣고, 두 사람이 볼 영화와 시작 시간이 바르게 된 것을 고르시오.

Good Movie Theater

Finding Sora	Who's There	Don't Touch
4:30	① 1:30	② 1:30
③ 5:30	④ 2:00	2:30
6:00	5:00	⑤ 5:00

5 다음 표를 보면서 대화를 듣고, 두 사람이 예약할 호텔을 고르시오.

Room Options

	Bed	View	Breakfast	Price
①	Double	Ocean	○	$120
②	Double	Ocean	×	$110
③	Double	Mountain	○	$100
④	Twin	Ocean	×	$90
⑤	Twin	Mountain	×	$70

6 다음 표를 보면서 대화를 듣고, 여자가 여행할 장소의 순서가 바르게 된 것을 고르시오.

Trip to Australia

	1st destination	2nd destination	3rd destination	4th destination
①	Uluru	Brisbane	Sydney	Melbourne
②	Melbourne	Uluru	Brisbane	Sydney
③	Melbourne	Brisbane	Uluru	Sydney
④	Brisbane	Sydney	Melbourne	Uluru
⑤	Brisbane	Uluru	Melbourne	Sydney

7 다음 표를 보면서 대화를 듣고, 다음 주 날씨가 바르게 표기되지 <u>않은</u> 것을 고르시오.

Weather Forecast

	Mon ~Tue	Wed	Thu	Fri	Sat ~ Sun
L.A.	① Sunny	Sunny	② Sunny	Sunny	③ Rainy
San Diego	Sunny	Cloudy	④ Rainy	Cloudy	⑤ Rainy

8 다음 표를 보면서 대화를 듣고, 두 사람이 선택한 활동을 고르시오.

Extreme Sports Program

	MTB	Hiking	Paragliding
①	×	○	×
②	○	○	×
③	×	○	With a pilot
④	○	○	With a pilot
⑤	×	○	Alone

9 다음 표를 보면서 대화를 듣고, 두 사람이 선택한 나이아가라 폭포 여행 상품을 고르시오.

Niagara Fall Tour Package

	Observatory	Cruise	Balloon
①	○	○	○
②	○	○	×
③	○	×	○
④	×	○	○
⑤	×	○	×

10 다음 표를 보면서 대화를 듣고, 여자가 등록하려고 하는 운동이 바르게 표기되지 <u>않은</u> 것을 고르시오.

Gym Schedule

	Mon	Tue	Wed	Thu	Fri	Sat & Sun
Yoga		① ○		② ○		③ ○
Squash			④ ○		⑤ ○	

A. Listening Web  MP3 12-01-A

Intro   I'm kind of (thirty / thirsty). Why don't we drink something?

Web1   Frappe is a drink with fruit pulp and (crush / crushed) ice in it.

Web2   I see. Then the difference between ade and frappe is the size of the ice seeing that an ade has (cube / cubed) ice.

Web3   I'd like mint ade. Do you want some syrup?

Ending   Me, (either / neither).

B. True / False  MP3 12-01-B

1. 바다 전망의 식당에서 이루어지는 대화이다.   (T / F)
2. 여자는 프라페를 먹어본 적이 없다.   (T / F)
3. 에이드와 프라페는 얼음의 크기만 다른 음료이다.   (T / F)
4. 남자가 음료값을 계산할 것이다.   (T / F)

C. Words and Phrases

pulp 과육 / crushed ice 잘게 부순 얼음 / cubed ice 각얼음 / it's on me 내가 낼게, 내가 살게

D. Dictation  MP3 12-01-B

W: Wow, it's so cool! Swimming in the sea is fantastic!

M: Yeah, the emerald color also looks cool.

W: I'm kind of thirsty. _____ _____ _____ _____ something?

M: Look! There's a snack bar over there. The snack bar _____ _____ _____ _____. That's interesting. Let's go.

W: Ade… and frappe… Frappe? What's frappe?

M: Frappe is a drink with fruit pulp and _____ _____ in it.

W: I see. Then the difference between ade and frappe is the size of the ice seeing that an ade has cubed ice.

M: That's right.

W: I'll have a cherry frappe. I've never had frappe before.

M: Excellent choice! _____ _____ _____ _____. Do you want some syrup?

W: No.

M: Me, neither. One lemon frappe and one mint ade.

W: No, cherry frappe for me.

M: Sorry. Wait here. _____ _____ _____.

W: Thanks.

A. Listening Web  MP3 12-02-A

Intro   Mom, my leg (is hurt / hurts).

Web1   You (should be / should've been) careful.

Web2   It seems it has nothing to do with it. My right leg is swollen and hurts (bad / badly).

Web3   The (calf / cap) under the knee is swollen.

Ending   The doctor's office will be (close / closed) because the day after tomorrow is the weekend.

B. True / False  MP3 12-02-B

1. 남자는 축구 경기를 하다 다리를 다쳤다.   (T / F)
2. 남자는 원래 목 디스크가 있다.   (T / F)
3. 내일은 병원 진료가 없다.   (T / F)
4. 주말 진료를 할 수 있다.   (T / F)

C. Words and Phrases

swollen 부은 / have nothing to do with ~와 관계가 없다 / calf 종아리 / cast 깁스

D. Dictation  MP3 12-02-B

M: Mom, my leg hurts.

W: What happened?

M: I think _____ _____ _____ _____ while I was playing football with my friends hours ago. I could stand it, but the pain is getting worse.

W: _____ _____ _____ _____. Always remember that you were treated for the disk problem in your neck.

M: It seems it _____ _____ _____ _____ with it. My right leg is swollen and hurts badly.

W: Isn't it the knee? Show me your leg.

M: The calf under the knee is swollen

W: Let's go to the hospital right now.

M: Do you think I'll have to _____ _____ _____?

W: I'm not sure.

M: Oh, no. I have an appointment tomorrow. I want to go to the hospital the day after tomorrow.

W: The doctor's office will be closed because _____ _____ _____ _____ is the weekend. Hurry up!

A. Listening Web  MP3 12-03-A

Intro Let's have lunch here.

Web1 Then I'll have a turkey sandwich, and I'll have diet coke, too.

Web2 They (sell / set) a ham and egg sandwich for half price. I'll have it.

Web3 Let's order (another / other) ham and egg sandwich and diet coke. And Caesar salad, too.

Ending A green salad is (included / including) for free with sandwiches at lunch. We don't need to order it.

B. True / False  MP3 12-03-B

1. 남자는 클럽 샌드위치를 먹을 것이다. (T / F)
2. 여자는 샌드위치를 두 개 먹을 것이다. (T / F)
3. 점심에는 샌드위치에 샐러드가 포함되어 있다. (T / F)
4. 두 사람은 사무실에 남아있는 동료에게 점심을 사다 줄 것이다. (T / F)

C. Words and Phrases

sheet 종이 / take a break 휴식을 취하다

D. Dictation  MP3 12-03-B

W: Let's have lunch here.

M: Yes, sandwiches are good because we don't have enough time.

W: It seems we have to check the menu on this sheet. _____ _____ _____ _____ to have?

M: A club sandwich and diet coke.

W: What else? _____ _____ _____?

M: Hmm. Mango salad.

W: Okay. Then I'll have a turkey sandwich, and I'll have diet coke, too.

M: Wait. They sell a ham and egg sandwich _____ _____ _____. I'll have it.

W: Do we need to buy Victoria lunch? She is in the office alone and I think she is too busy to _____ _____ _____ for lunch.

M: I think so. Let's order another ham and egg sandwich and diet coke. And Caesar salad, too. She loves it.

W: Oh, look! A green salad _____ _____ _____ _____ with sandwiches at lunch. We don't need to order it.

M: That's nice!

A. Listening Web  MP3 12-04-A

Intro How about going to a movie?

Web1 Then what about "Who's There"? It starts (at / on) 2 p.m.

Web2 I don't like (scared / scary) movies.

Web3 Then let's (see / sea) the scary movie you said.

Ending See you tomorrow in front of the theater 30 minutes before the movie (starts / will start).

B. True / False  MP3 12-04-B

1. 여자는 오늘 5시까지 집에 들어가야 한다. (T / F)
2. 내일 영화배우들이 극장에 방문할 예정이다. (T / F)
3. 여자는 내일 영화를 볼 수 없다. (T / F)
4. 남자는 어제 형과 영화를 보았다. (T / F)

C. Words and Phrases

come to think of it 생각해 보니 / scary 무서운

D. Dictation  MP3 12-04-B

M: How about going to a movie?

W: Cool. _____ _____ _____ now?

M: "Finding Sora" will _____ _____ tomorrow. The actors will come to the theater at 5:30 p.m. Maybe Jennifer Bake will come.

W: That's awesome. But _____ _____ _____ _____ it, I have a dinner appointment at 6 p.m. It's my grandmother's birthday tomorrow. I have to go home by 5 p.m.

M: Then what about "Who's There"? It starts at 2 p.m.

W: I don't like scary movies.

M: But you'll _____ _____ _____. It's had the top spot at the box office since last week.

W: What about "Don't Touch"?

M: My brother saw it yesterday, and he told me _____ _____ _____ the movie.

W: Really? Then let's see the scary movie you said. See you tomorrow in front of the theater 30 minutes before the movie starts. Don't be late! And don't forget that I have to go home by 5 p.m.

A. Listening Web

Intro Have you (reserve / reserved) a hotel?

Web1 I'd like an ocean view.

Web2 I (don't / won't) like the hotel breakfast buffet because I can't usually eat much in the morning.

Web3 Then we'll pay over $100 a night.

Ending We can save money (another / in other) areas. Don't worry.

B. True / False

1. 여자는 바다 전망을 원하고 있다.   (T / F)
2. 남자는 호텔 조식을 좋아하지 않는다.   (T / F)
3. 호텔은 지은 지 10년 되었다.   (T / F)
4. 총 여행 비용 중 숙박료가 가장 많은 부분을 차지한다.   (T / F)

C. Words and Phrases

ocean view 바다전망 / anniversary 기념일 / luxurious 호화로운 / buffet 뷔페

D. Dictation

M: Have you reserved a hotel?

W: Not yet. I'm looking at a hotel site now, and it looks clean and pretty. Will you come and see it?

M: Sure. Which one would you like?

W: I'd like _____ _____ _____. How about you?

M: _____ _____, _____ _____. You know, the hotel charge _____ _____ the largest part of our travel expenses.

W: Paul, it's _____ _____ _____. I don't think it should be luxurious, but I want it to be beautiful and comfortable.

M: I agree. But the mountain view is not bad. And I don't like the hotel breakfast buffet because I can't usually eat much in the morning. I don't think it's _____ _____ _____ _____.

W: I see, Paul. But I can't give up the ocean view.

M: You won't regret that you chose the mountain view.

W: Paul, please.

M: Okay, okay, then we'll _____ _____ $100 _____ _____.

W: Paul, we can save money in other areas. Don't worry.

A. Listening Web

Intro   I'm planning to go to (Australia / Austria) this winter.

Web1   Brisbane, Sydney, Melbourne, Uluru. Uluru is far away from the rest, so I'm thinking of Uluru as the first destination.

Web2   But there's no international flight that goes (direct / directly) to Uluru.

Web3   Then I'll go to Melbourne first, and then Brisbane, and then Uluru, and the last stop will be Sydney.

Ending   So I think Uluru (followed / following) by Brisbane is better.

B. True / False

1. 여자는 남자와 함께 호주에 가려고 한다.   (T / F)
2. 여자는 울룰루에 가기를 포기했다.   (T / F)
3. 브리즈번은 해안에서 가깝다.   (T / F)
4. 여자의 마지막 행선지는 시드니이다.   (T / F)

C. Words and Phrases

itinerary 여행 일정 / destination 도착지 / transfer 환승하다 / switch 맞바꾸다

D. Dictation

M: What's the matter?

W: I need your help. I'm planning to go to Australia this winter. It's not easy to _____ _____ _____. I heard you've traveled in Australia.

M: Yes. First of all, where do you want to go?

W: Brisbane, Sydney, Melbourne, Uluru. Uluru is _____ _____ _____ the rest, so I'm thinking of Uluru as the first destination.

M: But there's no _____ _____ that goes directly to Uluru. You have to drop by another city and transfer through a _____ _____.

W: I see. Then I'll go to Melbourne first, and then Brisbane, and then Uluru, and the last stop will be Sydney.

M: That's not bad. But traveling to Uluru is not easy. It's a desert. But Brisbane is near the beautiful beach. So I think Uluru _____ _____ Brisbane is better.

W: Then is it better to _____ _____ with each other?

M: I think so.

W: Thanks a lot. Now I have outlined my travel.

A. Listening Web

Intro Monday and Tuesday both in L.A. and San Diego are sunny and (cool / clear).

Web1 It'll be rainy (all / whole) weekend; we have to go during the weekdays.

Web2 What about going to San Diego on Wednesday?

Web3 It's cloudy.

Web4 Then what about Thursday?

Ending I mean L.A. It says it's (not / quite) sunny, but Wednesday is sunny and Friday is sunny.

B. True / False

1. 두 사람은 다음 주 출장 계획을 세우고 있다.   (T / F)
2. 화요일에는 로스앤젤레스와 샌디에이고는 모두 날씨가 맑다.   (T / F)
3. 여자는 화요일 약속을 옮기려 한다.   (T / F)
4. 여자는 샌디에이고의 날씨가 흐린 것을 좋아하지 않는다.   (T / F)

C. Words and Phrases

weather forecast 일기예보 / rearrange 재배치하다

D. Dictation

M: It's summer, Eunice! We need a break. Let's go to a beach next week.

W: I have a commitment next Tuesday. Where do you want to go?

M: What about L.A. or San Diego?

W: But it _____ _____ the weather.

M: Let's check the weather forecast.

W: Wow! Monday and Tuesday both in L.A. and San Diego are _____ _____ _____, but we cannot go anywhere because I have a commitment. It'll be rainy _____ _____; we have to go _____ _____ _____.

M: What about going to San Diego on Wednesday?

W: It's cloudy. I cannot imagine the San Diego beach without the sun.

M: Then what about Thursday?

W: Brian, it says it'll be raining.

M: No, I mean L.A. _____ _____ it's not sunny, but Wednesday is sunny and Friday is sunny. I think it can be sunny on Thursday.

W: Brian, come on. Why don't you go to L.A. on Wednesday or Friday?

A. Listening Web

Intro   Rachel, what are we going to do when we go to Canada?

Web1   We need to (climb / crime) up the beautiful mountain and see the emerald lake.

Web2   But I'm afraid of (ride a / riding a) mountain bike.

Web3   Then would you like to go (paraglide / paragliding)?

Ending   With a professional pilot? That's a (relief / relieve). I'll try it.

B. True / False

1. 여자는 혼자 캐나다에 갈 계획이다.   (T / F)
2. 여자는 산악자전거를 타고 싶어한다.   (T / F)
3. 남자는 패러글라이딩을 무서워한다.   (T / F)
4. 패러글라이딩은 전문 조종사와 함께 한다.   (T / F)

C. Words and Phrases

national park 국립 공원 / thrilling 흥분되는, 신 나는 / equipment 장비

D. Dictation

M: Rachel, what are we going to do when we go to Canada? You wanted to go to Banff National Park.

W: Yes. Look at this travel agency website. They provide ＿＿＿＿＿ ＿＿＿＿＿ ＿＿＿＿＿ activities. Everything looks fantastic. What do you want to do there?

M: Above all, we need to ＿＿＿＿＿ ＿＿＿＿＿ the beautiful mountain and see the emerald lake. What was the name?

W: Lake Louise. I'd like to go hiking, too.

M: And I want to ride an MTB. It's thrilling.

W: Yes, it's ＿＿＿＿＿ ＿＿＿＿＿ ＿＿＿＿＿. But I'm afraid of riding a mountain bike. I've ＿＿＿＿＿ ＿＿＿＿＿ ＿＿＿＿＿ ＿＿＿＿＿ when I was younger. I'll never do it again.

M: Then would you like to go paragliding? You've always been dreaming about it.

W: Yeah… but is it safe?

M: Yes, maybe. You need to wear the suit ＿＿＿＿＿ ＿＿＿＿＿ ＿＿＿＿＿, and you'll paraglide with a professional pilot.

W: With a professional pilot? ＿＿＿＿＿ ＿＿＿＿＿ ＿＿＿＿＿. I'll try it.

M: Okay, then I'll click this one.

A. Listening Web  MP3 12-09-A

Intro	What are we going to do there?
Web1	I think we have to go up to the (exhibitory / observatory) and look down at the huge Niagara Falls.
Web2	Can we go down to the water and get (above / on board) a cruise? I'd love to do it.
Web3	But getting on a (balloon / bloom) and going up to the observatory are almost the same thing.
Ending	Then I'd like the balloon.

B. True / False  MP3 12-09-B

1. 여자는 미국 여행이 처음이다. (T / F)
2. 남자는 나이아가라 폭포에 가본 적이 없다. (T / F)
3. 여자는 나이아가라 폭포에서 유람선 타는 것을 찬성한다. (T / F)
4. 남자는 전망대에 올라가지 않기로 했다. (T / F)

C. Words and Phrases

observatory 전망대 / cruise 유람선

D. Dictation  MP3 12-09-B

W: I'm so excited! It's the first time _____ _____ _____ _____ to America. Will we go to Niagara Falls?

M: Sure. We're going to stay there for two days. I can't believe I'll be there again!

W: What are we going to do there?

M: I think we have to go up _____ _____ _____ and look down at the huge Niagara Falls.

W: Wow! It must be amazing. And _____ _____? Just looking at the falls is all that we can do?

M: There are balloons and cruises.

W: Cruises? Can we go down to the water and _____ _____ _____ a cruise? I'd love to do it.

M: Me, too. And you can also look down Niagara Falls from a balloon.

W: That'll be fantastic, too. But getting on a balloon and going up to the observatory are almost the same thing.

M: Hmm… I think you're right.

W: Then _____ _____ _____ _____. We don't need to spend money doing the same thing twice.

M: Then I'd like the balloon. It can be kind of scary, but I want to try it.

W: Okay.

A. Listening Web

Intro I'll (walk / work) out during the vacation.

Web1 But yoga class is every (another / other) day. I need to choose a Monday, Wednesday, and Friday class or a Tuesday, Thursday, and Saturday class.

Web2 Then you can do (another / some other) things when you don't have a yoga class, like swimming or squash…

Web3 The beginner class is on Monday and Wednesday.

Ending Then you can do (all / both) yoga and squash.

B. True / False

1. 남자는 이 체육관에 다닌 지 오래되었다.   (T / F)
2. 여자는 요가가 정적인 운동이라 좋아하지 않는다.   (T / F)
3. 여자는 스쿼시를 배울 계획이다.   (T / F)
4. 남자는 여자와 같은 운동을 할 예정이다.   (T / F)

C. Words and Phrases

registration form 신청서 / every other day 격일로 / squash 스쿼시

D. Dictation

M: Hey, what's up?

W: Hi. _____ _____ _____ during the vacation. I have to lose weight. Do you go to this gym?

M: I'm new, like you. _____ _____ _____. What are you going to do?

W: Well, I've never worked out regularly before. I don't know what to do. Can you help me?

M: Sure. _____ _____ _____ _____ and check which classes you want to join. How about yoga? It's a kind of stretching, so it's not that hard, but you'll _____.

W: Oh! That's exactly my style. But yoga class is _____ _____ _____. I need to choose a Monday, Wednesday, and Friday class or a Tuesday, Thursday, and Saturday class.

M: Then you can do some other things when you don't have a yoga class, like swimming or squash…

W: I've wanted to try squash. But squash class is only on Friday.

M: That's _____ _____ _____. Have you ever learned squash?

W: No. A-ha, the beginner class is on Monday and Wednesday.

M: Then you can do both yoga and squash.

W: All right. Thank you.

이 유형은 유형 1의 확장형으로 생각하면 된다. 유형 1은 짧은 대화 끝에 이어질 응답을 찾는 것이라면, 이번 유형은 긴 대화 끝에 이어질 응답을 찾는 것이다. 따라서 듣기의 호흡을 길게 가져가는 것이 중요하다. 대화가 어떤 내용으로 흘러가는지, 중간에 대화의 주제가 바뀌거나 화자의 생각이 변화하지는 않는지 주의하면서 대화의 흐름을 잘 따라가도록 해야 한다. 이 유형은 수능 영어에서 항상 비율을 많이 차지해 왔고, 앞으로도 두 문제 이상의 비율을 차지할 것으로 예상되므로 고득점을 노리는 수험생이라면 절대 놓쳐서는 안 될 유형이다.

● Example

1　대화를 듣고, 여자의 마지막 말에 대한 남자의 응답으로 가장 적절한 것을 고르시오.
[2011 수능기출]

M: Hey, Lisa. Is something the matter?

W: I think I hurt my back helping my brother move yesterday.

M: Oh, no! How did it happen?

W: Well, I bent over to pick up this box and the next thing you know, I was in so much pain.

M: That's terrible. Did you go see a doctor about it?

W: No. I just put some ice on it to relieve the pain.

M: That's a smart thing to do, but that's only a temporary remedy.

W: Don't worry. I'll be up and running in no time.

M: Hurting your back is a serious matter. I think you'd be better off getting a professional opinion.

W: Hmm… Do you really think that's necessary?

M: ＿＿＿＿＿＿＿＿＿＿＿＿＿＿＿＿＿＿＿＿＿

Man: ＿＿＿＿＿＿＿＿＿＿＿＿＿＿＿＿＿＿＿

① Don't fix what isn't broken.
② I'd move mountains for you.
③ It's better to be safe than sorry.
④ You can't please the whole world.
⑤ Time flies when you're having fun.

* 여자는 처음에 얼음찜질만으로도 괜찮다고 생각하지만, 남자는 의사에게 가보는 것이 좋겠다고 말한다. 꼭 그럴 필요 있겠느냐는 여자의 질문으로 대화는 마무리된다. 선택지 중 병원에 가는 것이 그냥 있는 것보다는 낫다는 남자의 의견을 반영하고 있는 것은 ③번이다.

유형 13

적절한
응답 찾기

적절한 응답 찾기

1 대화를 듣고, 남자의 마지막 말에 대한 여자의 응답으로 가장 적절한 것을 고르시오.

Woman: _____

① You can renew the book by phone.
② Sorry, I can't connect him. The line is busy.
③ We'll let you know as soon as the book is returned.
④ The message about the book has been sent to your phone.
⑤ We'll give you a call when the computer has been repaired.

2 대화를 듣고, 남자의 마지막 말에 대한 여자의 응답으로 가장 적절한 것을 고르시오.

Woman: So you mean _____, right?

① the minor film industries need their own theaters
② Spiderman will never be shown again at the theaters
③ the Hollywood blockbusters need to be shut down right away
④ all the film companies share profits to develop the film industry
⑤ experimental movies need to have chances to be shown to people

3 대화를 듣고, 남자의 마지막 말에 대한 여자의 응답으로 가장 적절한 것을 고르시오.

Woman: _____

① Those bottles are not empty yet.
② Because we are supposed to reuse them.
③ I'm going to read the newspaper tomorrow.
④ Recyclable trash is collected every Tuesday.
⑤ You have to finish reading the newspaper by tomorrow.

4 대화를 듣고, 여자의 마지막 말에 대한 남자의 응답으로 가장 적절한 것을 고르시오.

Man: _____

① Practice makes perfect.
② Safety is more important than fashion.
③ Then, put on something else you want.
④ I can show you another set of helmet and sneakers.
⑤ Don't forget to ring the bell when you're in trouble.

5 대화를 듣고, 여자의 마지막 말에 대한 남자의 응답으로 가장 적절한 것을 고르시오.

Man: _____

① Keep the pictures on file.
② Have medical checkups regularly.
③ Keep the files according to the date.
④ Make hard copies of the image files.
⑤ Take as many pictures as possible when you travel.

6 대화를 듣고, 여자의 마지막 말에 대한 남자의 응답으로 가장 적절한 것을 고르시오.

Man: _____

① Shall we sit by the window?
② Please have a seat while you wait.
③ I hope you'll dine with us some other time.
④ I'm sorry, but I'd like to move to a quieter room.
⑤ The computer has already been placed in the room.

7 대화를 듣고, 여자의 마지막 말에 대한 남자의 응답으로 가장 적절한 것을 고르시오.

Man: _____

① I'm sure it will work out all right tomorrow.
② You have to check your answers after the exam.
③ The bedroom is kind of noisy, so it can irritate you.
④ A quick review at the last moment is always helpful.
⑤ Anyway, you'll feel a load off now that all the exams are over.

8 대화를 듣고, 여자의 마지막 말에 대한 남자의 응답으로 가장 적절한 것을 고르시오.

Man: _____

① Money will do anything.
② Drop by drop fills the tub.
③ Children are father to a man.
④ Life is full of ups and downs.
⑤ Empty vessels make the most sound.

9 대화를 듣고, 남자의 마지막 말에 대한 여자의 응답으로 가장 적절한 것을 고르시오.

Woman: _____

① We have a lot in common.
② Thank you for your advice.
③ Yes, winter fruit is quite scarce.
④ You have a good sense of humor.
⑤ Your choices are always excellent.

10 대화를 듣고, 여자의 마지막 말에 대한 남자의 응답으로 가장 적절한 것을 고르시오.

Man: _____

① Do to others as you would be done.
② You should've returned the books on time.
③ Early training means more than late learning.
④ Just say no when you don't want to do something.
⑤ You should have a medical checkup sooner or later.

해답/해설 293p

문항 1

△ 심화 학습

A. Listening Web

Intro   I cannot find the book I'm looking for. Can you help me to (find it / find out)?

Web1   "Language and Culture." The author is Amy Baker.

Web2   It's been checked (out / up).

Web3   Do you want us to (reserve / research) the book for you?

Ending   And give me your phone number, please.

B. True / False

1. 남자는 컴퓨터로 도서 검색을 시도했었다.   (T / F)
2. 남자가 찾는 책은 어학책이다.   (T / F)
3. 남자가 찾는 책은 현재 대출 중이다.   (T / F)
4. 남자가 빌리려는 책은 대출 예약을 할 수 없다.   (T / F)

C. Words and Phrases

tribe 부족, 종족 / check out (도서관의 책을) 대출하다

D. Dictation

M: Excuse me. I cannot find the book _____ _____ _____. Can you help me to find it?

W: Why don't you check on the computer?

M: I tried to, but there are too many books whose titles _____ _____ _____ each other.

W: What's the title?

M: "Language and Culture." The author is Amy Baker.

W: Is it about _____ _____ _____?

M: Yes, that's right.

W: It's been _____ _____. It's _____ on December 28th. Do you want us to reserve the book for you?

M: Yes, please.

W: Can I see _____ _____ _____? Thank you. And give me your phone number, please.

M: 013-4236-9395.

A. Listening Web

Intro   Almost all the theaters show only Hollywood blockbusters.

Web1   Minor films cannot have (opportunities / opportunity) to be (released / release it).

Web2   But the theaters have (right / rights) to show any profitable films.

Web3   That would be short-(sighted / site).

Ending   Money is not everything. We have to think of the future of the (film / firm) industry.

B. True / False

1. 남자는 스파이더맨 영화를 싫어한다.   (T / F)
2. 여자는 비주류 영화가 너무 많은 곳에서 상영되는 것은 문제가 있다고 생각한다.   (T / F)
3. 여자는 영화관이 수익을 중요시할 수 있다고 생각한다.   (T / F)
4. 남자는 영화의 수익성에만 신경 쓰는 것은 근시안적인 발상이라고 생각한다.   (T / F)

C. Words and Phrases

blockbuster (책이나 영화) 흥행작 / charity 자선사업 / make profits 수익을 올리다 / short-sighted 근시안적인

D. Dictation

M: Wow, almost all the theaters show only Hollywood blockbusters.

W: Is that a problem?

M: Minor films cannot have opportunities _____ _____ _____.

W: Theaters don't work as a _____. They want to _____ _____.

M: But some people want to see other films. Think about this situation: you went to the theaters, and all of them showed only Spiderman. You cannot _____ _____ _____.

W: You're right. But the theaters have rights to show any profitable films.

M: That would be _____.

W: What do you mean?

M: Money is not everything. We have to think of the future of the film industry.

A. Listening Web  MP3 13-03-A

Intro We have to (clean / clear) the house today.

Web1 Can we just (white / wipe) the floor with a cloth today?

Web2 There is a lot of dust so it's better to vacuum.

Web3 Put the newspapers and empty bottles into the recycling (bean / bin). We need to get them out tomorrow morning.

Ending I'll throw them away now. Why do we have to wait until tomorrow?

B. True / False  MP3 13-03-B

1. 남자는 런던에 다녀왔다. (T / F)
2. 남자는 바닥만 닦을 것이다. (T / F)
3. 청소하는 동안 음악을 들을 것이다. (T / F)
4. 여자는 남자에게 재활용품을 청소 후 바로 내놓으라고 했다. (T / F)

C. Words and Phrases

wipe 닦다 / vacuum 진공청소기로 청소하다 / neat 깔끔한 / bin 쓰레기통

D. Dictation  MP3 13-03-B

W: Hmm. We have to clean the house today.

M: Sarah, I've just come back from London. I'm so tired. Can we just _____ _____ _____ with a cloth today?

W: There is a lot of dust so it's better to _____.

M: Okay. The house will be clean because of my neat sister.

W: If the house is clean, we'll feel better and you can _____ _____ _____ your studying.

M: What about listening to music while cleaning?

W: That's nice!

M: Now, _____ _____ _____ _____ first?

W: Put the newspapers and empty bottles into the _____ _____. We need to get them out tomorrow morning.

M: I'll _____ _____ _____ now. Why do we have to wait until tomorrow?

A. Listening Web  MP3 13-04-A

Intro   Hey, why (are / aren't) you ready?

Web1   If you fall without it, you'll have a (messed / missed)-up head.

Web2   What do you think will happen when those bell-bottoms (flap / flat) into your bike chain?

Web3   You cannot say for sure. Go inside and change.

Ending   Helmet, sneakers… I don't like them.

B. True / False  MP3 13-04-B

1. 남자와 여자는 자전거를 타러 가려고 한다.   (T / F)
2. 여자는 지금 나팔바지를 입고 있다.   (T / F)
3. 남자는 여자의 옷차림이 자전거 타기에 좋다고 생각한다.   (T / F)
4. 여자는 남자의 충고에 대해 여전히 불만을 품고 있다.   (T / F)

C. Words and Phrases

mess ~을 망쳐놓다, 어지러뜨리다 / bell-bottoms 나팔바지 / flap 펄럭이다 / sneakers 스니커즈 운동화

D. Dictation  MP3 13-04-B

M: Hey, why aren't you ready?

W: I am ready.

M: I don't think so. First of all, where is your helmet?

W: It _____ _____ _____ _____.

M: If you fall without it, you'll have a messed-up head.

W: Oh, be serious.

M: I am serious. And what is up with those bell-bottom pants?

W: Don't you like them?

M: Sure. But _____ _____ _____ _____. What do you think will happen when those bell-bottoms _____ _____ your bike chain?

W: They won't.

M: You cannot say _____ _____. Go inside and change.

W: Okay. But I can't take off my lovely pink sandals.

M: Come on. Put on some real shoes. You can't _____ _____ on a bike.

W: Helmet, sneakers… I don't like them.

A. Listening Web  MP3 13-05-A

Intro I took a week (off / up) and traveled to Spain by myself.

Web1 It was quite good. It wasn't (raining / rainy) a lot. Do you want to see the pictures?

Web2 By the way, do you store all your pictures as image files?

Web3 Actually I used to (stall / store) all my pictures as image files, but one day my computer was (broke / broken), and all my picture (files / piles) had gone.

Ending I am sorry to hear that. Then what am I supposed to do?

B. True / False  MP3 13-05-B

1. 여자는 지난주에 출장 갔었다.   (T / F)
2. 여자는 지난주에 스페인에 다녀왔다.   (T / F)
3. 지난주 스페인에는 비가 많이 오지 않았다.   (T / F)
4. 남자는 사진 파일을 전부 날린 적이 있다.   (T / F)

C. Words and Phrases

turn up (사람이) 나타나다, 도착하다 / be supposed to ~해야 한다

D. Dictation  MP3 13-05-B

M: Hey, what's up? You haven't _____ _____ for a while.

W: I was in Spain last week.

M: A business trip?

W: No, I _____ _____ _____ _____ and traveled to Spain by myself.

M: That's cool. How was the weather? I heard it's rainy during winter in Europe.

W: Yeah, but it was quite good. It wasn't raining a lot. Do you want to see the pictures?

M: Of course. Let me see.

W: Look. This is my first day in Spain.

M: Beautiful. By the way, do you _____ all your pictures as image files?

W: Yes, does it matter?

M: Actually I _____ _____ _____ all my pictures as image files, but one day my computer was broken, and all my picture files _____ _____.

W: I am sorry to hear that. Then what am I _____ _____ _____?

A. Listening Web  MP3 13-06-A

Intro   I have a reservation (for / of) Lisa Smith.

Web1   But we don't have your name (on / in) the list. Did you happen to make a reservation on the Internet?

Web2   Sometimes the on-line reservation system doesn't work. We've been working (in / on) it since last week.

Web3   Do you have a table (for / of) five available now?

Ending   We don't have one right away, but one should be available soon. Do you want to (leave / live) your name on the list?

B. True / False  MP3 13-06-B

1. 여자는 식당에 오기 전 이미 예약을 했다.   (T / F)
2. 여자의 일행은 여자를 제외하고 다섯 명이다.   (T / F)
3. 남자는 웹사이트에 경고문이 없었던 것에 대해 사과했다.   (T / F)
4. 여자는 결국 이 식당에서 식사하기를 포기했다.   (T / F)

C. Words and Phrases

work on ~에 애쓰다, 공들이다 / warn against ~을 주의하라고 말하다

D. Dictation  MP3 13-06-B

M: May I help you? Do you have a reservation?

W: Yes, I have a _____ _____ Lisa Smith.

M: I'm sorry, but we don't have your name _____ _____ _____. Did you happen to make a reservation on the Internet?

W: Yes, I did it three days ago.

M: I'm really sorry. Sometimes the on-line reservation system doesn't work. We've been _____ _____ _____ since last week.

W: But there was nothing to warn against.

M: We put the notice not to use the on-line reservation service on the top of the website with blinking letters. You may have missed it.

W: Really? Do you have a _____ _____ _____ available now?

M: We don't have one right away, but one should be _____ _____. Do you want to leave your name on the list?

W: Yes. My name is Lisa Smith. _____ _____, please.

A. Listening Web  MP3 13-07-A

Intro   I stayed (off / up) all night studying, but I screwed up the science exam.

Web1   I spent too much time (in / on) the first question, so I just marked the answer sheet (random / randomly) after number 20.

Web2   The problem was that I should have (kept / skipped) the difficult question during the exam.

Web3   Just forget it. It's already over. Get a sound sleep tonight. It'll help you to concentrate (in / on) the exam tomorrow.

Ending   Thank you for your advice. I'll review it quickly and go to bed early tonight.

B. True / False  MP3 13-07-B

1. 과학 시험 문제는 모두 20문제였다.   (T / F)
2. 여자는 시험 보는 도중에 잠들었다.   (T / F)
3. 여자는 오늘 다시 밤을 새워서 공부할 계획이다.   (T / F)
4. 남자는 여자가 잠을 푹 자야 한다고 충고한다.   (T / F)

C. Words and Phrases

screw up ~을 망치거나 엉망으로 만들다 / stay up 일어나(자지 않고) 있다 / randomly 닥치는 대로, 무작위로 / skip 건너뛰다

D. Dictation  MP3 13-07-B

M: Hey, what's up? You don't look good.

W: I _____ _____ all night studying, but I screwed up the science exam.

M: I'm sorry to hear that.

W: It was _____ _____. I spent too much time on the first question, so I just marked the answer sheet randomly after number 20.

M: Don't worry. The other students are in the same situation, aren't they?

W: The problem was that _____ _____ _____ _____ the difficult question during the exam.

M: You might have been able to save some time.

W: I can't _____ _____ preparing for the next exam.

M: Just forget it. It's already over. Get a _____ _____ tonight. It'll help you to concentrate on the exam tomorrow.

W: Thank you for your advice. I'll _____ _____ _____ and go to bed early tonight.

A. Listening Web    MP3 13-08-A

Intro That's my favorite program. I like the (horse / host).

Web1 When I watch her talk show, I feel like I'm (taking / talking) with a friend.

Web2 I heard her childhood was very (touched / tough), though.

Web3 She was raised by her grandmother, and then (handed / hand it) over to her mother, and then over to her father.

Web4 She was (invited / inviting) to a local radio program after she (wanted / won at) the contest, and she got a chance to work for a broadcasting studio.

Ending Now she is a famous show host, and also a millionaire.

B. True / False    MP3 13-08-B

1. 여자는 토크쇼 진행자를 좋아한다.   (T / F)
2. 토크쇼 진행자는 고아로 자랐다.   (T / F)
3. 토크쇼 진행자는 미인대회에서 탈락했었다.   (T / F)
4. 토크쇼 진행지는 지방 방송국에서 처음 방송 일을 했다.   (T / F)

C. Words and Phrases

host 주인, 진행자 / hand over 넘겨지다 / beauty contest 미인대회 / broadcasting studio 방송국

D. Dictation    MP3 13-08-B

W: That's my favorite program. I like _____ _____ .

M: I think almost all women like her.

W: Yes. When I watch her talk show, I feel like I'm talking with a friend.

M: You mean she makes people very comfortable.

W: That's right. Sometimes she cries and _____ _____ _____ for a hug when the guest's story moves her.

M: I heard her childhood was very tough, though.

W: Yeah. I've read an article on her. She was _____ _____ her grandmother, and then _____ _____ _____ her mother, and then over to her father.

M: But do you know that she won a beauty contest?

W: Really? I didn't know that!

M: She was invited to a local radio program after she won at the contest, and she got a chance to work for _____ _____ _____.

W: That's interesting. Now she is a famous show host, and also a _____.

A. Listening Web

Intro It's (freezing / freeze) out here. I don't like winter.

Web1 Me, (either / neither).

Web2 I love summer. We can have lots of delicious fruit, and imagine (lie / lying) down on the beach and (enjoy / enjoying) the sun.

Web3 I love fruit, too.

Ending Well, you don't like winter, and neither (do / don't) I. You like fruit, and so do I. It's interesting, isn't it?

B. True / False

1. 여자는 겨울을 싫어한다. (T / F)
2. 남자는 겨울에 옷을 많이 껴입으면 별로 추위를 느끼지 않는다. (T / F)
3. 남자는 과일을 좋아한다. (T / F)
4. 여자는 보통 겨울보다 여름을 좋아한다. (T / F)

C. Words and Phrases

frozen 냉동된 / lie down 눕다 / in the mood for ~할 기분이 나서 / imported 수입된

D. Dictation

W: It's _____ out here. I don't like winter.

M: Me, neither.

W: It's too cold. I feel like my ears are frozen.

M: Yeah. No matter how many clothes I wear, I still feel cold. Winter in Korea is really long and cold.

W: Right. I love summer. We can have _____ _____ _____ _____, and imagine lying down on the beach and enjoying the sun.

M: I love fruit, too. My favorite fruit is pineapple. It doesn't look good, and it's a little hard to cut it, but it's really sweet.

W: Oh, no. Now I'm _____ _____ _____ for pineapple.

M: You know they're really expensive in winter _____ _____ they're imported.

W: I'll get some _____ _____ _____.

M: Well, you don't like winter, and neither do I. You like fruit, and _____ _____ _____. It's interesting, isn't it?

A. Listening Web  MP3 13-10-A

Intro I'm going to the library to return these books.

Web1 I have to return them quickly and go to swimming class. It's already (started / starting). I'll be late today.

Web2 Then why did you do her a favor? I think you (should / should've) refused it.

Web3 No, you should've said that you had a (class / glass). You went to the library to check out a book for David the other day.

Ending I can't refuse somebody a (favor / flavor). I think I have a hole in my head.

B. True / False  MP3 13-10-B

1. 여자는 Erin에게 책을 빌렸다.   (T / F)
2. 여자는 수공예에 관심이 없다.   (T / F)
3. 남자는 David 대신 도서관에서 책을 빌렸다.   (T / F)
4. 여자는 머리에 상처가 있다.   (T / F)

C. Words and Phrases

handicraft 수공예 / be all thumbs 손재주가 없다 / I think I have a hole in my head. 나 바보인가 봐.

D. Dictation  MP3 13-10-B

M: Where are you going?

W: I'm going to the library _____ _____ _____ _____.

M: Wow, I didn't know that you're interested in handicrafts.

W: No, _____ _____ _____. Erin asked me to return them.

M: Erin is really good at art. By the way, it's so hot and humid. Shall we drop by the store and have some ice cream?

W: No, I have to return them quickly and go to swimming class. _____ _____ _____. I'll be late today.

M: Then why did you do her a favor? I think you should've _____ _____.

W: Erin said she had a project to do with her friends, and these books are due today.

M: No, you should've said that you had a class. You went to the library to check out a book for David the other day.

W: I can't refuse somebody a favor. I think I have a _____ _____ _____ _____.

짧은 상황 설명을 듣고, 등장인물이 할 말을 고르는 유형이다. 누가 어떤 상황에 처해 있는지, 또 누가 누구에게 할 말을 고르는 것인지를 정확히 파악함과 동시에 선택지의 내용을 빠르게 읽고 이해하는 것이 관건이다.

● **Example**

1 **다음 상황 설명을 듣고, Jessica가 선생님에게 할 말로 가장 적절한 것을 고르시오.**
[2012 수능기출]

M: Jessica is in an English class with her friend Tom sitting next to her. Suddenly, she notices that Tom doesn't look well, and asks him if there's something wrong with him. He replies he has a stomachache. but he says he can stand the pain until the end of the class. But Jessica thinks his condition is serious because he looks awfully pale and is sweating all over. So, Jessica wants to let her teacher know of Tom's condition. In this situation, what would Jessica most likely say to her teacher?

Jessica: _____
① I think Tom needs some medical help.
② I'm sorry, but I have to go to the hospital.
③ May I go to the bathroom, please?
④ My condition couldn't be better.
⑤ What's going to be on the exam tomorrow?

* 배가 아픈 사람은 Tom이고, Tom을 대신하여 Jessica가 선생님께 Tom의 상태를 알리려고 하는 것이므로 정답은 ①번이다.

유형 14

설명을 듣고
상대방에게
할 말 찾기

설명을 듣고 상대방에게 할 말 찾기

1 다음 상황 설명을 듣고 Lucy가 Jessica에게 할 말로 가장 적절한 것을 고르시오.

Lucy: Jessica, _____

① no pain, no gain.
② when it rains, it pours.
③ a rolling stone never gets moss.
④ a friend in need is a friend indeed.
⑤ a journey of a thousand miles begins with single step.

2 다음 상황 설명을 듣고 Eunice가 Sarah에게 할 말로 가장 적절한 것을 고르시오.

Eunice: Sarah, _____

① I'm not sure I've helped you.
② people are so mean. Just forget it.
③ I didn't do it on purpose. It's just an accident.
④ it is only beginning. You've worked very hard.
⑤ people gave you an enthusiastic welcome. Don't worry.

3 다음 상황 설명을 듣고 엄마가 Liz에게 할 말로 가장 적절한 것을 고르시오.

Mom: Liz, _____

① Internet shopping malls are not trustworthy.
② in reality, celebrities don't always look as pretty as on TV.
③ fame doesn't always guarantee the reliability of a business.
④ customers' reviews are the best tip for choosing items online.
⑤ some celebrities are so immoral that they are often neglected.

4 다음 상황 설명을 듣고 엄마가 Christine에게 할 말로 가장 적절한 것을 고르시오.

Mom: Christine, _____

① get some more sleep.
② have some more spaghetti.
③ lead yourself a regular life.
④ why didn't you go to school?
⑤ set the alarm to earlier than 6 a.m.

5 다음 상황 설명을 듣고 Erin이 Julie에게 할 말로 가장 적절한 것을 고르시오.

Erin: Julie, _____

① please wash the dog in the morning.
② I want you to be more considerate of me.
③ would you mind preparing more for breakfast?
④ will you pick up the phone when I am not home?
⑤ why don't we clean the house together every day?

6 다음 상황 설명을 듣고 선생님이 Chloe에게 할 말로 가장 적절한 것을 고르시오.

Teacher: Chloe, _____

① why did you choose this topic?
② congratulations on your graduation.
③ I'm sorry, but what about asking to some other teachers?
④ I have the results of two other surveys on the same topic as yours.
⑤ I'm sorry, but I'm so busy that I can't go out for breakfast with you.

7 다음 상황 설명을 듣고 상담 선생님이 Susie에게 할 말로 가장 적절한 것을 고르시오.

Counselor: Susie, _____

① you should take enough rest for your health.
② it's better to share problems with your friends.
③ the quality is more important than the quantity.
④ you need to not hang out with friends before the exam.
⑤ sit at the desk longer and don't go out for trivial things.

8 다음 상황 설명을 듣고 Cindy가 선생님에게 할 말로 가장 적절한 것을 고르시오.

Cindy: _____

① I want you to proofread my report.
② This USB is very safe because it's waterproof.
③ Would you please help me to come to a conclusion?
④ I'm really sorry to have dropped your report in water.
⑤ Could you please give me two more days to finish the report?

9 다음 상황 설명을 듣고 Kelly가 매니저에게 할 말로 가장 적절한 것을 고르시오.

Kelly: _____

① I'm so sorry for the late delivery.
② Your website doesn't work properly.
③ Thank you for your convenient service.
④ I got different things than what I ordered.
⑤ Everything is too expensive and the food is not fresh.

10 다음 상황 설명을 듣고 Amy가 소년들에게 할 말로 가장 적절한 것을 고르시오.

Amy: _____

① How do you do?
② Excuse me, I'm in line.
③ Do you like jungle, too?
④ Are you in our company?
⑤ Welcome to "Jungle Adventure."

해답/해설 298p

A. Listening Web  MP3 14-01-A

Intro Jessica got up a little bit later than (usual / usually).

Web1 When she ran (about / around) the corner, she saw the bus still waiting for her.

Web2 But when she almost got (them / there), the bus left.

Web3 She realized that she didn't bring her science homework.

Ending It was due today, so she (tried / try) to call her mom to bring the homework, but the battery was out.

B. True / False  MP3 14-01-B

1. Jessica는 평소와 똑같이 일어났다.   (T / F)
2. Jessica는 가까스로 학교 버스를 탔다.   (T / F)
3. Jessica는 Lucy와 함께 과학 숙제를 했다.   (T / F)
4. 오늘은 과학 숙제 제출 마감일이다.   (T / F)

C. Words and Phrases

recharge 충전하다

D. Dictation  MP3 14-01-B

W: This morning, Jessica got up a little bit _____ _____ _____. She took a _____ _____ and got dressed, and ran out of the house to catch the school bus. When she ran around the corner, she saw the bus still waiting for her. But when she almost got there, the bus left. After the morning classes, while she was talking with her friend Lucy about _____ _____ _____ _____ that morning, she realized that she didn't bring her science homework. It was _____ today, so she tried to call her mom to bring the homework, but _____ _____ _____ _____. She forgot _____ _____ _____ last night. In this situation, what would Lucy most likely say to Jessica?

A. Listening Web

Intro   She has (complete / completed) her first film after working on it for six years.

Web1   On the day (of / on) which her film was released, she invited her best friend Eunice to the theater.

Web2   When they got there, they were (surprised / surprising) because there was nobody but them.

Web3   She looked so (disappointed / disappointing).

Ending   In the end, (no / one) more people came into the theater until the movie was over.

B. True / False

1. Eunice의 첫 영화가 개봉했다.   (T / F)
2. Eunice는 영화를 6개월 동안 만들었다.   (T / F)
3. Eunice와 Sarah는 영화가 시작되고 5분 후에 영화관에 들어갔다.   (T / F)
4. Eunice는 관객이 없어서 매우 실망했다.   (T / F)

C. Words and Phrases

rookie 초심자, 신인

D. Dictation

M: Sarah is a _____ _____. Actually she is a _____. She has completed her first film after working on it for six years. On the day on which _____ _____ _____ _____, she invited her best friend Eunice to the theater. Eunice was willing to go to the theater with Sarah. Both of them were so excited. However, when they got there, they were surprised because _____ _____ _____ _____ them. It was only _____ _____ _____ _____ before the movie started. Eunice looked at Sarah. She looked so _____. In the end, no more people came into the theater until the movie was over. In this situation, what would Eunice most likely say to Sarah?

A. Listening Web  MP3 14-03-A

Intro   Liz is (dissatisfied / satisfied) with a skirt.

Web1   She bought a skirt on an online shopping mall that a famous singer (learns / runs).

Web2   She depended on the pictures and the comments that the customers wrote on the (idols / items) after purchase.

Web3   She trusted everything about the shopping mall (because / because of) a celebrity runs the business.

Ending   But the skirt she (receive / received) today looks totally different from what she saw online.

B. True / False  MP3 14-03-B

1. Liz는 유명한 가수가 운영하는 쇼핑몰에서 치마를 샀다.   (T / F)
2. Liz는 치마 구매 시 구매자의 상품평을 참고했다.   (T / F)
3. Liz는 유명인이 입었던 것과 똑같은 치마를 샀다.   (T / F)
4. Liz는 구매한 치마를 마음에 들어 한다.   (T / F)

C. Words and Phrases

dissatisfied 불만족스러운 / celebrity 유명인사

D. Dictation  MP3 14-03-B

W: Liz _____ _____ _____ a skirt. Three days ago, she bought a skirt on an online shopping mall that a _____ _____ _____. It doesn't have an off-line mall, so she depended on the pictures and the comments that the customers wrote on the items _____ _____. She trusted everything about the shopping mall because a celebrity _____ _____ _____. But the skirt she received today _____ _____ _____ _____ what she saw online. The color is different, the quality is different, and the size is different. In this situation, what would her mom most likely say to Liz?

A. Listening Web

Intro   The winter vacation (has / was) started.

Web1   When the alarm went (off / on) at 6 a.m., Christine recognized that she didn't need to get up early, so she turned it off and went back to sleep.

Web2   Around 10 a.m. she got up, but didn't have an (apartment / appetite).

Web3   She felt her back (hurt / hurts) and it was hard to digest.

Ending   Her mom thought Christine should have gotten up earlier and (exercise / exercised) more.

B. True / False

1. 오늘은 겨울 방학식 날이다.   (T / F)
2. 새벽 6시에 알람이 울렸다.   (T / F)
3. 10시에 다시 일어났을 때 몹시 배가 고팠다.   (T / F)
4. 일어나자마자 컴퓨터로 바쁘게 일을 했다.   (T / F)

C. Words and Phrases

appetite 식욕, 입맛 / digest 소화하다

D. Dictation

M: The winter vacation has started. When _____ _____ _____ _____ at 6 a.m., Christine recognized that she didn't need to get up early, so she turned it off and went back to sleep. Around 10 a.m. she got up, but didn't _____ _____ _____. She skipped breakfast and surfed the Internet, _____ _____ on pop singers or movie stars. At 1 p.m. her mom told Christine _____ _____ _____, but she felt her back hurt and it was hard to digest. Her mom thought Christine _____ _____ _____ _____ earlier and exercised more. In this situation, what would her mom most likely say to Christine?

A. Listening Web

Intro Julie is Erin's roommate.
Web1 They had gotten (alone / along) with each other before they came to live together.
Web2 At first, they decided who would do what so as not to get (them / themselves) into trouble.
Web3 Julie didn't break her promise, but very often she got (an / on) Erin's (nerve / nerves).
Ending Finally, Erin was very upset with Julie, but she wanted to (keep / kick) their friendship.

B. True / False

1. Erin과 Julie는 룸메이트가 되기 전에는 서로 모르는 사이였다. (T / F)
2. Erin과 Julie는 서로의 임무를 정해두지 않았다. (T / F)
3. Julie는 주로 아침 식사를 만들고 설거지를 했다. (T / F)
4. Julie는 Erin이 집에 있을 때 전화를 받지 않았다. (T / F)

C. Words and Phrases

get along with ~와 잘 지내다 / junior (대학) 3학년생 / get on one's nerves ~의 신경을 거스르다

D. Dictation

W: Julie is Erin's roommate. They had _____ _____ _____ each other before they came to live together. At first, they decided who would do what so as not to get themselves _____ _____. For example, Julie would make breakfast every morning, and Erin would clean the house twice a week. Julie didn't break her promise, but very often she _____ _____ Erin's _____. Julie made breakfast every morning, but didn't wash the dishes. And she never answered the phone when Erin was home. Finally, Erin was very _____ _____ Julie, but she wanted to _____ _____ _____. In this situation, what would Erin most likely say to Julie?

A. Listening Web  MP3 14-06-A

Intro Chloe decided to write about the (relations / relationships) between breakfast and grades.

Web1 First, she needed to (do a / doing) survey targeting more than three hundred high school seniors.

Web2 So she went to the high school she graduated from, and (met / met with) her teacher.

Web3 She asked if he could do a survey for her paper instead of her.

Ending But he had already been asked to do two other surveys on different topics, and he was too busy to do (another / other) survey.

B. True / False  MP3 14-06-B

1. Chloe 글의 주제는 규칙적인 식습관과 학업 성적 간의 관계이다. (T / F)
2. Chloe는 모교의 재학생을 대상으로 설문조사 하려고 했다. (T / F)
3. Chloe의 선생님은 이미 다른 설문조사 요청을 받았다. (T / F)
4. Chloe의 선생님은 Chloe의 부탁을 받아주었다. (T / F)

C. Words and Phrases

do a survey 설문조사 하다 / high school senior 고등학교 3학년생

D. Dictation  MP3 14-06-B

M: Chloe decided to write about _____ _____ _____ breakfast and grades.

She thought that students who eat breakfast every day would _____ _____ _____ _____ on a test. First, she needed to _____ _____ _____ _____ more than three hundred high school seniors. So she went to the high school she _____ _____, and met with her teacher. She asked if he could do a survey for her paper instead of her. But he _____ _____ _____ _____ to do two other surveys on different topics, and he was too busy to do another survey.

In this situation, what would the teacher most likely say to Chloe?

A. Listening Web  MP3 14-07-A

Intro   Susie got a (disappointed / disappointing) grade on the final exam again.

Web1   Finally she decided to go see a counselor and (discuss / discuss on) this problem.

Web2   The counselor asked her how she had studied.

Web3   Come to think of it, she just sat (at / on) the desk for a long time, not focusing on studying.

Ending   And she thought she (had studied / studied) a lot.

B. True / False  MP3 14-07-B

1. Susie는 이번 시험에서 처음으로 낮은 점수를 받았다.   (T / F)
2. Susie는 이번 시험을 준비하면서 잠을 충분히 못 잤다.   (T / F)
3. 상담 선생님은 놀지도 못하고 열심히 공부한 Susie를 격려해 주셨다.   (T / F)
4. Susie는 집중하지 않고 책상에만 오래 앉아있는 편이다.   (T / F)

C. Words and Phrases

hang out 시간을 보내다 / come to think of it 그러고 보니, 생각해 보니

D. Dictation  MP3 14-07-B

W: Susie got a _____ grade on the final exam again. No matter how hard she thought about it, she couldn't _____ _____ _____ a reason. Finally she decided to go see a counselor and discuss this problem. The counselor asked her _____ _____ _____ _____. She thought for a while, and then said that she didn't sleep a lot and didn't hang out with friends, either. The counselor said that _____ _____ _____. Come to think of it, she just sat at the desk for a long time, _____ _____ _____ _____. And she thought she had studied a lot. In this situation, what would the counselor most likely say to Susie?

A. Listening Web  MP3 14-08-A

Intro   The report is (done / due) today, but Cindy is still (working / working on) it.

Web1   Actually (she / she's) already finished the report a week ago, and was proofreading it.

Web2   She dropped her USB into water by mistake.

Web3   She tried to rewrite everything again (in / on) time, but two days were not enough.

Web4   Moreover, the teacher is well-known for (none / not) collecting late homework.

Ending   But Cindy couldn't hand in the homework (with / without) a conclusion.

B. True / False  MP3 14-08-B

1. 오늘 Cindy는 보고서를 끝냈다.   (T / F)
2. Cindy의 보고서는 물에 대한 USB의 반응이다.   (T / F)
3. Cindy는 보고서를 두 번 작성했다.   (T / F)
4. 선생님은 보통 늦게 제출하는 숙제는 받아주지 않으신다.   (T / F)

C. Words and Phrases

proofread 교정을 보다 / drop 떨어뜨리다 / in time 시간에 맞춰, 늦지 않게

D. Dictation  MP3 14-08-B

M: The report is _____ _____, but Cindy is still working on it. Actually she already finished the report a week ago, and _____ _____ _____. Two days ago, she _____ her USB _____ _____ by mistake. She quickly took it out and checked if there was any problem. Unfortunately, the computer couldn't read any files on the USB. She tried to rewrite everything again in time, but two days were not enough. Moreover, the teacher is well-known for not _____ _____ _____. But Cindy couldn't hand in the homework without a conclusion. In this situation, what would Cindy most likely say to the teacher?

△ 심화 학습

A. Listening Web  MP3 14-09-A

Intro Kelly is (though / throwing) a party this evening.

Web1 The website said that everything could be (order / ordered) online and would be (delivered / delivery) in thirty minutes.

Web2 So she ordered (a line / online) what she needed, but it never came.

Web3 However, they were not what she (order / ordered).

Ending She was upset and decided to (complain / complete) to the manager about it.

B. True / False  MP3 14-09-B

1. Kelly는 파티에 초대받았다.   (T / F)
2. Kelly는 온라인으로 필요한 물건을 주문했다.   (T / F)
3. 주문한 물건들이 예상 시간보다 15분 일찍 도착했다.   (T / F)
4. Kelly가 받은 물건은 그녀가 주문한 물건이 아니었다.   (T / F)

C. Words and Phrases

throw a party 파티를 열다 / in the meantime 그러는 동안 / deliver 배달하다 / complain 항의하다

D. Dictation  MP3 14-09-B

W: Kelly is _____ _____ _____ this evening. She was going to cook a special dinner. In the meantime, she found an online market. The website said that everything could be _____ _____ and would be _____ _____ _____ _____. So she ordered online what she needed, but it never came. She called the online market, and they said everything would be _____ _____ _____ _____. Fifteen minutes later, she finally got the food items. However, they were not _____ _____ _____. She was upset and decided to complain to the manager about it. In this situation, what would Kelly most likely say to the manager?

A. Listening Web

Intro   Amy went on a picnic to an amusement park with her family.

Web1   As soon as she arrived at the amusement park, she (rushed / rush it) to "Jungle Adventure."

Web2   She was standing (in / on) line with her family.

Web3   At that time, several boys were going to go (through / to) in front of Amy.

Ending She stepped (aside / side) for them to pass by, but she was embarrassed because they stopped in front of her.

B. True / False

1. Amy는 일요일에 가족과 함께 놀이공원에 갔다.   (T / F)
2. Amy는 놀이공원에 도착하여 무엇을 먼저 할지 고민했다.   (T / F)
3. Amy는 혼자 Jungle Adventure를 타기로 했다.   (T / F)
4. Amy는 새치기로 당황스러운 일을 겪었다.   (T / F)

C. Words and Phrases

amusement park 놀이공원 / rush 돌진하다 / commercial (TV, 라디오) 광고 / brand new 신형의, 완전 새것의 / ride 놀이기구 / stand in line 줄을 서다 / step aside 길을 비켜주다 / pass by 지나가다

D. Dictation

M: Amy went on a picnic to an amusement park with her family. It was Sunday and the weather was fine, so it was _____ _____ _____. As soon as she arrived at the amusement park, she _____ _____ "Jungle Adventure." She had seen it on a TV commercial. It was a brand new ride, and she had been _____ _____ _____ it. She was _____ _____ _____ with her family. At that time, several boys were going to go through in front of Amy. She _____ _____ for them to pass by, but she was embarrassed because they stopped in front of her. In this situation, what would Amy most likely say to the boys?

대본의 길이가 가장 긴 유형으로, 두 문제가 세트로 출제된다. 무엇보다도 대본의 길이가 긴 만큼 중간에 주의집중이 흐트러지지 않도록 주의한다. 첫 번째 문제는 주제, 목적 등을 묻는 문제로 출제되며, 두 번째 문제는 세부 사항을 묻는 문제가 출제된다. 따라서 방송이 시작되기 전 재빨리 문제를 읽고 문제의 내용을 파악한 뒤, 들으면서 두 번째 문제를 먼저 푸는 것이 요령이다.

1 다음을 듣고, 물음에 답하시오. [2012 수능모의]

Today let's talk about what's best for your children's well-being. Do you know the proper way to prevent children's injuries in the car? Previously, it was recommended that only children 12 and under not ride in the front seat of air bag equipped cars. Recently, a study of automobile crashes disproved this and found that front-seat air bags protected only those ages 15 and over. So, keep those kids under 15 buckled up in the back seat. My second tip is about asthma, a breathing disorder. Many people already know that exposure to secondhand smoke and pets can lead to this difficulty in breathing. However, giving infants bananas, sweet potatoes, or other solid foods before 4 months can also be a cause, so keep this in mind. Also, when you cook, open your kitchen windows. Indoor air pollution is directly linked to asthma. Children who are not exposed to these factors are 56% less likely to have asthma at age 7. That does it for our program on child safety and health.

1-1. 남자가 하는 말의 목적으로 가장 적절한 것을 고르시오?
① to promote a new children's hospital
② to advise parents on their children's welfare
③ to warn people of an unknown disease
④ to notify children of seat belt safety in cars
⑤ to give tips on how to feed family pets

1-2. asthma의 원인으로 언급되지 <u>않는</u> 것은?
① 애완동물
② 꽃가루
③ 간접흡연
④ 고구마
⑤ 오염된 실내 공기

* 남자가 하는 말의 목적은 대본 처음에 선명하게 나타나 있다. "children's well-being"에 관해서 이야기 하겠다고 했으므로, 1번 문제의 정답은 ②번. asthma의 원인으로는 간접흡연, 애완동물, 바나나, 고구마, 딱딱한 음식, 실내 공기 오염을 언급하고 있으므로, 2번 문제의 정답은 ②번이다. 대본에서 언급이 되었는지를 반드시 확인해야 하며, 상식에 의존하여 문제를 해결하지 않도록 주의한다.

세트형 문제

Unit 15

유형 15

세트형 문제 (대화문이나 담화문은 각 2번씩 들려줍니다.)

1 다음을 듣고, 물음에 답하시오.

1-1. 남자가 하는 말의 주제로 가장 적절한 것을 고르시오.
① the nature of wolves
② the examples of mammals
③ the major characters of mammals
④ the ways for wolves to hunt other animals
⑤ the similarities and differences of wolves and dogs

1-2. 개와 늑대의 공통점으로 언급되지 <u>않는</u> 것을 고르시오.
① 털이 있음
② 새끼에게 젖을 먹임
③ 이빨이 날카로움
④ 육식을 함
⑤ 독립적인 생활을 함

2 다음을 듣고, 물음에 답하시오.

2-1. 여자가 하는 말의 목적으로 가장 적절한 것을 고르시오.
① to boast of her university
② to employ new professors
③ to promote to choose the university
④ to explain the merits of the university
⑤ to ask for advice on how to choose a university

2-2. 글로리아 대학에 대한 설명으로 일치하지 <u>않는</u> 것을 고르시오.
① 학생 개인마다 지도 교수가 있다.
② 취업을 위한 모의 면접을 실시한다.
③ 한동안 지원자가 가장 많았다.
④ 궁금한 점은 이메일로 문의할 수 있다.
⑤ 이번 달 안으로 지원해야 한다.

3 다음을 듣고, 물음에 답하시오.

3-1. 남자가 하는 말의 주제로 가장 적절한 것을 고르시오.
① The important things in studying English
② The problems of studying English alone
③ The various ways to study English in Korea
④ The ways to study English without teachers
⑤ The things you have to do in English speaking countries

3-2. 다음 중 화자의 주장과 일치하지 <u>않는</u> 것을 고르시오.

① 취업과 진학에서 영어 능력은 중요한 자질로 평가받는다.
② 영어권 국가로 어학연수를 가는 것은 요즘 대학생들에게 필수적이다.
③ TV를 보면서 영어 듣기 연습을 할 수 있다.
④ 한국어를 가르쳐 주면서 영어를 배우는 방법이 있다.
⑤ 어휘를 많이 알고 있으면 자신감이 생긴다.

4 다음을 듣고, 물음에 답하시오.

4-1. 여자가 하는 말의 목적으로 가장 적절한 것을 고르시오.

① 공원 이용 수칙을 안내하기 위해
② 공중화장실의 관리 실태를 파악하기 위해
③ 쾌적한 공원 환경 조성을 위한 조언을 하기 위해
④ 잘못된 공중화장실 사용 습관에 대해 경고하기 위해
⑤ 공공장소에서의 부도덕한 행농 예시를 보여주기 위해

4-2. 에티켓이 지켜지지 않는 행동으로 언급되지 않는 것을 고르시오.

① 애완동물의 배설물
② 악취
③ 낙서
④ 담배꽁초
⑤ 파손된 전등

5 다음을 듣고, 물음에 답하시오.

5-1. 남자가 하는 말의 주제로 가장 적절한 것을 고르시오.

① 기업의 인식 변화
② 교육 환경의 변화
③ 소비자 역할의 변화
④ 생산자와 소비자의 역할
⑤ 앨빈 토플러의 제3의 물결

5-2. 프로슈머에 대한 예시로 언급되지 <u>않는</u> 것을 고르시오.

① DIY 제품
② 위키피디아 집필
③ 인터넷 쇼핑 후기 작성
④ 소비자의 신제품 체험 기회
⑤ 학생과 학부모의 교육 참여

6 다음을 듣고, 물음에 답하시오.

6-1. 여자가 하는 말의 목적으로 가장 적절한 것을 고르시오.
① to introduce lacrosse
② to show how to play lacrosse
③ to inform the history of lacrosse
④ to advertise the new tools of lacrosse
⑤ to persuade people not to play lacrosse

6-2. Lacrosse와 아이스하키의 다른 점으로 언급된 것을 고르시오.
① 선수의 수
② 경기 장소
③ 경기 규칙
④ 점수 체계
⑤ 운동의 기원

7 다음을 듣고, 물음에 답하시오.

7-1. 남자가 하는 말의 주제로 가장 적절한 것을 고르시오.
① the Spanish invasion
② the brave Spanish conquerors
③ the people living in Machu Picchu
④ the flourishing culture of Machu Picchu
⑤ the paradoxical preservation of Machu Picchu

7-2. Machu Picchu 멸망의 원인으로 언급된 것을 고르시오.
① 전쟁
② 물 부족
③ 화산 폭발
④ 과도한 문명화
⑤ 원주민들의 이주

8 다음을 듣고, 물음에 답하시오.

8-1. 여자가 하는 말의 목적으로 가장 적절한 것을 고르시오.
① to inform on how archaeologists work
② to explain the best way to dig up artifacts
③ to advise on how to become an archaeologist
④ to notify freshmen what to study in archaeology
⑤ to warn people of the danger of archaeological sites

8-2. 발굴작업에 사용되는 도구로 언급되지 <u>않는</u> 것을 고르시오.

① 지도
② 격자판
③ 녹음기
④ 삽
⑤ 칫솔

9 다음을 듣고, 물음에 답하시오.

9-1. 남자가 하는 말의 주제로 가장 적절한 것을 고르시오.

① when dinosaurs thrived
② why dinosaurs disappeared
③ where dinosaurs lived on the earth
④ what kinds of plants dinosaurs ate
⑤ what kinds of dinosaurs lived on the earth

9-2. 소행성 충돌 시 일어난 일로 언급되지 <u>않는</u> 것을 고르시오.

① 먼지 구름
② 암흑
③ 새로운 별 생성
④ 식물의 죽음
⑤ 공룡의 죽음

10 다음을 듣고, 물음에 답하시오.

10-1. 여자가 하는 말의 주제로 가장 적절한 것을 고르시오.

① The ways to send messages
② The development of sending messages
③ The history of the post office in the U.S.
④ The history of a mail delivery company
⑤ The ways to become a good horse-riders

10-2. Pony Express에 대한 설명으로 언급되지 <u>않는</u> 것을 고르시오.

① 창립 배경
② 회사 위치
③ 창립 연대
④ 창립자
⑤ 회사 규모

A. Listening Web  MP3 15-01-A

Intro   A mammal is an animal that has hair, gives birth to (life / live) young, and feeds them milk.
Web1   In fact, dogs and wolves are closely (related / relatives).
Web2   (Thousand / Thousands) of years ago, humans came into contact with wolves and tamed some of them, just like what we do with dogs these days.
Web3   Wolves and dogs are both (carnivores / predators).
Web4   The (big / biggest) difference between dogs and wolves, though, is that wolves are wild.
Ending   They live in their (one / own) group and hunt together.

B. True / False  MP3 15-01-B

1. 인간은 과거에 늑대를 키우며 함께 살기도 했다.   (T / F)
2. 시베리안 허스키는 사실상 늑대의 한 종류이다.   (T / F)
3. 늑대는 잡식성이다.   (T / F)
4. 늑대는 혼자 사냥을 한다.   (T / F)

C. Words and Phrases

tame ~을 길들이다, 다스리다 / pup (동물) 새끼 / domesticate 길들이다 / carnivore 육식동물 / wild 야생의 / roam 이리저리 돌아다니다, 배회하다

D. Dictation  MP3 15-01-B

M: Wolves are mammals. A mammal is an animal that has hair, gives birth to live young, and _____ _____ _____. You are a mammal, too. So are mice, cats, and dogs. In fact, dogs and wolves are _____ _____. Thousands of years ago, humans came into _____ _____ wolves and tamed some of them, just like what we do with dogs these days. They may also have taken in lost wolf pups. If it happened, wolves became _____. Humans were able to use them to help with work. Over time, dog species were developed from the wolves. Siberian huskies and German shepherds are dog species that look and act a lot like wolves. Wolves and dogs are both carnivores. Carnivores are animals that eat meat. That's why they have sharp teeth. The biggest difference between dogs and wolves, though, is that wolves are wild. They don't depend on humans for _____ _____ _____ _____. Wolves will become unhappy if they cannot roam free. They live in their own group and hunt together. When they chase a large animal, they cooperate with each other. One wolf starts the chase first. Then as it gets tired, another wolf _____ _____ _____.

A. Listening Web  MP3 15-02-A

Intro I'm so (please / pleased) to have a chance to introduce you to Gloria.

Web1 Every individual student has his or her own personal advisor who will take care of you from entrance to graduation.

Web2 When you (choose / chose) your major, you can consult with your advisor, and when you're a senior, you can conduct a mock interview to get a job.

Web3 Gloria University has had the (larger / largest) number of applicants for the last six years.

Web4 If you have any questions about Gloria, you can email us at the address below the bulletin, or call the (admission / mission) department.

Ending It's (open / opened) for 24 hours this month to help you as much as possible. Thank you very much.

B. True / False  MP3 15-02-B

1. 전공을 선택할 때 지도 교수와 상의할 수 있다. (T / F)
2. 가장 만족스러운 대학 1위로 뽑힌 바 있다. (T / F)
3. 이메일이나 전화로 문의할 수 있다. (T / F)
4. 전화 문의는 자정 이후 불가능하다. (T / F)

C. Words and Phrases

advisor 지도 교수 / consult 상의하다 / mock interview 모의 면접 / admission 입학

D. Dictation  MP3 15-02-B

W: Good evening, I'm Irene Taylor from Gloria University. I'm so pleased to have a chance to introduce you to Gloria. I understand it's not easy for you to choose a university. There are hundreds of universities, and every university insists that they have a special program and _____ _____ _____ _____. But Gloria is different. We provide the unique Personal Guide program. Every individual student has his or her own personal advisor who will take care of you from entrance to graduation. When you choose your major, you can _____ with your advisor, and when you're a senior, you can _____ _____ _____ _____ to get a job. Gloria University has had the largest number of applicants for the last six years, and last year it was listed at the top of _____ _____ _____ _____ by the national survey. Now all you have to do is to choose Gloria. If you have any questions about Gloria, you can email us at the address below the bulletin, or call the admission department. It's open for 24 hours this month to help you _____ _____ _____ _____. Thank you very much.

A. Listening Web

Intro   English proficiency is a (critical / crucial) quality these days.

Web1   A lot of college students tend to think that it is (inventory / mandatory) to take an English language training course in the U.S. or England. You have many chances to study English in Korea.

Web2   There are some TV cable channels with which you can practice listening to English.

Web3   It is a good idea to participate in a language (change / exchange) program if your school provides one.

Ending   The last tip to improve your English is to memorize a large (account / amount) of vocabulary.

B. True / False

1. 요즘 취업을 하기 위해서는 상당한 수준의 영어 실력이 필요하다.   (T / F)
2. 영어권 국가로 어학연수를 다녀와야만 상당한 수준의 영어를 구사할 수 있게 된다.   (T / F)
3. 채팅은 주로 슬랭으로 이루어지기 때문에 외국어 학습에 좋지 않다.   (T / F)
4. 단어를 많이 외우는 것은 영어 학습에 자신감을 불어넣는다.   (T / F)

C. Words and Phrases

proficiency 숙달, 능수, 능란 / critical 중요한 / English proficiency test 영어능력시험 / significant 상당한 / mandatory 필수의 / listen for 귀담아듣다, 주의 깊게 듣다 / colloquial 구어의, 일상적인 대화체의 / participate in 참여하다 / exchange 교환 / a wide range of 광범위한, 다양한 / confident 자신감 있는

D. Dictation   MP3 15-03-B

M: English proficiency is a _____ _____ these days. In order to get a job, or enter a university or a graduate school, you need not only an excellent grade on an English proficiency test, but also ability in speaking and listening _____ _____ _____ _____. A lot of college students tend to think that it is _____ to take an English language training course in the U.S. or England. But you don't need to go to English speaking countries. You have many chances to study English in Korea. There are some TV cable channels with which you can practice listening to English. _____ _____ _____ foreign friends helps you to improve colloquial English. It is a good idea to _____ _____ a language exchange program if your school provides one. You can teach Korean to somebody who wants to learn Korean, and you can be taught English by them. The last tip to improve your English is to memorize a large amount of vocabulary. Vocabulary is not everything in studying English, but if you have a wide range of vocabulary, _____ _____ _____ when you encounter English at an unexpected moment.

A. Listening Web  MP3 15-04-A

Intro These days you can see many people in the park.

Web1 However, very often our attitude (to / towards) public toilets goes against proper etiquette.

Web2 A lot of people want to avoid (use in / using) public toilets when they are out of their house.

Web3 It reflects our attitude toward public (facilities / facility) that we don't think of them as valuable as our own (staff / stuff).

Ending If we keep using the public toilet the way that we used to do, we'll be the victims of a dirty (atmosphere / hemisphere) in the end.

B. True / False  MP3 15-04-B

1. 공원을 이용하는 사람들이 많다.   (T / F)
2. 공원 화장실은 쾌적한 경우가 많다.   (T / F)
3. 집 밖에서 공중화장실을 이용하기 꺼리는 사람들이 많다.   (T / F)
4. 화장실 쾌적 여부는 시 공무원에게 달려있다.   (T / F)

C. Words and Phrases

needless to say 말할 필요 없이 / scribbles 낙서 / flicker (전깃불이나 불빛이) 깜박거리다 / public facilities 공공시설

D. Dictation  MP3 15-04-B

W: These days you can see many people in the park. Some of them are _____ _____ _____; some jogging or exercising; some others sitting and chatting with friends. Everybody looks happy and peaceful. However, very often _____ _____ _____ public toilets goes against proper etiquette. _____ _____ _____, that the smell is often too bad to even enter the toilet. The walls are covered with a mass of scribbles, the light bulbs and sink are broken. So the lights flicker or have gone out. There's no water in the sink, and sometimes cigarettes have been thrown away in the sink. A lot of people want to _____ _____ _____ _____ when they are out of their house. This is not a situation of a particular area. It reflects our attitude toward public facilities that we don't think of them _____ _____ _____ our own stuff. If we keep using the public toilet the way that we used to do, we'll be the victims of a dirty atmosphere in the end. You may use a toilet in a clean and pleasant atmosphere, or in a dirty and smelly atmosphere. It depends on you.

문항
4

△
심
화
학
습

A. Listening Web  MP3 15-05-A

Intro Last class, we talked about the roles of producers and consumers. Today we're going to talk about this issue in (another / other) aspect.

Web1 You might have found a very interesting word, "prosumer." It is a (combination / conversation) of producer and consumer.

Web2 It means consumers who take (part / parts) in producing (good / goods) or services.

Web3 After you (punch / purchase) a shirt or a printer at an online shopping mall, some of you may write what you think of it on the Internet.

Ending You are (directly / indirectly) taking (part / parts) in producing the items.

B. True / False  MP3 15-05-B

1. 지난 시간에는 생산자와 소비자의 역할에 대해 배웠다. **(T / F)**
2. 프로슈머라는 용어는 앨빈 토플러의 책에 등장한다. **(T / F)**
3. 기업들이 신제품 사용 기회를 통해 소비자의 생각을 받아들인다. **(T / F)**
4. 교육 서비스는 프로슈머의 영향을 받지 않는 예외적인 분야이다. **(T / F)**

C. Words and Phrases

combination 조합 / purchase 구매하다 / potential 잠재력 있는 / passive 수동적인

D. Dictation  MP3 15-05-B

M: Last class, we talked about the roles of producers and consumers. Today we're going to talk about this issue _____ _____ _____. I told you to read Alvin Toffler's "The Third Wave." You might have found a very interesting word, "prosumer." It is a _____ _____ _____ _____ consumer. It means consumers who take part in producing goods or services. It means consumers no longer just consume what the producers _____ _____ _____. After you purchase a shirt or a printer at an online shopping mall, some of you may write what you think of it on the Internet. What do you think will happen next? The producers will accept your idea, and it'll _____ _____ in the next items. You are indirectly taking part in producing the items. Several years ago, businesses started to give _____ _____ chances to use their brand new items, and get very practical feedback. In addition, in the field of education, students and parents are not passive any more. They often ask for the educational services they want. The writers of Wikipedia are also prosumers because they directly take part in producing and sharing information.

A. Listening Web  MP3 15-06-A

Intro   This is a game that was (original / originally) invented by Native Americans. But its name, lacrosse was given by a French missionary.

Web1   Later in the late 1800s, lacrosse had (became / become) the national sport of Canada, and now a lot of people throughout the world play lacrosse.

Web2   Lacrosse looks similar (to / with) ice hockey in many ways.

Web3   But it is different, too. It is played on grass, not ice, as you see.

Ending   Now, it's your (term / turn) to enjoy lacrosse yourself.

B. True / False  MP3 15-06-B

1. Lacrosse는 북미에 정착한 프랑스 사람들이 만들어낸 경기이다.   (T / F)
2. Lacrosse 경기는 현재 캐나다와 프랑스에서만 한다.   (T / F)
3. Lacrosse에서는 골에 넣은 공의 개수가 그 팀의 점수가 된다.   (T / F)
4. Lacrosse의 스틱의 모양은 아이스하키 스틱과 매우 흡사하다.   (T / F)

C. Words and Phrases

missionary 선교사 / puck 아이스하키 공 (고무 원반) / scoop up 퍼 올리다

D. Dictation  MP3 15-06-B

W: This is a game that was _____ _____ by Native Americans. But its name, lacrosse was given by a French missionary. When the French arrived in North America, they saw the Native Americans playing this game. They _____ _____ their own team, and wanted to play each other. Later in the late 1800s, lacrosse had become the national sport of Canada, and now a lot of people throughout the world play lacrosse. Lacrosse looks _____ _____ ice hockey in many ways. It's a very speedy game like ice hockey. You need to _____ _____ _____ into the goal as many times as possible. And _____ _____ _____ _____ will be your score. It's quite simple, isn't it? But it is different, too. It is played on grass, not ice, as you see. And the players use a ball instead of a puck. These are lacrosse sticks. They are shaped differently. This shape allows the player to _____ _____ _____ _____ and throw it, like this. See it? That's all I can tell you about lacrosse. Now, it's your turn to enjoy lacrosse yourself. Have fun!

A. Listening Web  MP3 15-07-A

Intro The (Spain / Spanish) invaded and conquered the Incas in the middle of the 1500s. But Machu Picchu was already deserted at that time.

Web1 Some people say the reason is that its (geographical / geological) conditions were not very good.

Web2 Some scientists think the water (ran / rang) out.

Web3 Whatever the reason, the most interesting thing is that this (desert / desertion) saved the city in the long run.

Ending That's why now we can enjoy the beautiful buildings and culture of Machu Picchu.

B. True / False  MP3 15-07-B

1. 스페인이 침략했을 때 Machu Picchu는 이미 멸망해 있었다.   (T / F)
2. Machu Picchu에 살던 사람들은 빗물을 받아서 식수로 사용했다.   (T / F)
3. 스페인 군대는 잉카에서 값진 물건들을 약탈했다.   (T / F)
4. 지금 Machu Picchu는 완전히 폐허가 되어 흔적이 남아있지 않다.   (T / F)

C. Words and Phrases

conquer 정복하다 / desert 버리다, 유기하다 / geographical 지리학의, 지리적인 / thrive 번창하다 / desertion 내버림, 탈주 / flourishing culture 문화 번성 / paradoxical preservation 역설의 보존

D. Dictation  MP3 15-07-B

M: Have you ever heard about Machu Picchu? It is believed that people lived in Machu Picchu until the early 1500s. The Spanish _____ _____ _____ the Incas in the middle of the 1500s. But Machu Picchu was already _____ at that time. Nobody knows why this city was built or why it was deserted. Some people say the reason is that its _____ _____ were not very good. It was located too high between two mountain peaks. It may have been too hard for it to thrive. Some scientists think _____ _____ _____ _____. The springs from underground the main source of water, but they dried up. Whatever the reason, the most interesting thing is that this desertion saved the city in the long run. The Spanish army destroyed everything in the Inca Empire. They killed many people and took away many valuable things. However, they never found this _____ _____ _____ _____, Machu Picchu, because it was _____ high in the Andes Mountains. That's why now we can enjoy the beautiful buildings and culture of Machu Picchu.

A. Listening Web

Intro Archaeologists don't just go (about / around) digging things up. Like other scientists, they have a lot of work to do.

Web1 They come up with a hypothesis. Then they go about trying to (proof / prove) their hypothesis.

Web2 They are in (research / search) of data to collect, looking for artifacts.

Web3 They draw conclusions. They decided whether their findings prove that their hypothesis is (correct / incorrect).

Ending Many times, what they dig up makes them ask even more questions.

B. True / False

1. 고고학자들은 유품을 발견한 뒤 물건에 대한 가설을 세운다.   (T / F)
2. 그들은 옛 지도를 보며 고고학적 가치가 있는 장소를 알아본다.   (T / F)
3. 고고학자들은 일의 효율성을 위해 큰 삽을 이용하여 발굴 작업을 한다.   (T / F)
4. 발굴 장소는 먼지가 많이 나므로 고고학자들은 자주 양치를 한다.   (T / F)

C. Words and Phrases

dig ~을 파다 / hypothesis 가설 / in search of ~을 찾아서 / artifact 인공 유물 / grid 격자판 / pottery 도기 / shovel 삽 / date ~의 연대를 추정하다

D. Dictation

W: Archaeologists don't just go around digging things up. Like other scientists, they have a lot of work to do. They start with a problem or idea and _____ _____ _____ a hypothesis. Then they go about trying to prove their hypothesis. They do surveys and study old maps to find good places to dig. They look in riverbeds, in deserts, in the jungle. They also dig in mountains and under the ocean. They are in search of data to collect, _____ _____ _____. Then they use a grid to _____ the site _____ small areas. That way, they can record where they found a bit of pottery, an old tool, or a piece of bone. Archaeologists dig very carefully, using tiny shovels. Then they use toothbrushes to brush away dirt. They _____ _____ how old the objects are and they date them. Archaeologists must complete one more step. They _____ _____. They decided whether their findings prove that their _____ _____ _____. Many times, what they dig up makes them ask even more questions. And they get to have a lot to study and examine.

A. Listening Web

Intro People have many theories about what happened to the dinosaurs.

Web1 When a huge asteroid hit, it (throw / threw) up a huge cloud of dust. The dust was so (sick / thick) that it blocked the sunlight.

Web2 However, the plants on the earth could not (survive / thrive) without sunlight. In time, many or most of the plants died.

Web3 The dinosaurs that ate plants no longer had anything to eat. They (starved / started).

Web4 Then the dinosaurs that (ate / gate) other dinosaurs starved and died at last.

Ending An asteroid hit is (one / only) theory that might explain why the dinosaurs died.

B. True / False

1. 소행성 충돌은 현재 공룡의 멸종을 설명하는 현재의 유일한 이론이다. (T / F)
2. 먼지 구름으로 햇빛이 차단되면서 공룡이 죽기도 했다. (T / F)
3. 공룡이 멸종할 때쯤 먼지 구름으로 인해 새로운 별들이 생겨났다. (T / F)
4. 먼지 구름은 초식 공룡과 육식 공룡 모두에게 영향을 끼쳤다. (T / F)

C. Words and Phrases

asteroid 소행성 / block ~을 못 들어오게 하다 / starve 굶주리다, 아사하다 / thrive 번성하다

D. Dictation

M: People have many theories about _____ _____ _____ the dinosaurs. The most popular theory is that an asteroid struck the earth about 65 million years ago. When a _____ _____ _____, it threw up a huge cloud of dust. The dust was so thick that it blocked the sunlight. The cloud might have stayed in the sky for months or years. It caused the longest night ever. At that time, it _____ _____ _____ a few dinosaurs, but not many. However, the plants on the earth could not survive without sunlight. In time, many or most of the plants died. By the way, how did the dinosaurs die? The dinosaurs that ate plants no longer had _____ _____ _____. They starved. Then the dinosaurs that ate other dinosaurs starved and died at last. An asteroid hit is one theory that might explain why the dinosaurs died. How can anyone be sure the _____ _____ _____ _____ of dinosaurs? Scientists will keep researching this question. Someday, we will know the answer for sure.

A. Listening Web

Intro In the 1800s, most people (live / living) on the west (coast / cost) went there hoping to find gold.

Web1 But they still wanted to stay in touch (in / with) their families back east.

Web2 So, in 1860, William Russell started a new company, "Pony Express," whose riders on (speed / speedy) horses would carry mail and news overland.

Web3 The "Pony Express Company" had 500 horses and 120 stations along the route. When it was time for a rider to come by, the station man got a (flash / fresh) horse ready.

Ending And two days later, "Pony Express" (caused / closed). There was no longer a need for it.

B. True / False

1. 서부 해변에 살던 사람들은 금을 찾아온 사람들이었다.   (T / F)
2. William Russel은 육로로 편지를 배달하는 회사를 세웠다.   (T / F)
3. Pony Express의 배달 경로는 매우 안전했다.   (T / F)
4. Pony Express의 최초 배달 경로는 샌프란시스코에서 워싱턴 D.C. 구간이다.   (T / F)

C. Words and Phrases

Morse code 모스 부호 / come by 들르다 / chase 뒤쫓다, 추적하다 / telegram 전보

D. Dictation

W: In the 1800s, most people living on the west coast went there hoping to find gold. But they still wanted to _____ _____ _____ _____ their families back east. The only way to send messages long distances was in Morse code. If they sent letters by ship, it took six months. Sending mail overland seemed like a better idea. So, in 1860, William Russell started a new company, "Pony Express," whose riders on speedy horses would _____ _____ and _____ _____. Russell promised that the riders could deliver mail in ten days even though the route would be tough especially in winter. The "Pony Express Company" had 500 horses and 120 stations _____ _____ _____. When it was time for a rider to come by, the station man got a _____ _____ _____. Often they were attacked or chased by robbers. They knew the mail might contain gold or money. On October 24, 1861, the first telegram was sent from San Francisco to Washington D.C. And two days later, "Pony Express" closed. There was _____ _____ _____ _____ for it.

읽기 부문에서만 출제되었던 유형이 듣기에도 출제되기 시작한다. 사실상 담화를 요약하는 것은 쉬운 일이 아니다. 그러나 수능시험이 선다형임을 고려하면, 의외로 쉽게 접근할 수 있다. 요약문을 미리 읽어두면 어떤 부분에 착안하여 들어야 할지 파악할 수 있다. 이렇게 되면 사실상 주제 및 요지를 찾는 요령과 크게 다르지 않다. 다만 요약문 부분과 다섯 개의 선택지를 빠르게 읽고 정답을 골라야 하므로, 속도 조절에 주의를 기울여야 한다. 또한 요약이란 전체 내용을 아우를 수 있어야 하므로, 선택지 중 옳은 정보라도 내용의 일부만을 담고 있다면 오답이 될 수 있다는 점에 주의해야 한다.

● **Example**

1 **다음을 듣고, 남자의 말을 요약할 때 빈칸에 들어갈 말로 알맞은 것을 고르시오.** [2012 수능기출]

Mediation is a process that has much in common with advocacy but is also crucially different. It parallels advocacy in so far as it tends to involve a process of negotiation, but differs in so far as mediation involves adopting a neutral role between two opposing parties rather than taking up the case of one party against another. At times, particularly in very complex situations, the processes of advocacy and mediation can overlap, perhaps with very problematic results, as one loses clarity over this or her role. It is therefore important, if not essential, to maintain a clear focus in undertaking advocacy or mediation in order to ensure that the roles do not become blurred and therefore potentially counterproductive. For example, a mediator who 'takes sides' is likely to lose all credibility, as is an advocate who seeks to adopt a neutral position.

> Although both deal with negotiation, a mediator needs to maintain _____(A)_____ and an advocate partiality in order to _____(B)_____ crossing over into each other's role.

	(A)	(B)
①	neutrality	avoid
②	neutrality	encourage
③	potentiality	reinforce
④	creativity	facilitate
⑤	creativity	prevent

* 'mediation involves adopting a neutral role between two opposing parties rather than taking up the case of one party against another. (중재는 한쪽의 편을 들어주기보다는 상반되는 둘 사이에서 중립적인 역할을 취한다.)' 라고 했으므로, (A)에 들어갈 말은 neutrality이다. 이와 반대로 지지하는 것은 한 쪽의 편을 들어주는 것인데, 지지와 중재의 역할이 서로 모호해지지(crossing over) 않도록 지지하는 사람은 한 쪽의 편을 들어주어야 한다. 따라서 (B)에 들어갈 말은 avoid이다. 정답은 ①번이다.

유형 16

장문을 듣고
요약하기

장문을 듣고 요약하기

1 다음을 듣고, 여자의 말을 요약할 때 빈칸에 들어갈 말로 알맞은 것을 고르시오.

> The study of history _____

① literally means to study European history.
② puts a strong emphasis on the chronology.
③ requires memorizing a lot of specific events.
④ is recording all the facts from the past to the present.
⑤ requires both the chronology and spatial information.

2 다음을 듣고, 남자의 말을 요약할 때 빈칸에 들어갈 말로 알맞은 것을 고르시오.

> The most effective leader _____

① expresses his (or her) emotions honestly.
② gives the group members an expectation of success.
③ presents a high standard of life to the group members.
④ believes that the leader himself (or herself) will succeed.
⑤ considers both positive and negative aspects of things.

3 다음을 듣고, 여자의 말을 요약할 때 빈칸에 들어갈 말로 알맞은 것을 고르시오.

> Shakespeare's strong influence on English was _____
> _____

① to define a lot of English literary terms.
② to write great literary works in all genres.
③ to extend the amount of English vocabulary.
④ to make many new words and sophisticated expressions.
⑤ to create new characters in his works which had not existed before.

4 다음을 듣고, 남자의 말을 요약할 때 빈칸에 들어갈 말로 알맞은 것을 고르시오.

> There are two sides to Internet when it comes to finding people.
> One is _____(A)_____; the other _____(B)_____.

	(A)	(B)
①	finding them quickly	applying strict regulations
②	finding childhood friends	releasing their identities in public
③	finding them quickly	violating human personal rights
④	finding childhood friends	violating human personal rights
⑤	finding the victims quickly	releasing their identities in public

5 다음을 듣고, 여자의 주장을 요약할 때 빈칸에 들어갈 말로 알맞은 것을 고르시오.

> People of high social or economic status sometimes feel they are not
> always happy because _____

① they haven't ever felt their parents' love.
② stress is an inevitable factor for everyone.
③ they have no knowledge about the IT industry.
④ the condition of happiness is highly subjective.
⑤ their parents didn't have enough time to play with them.

6 다음을 듣고, 남자의 말을 요약할 때 빈칸에 들어갈 말로 알맞은 것을 고르시오.

> The major causes of drinking water problems are that _____(A)_____,
> and that some countries cannot _____(B)_____.

	(A)	(B)
①	water is polluted	purify or substitute water
②	the demand grows	convey or purify water
③	the population grows	make access to water
④	people suffer from poverty	develop the drinking water
⑤	there is a lack of infrastructure	purify or substitute water

7 다음을 듣고, 여자의 주장을 요약할 때 빈칸에 들어갈 말로 알맞은 것을 고르시오.

> It is important to _____

① select the trustworthy mass media.
② select the information that we need.
③ look at things from different viewpoints.
④ look at the world throughout mass media.
⑤ have a partial attitude towards mass media.

8 다음을 듣고, 남자의 주장을 요약할 때 빈칸에 들어갈 말로 알맞은 것을 고르시오.

> Because the crimes attributed to poverty or ignorance are not
> _____(A)_____, society should _____(B)_____.

	(A)	(B)
①	moral issues	reduce the economic gap
②	social problems	punish the criminals
③	individual problems	share the responsibility
④	social problems	get rid of the criminals
⑤	individual problems	provide educational opportunities

9 다음을 듣고, 여자의 말을 요약할 때 빈칸에 들어갈 말로 알맞은 것을 고르시오.

Because of _____(A)_____, we don't need to _____(B)_____.

	(A)	(B)
①	cell phones	remember phone numbers
②	smart people	recite all of Homer
③	great inventions	recite all of Homer
④	smart people	remember many things
⑤	great inventions	remember many things

10 다음을 듣고, 남자의 주장을 요약할 때 빈칸에 들어갈 말로 알맞은 것을 고르시오.

We all define risk in different ways, and _____(A)_____ can _____(B)_____ the threat of risk.

①	the crowd	provoke
②	the high salary	reduce
③	the fear for death	exaggerate
④	the potential reward	disguise
⑤	the social admiration	distort

해답/해설 307p

A. Listening Web  MP3 16-01-A

Intro   Learning history is very important because it teaches us the wisdom of (life / live).

Web1   In order to study history, you should make sure about the (chronology / technology).

Web2   For example, when you study (Europe / European) history, you need to set the timeline.

Web3   In addition, you have to check what (happen / happened) in other places in the world over the same period.

Ending   For example, the ancient Chosun Dynasty was in the same era as the ancient (Egypt / Egyptian) Empire.

B. True / False  MP3 16-01-B

1. 역사는 삶의 지혜를 알려준다.   (T / F)
2. 역사는 사실의 기록이다.   (T / F)
3. 역사를 공부할 때는 연대기 정리만 하면 된다.   (T / F)
4. 고조선과 고대 이집트 왕국은 같은 시대 다른 곳에 있었던 역사적 사실이다.   (T / F)

C. Words and Phrases

chronology 연대순, 연대표 / the Middle Ages 중세 / Early Modern Period 근세 / civil revolution 시민혁명 / era 시대 / spatial 공간적인

D. Dictation  MP3 16-01-B

W: Learning history is very important because it teaches us the _____ _____ _____. Literally, history is _____ _____ _____ all the facts from the past to the present. Carr, a historian, has said that history is an endless conversation between the past and the present. In order to study history, you should _____ _____ _____ the chronology. For example, when you study European history, you need to set the timeline, such as the birth of ancient civilization, the Middle Ages, the fall of the Western Roman Empire, the Early Modern Period, the civil revolution, the Modern Era, and then the era after World War I and so on. In addition, you have to check what happened _____ _____ _____ in the world over the same period. For example, the ancient Chosun Dynasty was _____ _____ _____ _____ as the ancient Egyptian Empire.

A. Listening Web

Intro   What makes (an effective / ineffective) (leader / reader)?

Web1   However it is true that the most effective leader (heard / holds) the group members to very high standards of performance.

Web2   In other words, the leader's expectation of success or failure becomes a self-fulfilling (proficiency / prophecy).

Web3   Conversely, if the leader thinks the group members will fail, the leader expresses (disappointed / disappointment) without realizing he or she is doing so.

Ending   And the leader's attitude (constitutes / contributes) to the failure in reality in the end.

B. True / False

1. 효과적인 지도자의 자질을 구성하는 결정적인 한 가지 특징이 있다. (T / F)
2. 피그말리온 효과는 눈치채지 못하는 사이에 작용한다. (T / F)
3. 지도자의 실패에 대한 부정적인 기대는 은연중에 구성원들에게 드러나기 마련이다. (T / F)
4. 훌륭한 지도자는 구성원들을 긍정적으로 이끌 수 있다. (T / F)

C. Words and Phrases

productivity 생산성 / live up to ~에 부응하다 / self-fulfilling prophecy 자기 충족적 (예언대로 성취되는) 예언 / phenomenon 현상 / unconscious 무의식적인 / conversely 역으로 / contribute to ~에 기여하다

D. Dictation

M: What makes an effective leader? To be sure, only one characteristic does not _____ an effective leader. However it is true that the most effective leader holds the group members to very _____ _____ _____ _____. Setting such standards increases productivity because they try to live up to the expectation which has already been set for them by the leader. In other words, the leader's expectation of success or failure becomes a self-fulfilling prophecy. We call this phenomenon Pygmalion effect, and it works in a subtle and almost _____ _____. For example, when the leader believes that the group members will succeed, the leader communicates with them positively with that _____ _____. Conversely, if the leader thinks the group members will fail, the leader expresses disappointment without realizing he or she is doing so. And the leader's attitude _____ _____ the failure in reality in the end.

A. Listening Web  MP3 16-03-A

Intro Shakespeare has strongly (inflated / influenced) the English language.

Web1 He has no rivals in regard to the (extension / extent) and the depth of his influence on the English language.

Web2 He created a lot of new English words, so he (expanded / extended) the volume of English vocabulary.

Ending In addition, he put a large (number / numbers) of sophisticated expressions in his writings.

B. True / False  MP3 16-03-B

1. 셰익스피어는 영어에 가장 큰 영향을 끼친 인물이다.   (T / F)
2. 셰익스피어가 만들어낸 단어들이 지금도 쓰이고 있다.   (T / F)
3. Venice는 셰익스피어가 만들어낸 이름이다.   (T / F)
4. 햄릿에는 제시카라는 인물이 나온다.   (T / F)

C. Words and Phrases

in regard to ~과 관련하여, ~에 대하여 / volume 양 / sophisticated 세련된, 기교를 부린 / eyeball 눈알 / revenge 복수

D. Dictation  MP3 16-03-B

W: Shakespeare has strongly influenced the English language. He has no rivals _____ _____ _____ the extent and the depth of his influence on the English language. He created a lot of new English words, so he _____ _____ _____ of English vocabulary. In addition, he put a large number of sophisticated expressions in his writings. Some of them have become _____ _____, and some others have entered into our daily conversation nowadays. For example, 'lonely,' 'gloomy' or 'eyeball' are words Shakespeare created. Interestingly, a woman's name, Jessica, _____ _____ in "The Merchant of Venice." There had been no Jessica before "The Merchant of Venice" was published. All of you may have heard or read the famous phrase 'to be, or not to be, that is the question,' which comes from Hamlet. It poetically represents that Hamlet was _____ _____ _____ and full of doubts about life.

A. Listening Web  MP3 16-04-A

Intro Sometimes the Internet takes a (critical / crucial) role in finding people.

Web1 The Internet has the advantage of making it possible to (capture / catch up) the suspect in a short time.

Web2 But the problem is that the (identification / identity) of the suspect can be released on the Internet.

Web3 It could be a (violate / violation) of human personal rights.

Ending When the police openly search on the Internet for the (wanted / wanting) person, there should be strict regulations.

B. True / False  MP3 16-04-B

1. 인터넷은 사람을 찾는데 매우 효과적이다. (T / F)
2. 일반인이 인터넷을 통해 가해자를 잡기도 한다. (T / F)
3. 경찰은 용의자에 한해서는 인터넷으로 공개수배를 할 수 있다. (T / F)
4. 인터넷 공개수배가 때로는 인권침해가 될 수 있다. (T / F)

C. Words and Phrases

violation 위반, 위배 / the wanted 지명 수배자 / hasty 성급한 / irrevocably 돌이킬 수 없게

D. Dictation  MP3 16-04-B

M: Sometimes the Internet takes a _____ _____ _____ finding people. Very often, we find childhood friends on the Internet. By the way, some victims use the Internet to find the suspect. The Internet has the advantage of making it possible to _____ _____ _____ in a short time. If you had an accident and the police said it would be difficult to catch the suspect, how would you feel? Maybe you'd want to find the suspect _____ _____ _____ _____ the Internet. But the problem is that the identity of the suspect can be released on the Internet, so everybody can see it. It could be a violation of _____ _____ _____. The suspect is not the criminal yet. At worst, _____ _____ _____ can hurt an innocent person irrevocably. And it really happens. When the police openly search on the Internet for the wanted person, there should be _____ _____.

A. Listening Web  MP3 16-05-A

Intro A (service / survey) shows that even more Australians feel happy than Koreans.

Web1 The people who are rich or in a high social position are (expected / expecting) to be happy.

Web2 They suffer from stress because they cannot avoid (competition / condition).

Web3 To win the competition, they should (inquest / invest) more time and effort into work, and they cannot spend a lot of time with their loving family or friends.

Ending Parents' love cannot be (replace / replaced) by expensive toys.

B. True / False  MP3 16-05-B

1. 한국 사람들은 호주 사람들보다 행복감을 덜 느낀다. (T / F)
2. 행복에는 몇 가지 필수적인 조건들이 있다. (T / F)
3. 사회적 지위가 높은 사람들은 경쟁으로 인한 스트레스에 시달린다. (T / F)
4. 어린아이들은 장난감 선물을 통해 부모의 사랑을 느낀다. (T / F)

C. Words and Phrases

desire 열망 / absolute 절대적인 / competition 경쟁 / inevitable 불가피한 / subjective 주관적인

D. Dictation  MP3 16-05-B

W: A survey shows that even more Australians feel happy than Koreans. But it's strange. Korea is a powerful country in the IT industry, and Korean people have a _____ _____ for education. But they feel they are not as happy as they are expected to be. The reason is simple. There's no _____ _____ of happiness. The people who are rich or in a high social position are expected to be happy. However, they _____ _____ stress because they cannot avoid competition. Moreover, to _____ _____ _____, they should invest more time and effort into work, and they cannot spend a lot of time with their loving family or friends. That's why they feel lonely and unhappy. Children may not feel happy if their parents don't have time enough to play with them. Parents' love _____ _____ _____ by expensive toys. Nobody thinks children will be happy as long as they are put into a toy factory.

A. Listening Web  MP3 16-06-A

Intro   We've suffered from a lack of drinking water for (decay / decades).

Web1   First, it's because of population (grows / growth).

Web2   (Another / The other) reason is a lack of infrastructure.

Web3   Water is (absolute / essential) to every living thing and there's no substitute.

Ending   So we need to take swift action to (stabilize / standardize) the water supply.

B. True / False  MP3 16-06-B

1. 물 부족 현상은 개발도상국과 저개발국가에서만 일어나는 특수한 현상이다.   (T / F)
2. 물 부족 현상이 나타나기 시작한 지 수십 년이 지났다.   (T / F)
3. 식수 정화 시설이나 수도 시설이 부족한 것도 물 부족 현상의 원인이 된다.   (T / F)
4. 안정적인 식수 공급을 위한 즉각적인 조치가 이루어져야 한다.   (T / F)

C. Words and Phrases

infrastructure 사회 공공 기반 시설 / access 접근 / substitute 대용품 / swift 즉각적인 / stabilize 안정시키다 /
convey 전달하다

D. Dictation  MP3 16-06-B

M: We've suffered from _____ _____ _____ drinking water for decades. Research has shown that the amount of drinking water has decreased since the 1970s, and that slightly less than 3 billion people on earth suffer from a lack of drinking water for more than a month a year. What is the reason for it? First, it's because of population growth. As the population grows, a large amount of water is in demand, and the supply cannot _____ _____ _____. Another reason is a lack of infrastructure. For example, some developing countries have no facilities _____ _____ _____ _____. Or some underdeveloped countries have water, but do not have facilities to carry water. That is, they don't have _____ _____ a water supply. Water is essential to every living thing and there's no substitute. So we need to _____ _____ _____ to stabilize the water supply.

A. Listening Web  MP3 16-07-A

Intro People tend to select only the information or ideas they (could / would) like to read or listen to.

Web1 Of course, it is a great ability to select only what they need in the (auction / ocean) of information.

Web2 But just as eating only what they want is not good, (selected / selecting) only the information that they want is not good, either.

Web3 This kind of partial attitude towards information interrupts us (for / from) taking the world as it is.

Ending Therefore we should remember that there could be more than one (argument / element) about an issue.

B. True / False  MP3 16-07-B

1. 인터넷은 사실상 우리에게 유익한 정보를 제공해주지 못한다. (T / F)
2. 수많은 정보 중에서 필요한 정보를 취하는 것은 위험한 것이다. (T / F)
3. 정보를 선택하는 과정에서 편향된 사고를 하게 될 수 있다. (T / F)
4. 하나의 문제를 여러 시각으로 볼 필요가 있다. (T / F)

C. Words and Phrases

beneficial 이로운, 유익한 / partial 편애하는, 편파적인 / interrupt 방해하다, 가로막다 /
take the world as it is 세상을 있는 그대로 받아들이다

D. Dictation  MP3 16-07-B

W: Mass media including the Internet _____ _____ _____ a wide variety of information. However, it is not always beneficial to us. People tend to select only the information or ideas they would like to read or listen to. Of course, it is a great ability to select only what they need in the ocean of information. But just as eating only what they want is not good, selecting only the information that they want is not good, either. This kind of _____ _____ towards information interrupts us from taking the world _____ _____ _____. That is, we look at the world through the newspaper, TV or Internet, which decide what we should _____ _____. Therefore we should remember that there could be _____ _____ _____ _____ about an issue.

A. Listening Web  MP3 16-08-A

Intro I don't think we can avoid our (collected / collective) responsibility for the crimes (committed / committing) in our community.

Web1 If somebody cannot get proper educational opportunities in time, he will try to improve his social (stations / status) by all means available.

Web2 Even though he behaves against common sense at the time, we cannot (punish / push) him for his ignorance.

Web3 In addition, if a person grows up in an environment without (replied / refined) manners or moral guidance, he never knows what standards are (expecting / expected) in society.

Ending Now we're supposed to take measures to lessen the (economic / economical) gap and get rid of ignorance.

B. True / False  MP3 16-08-B

1. 배우자가 빚이 있으면 상대 배우자에게도 이에 대한 법적인 책임이 있다. **(T / F)**
2. 교육을 제대로 받지 못한 사람은 결국 반드시 상식에 어긋나는 행동을 하게 된다. **(T / F)**
3. 도덕성이 결핍된 환경에서 자란 사람이 사회적 규범을 지킬 것을 기대하는 것은 무리이다. **(T / F)**
4. 사회 격차를 줄이고 무지를 없애는 것이 복지 국가이다. **(T / F)**

C. Words and Phrases

legally 법률적으로 / spouse 배우자 / if any 만약 있다면 / collective responsibility 연대 책임 / commit (범죄를) 저지르다, 범하다 / ignorance 무지 / refined 세련된 / take measures 조치를 취하다 / lessen 줄이다 / welfare state 복지 국가

D. Dictation  MP3 16-08-B

M: You may have heard that you're _____ _____ _____ your spouse's debts, if any. Likewise, the same rules should apply in society. I don't think we can avoid our collective responsibility for the _____ _____ in our community. If a person is starving to death, who can blame a person for stealing some food? If somebody cannot get proper educational opportunities in time, he will try to improve his social status _____ _____ _____ available. Even though he behaves against common sense at the time, we cannot _____ him _____ _____ _____. In addition, if a person grows up in an environment without refined manners or moral guidance, he never knows what standards are expected in society. Now we're supposed to _____ _____ to lessen the economic gap and get rid of ignorance. It is the welfare state that many countries pursue these days.

A. Listening Web  MP3 16-09-A

Intro The Greeks used to be able to recite all of Homer, because they (had / have) learned his works by heart.

Web1 Now we can't even remember the names of our classmates only a few years after graduation.

Web2 I don't think many of you remember your (close / closed) friend's phone number.

Web3 Navigation systems tell us the smartest route in traffic, but thanks to them, we don't need to remember the (map / mat).

Ending Smart people have created great inventions, but people seem to be (moving / losing) their memory.

B. True / False  MP3 16-09-B

1. 오늘날 그리스 사람들은 호머의 시집 전체를 암송한다. (T / F)
2. 졸업한 뒤 친구의 이름을 기억하지 못하는 경우가 종종 있다. (T / F)
3. 친구의 전화번호를 외우는 사람은 많지 않다. (T / F)
4. 위대한 발명품들은 우리가 중요한 것을 우리 스스로 기억하는데 도움을 준다. (T / F)

C. Words and Phrases

recite 암송하다 / Homer 호머(고대 그리스의 서사시인) / by heart 외워서, 기억하여 / destroy 파괴하다 /
look up 찾아보다 / manage to 가까스로 ~하다

D. Dictation  MP3 16-09-B

W: The Greeks _____ _____ _____ able to recite all of Homer, because they had learned his works _____ _____. Printing techniques had not been developed yet, so there wasn't a large volume of books. Reciting the whole book or story was the only way to share knowledge. Now we can't even remember the names of our classmates only a few years after graduation. We think we can look up the old buddy's name in the album any time. The printing press has destroyed our memory. I don't think many of you remember your close friend's phone number. We _____ _____ _____ _____ in a tiny and handy cell phone, and manage to remember the fact that we have the number in the phone. Navigation systems tell us the smartest route in traffic, but thanks to them, we don't need to remember the map. Smart people have created _____ _____, but people seem to be _____ _____ _____.

A. Listening Web  MP3 16-10-A

Intro   Why are some people willing to take risks (whereas / while) others want to be safe?

Web1   Although the risk of danger may be real, (perception / reception) of the risk can vary from person to person, or from time to time.

Web2   Age tends to (convenience / convince) us that death is a reality while the young people think it will happen to somebody else.

Web3   Sometimes the (visional / vision of) future rewards can cloud our assessment of danger.

Web4   They think money is (worked / worth) taking risks.

Ending   And some young adults drive a car very fast with a (designer / desire) for social admiration.

B. True / False  MP3 16-10-B

1. 시기에 따라 위험을 감지하는 정도가 다르다.   (T / F)
2. 10미터 높이의 줄 위에서 걷는 것은 사실 예사로운 일이다.   (T / F)
3. 나이 든 사람은 젊은 사람보다 죽음에 대해 현실적으로 느낀다.   (T / F)
4. 젊은 사람이 과속하는 것은 사람들의 찬사를 받고 싶기 때문이기도 하다.   (T / F)

C. Words and Phrases

take risk 위험을 감수하다 / on a daily basis 매일 / cloud (기억력, 판단력 등을) 흐리다 / admiration 감탄, 존경 / provoke 유발하다 / exaggerate 과장하다 / potential reward 잠재적 보상 / disguise 위장하다 / distort 왜곡하다

D. Dictation  MP3 16-10-B

M: Why are some people _____ _____ _____ _____ whereas others want to be safe? Although the risk of danger may be real, _____ of the risk can _____ from person to person, or from time to time. How many among you would walk on a line strung ten meters above the ground? But some people do it on an almost daily basis and _____ _____ _____ _____. Most people won't take the same risks at fifty as they did at twenty. Age tends to convince us that death is a reality while the young people think it will happen to somebody else. Sometimes the _____ of future rewards can _____ _____ _____ of danger. Some people are willing to work in very dangerous environments for a high salary. They think money is worth taking risks. And some young adults drive a car very fast with a desire for social admiration.

Answer Key

Answer Key

Unit 01 유형 1 - 짧은 대화 응답 찾기

문항 1 ③

Script & Dictation

M: Hurry up and **finish your coffee**. We'll be late!

W: I can't. This coffee is too hot **for me to drink**.

M: Why don't you put some cold **milk in it**?

W: I don't take milk in my coffee.

남: 서둘러서 커피 빨리 마셔. 우리 늦겠어!

여: 빨리 마실 수가 없어. 이 커피 마시기에 너무 뜨거워.

남: 차가운 우유를 좀 넣어봐.

여: 난 커피에 우유 안 넣어.

해설: 남자는 여자에게 커피를 빨리 마시라고 재촉하면서, 찬 우유를 넣을 것을 권유하고 있다.

Listening Web

Intro: late   Web 1: drink

Ending: cold

True / False

1. T   2. T   3. F   4. F

문항 2 ③

Script & Dictation

M: Sally, I'm **walking on air** now.

W: Oh! What happened to you?

M: **My debate team** has gone Intro the semi-final.

W: The speech practice really worked!

남: Sally, 나 지금 하늘을 나는 기분이야.

여: 오! 너 무슨 일 있니?

남: 우리 토론팀이 준결승에 진출했어.

여: 연설 준비가 정말 효과 있었네!

해설: 남자의 토론팀이 준결승에 진출한 것이므로 말하기 연습과 관련된 응답이 가장 자연스럽다.

Listening Web

Intro: walking   Web 1: happened

Ending: debate

True / False

1. F   2. T   3. F   4. T

문항 3 ④

Script & Dictation

M: Look who's here! I haven't seen you **for ages**.

W: I should say so. It's been a long time, **hasn't it**? How have you been?

M: Quite well. **Where have you been**?

W: I've been out of town on business.

남: 이게 누구시더라! 정말 오랜만이에요.

여: 그러게요. 정말 오랜만이죠? 어떻게 지내셨어요?

남: 잘 지냈어요. 어디에 계셨어요?

여: 전 외지로 출장 갔었어요.

해설: 남자가 마지막으로 그동안 어디에 있었느냐고 물었으므로, 여자가 그동안 어디에 있었는지에 관한 대답이 와야 한다.

Listening Web

Intro: haven't   Web 1: long

Ending: been

True / False

1. T   2. F   3. T   4. F

문항 4 ⑤

Script & Dictation

W: Congratulations on your graduation! I'm so **proud of you**.

M: Mom, it's no big deal. It happens to everyone.

W: No, you did a good job. You **deserve it**.

M: Thank you for your support.

여: 졸업을 축하한다! 네가 무척 자랑스럽구나.

남: 별것도 아닌데요, 엄마. 모두에게 있는 일이에요.

여: 아니야, 정말 장하다. 넌 축하 받을 만해.

남: 응원해주셔서 고마워요.

해설: 졸업을 축하해주는 엄마의 말에 가장 자연스러운 응답은 부모님의 도움에 고마움을 표시하는 것이다.

Listening Web

Intro: Congratulations   Web 1: deal

Ending: deserve

True / False

1. F   2. T   3. F   4. F

문항 5 ③

Script & Dictation

M: Do you mind helping me **find my glasses**?

W: Have you looked in the bathroom?

M: Yes, I have, but they weren't there. I put them on the desk **as far as** I know, but I can't find them anywhere.

W: Are these what you are looking for?

남: 안경 찾는 것 좀 도와줄래?

여: 화장실 안에 봤어?

남: 응, 봤는데 거기 없었어. 내가 기억하기로는 책상에 뒀는데, 아무리 찾아도 없어.

여: 이게 네가 찾는 거니?

해설: 남자가 잃어버린 안경 (glasses)을 찾고 있다. 선택지에 있는 glass (유리잔)와 혼동하는 일이 없도록 한다.

Listening Web

Intro: glasses   Web 1: bathroom

Ending: can't

True / False

1. T   2. F   3. F   4. T

문항 6 ④

Script & Dictation

M: What are you doing this weekend?

W: We're having a **farewell party** for Melissa.

M: Right. She will **leave for** England soon.

W: I'd love to **have you join us**. Will you come?

M: Oh, thank you. How nice of you to ask me.

남: 이번 주말에 뭐해?

여: Melissa 환송회를 할 거야.

남: 맞다. 그 애는 곧 영국으로 떠나지.

여: 네가 와주었으면 좋겠어. 올 거니?

남: 오, 고마워. 물어봐줘서.

해설: 여자는 남자에게 파티에 올 수 있는지 여부를 묻고 있으므로, 자신에게 물어봐주어서 고맙다는 말이 이어질 응답으로 가장 자연스럽다.

Listening Web

Intro: doing   Web 1: farewell

Web 2: leave   Ending: join

True / False

1. F   2. F   3. T   4. T

문항 7 ④

Script & Dictation

M: Why are you **pulling the long face**?

W: I had a **terrible argument** with my friend. She never wants to talk to me again.

M: I'm sorry to hear that. Is there anything I can do for you?

W: Don't worry about it. I can get over it.

남: 왜 이렇게 시무룩해?

여: 친구랑 심하게 다퉜어. 걔가 나랑 말을 아예 안 하려고 해.

남: 그 말을 들으니 유감이구나. 내가 뭐 도와줄 게 없을까?

여: 걱정하지 마. 난 극복할 수 있어.

해설: 이어질 여자의 응답으로는 남자의 도움이 필요한지 아니면 스스로 해결할지를 말해주는 내용이 와야 한다.

Listening Web

Intro: pulling, face   Web 1: terrible

Ending: anything

True / False

1. F   2. F   3. T   4. F

문항 8 ④

Script & Dictation

W: Excuse me. The air conditioner is never **turned on**.

M: I'm really sorry. We'll **take care of it** right away. What's your room number?

W: I'm staying in room **630**.

M: We'll send someone up in a minute.

여: 실례합니다. 에어컨이 켜지지 않아요.

남: 정말 죄송합니다. 바로 처리해드리겠습니다. 몇 호실이십니까?

여: 630호에 있습니다.

남: 곧 사람을 올려 보내겠습니다.

해설: 여자가 호텔 방의 에어컨이 켜지지 않는다고 했으므로, 호텔 직원인 남자는 이 문제를 해결해준다는 말을 하는 것이 자연스럽다.

Listening Web

Intro: on   Web 1: of

Ending: 630

True / False

1. T   2. F   3. F   4. T

문항 9 ③

Script & Dictation

W: I'd like a bottle of ice water, please.

M: I'm sorry. The **power is off** now and the fridge isn't working. Cold items are not **available** right now.

W: What time are you **going to be ready** again?

M: I'm sorry, but we can't make a guarantee.

여: 얼음물 한 병 주세요.

남: 죄송합니다. 지금 전기가 나가서 냉장고가 작동하지 않습니다. 지금은 찬 제품들은 제공해드릴 수 없습니다.

여: 몇 시에 다시 준비되나요?

남: 죄송합니다만, 확답을 못드리겠습니다.

해설: 여자는 몇 시에 냉장 음료가 준비되는지를 묻고 있다. 따라서 언제 냉장고가 고쳐질지 알 수 없다는 내용이 오는 것이 가장 자연스럽다.

Listening Web

Intro: a bottle of   Web 1: available

Ending: ready

True / False

1. T   2. F   3. F   4. T

문항 10 ①

Script & Dictation

W: Where are you going? Have you already finished studying?

M: Mom, I promise I'll be back **in an hour** and prepare for the exam. **I need a break.**

W: Daniel, you're constantly **making excuses**.

M: Okay, I'll study first.

여: 어디 가니? 벌써 공부 다 했니?

남: 엄마, 한 시간 내로 꼭 돌아와서 공부할게요. 휴식이 필요해요.

여: Daniel, 넌 계속해서 핑계만 대는구나.

남: 알았어요. 공부 먼저 할게요.

해설: 엄마는 쉴 구실을 찾고 있는 아들을 다그치고 있으므로, 우선 공부를 하겠다는 아들의 응답이 가장 자연스럽다.

Listening Web

Intro: studying   Web 1: break

Ending: making excuses

True / False

1. T   2. F   3. T   4. T

Unit 02 유형 2 - 적절한 의견 찾기

문항 1 ④

Script & Dictation

M: I can't breathe. There are a lot of cars on the street, fuming out exhaust gas.

W: The government should **take some strong actions** against those kinds of car owners. They're polluting the air, causing a lot of environmental problems...

M: You're right.

W: But **who do you think** has responsibility for these environmental problems like air pollution?

M: What do you mean?

W: Who spoiled the earth? Now that the **developed countries** face some serious environmental problems, they want to share the responsibility with **underdeveloped countries**.

M: Well, we have only one earth and limited natural resources. We all should protect the environment.

W: Yes. But I think **it's unfair** to share the same **amount of** responsibility with them.

남: 난 숨을 쉴 수가 없어. 길에 많은 차들이 매연을 내뿜고 있어.

여: 정부는 그런 자동차 주인들에 대해서 강력한 조치를 취해야 해. 공기도 오염시키고 있고, 많은 환경 문제도 일으키고…

남: 맞아.

여: 그런데 넌 공기 오염 같은 이 환경 문제의 책임이 누구에게 있다고 생각하니?

남: 무슨 말이야?

여: 누가 지구를 망가뜨렸을까? 선진국들은 이제 환경 문제에 당면하니까 후진국과 함께 책임을 나누려고 해.

남: 글쎄, 지구는 하나뿐이고, 자원도 한정되어 있어. 우리 모두가 환경을 보호해야지.

여: 그래. 하지만 똑같이 책임을 나누는 것은 부당하다고 생각해.

해설: 여자는 선진국들이 이미 자연을 훼손해 놓고, 환경 문제가 대두되자 후진국들과 책임을 나누려고 하는 태도를 비판하고 있다.

Listening Web

Intro: exhaust   Web 1: against

Web 2: countries   Ending: unfair

True / False

1. T   2. F   3. F   4. T

문항 2 ④

Script & Dictation

W: What are you going to do this summer vacation?

M: I'm planning to go to America to study English.

W: Where are you going in America?

M: L.A. My uncle lives there. Maybe I'll stay there and **commute to school**.

W: Why don't you **live in a dorm**?

M: It's expensive, and maybe there are **strict rules**...

W: But you'll speak only Korean when you're home. You need to **practice English** every day for 24 hours, don't you?

M: Yes, but I don't want to share a room with somebody **I don't know**.

W: Make friends with them. Making foreign friends, speaking in English all the time, and experiencing American students' lives, will all **help you to improve** your English.

M: Well, I think you're right. I'll **discuss it** with my parents again.

여: 이번 여름 방학에 뭐 할 거니?

남: 영어 공부하러 미국에 가려고 계획 중이야.

여: 미국 어디로 가는데?

남: L.A. 우리 삼촌이 거기에 살고 계셔. 거기 머무르면서 학교에 통학하려고.

여: 기숙사에 들어가는 게 어때?

남: 비싸잖아, 그리고 규칙도 엄격할 거고…

여: 하지만 넌 집에 있으면 한국말만 쓰게 될 거야. 매일매일 24시간 영어 연습해야 하잖아.

남: 맞아, 하지만 모르는 사람이랑 방 같이 쓰는 것도 별로야.

여: 친구를 사귀면 되지. 외국 친구를 사귀고, 항상 영어를 쓰고, 미국 학생들의 생활을 경험하는 것 전부가 영어 실력을 높이는 데 도움이 될 거야.

남: 음, 네 말이 맞는 것 같아. 이 문제를 부모님과 다시 상의해 봐야겠어.

해설: 여자는 기숙사에 들어가면 새로운 친구를 사귀어서 영어를 사용할 기회가 더 많아진다고 남자를 설득하고 있다.

Listening Web

Intro: planning

Web 1: commute to

Web 2: live in

Ending: discuss

True / False

1. T   2. F   3. T   4. F

문항 3 ⑤

Script & Dictation

W: Is everybody here? Am I the last?

M: No. David is still coming.

W: It took about three hours. It was a long journey. I was **kind of scared** because it's so dark and I almost **hit an animal**.

M: You have to be careful. There are some wild animals around here.

W: Did you also **encounter a wild animal** on the way?

M: Yes, but I only saw a dead animal body.

W: No way. I think it's very dangerous to **let wild animals live** that way. They are always injured **by cars**.

M: I think the National Park authorities need to **make regulations** to protect them.

W: Like fencing or a trail for the wild animals.

M: Yes, we must not hurt them.

W: Oh! Here comes David! Hi, David!

여: 다 왔어? 내가 제일 마지막이야?

남: 아니, David가 아직 오는 중이야.

여: 세 시간이나 걸렸어. 오래 걸렸지. 어두워서 좀 무서운데다 동물을 칠 뻔했어.

남: 조심해야 해. 이 근처에 야생동물들이 있어.

여: 너도 오는 길에 야생동물이랑 마주쳤어?

남: 응, 그런데 난 시체를 봤을 뿐이야.

여: 이럴 수가. 야생동물을 그런 식으로 내버려 두는 건 위험한 것 같아. 항상 차들로부터 공격을 받잖아.

남: 내 생각엔 국립 공원 당국이 야생동물을 보호할 규제를 만들어야 해.

여: 울타리를 치거나 야생동물 길을 놓아주거나 하는 거 말이지.

남: 그래, 동물들을 해치면 안 되지.

여: 어! David가 저기 온다! 안녕, David!

해설: 남자는 야생동물을 보호할 규제를 만들어야 한다 (need to make regulations to protect them)고 자신의 의견의 요지를 언급하고 있다.

Listening Web

Intro: hit

Web 1: dead

Web 2: dangerous

Web 3: authorities

Ending: hurt

True / False

1. T   2. T   3. F   4. F

문항 4 ①

Script & Dictation

M: Eunice, did you hear the news?

W: What?

M: Steve **got accepted to** Blooming University. It doesn't **make sense**!

W: **Good for him**. What's the matter?

M: He didn't do well in school. I got **straight** A's last semester, but I failed to get accepted. And he's a Blooming student now.

W: Calm down. Steve is worth it. He has been **eager to make** his own portfolio. Do you remember that he was the leader of our summer camp last year? He was enthusiastically **involved in** a lot of activities.

M: You know **I've been honored** through all three years.

W: Brian, grades are not everything. Maybe Blooming University wants more active students, and Steve had an **excellent strategy**.

M: I cannot **accept** this situation.

W: You're a smart student, Brian. Some other good universities will want you to come.

남: Eunice, 소식 들었어?

여: 뭔데?

남: Steve가 Blooming 대학교에 입학 허가를 받았대. 말도 안 돼!

여: 잘 됐네. 뭐가 문제인데?

남: 그 애는 공부도 못했잖아. 난 지난 학기에 전 과목 A를 받았어. 그런데 난 떨어지고, 그 애는 이제 Blooming 학생이야.

여: 진정해. Steve는 그럴 만해. 그 애가 자기 포트폴리오 만드는데 얼마나 열정을 쏟았다고. 작년 우리 여름 캠프에 그 애가 리더였던 거 기억하지? 그 애는 많은 활동에 열정적으로 참여했어.

남: 너도 내가 3년 내내 우등상 받은 거 알잖아.

여: Brian, 성적이 전부는 아니야. 아마도 Blooming 대학교는 더 적극적인 학생을 원하나 보지. 그리고 Steve는 정말 전략을 잘 세웠던 거고.

남: 난 이 상황을 도저히 받아들일 수가 없어.

여: Brian, 넌 정말 똑똑한 학생이야. 다른 좋은 대학교들이 네가 와주길 원할 거야.

해설: 여자는 Steve가 다양한 활동에 적극 참여하며 자신의 포트폴리오를 만드는 전략을 통해 대학 입학에 성공한 것이라고 말하고 있다.

Listening Web

Web 1: accepted   Web 2: eager, involved in

Web 3: active   Ending: come

True / False

1. T   2. T   3. T   4. F

문항 5 ②

Script & Dictation

W: What time are we leaving tomorrow?

M: Five in the morning.

W: That's too early. I'm not sure I can get up so early.

M: The holiday season started yesterday, so I think there is **a lot of traffic.**

W: But it's hard for the kids to get up before five.

M: If we leave after seven, we'll be **stuck in traffic.**

W: But we need to have breakfast before leaving.

M: What about eating at a highway service area, or carrying a breakfast box?

W: I don't think we'll have **enough time to pack** a breakfast box tomorrow morning.

M: But if we don't leave at five, it'll take more than five hours. It'll make **all of us tired** way before we get there.

여: 우리 내일 몇 시에 출발할까?

남: 새벽 5시.

여: 너무 이른데. 내가 그렇게 일찍 일어날 수 있을지 모르겠어.

남: 어제 휴가철이 시작됐기 때문에, 차가 많을 거야.

여: 하지만 아이들은 5시 전에 일어나기 어려워.

남: 만약 우리가 7시 넘어서 출발하면 우린 교통체증으로 갇혀 버릴 거야.

여: 그래도 떠나기 전에 아침 식사는 해야지.

남: 고속도로 휴게소에서 먹거나 아침 도시락을 싸가는 건 어때?

여: 내일 아침에 도시락 쌀 시간도 없을 것 같아.

남: 하지만 5시에 출발하지 않으면 다섯 시간 이상 걸릴 거야. 그럼 도착하기 훨씬 전에 우리가 지쳐버릴걸.

해설: 남자는 휴가철에 길이 막힐 것을 염려하여 내일 아침 일찍 집을 나설 것을 주장하고 있다.

Listening Web

Intro: leaving   Web 1: season, traffic

Ending: don't

True / False

1. T   2. T   3. F   4. F

문항 6 ④

Script & Dictation

M: How much is the ticket to Springville?

W: There's no ticket to only Springville.

M: What do you mean?

W: **The board says** the ship goes to both Springville and Summerfield on Sunday. There's no ship that goes to only **one of them.**

M: But Summerfield wasn't on our itinerary.

W: But it's not bad to travel to both. It takes only two more hours and Summerfield is very **famous for** its beautiful buildings with orange roofs.

M: How much is the **ticket for** both of them?

W: $25. Transportation and admission **are included.**

M: Then we need to spend $50 for both of us. It's too expensive. I'm not **in the mood for** Summerfield.

W: We didn't plan to go to Summerfield this time, but I want to go there someday. I think this is the chance.

M: It's close to our town, and we can come again any time. Let's take **a rain check.**

W: Okay.

남: Springville 가는 표가 얼마지?

여: Springville만 가는 표는 없어.

남: 무슨 소리야?

여: 일요일에는 배가 Springville이랑 Summerfield 둘 다 간다고 게시판에 쓰여있어. 둘 중 한 곳만 가는 배는 없대.

남: 하지만 Summerfield는 우리 일정에 없던 거잖아.

여: 그렇지만 둘 다 가는 것도 나쁘지 않아. 세 시간밖에 더 안 걸리는데다가, 거긴 주황색 지붕의 예쁜 건물들로 아주 유명해.

남: 둘 다 가는 건 얼마인데?

여: 25달러. 교통비랑 입장료 포함이야.

남: 그럼 우리 둘이 합쳐서 50달러 내야 하잖아. 너무 비싸. 난 Summerfield에 별로 가고 싶지 않아.

여: 이번에 Summerfield에 갈 계획은 없었지만, 언젠가 가보고 싶어. 이번이 기회인 것 같아.

남: 우리 동네에서 가깝고, 우린 언제든지 또 올 수 있어. 다음 기회로 미루자.

여: 알았어.

해설: 지금은 Springville에만 갈 수 있는 표가 없다. 남자의 마지막 발언 Let's take a rain check. (다음 기회로 미루자.) 라는 말에서 여행을 미루고 있음을 알 수 있다.

Listening Web

Intro: ticket   Web 1: no

Web 2: wasn't   Ending: close

True / False

1. T   2. T   3. F   4. F

문항 7 ③

Script & Dictation

M: I'm feeling a little hungry, Mom. What about having some fried potatoes?

W: Do you **want me to fry** potatoes or to go buy fried potatoes?

M: Well, let's fry them at home. Your fried potatoes are more delicious.

W: But we don't have any potatoes. Will you go to the mart and buy some potatoes?

M: Then it'll take a lot of time. It'll take about 30 minutes to buy potatoes and about 15 more **minutes** to cook them.

W: Yes, maybe the fried potatoes would be ready **in about** 45 minutes.

M: Mom, I think it's better to buy fried potatoes at a fast food restaurant.

W: But we need milk and salad dressing. How about going to the mart and getting some milk and potatoes, and a salad dressing **you'd like**?

M: Mom, you want me to **run an errand**.

W: Brian, it's all for you anyway.

M: Okay, Mom.

남: 엄마, 출출해요. 감자튀김 먹는 게 어때요?

여: 감자를 튀겨 줄까, 감자튀김을 사줄까?

남: 음. 집에서 튀겨 먹어요. 엄마가 해주시는 감자튀김이 더 맛있어요.

여: 그런데 감자가 없단다. 네가 가게에 가서 감자 좀 사올래?

남: 그럼 시간이 오래 걸리잖아요. 감자 사오는데 한 30분 걸릴 거고, 요리하는데 한 15분 걸릴 거고.

여: 그렇지. 아마도 한 45분이면 감자튀김이 완성되겠지.

남: 엄마, 그냥 패스트푸드점에 가서 감자튀김을 사오는 게 낫겠어요.

여: 그런데 우유랑 샐러드 드레싱도 필요하단다. 시장 가서 우유, 감자와 네가 먹고 싶은 샐러드 드레싱을 사오는 게 어떻겠니?

남: 엄마, 저보고 심부름 다녀오라는 말씀이시죠.

여: Brian, 다 너를 위한 거잖니.

남: 알았어요, 엄마.

해설: 엄마는 아들에게 우유와 감자, 샐러드 드레싱을 사오라고 심부름을 시키고 있다.

Listening Web

Intro: fried   Web 1: fry

Web 2: potatoes   Web 3: getting

True / False

1. T   2. T   3. F   4. F

문항 8 ①

Script & Dictation

M: Wow! The view is really fantastic!

W: Yeah, this is the most beautiful scenery **I've ever seen**.

M: Now let's **move on to** the next destination.

W: Okay. Let's go down to the parking lot. Andy, Look! There are two paths to go down.

M: The sign says **this way is** for the parking lot.

W: Yes, but we came up that way.

M: I think we need to follow the sign to the mountain.

W: But we can **make a detour** around the mountain, or what if the parking lot isn't the very parking lot where we parked?

M: No way.

W: But if I'm right, we'll spend a lot on riding a taxi.

M: **It shouldn't be** the case! Don't worry. This way is tree-shaded and it looks much better. Follow me.

W: Oh, Andy, please.

남: 와! 경치 끝내준다!

여: 그래, 내가 지금까지 본 것 중에 제일 아름다운 경치인 것 같아.

남: 이제 다음 장소로 이동하자.

여: 좋아. 주차장으로 내려가자. Andy, 봐봐! 내려가는 길이 두 개야.

남: 이쪽이 주차장 방향이라고 되어 있어.

여: 그래, 그런데 우린 저 길로 올라왔어.

남: 내 생각에 우리는 산쪽으로 난 표지판을 따라가야 할 것 같아.

여: 그렇지만 산을 돌아가게 될 수도 있어. 아니면 주차장이 우리가 주차한 그곳이 아니면 어떡해?

남: 설마.

여: 하지만 내 말이 맞으면, 우린 택시비가 엄청나게 들 거야.

남: 그럴 일은 없어! 걱정 마. 이 길이 숲도 우거지고 더 좋아 보이는데. 따라와.

여: 아, Andy. 제발 좀.

해설: 여자는 "we came up through that way. (우린 저쪽으로 올라왔어.)" 라고 말함으로써 왔던 길로 내려갈 것을 권하고 있다.

Listening Web

Intro: on   Web 1: paths

Web 2: we came up   Web 3: detour, around

Ending: on

True / False

1. T   2. T   3. T   4. F

문항 9 ③

Script & Dictation

M: The soap opera you like has just started. Come on!

W: No. See any other program you'd like to see.

M: Why? Isn't it interesting anymore?

W: No.

M: What happened?

W: Once the soap operas become popular, they're **always extended**.

M: Because people keep asking for extensions on the website.

W: I know. But it's not right. It almost got close **to the ending**, but it seemed to **develop another topic**. Now it's a quite different story.

M: It happens **all the time**. Do you know that Charles Dickens' "Great Expectations" has **two different endings**?

W: No, I didn't know that.

M: The novel was so popular and people back then asked for a happy ending. So the author **couldn't help accepting** it. And he wrote the original ending and also a more **reader-friendly version**.

W: That's interesting. But that extended soap opera isn't interesting.

남: 너 좋아하는 드라마 시작했어. 빨리 와!

여: 아니야. 너 보고 싶은 거 봐.

남: 왜? 이제 재미없어?

여: 응.

남: 무슨 일이야?

여: 드라마들은 인기 많아지면 꼭 연장하더라.

남: 사람들이 웹사이트에 연장해달라고 요청하니까 그렇지.

여: 맞아. 하지만 그건 옳지 않아. 결론에 다 왔는데, 또 다른 주제가 시작되는 느낌이야. 이제 아주 다른 이야기가 되어버렸어.

남: 그런 일은 항상 있는 일이야. 찰스 디킨스의 '위대한 유산'이 결말이 두 개인 것 알아?

여: 아니, 몰랐어.

남: 그 소설이 인기가 많아서 그 당시에 사람들이 행복한 결말로 해달라고 요청했었어. 그래서 작가가 어쩔 수 없이 받아들였지. 그리고 원래 결말과 독자들이 더 원하는 결말 버전을 쓴 거야.

여: 재미있구나. 하지만 연장된 저 드라마는 재미없어.

해설: 여자는 드라마가 인기에 힘입어 결말을 연장하는 것에 반대하고 있다.

Listening Web

Intro: has   Web 1: extended

Web 2: for

True / False

1. F   2. F   3. T   4. F

문항 10 ③

Script & Dictation

W: How is the steak?

M: Very delicious. Is it different from **what we used to** eat?

W: Yes, it's 'freedom food.'

M: 'Freedom food'? What is that?

W: A lot of animals are **unethically raised**. For example, calves are **locked up** in a small box and can't move.

M: Why is that?

W: Because a lack of **physical activity** makes tender meat.

M: The farmers take the freedom away from the animals to make money.

W: That's right.

M: So 'freedom food' means that this food is from animals **raised on** a large farm.

W: Exactly. I think we need to consume this kind of food and encourage the ethical farmers.

M: Wow. You're like an **animal rights activist**.

여: 스테이크 어때?

남: 아주 맛있어. 우리가 먹던 거랑 다른 거야?

여: 응, 이건 프리덤 푸드야.

남: 프리덤 푸드? 그게 뭔데?

여: 많은 동물들이 비윤리적으로 키워져. 예를 들면 송아지가 움직이지 못하게 작은 상자에 가둬.

남: 왜 그러는데?

여: 왜냐하면 운동량이 적어야 부드러운 고기가 부드러워지거든.

남: 농부들이 돈을 벌기 위해서 동물들이 자유를 빼앗아 간다는 것이구나.

여: 맞아.

남: 그러니까 프리덤 푸드라는 것은 넓은 목장에서 기른 동물로부터 나온 음식이라는 것이고.

여: 바로 그거야. 우리가 이런 식품들을 소비해서 윤리적인 농부들에게 힘을 실어주어야 해.

남: 와. 너 동물 보호 운동가 같아.

해설: 여자가 프리덤 푸드의 윤리성을 강조하고 있는 것으로 보아, 동물들이 자유로운 환경에서 길러져야 함을 주장하고 있다는 것을 알 수 있다.

Listening Web

Web 1: unethically   Web 2: farm

Ending: consume

True / False

1. T   2. F   3. F   4. F

Unit 03 유형 3 - 주제 및 목적 찾기

문항 1 ④

Script & Dictation

W: Good evening, visitors. This is Green Park's main office. We hope you're enjoying summer with your family or friends at Green Park. Our staff is always doing its best for you to have a great time at Green Park. Also we're always ready to help you **with any inconveniences** and to listen to your opinion. According to the Nature Protection Regulations, we cannot **light up** the lamps at night in the park. So please **strike your tents** before 9 p.m. for your safety. We are temporarily allowing you to **set up tents** or awnings during the daytime since there are few trees and little shade. But if you **leave your tent up** in the dark, it can stand in others' way. Thank you **in advance** for your cooperation.

여: 방문객 여러분, 안녕하십니까. Green Park 사무실에서 알려드립니다. 가족, 친구들과 Green Park에서 즐거운 여름을 보내고 계시기를 바랍니다. 저희 직원들은 언제나 여러분의 즐거운 휴식을 위해 최선을 다하고 있습니다. 또한 불편한 사항에 대해 언제나 여러분들을 도와드릴 준비가 되어 있으며, 여러분들의 의견을 들을 준비가 되어 있습니다. 자연보호 규정에 따라 야간에는 공원 내에 불을 밝힐 수가 없습니다. 따라서 여러분의 안전을 위해 밤 9시 이전까지 모두 텐트를 철수해 주시기 바랍니다. 공원 내 나무가 거의 없고 그늘이 많지 않아 낮 시간 동안에는 일시적으로 텐트와 차양 설치를 허용하였습니다. 하지만 어둠 속에 텐트를 그대로 두면, 다른 사람들의 보행에 방해가 될 수 있습니다. 협조해 주셔서 감사합니다.

해설: 낮에는 한시적으로 텐트 사용을 허가하나, 밤 9시 이후에는 텐트를 걷어야 함을 알리고 있다.

Listening Web

Web 1: safety   Web 2: few, little

Web 3: in others'   Ending: cooperation

True / False

1. F   2. T   3. T   4. F

문항 2 ①

Script & Dictation

M: Good afternoon. I'm Jacob Smith, a 3rd grader. First of all, I'd like to thank Hankuk High School Broadcast Studio for giving me this opportunity to give a guest announcement. I have only three minutes, so I'll just **get to the point**. Now it's summer, and it's so **hot and humid**. But there is only one air conditioner for over 30 students in a classroom. Unfortunately it is not **beneficial** to everybody. Some of the students sitting at the corner never enjoy air conditioning all day long. Furthermore, we cannot **control the temperature**. However, I heard the demand for electricity soars during daytime these days because of this awfully hot weather. So the electricity supply cannot **meet the demand**. So I'll not say we need more air conditioning. I just want our summer uniforms to be short pants. I think it is the best way to save electricity.

남: 안녕하세요. 저는 3학년 Jacob Smith 입니다. 우선, 저에게 초대 연설의 기회를 준 한국고등학교 방송부에 감사의 인사를 전하고 싶습니다. 저에게 3분 밖에 허락되어 있지 않으므로, 바로 본론으로 들어가도록 하겠습니다. 이제 여름이고, 너무나 덥고 습합니다. 하지만 30명이 넘는 학생들이 있는 교실에는 에어컨이 오직 한 대 뿐입니다. 애석하게도 에어컨은 모두에게 혜택이 가지 않습니다. 코너에 앉은 몇몇 학생들은 하루 종일 에어컨 바람을 쐬지 못합니다. 더욱이 우리가 온도를 조절할 수도 없습니다. 하지만 요즘 몹시 더운 날씨 때문에 낮 동안 전기 수요가 급증한디고 합니다. 그래서 전기 공급이 수요를 맞추지 못한다고 하더군요. 따라서 저는 에어컨을 더 틀어달라고는 말씀 드리지 않겠습니다. 다만 여름 교복이 반바지이기를 바랍니다. 이것이 전기를 절약하는 가장 좋은 방법이라고 생각합니다.

해설: 날씨가 덥지만 전기를 절약해야 하는 상황이므로, 교복을 반바지로 입게 해줄 것을 건의하고 있다.

Listening Web

Web 1: conditioner   Web 2: demand

Web 3: short   Ending: electricity

True / False

1. F   2. F   3. F   4. T

문항 3 ①

Script & Dictation

W: The best choice for your trip! Summerfield Hotel will be open next month. It will be the symbol of a cozy and relaxing atmosphere. **Located at the center** of downtown, it is complete with guest rooms, authentic Chinese and Japanese restaurants, and a fitness center. All the guests can enjoy **free Internet access** with Wi-Fi in the rooms. They are fully **equipped with** individual air-conditioning and heating system controls, and 100 channels with English, Japanese, and Chinese. Summerfield Hotel **invites you to** its Grand Opening Banquet on September 1st. Please come and see our beautiful interior and modern amenities, and have a wonderful night with a lot of celebrities. Everybody who will join our banquet will be given a 50% discount coupon for a poolside BBQ **valid until** the end of this year.

여: 당신의 여행을 위한 최고의 선택! Summerfield 호텔이 다음 달에 문을 엽니다. 호텔은 아늑하고 편안한 분위기의 대명사가 될 것입니다. 시내 중심부에 위치한 호텔은 객실, 정통 중식당과 일식당, 휘트니스 센터까지 완비되어 있습니다. 모든 투숙객들은 객실 내에서 와이파이로 무료 인터넷을 사용할 수 있습니다. 모든 객실에는 냉난방 시설이 되어 있으며, 영어, 중국어, 일본어가 나오는 100개의 TV 채널을 이용할 수 있습니다. Summerfield 호텔은 9월 1일 오프닝 연회에 여러분을 초대합니다. 꼭 오셔서 아름다운 인테리어와 현대적 감각의 편의시설을 돌아보시고, 많은 유명인사들과 멋진 밤을 보내시길 바랍니다. 저희 연회에 오시는 모든 분께 올해 말까지 사용 가능한 풀사이드 바비큐 50% 할인 쿠폰을 드립니다.

해설: 현대적 시설을 갖춘 호텔의 오프닝 연회에 초대하기 위한 글이다.

Listening Web

Intro: open	Web 1: relaxing
Web 3: modern	Ending: join

True / False

1. T	2. F	3. T	4. F

문항 4 ③

Script & Dictation

M: Waste is a big problem for our planet. We have to find places to put all the waste **we throw away**, and we are running out of space. Besides, every time we throw something away, we waste precious materials. We need to find ways to throw less waste away. There are three ways to do this. These are known as the three Rs. The first R is **for reduce**, which means cutting down on the things we buy so that we have to throw less away. The second R is **for reuse**, which means using old things again **instead of** throwing them away. The third R is **for recycle**, which means making new things **out of old**. Things should only be thrown away when we cannot reuse or recycle them.

남: 쓰레기는 지구의 큰 문제 거리입니다. 우리는 우리가 버리는 쓰레기를 모아 놓을 장소를 찾아야 하고, 공간을 낭비하게 됩니다. 뿐만 아니라 우리가 물건을 버릴 때마다 소중한 자원을 낭비하게 됩니다. 우리는 쓰레기를 적게 버릴 방법을 찾아야 합니다. 이를 실천하기 위한 세 가지 방법이 있습니다. 그것은 세 가지 R이라고 알려져 있는 것들입니다. 첫 번째 R은 reduce (줄이다)의 R인데, 이는 버리는 양이 적어지도록 적게 사는 것을 의미합니다. 두 번째 R은 reuse (재사용하다)의 R인데, 이는 물건을 버리지 말고 이미 사용한 물건을 다시 사용하는 것을 말합니다. 세 번째 R은 recycle (재활용하다)의 R인데, 이는 오래된 물건으로부터 새 물건을 만들어내는 것을 의미합니다. 물건은 재사용하거나 재활용할 수 없을 때만 버리도록 해야 하겠습니다.

해설: 쓰레기를 줄일 수 있는 방법을 세 가지 R을 예로 들어 설명하고 있다.

Listening Web

Intro: planet	Web 1: known
Web 2: cutting	Web 3: old

True / False

1. F	2. T	3. F	4. T

문항 5 ②

Script & Dictation

W: There is a saying that too much is **as bad as** too little. As with all other things, Aldous Huxley said, reading is not always good. That is, if you are **indulged in** reading to excess, it can be a vice. Reading is not usually **thought to be** a vice, so excessive reading can be more dangerous because you don't recognize that it's dangerous. One of the main objectives of reading, generally, is to have an **ability to observe** yourself and other people candidly. Therefore, to anyone who is already able to do so, excessive reading is only a waste of time and energy. Sometimes it can **distract their attention** from reality.

여: 지나친 것은 부족한 것만 못하다는 말이 있습니다. Aldous Huxley에 따르면, 모든 것이 그러하듯이 독서도 언제나 좋은 것만은 아니라고 합니다. 즉 만약 여러분이 독서에 지나치게 탐닉한다면, 그것은 해악이 될 수도 있습니다. 독서는 일반적으로 악한 것으로 간주되지 않아서, 여러분이 위험을 감지하지 못하기 때문에 더욱 위험해 질 수 있다는 것입니다. 일반적으로 독서를 하는 가장 중요한 목적 중의 하나는 스스로와 타인을 있는 그대로 바라보는 능력을 갖기 위한 것입니다. 따라서 이미 그러한 능력을 갖고 있는 사람에게 지나친 독서는 시간과 에너지의 낭비일 뿐입니다. 때로는 그들의 주의를 현실로부터 벗어나게 하기도 합니다.

해설: 독서를 통해 얻을 수 있는 능력을 이미 갖춘 사람들에게 독서는 시간과 에너지 낭비일 뿐이라고 말하고 있다.

Listening Web

Web 1: indulged in	Web 2: objectives
Web 3: excessive	Ending: distract, attention

True / False

1. F	2. T	3. T	4. F

문항 6 ④

Script & Dictation

M: Many living things on the earth are disappearing now. Endangered species are in serious trouble. Think about this situation. People **keep taking up** more and more areas of the earth. Then the wildlife **that already lived there** has no place to live, and they have to move to find another place to live. But **what if** people keep building their houses along the beach? The animals living on the shore cannot move inland, so finally they may **become extinct**. Every species plays a **special role** in the ecosystem. For example, plants usually provide food for animals. If they become extinct, it may **cause the loss** of the whole ecosystem. That's why scientists and governments get involved with protecting endangered species.

남: 지구상의 많은 생물들이 사라지고 있습니다. 멸종 위기의 종은 심각한 위기에 처해있습니다. 이 상황을 생각해 보십시오. 사람들은 지구 상에서 점점 더 많은 영역을 차지해가고 있습니다. 그러면 이미 그 곳에 살고 있던 야생 생물들은 살 곳을 잃게 되어, 다른 서식지를 찾아 떠나야 합니다. 하지만 만약 사람들이 계속해서 해안에 집을 짓는다면 어떻게 되겠습니까? 해변에 살고 있던 동물들은 내륙에서 살 수 없으므로, 결국 멸종하게 되는 것입니다. 모든 종은 생태계 안에서 특별한 역할을 수행합니다. 예를 들어 식물은 주로 동물들의 먹이가 됩니다. 만약 식물이 멸종하게 된다면, 그것은 생태계 전반에 걸친 손실을 야기할지도 모릅니다. 그렇기 때문에 과학자들과 정부가 멸종 위기의 종을 보호하는데 주력하는 것입니다.

해설: 멸종 위기의 동식물을 보호해야 하는 이유를 설명하기 위해, 멸종의 원인과 그 영향에 대해 언급하고 있다.

Listening Web

Intro: Endangered   Web 1: place
Web 2: move inland   Web 3: whole
Ending: involved

True / False

1. F   2. F   3. F   4. T

문항 7 ③

Script & Dictation

W: Very often, you may think your dog understands you, and scientists say it's true. Moreover, new research shows that dogs can learn new words **the same way** children do. Scientists used to believe only humans learn and this makes us different from other animals, but now it is proved **to be false**. It was thought that gorillas, chimpanzees, and other primates can't speak. However, a researcher in the U.S. taught American Sign Language to a baby gorilla, and finally she was able to **communicate with her hands**. Surprisingly, she could use **more than** 1,000 signs. Animals can learn languages. In other words, they have the same **ability in learning** languages. The only difference is its degree.

여: 당신은 매우 자주 당신의 개가 당신의 말을 이해한다고 생각할 것입니다. 과학자들은 그것이 사실이라고 합니다. 심지어 새로운 연구 결과에 따르면 개는 아이들이 말을 배우는 것과 같은 방식으로 언어를 배울 수 있다고 합니다. 과거에 과학자들은 오직 인간만이 배울 수 있고, 이것이 동물과의 차이점이라고 믿어왔습니다. 하지만 이것은 사실이 아닌 것으로 밝혀졌습니다. 고릴라, 침팬지, 다른 영장류는 말을 할 수 없다고 여겨졌습니다. 하지만 미국의 한 과학자는 새끼 고릴라에게 수화를 가르쳤고, 마침내 고릴라는 손으로 의사소통을 할 수 있게 되었습니다. 놀랍게도 그 고릴라는 1,000개 이상의 수화를 사용할 수 있었습니다. 동물들도 언어를 배울 수 있는 것입니다. 다시 말해 이들도 언어 학습에 대하여 (사람과) 같은 능력을 갖고 있는 것입니다. 단지 정도의 차이가 있을 뿐입니다.

해설: 언어 학습은 인간의 고유한 영역으로 여겨져 왔으나, 과학적 연구를 통해 동물도 언어를 습득할 수 있는 것으로 밝혀졌다는 것에 대해 말하고 있다.

Listening Web

Web 1: research   Web 2: thought
Web 3: taught

True / False

1. F   2. T   3. T   4. F

문항 8 ③

Script & Dictation

M: Advertising today is an over $100 billion a year industry and affects all of us throughout our lives. The average adult will spend **one and a half** years of their life watching TV commercials. But the ads sell more than products. They sell values, images, concept of success, and so on. And usually adolescents are the prime target. However, adolescents are particularly **vulnerable to ads** because they are new and inexperienced consumers. They are in the **process of learning** their values and developing their self-concepts. Most teenagers are sensitive to **peer pressure** and find it difficult to resist or even question the dominant cultural message communicated by the ads.

남: 오늘날 광고는 1년에 1조 달러가 넘는 산업이며, 우리의 삶 전반에 영향을 미치고 있습니다. 보통 성인이라면 일생 동안 1년 반을 TV 광고를 보는데 소비하게 될 것입니다. 하지만 광고는 물건만을 파는 게 아닙니다. 광고는 가치와 이미지, 성공의 개념도 전달합니다. 그리고 청소년들이 보통 그 주 타겟층이 됩니다. 그러나 청소년은 경험이 없는 신규 소비자들이기 때문에 광고에 특히 취약합니다. 그들은 가치를 배우는 과정에 있으며 자아개념을 확립해가고 있는 중입니다. 대부분의 십대들은 또래들로부터 받는 압박에 예민하게 반응하고(또래들과 똑같이 생각하고 행동해야 한다는 압박이 있고), 광고로부터 형성되는 지배적인 문화적 메시지에 저항하거나 의문을 제시하기는 힘든 것입니다

해설: 청소년들은 광고가 전하는 메시지에 대해 주체적으로 판단하기 힘들다는 점을 말하고 있다.

Listening Web

Intro: lives   Web 2: target
Web 3: inexperienced   Ending: sensitive, resist

True / False

1. T   2. T   3. T   4. F

문항 9 ③

Script & Dictation

M: Mom, look at the dog. He's really cute. I want to go to **pat him**.

W: No. It's a seeing eye dog.

M: Seeing eye dog?

W: Yes, it's for blind people. The dog is **trained to help** the owner. It guides the owner on the street. If you touch the dog, it'll **bother the dog**.

M: I see. Look! The dog stopped its owner in front of the crosswalk.

W: Of course. And some dogs let the owner know when the telephone or doorbell rings. They are **for the deaf**.

M: Sometimes dogs are like family.

W: Yes. Many **disabled** people **depend on** their pets to improve the **quality of their lives**. Some monkeys help people who cannot move **by themselves**. They are very helpful.

남: 엄마, 저 개 좀 보세요. 귀엽게 생겼어요. 가서 쓰다듬어 주고 싶어요.

여: 안 돼. 그건 맹인 안내견이야.

남: 맹인 안내견이요?

여: 그래, 시각 장애인을 위한 개란다. 그런 개는 주인을 도와주도록 훈련되어 있어. 길에서 주인을 안내해준다. 네가 만약 그 개를 만지면, 그건 그 개를 방해하는 거야.

남: 알겠어요. 보세요! 개가 횡단보도 앞에서 주인을 세웠어요.

여: 그래. 어떤 개들은 전화벨이 울리거나 초인종이 울리는 것을 주인에게 알려주기도 해. 청각장애인들을 위한 개들이지.

남: 개가 가족 같은 때가 있군요.

여: 그래. 많은 장애인들이 삶의 질을 향상시키기 위해 애완동물에 의지한단다. 어떤 원숭이들은 혼자 움직일 수 없는 사람들을 돕기도 하지. 원숭이들이 큰 도움이 된단다.

해설: 두 사람은 시각, 청각 장애인을 돕는 개와 몸을 움직이지 못하는 장애인을 돕는 원숭이에 대해 이야기 하고 있다.

Listening Web

Web 1: trained   Web 2: deaf
Web 3: quality

True / False

1. F   2. T   3. F   4. F

문항 10 ②

Script & Dictation

M: You look so tired. What **made you exhausted**?

W: I'm thinking about quitting my job. My boss always irritates me.

M: Come on. It is a job. What do you expect?

W: He sends me on his **personal errands**. Today I went to the library to return his books.

M: My boss has had me pick up his son at school.

W: What? So you did it?

M: In addition, he always gives me a lot of work at once and then asks me if it's finished at **hourly intervals**.

W: Oh, he must make you crazy. Why aren't all bosses considerate?

M: They **might have been** considerate when they were clerks. They just forgot as time went on.

W: Nothing is easy. These days I wonder how my parents **have endured** their burdens **for decades**.

남: 너 피곤해 보인다. 뭐 땜에 그렇게 지치니?

여: 직장을 그만 둘까 생각 중이야. 상사가 날 너무 힘들게 해.

남: 진정해. 그게 직장이야. 뭘 기대해?

여: 상사가 개인적인 심부름을 시켜. 오늘은 도서관에 상사의 책을 반납하러 갔다니까.

남: 우리 직장 상사는 학교에서 자기 아들 데려오라고 시키기도 했어.

여: 뭐? 그래서 너 했어?

남: 뿐만 아니라 항상 일을 한꺼번에 많이 주고 한 시간 간격으로 다 했는지 물어봐.

여: 아, 상사가 널 정말 힘들게 했구나. 상사들은 다들 왜 배려심이 없을까?

남: 사원 때는 배려 깊은 사람들이었을 거야. 시간이 가면서 잊어버린 거지.

여: 쉬운 게 없어. 요즘에는 우리 부모님들은 어떻게 수십 년간 이 부담을 견뎌오셨는지 신기해.

해설: 남자와 여자는 각자가 직장 상사 때문에 겪는 괴로움에 대해 이야기 하고 있다.

Listening Web

Intro: quitting   Web 2: hourly

Web 3: considerate   Ending: endured

True / False

1. T   2. F   3. F   4. F

Unit 04 유형 4 - 장소·관계 추론하기

문항 1 ②

Script & Dictation

W: I'd like to **pick up** my pants.

M: What's your name?

W: Jessica Adams.

M: Here you are.

W: Oh, these haven't been ironed well, and the stain here didn't come out.

M: Let me see. I'm sorry. I tried to **get this stain out**, but I couldn't.

W: Could you try to remove the stain **once again**?

M: Okay, I will.

W: Can I buy a strong detergent here? There is a lot of oil paint on my clothes because I study oil painting.

M: Sorry, we don't sell any detergents. There is a big market **just around the corner**. You may find what you want there.

W: I see. Thanks. When will my pants be ready? Can I pick them up tomorrow?

M: We're very busy these days, so why don't you call me **the day after tomorrow**?

W: I will. Thank you.

여: 바지를 찾고 싶어요.

남: 성함이 어떻게 되시죠?

여: Jessica Adams입니다.

남: 여기 있습니다.

여: 아, 다림질이 제대로 되지 않았네요. 여기 얼룩도 빠지지 않았어요.

남: 어디 봅시다. 죄송합니다. 이 얼룩은 빼려고 노력했지만, 그러지 못했어요.

여: 얼룩을 다시 한 번 제거해 봐주실 수 있나요?

남: 그러지요.

여: 여기에서 강력 세제를 살 수 있나요? 제가 유화를 공부하고 있어서 옷에 유화 물감이 많이 묻어서요.

남: 죄송하지만, 저희는 세제를 판매하지 않습니다. 모퉁이만 돌아가시면 큰 시장이 있습니다. 거기에서 원하시는 물건을 찾을 수 있으실 거예요.

여: 알겠습니다. 고맙습니다. 바지는 언제 찾아갈 수 있을까요? 내일 찾아갈 수 있을까요?

남: 저희가 요즘 매우 바빠서 그러는데 모레 저희에게 전화 주시 겠습니까?

여: 그렇게 할게요. 감사합니다.

해설: 여자는 다림질과 얼룩 제거를 요청하고 있다. 따라서 대화가 이루어 지는 장소는 세탁소이다.

Listening Web

Web 1: haven't, ironed   Web 2: market

Web 3: When

True / False

1. T   2. F   3. F   4. F

문항 2 ③

Script & Dictation

M: Now we are at our last destination in Canada. What would you like to buy?

W: Anything to **remind me of** this trip.

M: What about maple syrup? It was so delicious and you liked it.

W: That's good, but we can get it in Korea, too. I want something unique, and something authentically Canadian.

M: Yes, that's why you should buy maple syrup. This is **made in** Canada, and **sells in** Canada, and you buy it in Canada. And above all, it is the symbol of Canada.

W: You mean you want to buy it?

M: You're **reading my mind**.

W: Then let's buy some maple syrup for you. And I'd like these fridge magnets.

M: That's good, too. They're quite practical.

W: Yes, and they have beautiful pictures of **tourist spots** in Canada. I'll be able to think of Canada whenever I see them.

남: 이제 캐나다에서의 마지막 행선지에 왔어. 넌 뭐 살 거야?

여: 이번 여행을 기억할 수 있는 거 아무거나.

남: 메이플 시럽 어때? 무척 맛있었던 데다 너도 좋아했잖아.

여: 좋아, 하지만 그건 한국에서도 구할 수 있어. 난 뭔가 특별하고 진정으로 캐나다다운 것을 원해.

남: 그래, 그러니까 메이플 시럽을 사야 하는 거야. 캐나다에서 만들어져서, 캐나다에서 팔리고, 넌 캐나다에서 그걸 사는 거지. 무엇보다 그게 캐나다의 상징이야.

여: 그러니까 넌 그것을 사고 싶다는 말이지?

남: 내 마음을 읽고 있구나.

여: 정 그러면 메이플 시럽을 사자. 그리고 나는 이 냉장고에 붙이는 자석이 좋겠어.

남: 그것도 멋져. 무척 실용적이겠는데.

여: 응, 그리고 이건 캐나다 관광지의 아름다운 사진들이 있어. 이걸 볼 때마다 캐나다를 떠올릴 수 있을 거야.

해설: 두 사람은 캐나다 여행을 기억할 수 있는 물건을 고르고 있으므로, 대화가 이루어지는 장소는 기념품 가게이다.

Listening Web

Intro: last	Web 1: trip
Web 2: unique, authentically	Web 3: fridge
Ending: whenever	

True / False

1. T   2. F   3. F   4. T

문항 3 ⑤

Script & Dictation

M: Don't run! It's dangerous.

W: But it's really spacious.

M: The floor is slippery, and there are many people. Watch out all the time **not to bump Intro** others.

W: Don't worry, Dad. I'll be careful.

M: Good.

W: How long is the lane?

M: It's 50 meters. It's for the Olympics, so it's even longer than the other pools that **you've been to**.

W: I see. Where are the kickboards?

M: Over there. Oh, it's too small.

W: That's for kids. I think this one **will fit me**.

M: Good. Now we need to **warm up** first. Remember that it's very cold in there and it can be dangerous if you just go in without exercise.

W: Dad, I know. I'm not a baby. It's getting chilly. We need to exercise right away.

M: Okay, don't forget to **put on the cap** in your hand. Now let's go! Practice makes perfect! Just follow the line. Come on.

남: 뛰지마! 위험해.

여: 그런데 정말 넓어요.

남: 바닥이 미끄럽고 사람들이 많잖니. 다른 사람들과 부딪히지 않도록 항상 주의해라.

여: 걱정하지 마세요, 아빠. 조심할게요.

남: 좋아.

여: 레인이 얼마나 길죠?

남: 50미터야. 올림픽 경기용이라 네가 가 봤던 다른 수영장보다 더 길어.

여: 그렇군요. 킥보드가 어디에 있죠?

남: 저기에 있구나. 오, 이건 너무 작은걸.

여: 그건 아동용이잖아요. 이게 맞을 것 같아요.

남: 그렇구나. 이제 준비운동을 먼저 하자. 저 안은 매우 차가운 데다 운동하지 않고 들어가면 위험할 수 있다는 걸 명심해라.

여: 아빠, 저 알아요. 전 아기가 아니에요. 추워져요. 당장 운동을 해야겠어요.

남: 그래, 손에 든 수영모자 쓰는 거 잊지 마라. 이제 가 보자! 계속 연습하면 잘하게 돼! 선만 따라가라. 자, 해 봐.

해설: 레인과 킥보드가 언급된 것으로 보아 대화가 이루어지는 장소가 수영장임을 알 수 있다.

Listening Web

Intro: lane	Web 2: pools
Web 3: kickboards	Ending: cap

True / False

1. T   2. T   3. F   4. F

문항 4 ⑤

Script & Dictation

W: Hello, I have an appointment at 3.

M: Oh, you're Ms. Green! Right this way and have a seat, please. What would you like? Do you have anything **special in mind**?

W: Well, I'd like to change my hair style. What style do you think **is the best** for me?

M: It's always a difficult question. These pictures will help you to **make a decision**. It seems you have an important promise.

W: Not really. I'll have **my picture taken** today.

M: How about the style on this model?

W: She looks very elegant. How much will it cost?

M: It costs $50 because your hair is long. But it **coordinates with** your dress now.

W: That's reasonable, I think. How long will it take?

M: About **two and a half** hours. Would you like to have some tea?

W: Yes, please. I'd like to have some hot tea. Thank you.

여: 안녕하세요. 3시에 예약했는데요.

남: 아, Green양이시죠! 이 쪽으로 와서 앉으세요. 어떻게 해드릴까요? 특별히 생각하고 계신 게 있나요?

여: 음, 머리 스타일을 바꾸고 싶어요. 어떤 스타일이 저에게 가장 좋을 것 같나요?

남: 그건 항상 어려운 질문이죠. 이 사진들 보시면 결정하는데 도움이 되실 겁니다. 중요한 일이 있으신가 봐요.

여: 그런 건 아니고요. 오늘 사진 찍을 거라서요.

남: 이 모델 스타일 어떠세요?

여: 세련되어 보이네요. 얼마죠?

남: 손님은 머리 길이가 길어서 50달러입니다. 하지만 지금 입고 계신 옷과 잘 어울려요.

여: 가격은 괜찮은데요. 얼마나 걸리죠?

남: 두 시간 반 정도 걸립니다. 차 좀 드릴까요?

여: 네. 따뜻한 차로 주세요. 감사합니다.

해설: 여자는 머리 스타일을 바꾸러 왔으므로 대화가 이루어지는 장소는 미용실이다.

Listening Web

Intro: an   Web 1: change

Web 2: model   Web 3: 50

Ending: coordinates

True / False

1. F   2. F   3. T   4. F

문항 5 ①

Script & Dictation

M: Excuse me, I didn't understand the announcement. Why **haven't we left yet**?

W: Another plane for Europe has just departed, so we need to **keep some distance** from it.

M: When are we going to take off?

W: In 50 minutes.

M: But I'll transfer at Prague for a flight to Rome. What if we're **behind schedule**?

W: We'll be in Prague in time. Don't worry. Would you like some snacks or drinks?

M: What kind of tea do you have?

W: We have green tea and black tea. We can **offer an iced one** if you want.

M: I'd like hot green tea, please.

W: And what else do you need?

M: Can I get a blanket? It's **kind of chilly**.

W: Of course. I'll bring them right away.

M: Thank you very much.

남: 죄송하지만, 방송을 못 들었습니다. 왜 아직 출발하지 않는 건가요?

여: 유럽 행의 다른 비행기가 방금 출발해서 그 비행기와 거리를 유지해야 되어서요.

남: 우리는 언제 떠나죠?

여: 50분 후에요.

남: 그런데 전 프라하에서 로마로 가는 비행기로 환승해야 합니다. 일정이 늦어지면 어떻게 하나요?

여: 저희는 프라하에 제시간에 도착할 거예요. 걱정하지 마세요. 스낵이나 마실 것 좀 드릴까요?

남: 어떤 종류의 차가 있죠?

여: 녹차와 홍차가 있습니다. 원하시면 얼음을 넣어드릴 수도 있습니다.

남: 따뜻한 녹차 부탁합니다.

여: 다른 건 필요한 거 없으세요?

남: 담요 한 장 얻을 수 있을까요? 쌀쌀하네요.

여: 물론이죠. 바로 가져다 드리겠습니다.

남: 감사합니다.

해설: 남자는 기내 안내방송을 듣지 못해 여자에게 안내방송의 내용을 묻고 있다. 따라서 대화가 이루어지는 곳은 비행기 안이다.

Listening Web

Web 1: plane, distance   Web 2: off

Web 3: flight   Ending: in

True / False

1. T   2. F   3. T   4. T

문항 6 ②

Script & Dictation

M: How many bedrooms do you want in your house?

W: Three. And I **want there to be** two bathrooms. One on the 1st floor, and the other on the 2nd floor.

M: Oh, you're thinking of **a two-story house**.

W: Yes. I want the living room and the kitchen to be **divided by an aisle**.

M: Look at these pictures. Which house would you like the most?

W: I like this one. I like this garden.

M: Do you want a garden to be on the list?

W: Yes. I want **there to be** a very big window around here, so I can see the garden while sitting in the living room.

M: Anything else? An attic or...

W: No. I just want the walls to be white and the roof to be blue.

M: Okay. **I'll have finished** the blueprint by next Friday, and we'll discuss more details then.

W: Thanks a lot.

남: 집에는 방이 몇 개이길 원하십니까?

여: 세 개요. 그리고 화장실은 두 개를 원해요. 하나는 1층에, 다른 하나는 2층에요.

남: 아, 2층짜리 집을 생각하시는군요.

여: 네. 거실과 부엌은 복도로 나뉘어져 있으면 좋겠어요.

남: 이 사진들을 보세요. 어느 집이 가장 마음에 드세요?

여: 이게 좋아요. 이 정원이 좋은데요.

남: 정원도 목록에 올릴까요?

여: 네. 여기쯤에 커다란 창문이 있으면 좋겠어요. 거실에 앉아서 정원을 내다 볼 수 있게요.

남: 다른 것은요? 다락이나…

여: 아니요. 그냥 벽은 흰색, 지붕은 파란색이면 좋겠네요.

남: 알겠습니다. 설계도를 다음주 금요일까지 완성할게요. 그리고 그 때 세부 사항에 대해 더 논의해 보도록 하지요.

여: 감사합니다.

해설: 여자는 건축가인 남자에게 자신의 원하는 집의 구성에 대해 이야기 하고 있다.

Listening Web

Intro: bedrooms　　　　　　　Web 1: story

Web 2: these pictures　　　　Ending: discuss, details

True / False

1. F　　　　　2. F　　　　　3. T　　　　　4. T

문항 7 ②

Script & Dictation

M: May I help you?

W: Yes, I'd like to remit some money to a travel agency in Australia.

M: First you'll have to **fill out this form**. Could I have your name and phone number, please?

W: Jennifer Lauren. And here's my phone number.

M: If you **have an account**, you can save the remittance charge.

W: How much is the remittance charge?

M: **It depends**. How much would you like to remit?

W: $500.

M: It's 30,000 won.

W: I have an account **with your bank** in Australia. I've just moved to Seoul…

M: Then, I don't think you need another account. I can arrange it for you. Please **be sure** that your phone number is correct on this form. It **keeps flashing** an error message.

W: Oh, this is a four, not a nine.

M: Thank you very much. Please be seated here for a second.

남: 무엇을 도와드릴까요?

여: 네, 호주에 있는 여행사에 송금하려고 합니다.

남: 우선 이 서류를 작성해 주십시오. 성함과 전화번호가 어떻게 되시나요?

여: Jennifer Lauren 입니다. 여기 전화번호 드릴게요.

남: 계좌가 없으시네요. 계좌가 있으면, 송금 수수료를 절약할 수 있습니다.

여: 송금 수수료가 얼마입니까?

남: 경우에 따라 다릅니다. 얼마를 송금하려고 하십니까?

여: 500달러요.

남: 수수료는 30,000원입니다.

여: 호주에 이 은행 계좌가 있습니다. 방금 서울로 이사를 와서…

남: 그럼 다른 계좌를 만드실 필요는 없으시겠는데요. 제가 처리 해드리겠습니다. 전화번호가 맞는지 확인해주세요. 자꾸 에러 메시지가 뜹니다.

여: 아, 이건 9가 아니고 4입니다.

남: 감사합니다. 여기 잠시만 앉아계세요.

해설: 여자는 호주로 송금하려고 한다. 따라서 이 대화가 이루어지는 장소는 은행이며 두 사람은 은행원과 손님이다.

Listening Web

Intro: agency　　　　　　　Web 1: account

Web 2: remit　　　　　　　Ending: arrange

True / False

1. T　　　　　2. F　　　　　3. T　　　　　4. T

문항 8 ⑤

Script & Dictation

M: Excuse me.

W: Yes?

M: Are you Erin Baker who stayed at the Grand Hill Inn?

W: Yes. I'm sorry, but who are you?

M: I'm Ted Johnson from the Grand Hill Inn. After you checked out, we found your passport in your room. It's yours, right?

W: I think so, but I have **mine in my bag** here… Oh, no! You've saved my life!

M: I remember your face because I was at the front desk when you checked out. That's why **I followed you** by taxi.

W: I'd have wasted a lot of time **looking for my passport** at this airport. I really appreciate it.

M: My pleasure. I'll carry your luggage to the **check-in counter**.

W: Thanks, but that's okay. The counter **is not open yet**.

M: I hope you'll **enjoy the journey home**.

W: Thank you very much.

남: 실례합니다.

여: 네.

남: Grand Hill Inn에서 묵으셨던 Erin Baker 씨 맞으시죠?

여: 네. 죄송하지만 누구시죠?

남: 저는 Grand Hill Inn에서 나온 Ted Johnson입니다. 체크아웃 하신 뒤에 저희가 방에서 여권을 발견했습니다. Baker 씨의 것이 맞죠?

여: 그런 것 같은데 제 여권은 여기 제 가방에… 오, 이런! 저에게 큰 도움을 주셨어요!

남: 손님께서 체크아웃 하실 때 제가 안내 데스크에 있어서 손님 얼굴을 기억하거든요. 그래서 택시를 타고 따라왔습니다.

여: 하마터면 여권 찾느라 이 공항에서 시간 낭비 할 뻔 했네요. 정말 고맙습니다.

남: 다행이네요. 탑승 수속하는 곳까지 짐을 들어드릴게요.

여: 고맙지만 괜찮습니다. 카운터가 아직 안 열렸어요.

남: 댁에 돌아가실 때까지 즐거운 여행 되시길 바랍니다.

여: 정말 감사합니다.

해설: 남자는 여자가 묵었던 호텔의 직원으로, 여자의 여권을 방에서 찾아 전해주기 위해 공항으로 왔다.

Listening Web

Intro: stayed   Web 1: found

Web 2: desk   Web 3: enjoy

True / False

1. F   2. T   3. F   4. F

문항 9 ①

Script & Dictation

M: Lie down **with your face down**.

W: Like this?

M: Yes. And **lift up your head**, and lift up your chest slowly. Now hold. One, two, three. Okay. Now lower your chest. Good.

W: It takes **a lot of strength** in the waist.

M: Yes. The surgery was a success. Now all you have to do is to strengthen the muscle around the waist. Do this exercise ten or fifteen times a day.

W: Then will the pain disappear forever?

M: The pain occurs simply because the muscle around your waist is too weak. Even though you work only a little, the muscle **begins to stiffen**. So if it gets stronger, the pain **will be relieved** much more. But I cannot guarantee you'll never get hurt again.

W: I understand. What if my waist is painful again?

M: Then you should come again and **get an injection** to relax the muscle.

W: I see. I think I need to exercise every day. Thanks.

남: 얼굴을 아래쪽으로 향하게 누우세요.

여: 이렇게요?

남: 네. 그리고 머리를 들어올리시고 가슴을 천천히 들어올리세요. 이제 멈추세요. 하나, 둘, 셋. 됐습니다. 내려오세요. 잘하셨 습니다.

여: 허리에 힘이 많이 들어가요.

남: 그렇죠. 수술은 잘 됐어요. 이제 하실 일은 허리 주변 근육을 강화시키는 것이지요. 이 운동을 하루에 열 번 또는 열다섯 번씩 하세요.

여: 그럼 통증이 완전히 없어지나요?

남: 통증은 단순히 허리 주변 근육이 약하기 때문에 생기는 거예요. 일을 조금만 해도 근육이 경직되기 시작하는 거죠. 그러니까 근육이 강해지면 통증이 훨씬 완화될 겁니다. 하지만 전혀 아프지 않을 거라고는 보장할 수 없습니다.

여: 그렇군요. 허리가 다시 아프면 어쩌죠?

남: 그럼 다시 오셔서 근육을 이완시켜주는 주사를 맞으셔야 해요.

여: 알겠습니다. 운동을 매일 해야겠군요. 고맙습니다.

해설: 수술이 잘 되었고 운동이 효과가 없을 경우 다시 와서 주사를 맞아야 한다고 남자가 말하고 있으므로, 두 사람의 관계는 의사와 환자이다.

Listening Web

Intro: lower   Web 1: strengthen

Web 2: relieved   Web 3: injection

True / False

1. T   2. T   3. F   4. F

문항 10 ①

Script & Dictation

W: Good afternoon.

M: Good afternoon. **What brought you** here again?

W: There seems to be a problem with the steering wheel.

M: I didn't notice any problem the other day.

W: No, but from this morning, whenever I steer to the right, I hear a strange sound.

M: **Did you happen to** have an accident again? Even a small accident, like you bumped Intro a pole at the parking lot or...

W: No, never. I **had not driven** the car until yesterday since I picked it up last week.

M: It can't be a problem with the steering wheel. I need to **inspect** all the **suspected parts**.

W: I **wonder if** the insurance will cover this kind of thing.

M: It depends. You need to contact your insurance agent about it.

W: I see.

M: Would you mind coming with me **to test-drive** the car? I need to hear the sound.

W: Of course not.

여: 안녕하세요.

남: 안녕하세요. 무슨 일로 다시 오셨어요?

여: 핸들에 문제가 있는 것 같아요.

남: 지난 번에 문제가 있는 걸 전혀 몰랐는데요.

여: 안 그랬었는데, 오늘 아침부터 핸들을 오른쪽으로 돌릴 때마다 이상한 소리가 나요.

남: 혹시 사고가 또 났었나요? 작은 사고라도, 주차장에서 기둥에 박았다든지…

여: 아니요, 절대 아니에요. 지난 주에 차를 찾아가고 나서 어제까지 운전을 하지 않았어요.

남: 핸들의 문제가 아닐 거예요. 의심되는 부분을 모두 살펴봐야겠네요.

여: 이런 것도 보험처리가 될지 모르겠네요.

남: 상황에 따라 다르죠. 그 문제에 관해서는 보험사와 연락을 해 보셔야 합니다.

여: 알겠어요.

남: 저와 같이 시운전 해주시겠어요? 소리를 들어봐야겠는데요.

여: 물론이죠.

해설: 여자는 핸들을 돌릴 때마다 소리가 나는 문제점을 호소하고 있다. 따라서 상대방의 직업은 기술공이다.

Listening Web

Intro: brought	Web 1: wheel
Web 2: steer	Web 3: suspected

True / False

1. T	2. F	3. F	4. F

Unit 05 유형 5 - 그림과 일치하지 않는 내용 찾기

문항 1 ④

Script & Dictation

M: How's **your new home**?

W: I love it! There's a big window. I put my bed **right under the window**, so that I can get up in the morning in the beautiful sunshine.

M: Wow! Beautiful!

W: And I put the computer **next to the bed**, so that I can go to bed quickly after work.

M: You're so funny. By the way, did you throw away your table **when you moved**? I remember you told me that the legs were broken.

W: My brother fixed it. And now it's **in the middle of** my room.

M: Where are your books? Did you bring all the books? You had a lot of books.

W: I made a really big bookshelf on the wall, but it's only **half full with** books.

M: Did you also bring your old TV?

W: No, I bought a new one. I **attached it to** the wall.

남: 새 집 어때?

여: 정말 좋아! 큰 창문도 있고. 아침 햇살을 받으면서 잠에서 일어날 수 있게 창문 바로 아래에 침대를 뒀지.

남: 와! 멋진걸!

여: 그리고 컴퓨터는 침대 바로 옆에 뒀어. 일 끝내고 곧장 잘 수 있게.

남: 너 참 재미있다. 그런데 이사하면서 탁자는 버렸어? 네가 탁자 다리 망가졌다고 말했던 기억이 나.

여: 그건 우리 남동생이 고쳤어. 지금은 내 방 한 가운데 뒀어.

남: 책은 어떻게 했어? 책 전부 다 가져갔어? 너 책 무척 많잖아.

여: 벽에 진짜 큰 서가를 만들었어. 그런데 책이 반밖에 안 차더라.

남: 오래된 TV도 가져갔어?

여: 아니, 새로 샀지. 벽에 걸어뒀어.

해설: 큰 서가를 만들었는데 책이 반밖에 차지 않았다고 했으므로, 책이 가득 차 있는 그림이 대화의 내용과 일치하지 않는다.

Listening Web

Intro: bed	Web 1: next to
Web 2: throw	Web 3: fixed
Ending: bookshelf	

True / False

1. F	2. F	3. F	4. F

문항 2 ④

Script & Dictation

M: Now **we're all done**.

W: It's not easy at all to set up the tent. I don't think I'll go camping again.

M: Don't worry. It's your first time.

W: I'm hungry anyway. Let's have dinner.

M: Okay, wait a second. I'll prepare dinner for you. Here's the burner, and dinner will be ready soon.

W: **Since we're surrounded by** trees, it's like a primitive life. Where is the radio? I want to hear the sound of civilization.

M: It's on the table. Take a rest in the hammock. You look so tired.

W: Where is the lamp? It's only 6:30 p.m., but it's getting dark. We need light.

M: Oh, my God! I **forgot to bring it**.

W: Oh, no. I think we have to have a quick dinner and make a bonfire. **I'll fix dinner**. You go get some firewood now.

M: This is not **what I planned**. Sorry about it.

남: 이제 다 끝났다.

여: 텐트 치는 건 전혀 쉽지 않은걸. 난 캠핑 다시 안 올 것 같아.

남: 걱정 마. 이번이 처음이잖아.

여: 아무튼 난 배고파. 저녁 먹자.

남: 그래, 조금만 기다려. 내가 저녁 해줄게. 버너가 여기 있으니, 저녁은 금방 될 거야.

여: 나무들에 둘러싸여 있으니 원시 생활 같군. 라디오는 어디 있어? 문명의 소리를 듣고 싶어.

남: 탁자 위에 있어. 해먹에 누워서 좀 쉬어. 너 피곤해 보인다.

여: 램프는 어디 있어? 겨우 오후 6시 30분인데 어두워지고 있어. 빛이 필요해.

남: 세상에! 가져오는걸 깜빡 했어.

여: 오 이런. 저녁을 얼른 먹고 모닥불을 피워야겠다. 저녁은 내가 할게. 넌 지금 가서 장작 좀 구해와.

남: 이럴 계획이 아니었는데. 미안해.

해설: 램프를 가져오지 않아서 모닥불을 피워야 하겠다고 말했으므로, 모닥불 그림이 대화의 내용과 일치하지 않는다.

Listening Web

Intro: set up   Web 1: burner

Web 3: on   Web 4: tired

Ending: bonfire

True / False

1. T   2. T   3. T   4. F

문항 3 ⑤

Script & Dictation

W: What lovely weather!

M: Yeah. Look at the sky. The sun is shining and **it's breezy**. It's perfect weather for going on a picnic.

W: Yes, and it's a perfect birthday present for me. Thanks, Andy.

M: My pleasure. I'm so glad that you like it.

W: Wow! Look! Sheep are **grazing on the grass**. It looks so peaceful.

M: Look at those sheep! They're sleeping under the trees.

W: Are they dreaming?

M: Maybe they are grazing in their dreams. Can we **try feeding** the sheep?

W: I think so. The girl over there is feeding the sheep with her father! The sheep is **almost standing upright** to eat grass. I'd like to do it.

M: Are you sure? You're **afraid of animals**.

W: Yes, but I want to try it. They are so cute. I think it'll be fun.

M: Okay. Let's go! **I'll take a picture** while you're feeding the sheep.

여: 날씨 좋다!

남: 그래. 하늘 좀 봐. 해도 빛나고 바람도 불고. 소풍 가기 딱 좋은 날씨야.

여: 그래, 그리고 내 생일 선물로도 딱이야. 고마워, Andy.

남: 천만해. 네가 좋다니 나도 기쁘네.

여: 와! 봐봐! 양들이 풀을 뜯고 있어. 참 평화롭게 보인다.

남: 저 양들 좀 봐! 나무 아래서 자고 있네.

여: 양들도 꿈꾸고 있을까?

남: 아마 꿈 속에서 풀 뜯고 있을 거야. 우리가 양한테 먹이를 줄 수 있을까?

여: 그럴걸. 저기에서 여자 아이가 아빠와 같이 양한테 먹이를 주고 있어! 양이 풀 먹으려고 거의 똑바로 일어났는걸. 나도 하고 싶다.

남: 정말? 너 동물 무서워하잖아.

여: 응, 그런데 해 보고 싶어. 양들이 정말 귀여워. 재미있을 것 같아.

남: 좋아. 가자! 네가 먹이 주는 거 사진 찍어줄게.

해설: 여자 아이가 아빠와 함께 양에게 먹이를 주고 있다고 했으므로, 사진을 찍고 있는 아빠 그림이 대화의 내용과 일치하지 않는다.

Listening Web

Intro: shining   Web 1: Sheep

Web 2: trees   Web 3: feeding

Ending: while

True / False

1. T   2. F   3. T   4. F

문항 4 ④

Script & Dictation

W: Did you decorate the tree by yourself?

M: With my nephews. They love to do it.

W: Yeah, children always **enjoy decorating** Christmas trees. The candy canes on the tree are cute.

M: Have a seat in front of the fireplace. I'll get some tea.

W: Thanks. Are these presents in front of the fireplace **for your nephews**?

M: Yes. They believe that Santa Claus will put the presents in their socks while they're sleeping. That's why they put their socks over the fireplace.

W: I **believed in** Santa Claus, too. I always put my socks **over the bed** on Christmas Eve. Oh! Now I see the Christmas wreath on the door. That's beautiful.

M: My mother makes it every year.

W: Is that turkey on the table what your mother made?

M: I cooked it with her. I learned **how to make it**.

W: I wish **everybody would come** early so we can taste that turkey!

여: 저 트리는 네가 직접 장식했니?

남: 내 조카들이랑 했어. 그 애들이 그걸 좋아해.

여: 그래, 애들은 크리스마스 트리 장식하는 거 언제나 좋아하지. 지팡이 모양 캔디가 귀여운데.

남: 벽난로 앞에 앉아. 차를 좀 내올게.

여: 고마워. 벽난로 앞에 있는 선물들은 조카 줄 거야?

남: 응. 그 애들은 자기들이 자는 동안 산타클로스가 양말 속에 선물을 넣어 줄 거라고 믿어. 그래서 벽난로 위에 양말도 걸어 놨어.

여: 나도 산타클로스를 믿었었는데. 난 항상 크리스마스 이브에 양말을 침대에 걸어두었어. 오! 문에 걸린 크리스마스 화환을 이제 봤어. 저거 예쁜데.

남: 우리 어머니께서 해마다 만드셔.

여: 식탁 위에 있는 칠면조도 너희 어머니께서 만드신 거니?

남: 내가 어머니와 같이 만들었어. 만드는 방법을 배웠거든.

여: 모두들 빨리 와서 저 칠면조 맛보고 싶다!

해설: 산타클로스의 존재를 믿고 크리스마스 전날 밤 침대에 양말을 걸어둔 것은 여자가 어릴 적 일이다.

Listening Web

Intro: decorate   Web 2: over

Web 3: wreath   Ending: what

True / False

1. F   2. F   3. T   4. T

문항 5 ①

Script & Dictation

W: Jack, **what kind of** costume do you want for Halloween Night?

M: I'm thinking of Dracula. I saw Brian's Batman costume and I want to **wear a long cape.**

W: Okay. Then you need gloves with long and sharp nails.

M: Yes, and I want to carry the jack-o'-lantern.

W: What about a hat? You have a wizard hat, like Harry Potter's.

M: Mom, Dracula never wears a hat. His hair **stands out like horns.**

W: Right, but you don't need to be **the same as** the real Dracula. Make **your own style.** And if you wear your black shoes, it'll be cute.

M: You mean the wizard shoes **with the sharp fronts**? Mom, I think you want me to reuse last year's costume. I'll wear the shoes, but I won't wear the hat. That's not Dracula.

W: Okay, Jack. Let's go get your Dracula costume.

여: Jack, 핼러윈 밤에 어떤 복장을 하고 싶니?

남: 드라큘라가 어떨까 생각 중이에요. Brian의 배트맨 복장을 봤는데, 긴 망토를 하고 싶어요.

여: 그래. 그럼 길고 뾰족한 손톱이 달린 장갑도 필요하겠구나.

남: 네, 그리고 호박 등도 들고 싶어요.

여: 모자는 어떻게 할 거니? 너 해리포터 마법사 모자 같은 거 있잖아.

남: 엄마, 드라큘라는 모자를 쓰지 않아요. 머리가 뿔처럼 솟아 있죠.

여: 그래, 하지만 꼭 진짜 드라큘라와 똑같을 필요는 없잖니. 너만의 스타일을 만들렴. 그리고 네 검정색 신발 신으면 귀여울 거야.

남: 앞 코가 뾰족한 마법사 신발 말이죠? 엄마, 엄마는 제가 작년 복장을 다시 사용하기를 바라시는 것 같아요. 그 신발은 신을게요. 그런데 모자는 싫어요. 그건 드라큘라가 아니에요.

여: 알았다, Jack. 나가서 드라큘라 복장을 사 보자.

해설: 엄마가 마법사 모자를 쓸 것을 권했으나, 아들은 드라큘라 머리를 하고 모자를 쓰지 않겠다고 말하고 있다.

Listening Web

Intro: long   Web 1: sharp

Web 3: horns   Ending: won't

True / False

1. T   2. F   3. F   4. T

문항 6 ②

Script & Dictation

W: I think we're **quite lost**. The road has **diverged Intro** three. Where should we go?

M: We just need to go south.

W: Do you have a map?

M: No, but I have a compass. Look at this. It will show us where south is.

W: Is the road **on the very right** heading south?

M: Yes. That's right. It's 12 p.m. now, and that's why the sun is over the road **on the very right**. By the way, it's very hot and humid.

W: If I didn't wear a hat, **I would melt.**

M: Yeah, the sun is too hot, and the backpack is too heavy. I want to take a rest in the shade for a second.

W: Cool. What's in your bag?

M: Water, cucumber, and some fruit. I thought we **would become thirsty.**

여: 우리 길을 완전히 잃은 것 같아. 길이 세 개로 갈라져 있어. 어디로 가야 하지?

남: 우린 그냥 남쪽으로 가면 돼.

여: 지도 있어?

남: 아니, 하지만 나침반이 있어. 이 나침반을 봐. 어디가 남쪽인지 알려줄 거야.

여: 제일 오른쪽에 있는 길이 남쪽 방향이지?

남: 응. 맞아. 지금이 정오야. 그러니까 제일 오른쪽 길 위에 태양이 있는 거지. 그런데 너무 덥고 습하다.

여: 내가 모자를 안 썼으면 난 아마 녹아버렸을 거야.

남: 그러게. 태양은 너무 뜨겁고, 배낭은 너무 무거워. 그늘에서 잠시 쉬고 싶어.

여: 좋아. 가방에 뭐가 있니?

남: 물, 오이, 그리고 과일. 목마를 것 같아서.

해설: 지도가 있냐는 여자의 질문에 남자가 없다고 답했으므로, 남자가 들고 있는 지도 그림이 대화의 내용과 일치하지 않는다.

Listening Web

Intro: diverged   Web 1: map

Web 2: right   Web 3: didn't

Ending: backpack

True / False

1. T   2. F   3. F   4. T

문항 7 ④

Script & Dictation

M: This street is **too messy**. A lot of cars are parked along the street.

W: Yeah, there's no police officer. Maybe **parking is allowed** because it's Sunday.

M: But it looks dangerous. The building is **under the construction**.

W: Tom, don't walk under the ladder. Come this way.

M: What's the problem?

W: It's a taboo. Americans think **you'll be unlucky** if you walk under the ladder.

M: It's just a superstition! I **can't see if** we're close to the hospital or not.

W: There are so many trees across the street that we cannot see what there is **on the opposite side**.

M: There's a crosswalk over there. Let's cross the street.

W: That's a good idea. Oh! It turned green. Run!

남: 이 길은 무척 정신 없군. 차들이 길을 따라 주차되어 있어.

여: 그러게. 경찰도 없어. 아마 일요일이라 주차가 허용되나 봐.

남: 그렇지만 너무 위험해 보인다. 건물은 공사 중이고.

여: Tom, 사다리 아래로 지나가지마. 이쪽으로 와.

남: 무슨 문제 있어?

여: 터부야. 미국 사람들은 사다리 아래로 지나가면 재수가 없다고 생각해.

남: 그건 미신일 뿐이야! 우리가 병원 근처에 왔는지 알 수가 없네.

여: 건너편에 나무가 많아서 저 쪽에 뭐가 있는지 안 보여.

남: 저기 횡단보도 있다. 건너가자.

여: 좋은 생각이야. 어! 녹색불로 바뀌었어. 뛰어!

해설: 여자가 공사 중인 복잡한 길에 경찰이 없다고 말했으므로, 경찰 그림이 대화의 내용과 일치하지 않는다.

Listening Web

Intro: cars   Web 1: no

Web 2: ladder   Web 3: across

Ending: a crosswalk

True / False

1. F   2. T   3. T   4. F

문항 8 ①

Script & Dictation

W: What are you doing?

M: Yesterday I saw my friend playing this game, and now I'm trying it.

W: It looks interesting. Will you show me how to do it?

M: Sure. **You're a chef**, who comes from the bakery on the top. You have to carry the cake to the princess **at the bottom** safely.

W: That's quite simple.

M: Yes, but you need to **jump over** these rocks. If you fall on them, the ghost will **catch up with** you. The ghost keeps following you, and you'll lose a chance if you're caught by him.

W: What are these diamonds **on the way for**?

M: If you jump up to a diamond, you'll get another chance.

W: How can I know how many chances are left?

M: The diamonds on the top show you how many chances you have.

W: So, the number of diamonds is **the number of** my lives.

M: That's right.

여: 뭐해?

남: 어제 친구가 이 게임을 하는 걸 봐서 지금은 내가 해 보는 거야.

여: 재미있어 보인다. 어떻게 하는 건지 알려줄래?

남: 물론이지. 너는 요리사야. 꼭대기에 있는 빵집에서 나오지. 너는 이 케이크를 맨 아래에 있는 공주에게 안전하게 전달해야 해.

여: 간단하구나.

남: 응. 하지만 이 바위들을 뛰어 넘어야 해. 만약 걸려 넘어지면 유령이 널 따라잡을 거야. 유령은 너의 뒤를 계속 쫓아 올 건데, 만약 잡히면 넌 기회를 한 번 잃게 돼.

여: 이 길에 있는 다이아몬드들은 뭐에 쓰는 거야?

남: 다이아몬드에 뛰어오르면, 또 다른 기회가 생겨.

여: 기회가 얼마나 남았는지 어떻게 알 수 있어?

남: 위에 있는 다이아몬드가 너에게 기회가 얼마나 남았는지 보여 주는 거야.

여: 그러니까 다이아몬드 개수가 내 목숨의 개수구나.

남: 그렇지.

해설: 화면 상단에 있는 다이아몬드의 개수가 남은 기회 [목숨]의 개수라고 말하고 있으므로, 하트 그림이 대화의 내용과 일치하지 않는다.

Listening Web

Intro: chef   Web 1: princess

Web 2: catch up   Web 3: up

Ending: on

True / False

1. T   2. F   3. T   4. T

문항 9 ④

Script & Dictation

M: Guess what?

W: What?

M: Look at this picture. I went there yesterday.

W: It's Sarah's room in the film "Sad Genius." I've always wanted to go there. How was it?

M: You should go. The big lamp was **still on** beside the desk, and lots of books were still stacked up on the desk.

W: Oh, you sat at the piano. Did you try playing it?

M: No, you are **not allowed to** touch it.

W: I remember Sarah picked a flower on the street and **put it** in the vase under the window. She stood in front of the window **rubbing the petals**.

M: This is a real flower. It's not artificial.

W: Really? Everything's **almost the same as** in the movie. But where is the cat on the rug?

M: She was always there in the movie, but you know, it's impossible to make a live cat stay still.

남: 맞춰봐.

여: 뭘?

남: 이 사진을 봐. 나 어제 여기 갔었어.

여: 영화 'Sad Genius'에 나왔던 Sarah의 방이잖아. 나 여기 항상 가보고 싶었는데. 어땠어?

남: 너 꼭 가봐야 해. 큰 램프도 책상 옆에 그대로 켜져 있고, 책들도 그대로 책상 위에 쌓여있어.

여: 와, 너 피아노에 앉았네. 피아노 쳐봤어?

남: 아니, 못 만지게 해.

여: Sarah가 길에서 꽃 꺾다 창문 아래 꽃병에 꽂아 두던 게 생각난다. 꽃잎을 만지작거리면서 창문 앞에 서있었는데.

남: 이거 진짜 꽃이야. 조화가 아니야.

여: 정말? 모든 게 영화와 거의 똑같네. 그런데 양탄자 위에 고양이는 어디 있어?

남: 고양이가 영화에서는 항상 거기에 있었지. 그렇지만 너도 알다시피 살아있는 고양이를 움직이지 않게 할 수는 없잖아.

해설: 영화에서는 양탄자 위에 고양이가 있었지만, 실제 고양이는 계속 움직이므로 지금은 양탄자 위에 고양이가 없다.

Listening Web

Intro: stacked   Web 1: sat at

Web 2: picked   Web 4: rug

Ending: a live

True / False

1. F   2. F   3. F   4. T

문항 10 ③

Script & Dictation

M: **You're so talented!** Do you really paint it yourself?

W: Thanks. It's just **an imitation I practiced** in art class. It's not the same as the original work. The couple at the bottom is my creation.

M: Was the window on the 2nd floor originally open?

W: Yes, **the rest** is almost the same.

M: This café **still exists**. Have you ever been there?

W: No, but I'd like to sit at one of these round tables and have dinner on a summer night, like in this picture.

M: Night? Ah-ha, that's why there are stars in the sky. At first I thought you **painted daytime** because it's so bright.

W: It's because I was going to draw a lamp on the wall last. But when I was about to paint it, **the time was up**.

남: 너 재능 있구나! 네가 다 그린 거야?

여: 고마워. 미술시간에 연습으로 따라 그린 거야. 원작하고 똑같지는 않아. 아래 커플은 내가 그려 넣은 거야.

남: 2층에 창문은 원래 열려 있었어?

여: 응. 나머지는 거의 똑같아.

남: 이 카페 아직도 있어. 거기 가봤니?

여: 아니, 하지만 이 그림에서처럼 여름 밤에 이 원형 테이블에 앉아 저녁을 먹어보고 싶어.

남: 밤? 아하, 그래서 하늘에 별이 있구나. 난 처음에 너무 밝아서 낮을 그렸는 줄 알았어.

여: 그게 왜냐하면 내가 벽에 램프를 마지막에 그리려고 했었거든. 그런데 막 그리려고 했을 때 시간이 끝나버렸어.

해설: 마지막에 여자가 시간이 없어서 램프를 그리지 못했다고 했으므로, 램프 그림이 대화의 내용과 일치하지 않는다.

Listening Web

Intro: creation   Web 2: round

Ending: up

True / False

1. F   2. F   3. T   4. F

문항 1 ①

Script & Dictation

M: Excuse me. Can I exchange this dress shirt?

W: Yes, of course. What seems to be the **problem with it**?

M: It was my birthday gift, but it's not **big enough**. Do you have this in a larger size?

W: I'm sorry. We don't.

M: Please show me another one in a larger size, then.

W: This way, please. How would you like this blue T-shirt?

M: That looks good, but do you have this **in another color**?

W: How about this pink one?

M: That's **too fancy**. I'll take the blue one **instead**.

W: No problem. It's cheaper than that dress shirt. Do you need anything else? Socks and neckties are **on sale**.

M: Those are good, but I want to see a women's T-shirt in the same design for my girlfriend.

W: Okay.

남: 실례합니다. 이 정장 셔츠를 교환할 수 있을까요?

여: 네, 물론이죠. 무슨 문제가 있나요?

남: 생일 선물로 받은 건데 좀 작아서요. 더 큰 치수 있나요?

여: 죄송합니다. 더 큰 치수는 없습니다.

남: 그럼 더 큰 치수로 다른 걸 보여주세요.

여: 이쪽으로 오세요. 이 파란색 티셔츠 어떠세요?

남: 좋긴 한데요, 다른 색깔은 없나요?

여: 분홍색은 어떠세요?

남: 너무 화려해요. 차라리 파란색으로 할게요.

여: 그러세요. 이게 정장 셔츠보다 저렴해요. 다른 건 필요한 거 없으세요? 양말과 넥타이가 할인 중이에요.

남: 그것도 좋지만, 여자친구에게 줄 같은 디자인으로 여성용 티셔츠를 보고 싶어요.

여: 알겠습니다.

해설: 남자는 자신의 옷을 교환하고 남는 금액으로 여자친구를 위한 여성용 티셔츠를 보려고 한다.

Listening Web

Intro: exchange	Web 1: larger
Web 2: another	Ending: women's

True / False

1. T	2. F	3. T	4. F

문항 2 ③

Script & Dictation

[Telephone rings.]

M: Hello?

W: Honey, it's me.

M: What's up?

W: I'm really sorry, but **I'll be late**.

M: No! It's your turn to pick up Amy at kindergarten.

W: I know. But I have an unexpected meeting at 5 p.m. with an important buyer.

M: Just tell them you **have already had plans**!

W: This is not a casual thing. There seems to be something wrong **with our contract**, and it will be a long conversation.

M: But... but I told you I have an appointment for dinner with my friends. I haven't seen them for years. I invited them to dinner. I cannot cancel it.

W: I know. But **what's your priority**, your daughter or dinner with friends?

M: Don't be upset. I'll go to the kindergarten right after work. But please call me if the meeting cancels.

남: 여보세요.

여: 여보, 나예요.

남: 무슨 일이에요?

여: 정말 미안한데, 나 오늘 늦어요.

남: 안 돼요! 오늘 당신이 유치원에서 Amy 데려올 차례잖아요.

여: 알아요. 그런데 중요한 바이어와 예상치 못했던 미팅이 5시에 잡혔어요.

남: 그 사람들한테 선약이 있다고 말해요!

여: 이건 단순한 문제가 아니에요. 우리 계약서에 문제가 생긴 것 같고, 이야기가 길어질 것 같아요.

남: 그렇지만… 그렇지만 오늘 난 친구들과 저녁 약속이 있다고 했잖아요. 정말 오랜만에 만나는 거란 말이에요. 내가 친구들을 저녁에 초대한 거예요. 취소할 수 없어요.

여: 알아요. 하지만 딸과 친구 중에 어느 것이 더 중요하죠?

남: 화내지 말아요. 내가 퇴근하는 대로 유치원으로 갈게요. 하지만 미팅이 취소되면 꼭 전화해줘요.

해설: 남자는 원래 퇴근 후 친구들과 약속이 있었지만, 여자가 회사에서 피치 못할 일이 생겼기 때문에 남자가 아이를 데리러 가야 한다.

Listening Web

Intro: late	Web 2: an unexpected
Web 3: for	

True / False

1. T	2. T	3. F	4. F

문항 3 ⑤

Script & Dictation

W: Jack, will you **give me a hand**, please?

M: Sure, what do you want me to do?

W: I'm trying to change the bulb, but I can't reach it.

M: That's a **walk in the park**.

W: What do you mean by that?

M: I mean it's easy for me to do it. It's the same expression as 'a piece of cake.'

W: I've heard of the expression. We have a similar expression in Korean. Have you ever heard of 'eating rice cake while **lying down**'?

M: Yeah, that's interesting. But actually eating rice cake while lying down is not a piece of cake. I've tried to, but I choked and I almost died.

W: Haha. I know what you mean.

M: I don't understand where that expression came from.

W: I **agree with you**, Jack. Now help me with this.

남: Jack, 나 좀 도와줄래?

남: 물론이지. 무엇을 해줄까?

여: 전구를 갈아 끼우고 있는데, 손이 안 닿아.

남: 그거야 공원 산책이지.

여: 무슨 뜻이야?

남: 내가 그것을 하는 건 쉬운 일이란 뜻이야. 'a piece of cake'과 같은 의미야.

여: 그 표현 들어봤어. 한국어에도 그와 비슷한 표현이 있어. '누워서 떡 먹기'라고 들어봤니?

남: 응, 그 표현 재미있지. 하지만 실제로 누워서 떡 먹기는 전혀 쉽지 않아. 내가 해 봤는데, 목 막혀서 죽는 줄 알았어.

여: 하하. 무슨 말인지 알아.

남: 이 표현이 어디에서 비롯된 것인지 모르겠어.

여: 동감이야, Jack. 이제 나 이것 좀 도와줘.

해설: 여자는 전구를 교환하는데 남자에게 도움을 요청했고, 남자는 요청을 수락했다.

Listening Web

Web 1: bulb   Web 2: walk

Web 3: piece

True / False

1. T   2. F   3. T   4. F

문항 4 ②

Script & Dictation

[Telephone rings.]

M: Hello?

W: Brad, I just now fell down the stairs, and I think I **sprained my ankle**.

M: Where are you now?

W: I'm in the Twinkle Tower in Summerfield town.

M: Can you walk? Or do you want me to go there?

W: It's kind of **far away from home**. It'll take a lot. I didn't try walking yet, but it's getting swollen.

M: Wait. I'll search where the **nearest hospital** is. *[Pause]* Christine, the hospital is just around the corner. Can you drive?

W: No, I can't.

M: Is there anybody who can help you?

W: Unfortunately no. I'll **try walking**. Ouch!

M: Don't do that! How about calling 911?

W: Well, that's okay. I can walk slowly by myself.

M: I'll **go to the hospital** right away. See you there.

남: 여보세요.

여: Brad, 나 지금 계단에서 넘어졌는데, 발목을 삔 것 같아.

남: 지금 어디야?

여: Summerfield 동네에 있는 Twinkle Tower에 있어.

남: 걸을 수 있겠어? 아니면 내가 그 쪽으로 갈까?

여: 집에서 좀 많이 멀어. 오래 걸릴 거야. 아직 걸어보지 않았는데, 부어 오르고 있어.

남: 잠깐만. 제일 가까운 병원이 어딘지 찾아볼게. *[잠시 후]* Christine, 병원이 바로 모퉁이 돌아서 있어. 운전할 수 있겠어?

여: 아니, 못 하겠어.

남: 너를 도와줄 만한 사람이 있어?

여: 불행히도 없어. 한번 걸어볼게. 아야!

남: 무리하지마! 911에 전화하는 건 어때?

여: 괜찮아. 내가 혼자 천천히 걸을 수 있어.

남: 내가 당장 병원으로 갈게. 거기에서 봐.

해설: 마지막에 여자가 혼자 걸을 수 있다고 했으므로, 여자는 혼자 병원으로 천천히 걸어갈 것이다.

Listening Web

Intro: sprained   Web 1: swollen

Web 2: around   Ending: by myself

True / False

1. T   2. T   3. F   4. F

문항 5 ③

Script & Dictation

W: Have you decided which class you would go to at Career Expo?

M: I'm thinking of the **diplomat course**.

W: I remember you told me that you're **interested in** learning foreign languages.

M: Yes, and I want to live in a foreign country.

W: That'll be interesting. Do you want to be a diplomat or are you just interested in **something global**?

M: I have wanted to be a diplomat since I was in elementary school. I think I can get some useful information. What about you?

W: I'm thinking of the food stylist and the fashion designer courses.

M: You like art. I heard a famous **photographer** will come, and the student response to him was very good last year.

W: Really? I'm interested in taking pictures, too.

M: Now you've changed **your mind**?

W: Yes, I think so.

여: 진로 박람회에서 무슨 강의를 들을지 결정했어?

남: 외교관 과정을 생각 중이야.

여: 네가 외국어 배우는데 관심 있다고 했던 거 기억나.

남: 응, 그리고 난 외국에서 살아보고 싶어.

여: 재미있겠다. 외교관이 되고 싶은 거야, 아니면 그냥 뭔가 국제적인 것에 관심이 있는 거야?

남: 초등학교 때부터 외교관이 되고 싶었어. 유용한 정보를 얻을 수 있을 것 같아. 넌 어때?

여: 나는 푸드 스타일리스트나 패션 디자이너 과정을 생각 중이야.

남: 예술을 좋아하는구나. 내가 듣기로 유명 사진작가가 오는데, 작년에 학생들 반응이 아주 좋았대.

여: 정말? 나 사진 찍는 것도 좋아해.

남: 지금 마음이 바뀐 거야?

여: 응, 그런 것 같아.

해설: 여자는 원래 푸드 스타일리스트와 패션 디자이너에 관심이 있었지만, 남자의 말을 듣고 작년에 인기가 많았던 사진작가의 강의를 듣기로 마음을 바꿨다.

Listening Web

Intro: would   Web 1: courses

Web 2: response   Web 3: pictures

Web 4: changed

True / False

1. T   2. F   3. T   4. T

문항 6 ①

Script & Dictation

[Telephone rings.]

W: Hello?

M: Hi, Emily. Let's go to school together. See you at 7:40 in front of the convenience store.

W: I'll leave for school early today to buy a sketchbook. We need it in **art class** today. Did you buy one?

M: Oh, I forgot to.

W: Buy one **on the way to** school. I'll leave home at 7:20 a.m.

M: Where is the nearest stationery store?

W: Across **from the hospital**.

M: It's too far away from my house. How much is it?

W: Around $5? I'm not sure, **either**.

M: I'm really sorry, but will you please buy one for me? I'll give you the money at school.

W: Okay. But what if there is a wide range **in quality**?

M: Then please get me one the same as yours.

W: I see.

여: 여보세요.

남: 안녕, Emily. 학교 같이 가자. 7시 40분에 편의점 앞에서 만나.

여: 나 오늘 스케치북 사야 해서 일찍 갈 거야. 우리 오늘 미술 시간에 필요하잖아. 넌 스케치북 샀어?

남: 아, 까먹었다.

여: 너도 학교 가는 길에 하나 사. 난 7시 20분에 나갈 거야.

남: 제일 가까운 문구점이 어디에 있지?

여: 병원 건너편에.

남: 우리 집에서는 너무 멀어. 얼마야?

여: 한 5달러쯤? 나도 잘 몰라.

남: 정말 미안한데, 내 것 좀 하나 사다 줄래? 학교에서 돈 줄게.

여: 그래. 그런데 종류가 다양하면 어떡하지?

남: 너랑 같은 걸로 사줘.

여: 알았어.

해설: 남자는 여자에게 여자의 것과 같은 종류의 스케치북을 사달라고 부탁하고 있다.

Listening Web

Intro: 40   Web 1: early

Web 3: quality   Ending: as

True / False

1. F   2. T   3. F   4. T

Script & Dictation

[Telephone rings.]

M: Hello?

W: Hi, this is Chloe. Have you finished the history homework?

M: I'm still **working on it**. Did you find all the pictures Mr. Green mentioned? Did he say that we should include at least five pictures?

W: Yes, I've already **put them in**. I found seven pictures.

M: Where did you get them?

W: At www.photophoto.com. You can find many pictures of New York **in the early 1900s** at the site.

M: I see. Thank you. How did you know about this site?

W: My sister is a **history major**. By the way, will you please print my report? My printer is out of ink. I'll email it to you.

M: I'm really sorry, but my printer doesn't work. I fixed it yesterday, but it's **out of order again**. Why don't you call David?

W: I see. I'd better hurry. I hope he's not in bed yet.

남: 여보세요.

여: 안녕, 나 Chloe야. 역사 숙제 다 끝냈니?

남: 아직 하는 중이야. Green 선생님께서 말씀하신 사진들은 다 찾았어? 5장 이상 붙여야 한다고 했지?

여: 응, 난 다 붙였어. 난 사진을 7장 찾았어.

남: 어디서 구했어?

여: www.photophoto.com에서. 그 사이트에는 초기 1900년대 뉴욕 사진들이 많이 있어.

남: 그렇구나. 고마워. 넌 이 사이트를 어떻게 알았어?

여: 우리 언니가 역사 전공이야. 그런데 내 보고서 출력 좀 해줄 수 있니? 내 프린터는 잉크가 떨어졌어. 내가 이메일로 보낼게.

남: 정말 미안한데, 우리집 프린터는 고장 났어. 어제 내가 고쳤는데, 또 고장이 났어. David에게 전화해 보는 게 어때?

여: 알았어. 서둘러야겠다. David가 아직 자고 있지 않아야 할텐데.

해설: 여자는 프린터 잉크가 떨어져서 남자에게 대신 출력을 해 줄 것을 부탁했지만 남자도 자신의 프린터도 고장 났다면서 David에게 전화로 물어보라고 하고 있다.

Listening Web

Intro: finished   Web 1: all

Web 2: I've already   Web 3: out of

Web 4: fixed

True / False

1. T   2. F   3. T   4. F

Script & Dictation

M: **It's pouring**. Do you have an umbrella?

W: Yes, I have one. But it's raining **cats and dogs**. I can't walk home.

M: Your home is far away from here. Will you wear my raincoat?

W: Then what are you going to wear?

M: Lend me your umbrella and you wear my coat. It takes only two or three minutes to my house. But you'll be **soaked** with only this umbrella.

W: How nice of you. But you'll be soaked, too. I'll call my roommate and ask if she can pick me up.

M: Then you'll have to wait for her for a long time here alone.

W: But I can't give you back your raincoat tomorrow because I'll be **on a business trip** for a week from tomorrow. So I'm very grateful, but I don't think it's a good idea.

M: Then I'll stay with you here until **your roommate comes**.

W: Thank you.

남: 비가 엄청나게 오는데. 우산 있어?

여: 응, 하나 있어. 그런데 비가 보통 많이 오는 게 아닌데. 난 집까지 못 걸어가겠다.

남: 너네 집이 여기서 멀지. 내 비옷 입을래?

여: 그럼 넌 뭘 입으려고?

남: 네 우산을 나한테 빌려줘. 그리고 네가 내 비옷을 입어. 난 집까지 2-3분 밖에 걸리지 않아. 하지만 넌 이 우산을 쓰고 가다가는 흠뻑 젖겠어.

여: 너 정말 친절하구나. 그렇지만 너도 흠뻑 젖을 거야. 난 룸메이트에게 전화해서 데리러 올 수 있는지 물어볼게.

남: 그럼 넌 여기서 한참 동안 혼자 기다려야 할 거야.

여: 그렇지만 내가 네 비옷을 내일 돌려줄 수가 없어. 내가 내일부터 일주일 동안 출장을 하거든. 정말 고맙지만, 별로 좋은 생각이 아닌 것 같아.

남: 그럼 네 룸메이트가 올 때까지 같이 기다려줄게.

여: 고마워.

해설: 여자는 내일부터 출장을 가서 남자의 비옷을 돌려 줄 수가 없기 때문에 룸메이트에게 데리러 와달라고 전화할 것이다.

Listening Web

Intro: pouring   Web 1: Lend

Web 3: back   Ending: stay

True / False

1. F   2. T   3. T   4. F

문항 9 ①

Script & Dictation

W: Kevin, I heard you have an awesome plan during this summer vacation.

M: Yeah. I've always been dreaming of international **voluntary** service. I applied for it last semester, and fortunately **I'm in**.

W: But aren't you afraid of going to Africa? We don't have lots of information about it.

M: That's why these days I'm reading a book about Brundi.

W: Brundi? What is it?

M: It's a country in Africa.

W: I see. What's the title?

M: "Dreaming with a Camera." It is about the students in Brundi who take pictures of their daily lives with **disposable cameras** and present their dreams in the pictures.

W: Interesting. I'd like to read the book. Could you lend me the book after **you finish it**?

M: I'm sorry. I borrowed it from my friend. I heard all the profits from the books are donated to the schools in Africa.

W: Wow, then I'm **willing to buy one** right now.

여: Kevin, 네가 이번 여름 방학에 아주 멋진 계획이 있다고 들었어.

남: 응, 국제 봉사활동은 내가 항상 꿈꿔왔던 거야. 지난 학기에 신청했는데, 운 좋게도 합류하게 됐어.

여: 하지만 아프리카에 가는 것이 두렵지 않니? 아프리카에 관한 정보도 많지 않잖아.

남: 그래서 요즘 브룬디에 관한 책을 읽고 있어.

여: 브룬디? 그게 뭐야?

남: 아프리카에 있는 나라야.

여: 그렇구나. 제목이 뭔데?

남: '카메라로 꿈꾸며'야. 자신들의 일상생활을 일회용 카메라로 찍고 그 사진을 통해 자신의 꿈을 보여주는 브룬디의 학생들에 관한 책이야.

여: 재미있는걸. 나도 그 책 읽어보고 싶어. 너 다 읽은 다음에 나 좀 빌려줄래?

남: 미안. 나도 친구한테 빌린 거야. 책에서 나오는 수익금은 전부 아프리카 학교에 기증된다고 들었어.

여: 와, 그렇다면 지금 당장 기꺼이 한 권 사겠어.

해설: 여자는 처음에 책을 남자에게 빌리려고 했으나, 수익금 전체가 기부된다는 말을 듣고 당장 책을 사겠다고 했다. 따라서 여자는 서점으로 갈 것이다.

Listening Web

Intro: and fortunately   Web 2: lives, disposable

Web 3: donated

True / False

1. T   2. F   3. F   4. F

문항 10 ②

Script & Dictation

W: What's up?

M: Hi, Irene. I'm on the way **to the bookstore**.

W: Really? Me, too. Let's go together. What are you looking for?

M: A score.

W: Score? Do you play a **musical instrument**?

M: I play clarinet. I promised to play "Nella Fantasia" to my girlfriend on her birthday, so I'm going to the bookstore to buy the score.

W: How sweet of you. By the way, you know my brother, Tom. He also plays the clarinet, and he has the score.

M: Are you sure?

W: Yes, I heard him practice it a week ago. Maybe he practiced it for the **music performance test**.

M: Can you lend it to me, please?

W: No problem. I think Tom wants to be friends with you. He is trying to make a club for **clarinet players**.

M: Wow, I'm interested in the club.

여: 별일 없어?

남: 안녕, Irene. 난 서점 가는 길이야.

여: 정말? 나도. 같이 가자. 뭐 살 건데?

남: 악보.

여: 악보? 너 악기 연주해?

남: 나 클라리넷 연주해. 여자친구에게 생일에 Nella Fantasia 연주해주기로 약속했거든. 그래서 악보 사러 가는 길이야.

여: 멋지구나. 그런데 너 내 동생 Tom 알지. 그 애도 클라리넷 연주하는데, 그 악보가 있어.

남: 정말이야?

여: 응, 일주일 전에 연습하는 거 들었어. 아마 음악 수행평가 때문에 연습한 거 같아.

남: 그거 나한테 빌려줄 수 있을까?

여: 물론이지. 내 생각에 Tom이 너와 친구되고 싶어 할 것 같아. 클라리넷 연주자 동아리를 만들려고 하고 있거든.

남: 와, 나 그 동아리에 관심 있어.

해설: 남자는 원래 악보를 사러 가는 길이었지만, 여자의 동생이 그 악보를 갖고 있는 말을 듣고 빌려줄 것을 부탁했다.

Listening Web

Web 1: on   Web 2: score

True / False

1. T   2. F   3. T   4. F

문항 1 ②

Script & Dictation

W: Springville District Police. May I help you?

M: Hi, I'm calling to see if I can **ask about tickets**.

W: What's the problem?

M: I got a ticket for speeding.

W: Then you have to pay the fine **within two weeks** at the nearest police office.

M: I know, but I **couldn't help speeding** at the time.

W: What happened?

M: My wife was giving birth to a baby, and I was on the way to the hospital.

W: Oh, congratulations. Then you need to hand in the proof of birth at the police office.

M: Then can I simply get the fine cancelled?

W: Yes. And **from now on** don't forget that speeding is very dangerous, especially in winter. The streets are very snowy and slippery.

M: Of course. I'm always **a safe driver**. Thanks.

W: You're welcome.

여: Springville 경찰서입니다. 무엇을 도와드릴까요?

남: 안녕하세요. 교통 딱지에 대해서 여쭈어 보려고 전화했습니다.

여: 무슨 문제가 있으신가요?

남: 과속 딱지를 받았습니다.

여: 그럼 2주 안에 가장 가까운 경찰서에 가셔서 벌금을 내셔야 합니다.

남: 알고 있습니다. 하지만 그 당시에는 어쩔 수 없는 상황이었습니다.

여: 무슨 일인가요?

남: 제 아내가 출산 중이어서 병원에 가는 길이었습니다.

여: 오, 축하드려요. 그럼 출생증명서를 경찰서에 제출하시면 됩니다.

남: 그럼 벌금은 그냥 면제받을 수 있는 건가요?

여: 네. 그리고 이제부터 과속은 위험하다는 것을 잊지 마세요. 특히나 겨울에는요. 길에 눈이 쌓여 있어서 미끄러우니까요.

남: 물론이죠. 전 언제나 안전하게 운전합니다. 감사합니다.

여: 별말씀을요.

해설: 남자는 과속을 한 이유로 "My wife was giving birth to a baby… (아내가 출산 중이어서…)"라고 말하고 있다.

Listening Web

Web 1: speeding   Web 2: to

Web 3: hand in   Ending: snowy

True / False

1. F   2. F   3. T   4. F

문항 2 ①

Script & Dictation

W: What did you do last weekend? I called you to go to a movie, but you didn't **get the phone**.

M: I'm sorry. I went to **my cousin's wedding** on Sunday. I recognized that **I'd missed your calls** too late, so I couldn't give you a return call.

W: That's okay. I **hung around** with my friends during the weekend.

M: But it was rainy a lot!

W: Yeah. That's why I spent **a lot of time** at the shopping mall, I got rain boots.

M: I see. I was going to ask you if you can go rafting next Friday.

W: I'd love to, but...

M: Are you **afraid of** water?

W: No way. I do love rafting. But actually I have a backache.

M: Did you go to the hospital?

W: Yes, the doctor said I need to **avoid active exercise** for a while.

M: I see. I hope you'll get better soon.

여: 지난 주말에 뭐했어? 영화 보러 가자고 전화했는데 안 받더라.

남: 미안해. 일요일에 사촌 결혼식에 갔었어. 네가 전화했던 것을 너무 늦게 알아서 다시 전화 못 했어.

여: 괜찮아. 난 주말에 친구들이랑 돌아다녔어.

남: 하지만, 비가 많이 왔잖아!

여: 응, 그래서 쇼핑몰에서 많은 시간을 보내다가 장화를 샀어.

남: 그랬구나. 다음 금요일에 래프팅 갈 수 있는지 물어보려고 했는데.

여: 정말 가고 싶다. 그런데…

남: 물을 무서워해?

여: 아니. 래프팅 정말 좋아한다니까. 그런데 사실 나 허리가 아파.

남: 병원에 가봤어?

여: 응, 의사 선생님께서 당분간 활동적인 운동은 하지 말래.

남: 그렇구나. 곧 좋아지길 바랄게.

해설: 래프팅 가자는 남자의 제안에 여자는 "…actually I have a backache. (사실 나 허리가 아파.)"라고 말하고 있다.

Listening Web

Web 1: return   Web 2: next

Web 3: rafting   Ending: avoid

True / False

1. F   2. F   3. T   4. F

문항 3 ⑤

Script & Dictation

W: Paul, what are you doing?

M: I'm looking at my friend's Buddy Book. She uploads **a lot of pictures** and comments every day.

W: Do you also have your own Buddy Book?

M: I don't have my own. I just surf my friends' Buddy Books.

W: Why don't you have one?

M: Well, it's very interesting, but I think it's **open to everyone**. I don't want somebody I don't know to know about my private life. What about you?

W: I just **look around** my friends', like you.

M: How often do you visit the Buddy Book site?

W: Only two or three times a month.

M: You're not interested in this kind of thing. I thought it was **kind of girlish.**

W: Well, some of my male friends like Buddy Book. I think I'm just **too lazy to visit** my friends' Buddy Books and put up some comments.

여: Paul, 뭐 하고 있어?

남: 내 친구의 Buddy Book을 보는 중이야. 얘는 매일 사진과 글을 올려.

여: 너도 네 Buddy Book이 있어?

남: 내 것은 없어. 난 그냥 친구들 것만 돌아다녀.

여: 너도 해 보지그래?

남: 음, 재미있긴 한데, 모든 사람들에게 열려있잖아. 내가 모르는 사람이 내 사생활에 대해서 아는 건 싫어. 넌?

여: 나도 너처럼 친구들 것만 돌아다녀.

남: Buddy Book 사이트에는 얼마나 자주 가?

여: 한 달에 두세 번.

남: 넌 이런 데에 별로 관심이 없구나. 난 이건 좀 여자애들이 하는 거라고 생각했는데.

여: 음, 몇몇 남자애들도 Buddy Book을 좋아해. 내 생각에 난 그저 너무 게을러서 친구 Buddy Book에 들어가서 글 남기고 그러질 못하는 것 같아.

해설: "I don't want somebody I don't know to know about my private life. [난 내가 모르는 사람이 내 사생활을 아는 게 싫어.]"라는 말에서 남자가 사생활 노출을 꺼림을 알 수 있다.

Listening Web

Web 1: surf   Web 2: private

Web 3: interested in   Ending: up

True / False

1. F   2. F   3. T   4. T

문항 4 ⑤

Script & Dictation

W: What are you looking at?

M: This is the performance of a K-pop star. I'm practicing this type of dance these days.

W: I didn't know that you like dancing.

M: I became **interested in** Korean pop songs after I saw some Korean **soap operas**. Do you like K-pop?

W: Well, I've heard only a few songs. What makes you like K-pop?

M: The rhythm is **so** simple **that** anybody can sing along.

W: But if the rhythm is simple, I don't think it's interesting.

M: The songs have a quick tempo. And the Korean pop singers are also professional **when it comes to** dancing, so their performances are not boring at all.

W: Really? I can't imagine. Can you let me listen to a Korean pop song?

M: Sure, why not? Oh! I'm planning a flash mob dance with a Korean pop song. Will you join?

W: No, Jack. I'm really **terrible at dancing**.

여: 뭘 보고 있니?

남: 이건 한국 대중가수의 공연이야. 나 요즘 이런 춤을 연습해.

여: 네가 춤을 좋아하는지 몰랐어.

남: 한국 드라마를 보고 나서 한국 대중가요에 관심이 생기게 되었어. 너도 한국 대중가요를 좋아하니?

여: 음, 난 몇 곡밖에 못 들어봤어. 한국 대중가요가 왜 좋아?

남: 리듬이 단순해서 아무나 따라 부를 수 있어.

여: 하지만 리듬이 단순하면 재미없을 것 같은데.

남: 노래들이 박자가 빨라. 그리고 한국 대중가요 가수들은 춤에 관해서도 프로야. 그래서 공연이 전혀 지루하지 않아.

여: 그래? 상상이 안 가. 한국 대중가요 좀 들려줄래?

남: 그럼, 물론이지. 아! 내가 한국 노래에 맞춰서 플래시 몹을 준비 중인데. 너도 할래?

여: 아니야, Jack. 난 춤 진짜 못 춰.

해설: "The rhythm is so simple that anybody can sing along. [리듬이 단순해서 아무나 따라 부를 수 있어.]"라는 말에서 남자가 한국 대중가요를 좋아하는 이유를 알 수 있다.

Listening Web

Intro: type   Web 2: along

Web 3: boring   Ending: flash

True / False

1. F   2. T   3. F   4. F

Script & Dictation

W: It's raining heavily.

M: You don't like rain, do you?

W: No. It's **humid and dark** all day long.

M: I don't like rain, either. But we haven't had rain for a long time, so the current drought has been extremely hard on farmers.

W: I've heard the news that farmers have **suffered from** drought damage.

M: Maybe this rain will be helpful. I think we need more rain. This is **not enough**.

W: You're right. Farmers are glad to have rain, but I'm worried **because of this rain**.

M: Why?

W: I'm going to take **a few days off** next week. The weather forecast says that it will last for about five days from now.

M: Uh-oh. I'm sorry to hear that. You can **enjoy indoor activities**, like swimming in an indoor swimming pool.

W: I've already reserved a hotel room near Sorak Mountain. I was going to go hiking.

여: 비 정말 많이 온다.

남: 너 비 안 좋아하지, 그렇지?

여: 응. 종일 습하고 어둡잖아.

남: 나도 비는 안 좋아해. 하지만 한동안 비가 안 와서 최근 가뭄은 농부들에게 무척 힘들었어.

여: 나도 농부들이 가뭄 피해로 고생했다는 뉴스를 들었어.

남: 아마 이 비가 도움이 될 거야. 내 생각엔 비가 좀 더 와야 해. 이걸로는 부족해.

여: 네 말이 맞아. 농부들은 이 비를 반가워하겠지만, 난 이 비 때문에 걱정스러워.

남: 왜?

여: 난 다음 주에 며칠 휴가를 쓸 거거든. 일기 예보에서 그러는데 비가 지금부터 닷새 동안 계속될 거래.

남: 이런. 그 말을 들으니 유감이야. 실내 활동을 즐길 수도 있잖아. 실내 수영장에서 수영을 하거나.

여: 벌써 설악산 근처에 호텔을 예약했어. 등산 가려고 했었지.

해설: 여자는 설악산에 가려고 예약을 해 놓은 상태인데, 일기 예보에서 여자의 휴가 동안 비가 온다고 하여 걱정하고 있다.

Listening Web

Intro: heavily   Web 1: hard on

Web 2: worried   Web 3: a

True / False

1. F   2. T   3. F   4. T

Script & Dictation

W: Yoon, will you **sign up for** English Conversation next semester?

M: Sure. It's a requirement **as far as** I know.

W: Not really. I'm thinking of changing one of my classes next semester.

M: What's **on your mind**?

W: I'll take 19th century American literature instead of English Conversation.

M: I heard it's **quite demanding**.

W: I know, but it's not an elective for English majors.

M: Who's going to teach it next semester?

W: Ms. Quinn. Will you sign up for this course with me? Why don't we help each other next semester? You told me that you need **another three credits** for graduation.

M: What time is the class?

W: **It meets on** Wednesday from 10 a.m. to 12 p.m.

M: Sorry, I have a part-time job then. Mina is an English major, too. Why don't you call her?

W: She **took this course** last semester.

여: 윤, 다음 학기에 영어 회화 수업 들을 거야?

남: 물론이지. 필수과목이라고 알고 있는데.

여: 그렇지는 않아. 난 다음 학기에 수업 하나를 바꾸고 싶어.

남: 뭐로 할 생각인데?

여: 영어 회화 대신 19세기 미국 소설을 들으려고.

남: 그거 좀 힘들다던데.

여: 알아, 하지만 영어 전공자들에게는 선택과목이 아니야.

남: 다음 학기에 누가 가르치셔?

여: Quinn 교수님. 너도 나랑 같이 이거 신청할래? 다음 학기에 우리 서로 도와주는 게 어때? 너 졸업하려면 3학점 더 남았다며.

남: 수업이 몇 시에 있는데?

여: 수요일 오전 10시부터 12시까지.

남: 미안, 난 그때 아르바이트가 있어. 미나도 영어 전공하잖아. 미나에게 전화해 봐.

여: 미나는 지난 학기에 이 수업 들었어.

해설: 마지막 남자의 발언 "I have a part-time job then. (난 그 시간에 아르바이트가 있어.)" 라는 말에서 남자가 수업을 들을 수 없는 이유를 알 수 있다.

Listening Web

Intro: of   Web 1: 19th

Web 2: up   Ending: took

True / False

1. T   2. T   3. F   4. F

문항 7 ③

Script & Dictation

M: Hi, Chelsea. You look tired.

W: I have a history test today, so I **crammed for the test** last night. Because I had to cover the entire Middle Ages, I slept for only four hours.

M: You don't review **what you learned** every day?

W: No. Do you?

M: **Me neither**.

W: Do you also have a test today? You look exhausted, too.

M: No, the **fire alarm went off** at midnight in my apartment. All of my family escaped from the house.

W: Was the fire in your house?

M: Fortunately, no. It was an accident. But the firefighters and the police officers investigated what the problem was, so I couldn't come back home until 6 a.m.

W: **It's a relief** that everything was okay, **though**.

M: Yes. But the problem is that I was going to do my homework this morning, and I couldn't after all.

남: 안녕, Chelsea. 너 피곤해 보인다.

여: 나 오늘 역사 시험 있어서 어젯밤에 벼락치기 했어. 중세 시대 전체를 다뤄야 해서 네 시간밖에 못 잤어.

남: 너 평소에 복습을 안 하는구나?

여: 안 해. 넌 해?

남: 나도 안 해.

여: 너도 오늘 시험 있어? 너도 피곤해 보여.

남: 아니. 어젯밤에 우리 아파트에 화재경보기가 울렸어. 우리 식구들 다 집에서 피신했지.

여: 너희 집에 불이 났던 거야?

남: 다행히도 아니야. 잘못 울린 거였어. 그런데 소방관과 경찰관이 와서 문제가 무엇이었는지 조사하느라 새벽 6시가 되어서야 집에 들어갔어.

여: 그래도 무사해서 다행이다.

남: 그렇지. 그런데 문제는 내가 오늘 아침에 숙제하려고 했었는데, 결국 못했다는 거야.

해설: 어젯밤 남자는 화재경보기가 잘못 울려서 새벽에 집에 들어갔다.

Listening Web

Intro: tired   Web 1: entire

Web 2: midnight   Web 3: investigated

Ending: couldn't

True / False

1. T   2. T   3. F   4. T

문항 8 ②

Script & Dictation

W: Where are you going?

M: I'm going to school.

W: During vacation? Do you attend summer school?

M: No. I have to prepare for the **annual school festival**.

W: Oh, I remember last year's festival. The musical was enthusiastically supported by the audience.

M: **They won** the grand prize. It was really impressive.

W: What will you do to at the festival? Will you play the piano again? Your piano recital last year was really excellent, too.

M: Thank you. But I'm **conducting** the school **orchestra** this year.

W: Good for you! That's what **you've been dreaming of**! Now you're a maestro.

M: Not really. I'm just practicing.

W: I **promise to go see** the orchestra.

여: 어디가?

남: 학교 가는 길이야.

여: 방학에? 여름 보충 수업 들어?

남: 아니. 학교 연례 축제를 준비해야 해.

여: 아, 작년 축제 생각난다. 뮤지컬이 열광적인 환호를 받았었지.

남: 그랑프리 받았잖아. 정말 인상적이었어.

여: 넌 축제에서 뭐해? 또 피아노 연주하니? 작년에 너의 피아노 독주도 정말 멋있었어.

남: 고마워. 그런데 올해는 학교 오케스트라를 지휘해.

여: 잘됐다! 네가 꿈꾸던 거잖아! 이제 넌 마에스트로구나.

남: 그렇다기보다는. 그냥 연습 중이야.

여: 오케스트라 꼭 보러 갈게.

해설: 남자는 작년 학교 축제 때 피아노 독주를 했지만, 올해는 오케스트라를 지휘한다고 말하고 있다.

Listening Web

Web 1: the annual   Web 2: recital

Web 3: conducting

True / False

1. T   2. F   3. T   4. F

Script & Dictation

W: I heard you've been chosen to take part in a training program as the **representative of** our school. Buy the way, what is it?

M: Well, I was going to participate in the global leadership training program, but **I gave up**.

W: What happened? There were so many applicants that it was very **competitive**, as far as I know.

M: Actually, Brian **was to attend** the program at first, but he gave up because he had to go on a retreat.

W: Yeah, he is a **devout churchgoer**.

M: So I was going to attend it instead of him, but I'll be traveling to Phuket.

W: Phuket? In Thailand?

M: Yes. My father **got a promotion**, and he got flight tickets to Phuket.

W: Wow! Congratulations! Have a nice vacation.

M: Thanks. You, too.

여: 네가 우리 학교 대표로 무슨 연수 프로그램에 참가한다고 들었어. 그런데 무슨 프로그램이야?

남: 음, 난 국제 리더십 연수에 참가하려고 했었는데, 포기했어.

여: 어떻게 된 거야? 내가 알기로는 지원자가 너무 많아서 경쟁이 아주 심했다던데.

남: 사실은 처음에 Brian이 가기로 했었어. 그런데 수련회에 가야 해서 포기했었지.

여: 그래, 그 애는 독실하게 교회 다니는 애야.

남: 그래서 내가 그 애 대신에 참여하려고 했던 거야. 그런데 난 푸껫 여행 갈 거거든.

여: 푸껫? 태국에 있는?

남: 응. 아버지께서 승진하셨는데, 푸껫 비행기 표가 생겼어.

여: 와! 축하해! 멋진 방학 보내.

남: 고마워. 너도 잘 지내.

해설: 남자는 원래 방학 중 연수를 받을 계획이었지만, 아버지가 승진하셔서 푸껫으로 여행을 가게 되었다.

Listening Web

Intro: part in
Web 1: training
Web 2: attend, retreat
Web 3: attend

True / False

1. T   2. F   3. T   4. F

Script & Dictation

W: You're the only person I've seen today.

M: You told me on the phone **you would go see** a dentist this afternoon.

W: I called the dentist's and found out that I had to wait for over an hour. So I **made an appointment** for next week.

M: I see. Where do you want to go for dinner?

W: Let's go to the nearest restaurant. I'm starving. **I skipped lunch**.

M: Do not skip three meals even if you're on a diet.

W: I had **a late breakfast**. I ate salad.

M: What did you do after that?

W: I went to the gym to exercise, but it's closed today.

M: So you came home?

W: Yes. And I **lay down** on the sofa surfing TV channels. And then maybe I fell asleep. Your call an hour ago **woke me up**.

M: That's why you skipped lunch.

W: That's right.

여: 네가 오늘 내가 만난 유일한 사람이야.

남: 너 나한테 전화로 오후에 치과 갈 거라고 했잖아.

여: 치과에 전화했더니 한 시간도 넘게 기다려야겠더라고. 그래서 다음 주로 예약했어.

남: 그랬구나. 저녁 어디로 먹으러 갈까?

여: 제일 가까운 식당으로 가자. 배고파 죽겠어. 점심을 안 먹었거든.

남: 다이어트 중이라도 세 끼니를 거르지는 마.

여: 나 늦게 아침을 먹었어. 샐러드를 먹었어.

남: 그리고 나서 뭐했어?

여: 운동하러 체육관 갔는데, 오늘 쉬는 날이더라고.

남: 그래서 집에 왔어?

여: 응. 그리고 소파에 TV 채널 돌리면서 누워있었지. 그러다가 잠이 들었나 봐. 한 시간 전에 네 전화 받고 깼어.

남: 그래서 점심을 걸렀구나.

여: 그런 거지.

해설: 여자는 오늘 아침 일어나서 치과에도 가지 못하고 운동하러 가지도 못했다. 집에 돌아와 TV를 보다가 잠이 들어서 점심을 거르게 되었다.

Listening Web

Intro: I've seen
Web 1: skipped
Web 2: late
Web 3: closed
Ending: surfing

True / False

1. F   2. T   3. T   4. F

문항 1 ②

Script & Dictation

W: Good evening. What can I do for you?

M: I'd like to make a reservation for a flight to Paris next Tuesday morning.

W: Would it be a **round-trip** ticket or one-way?

M: Round-trip, please

W: Hold on, please. I'll check to **see if** there's room. *[Pause]* We have a 10 a.m. flight on Tuesday morning.

M: Good. I'll take it. What's **the fare**?

W: Which class would you like?

M: First class, please.

W: It's $200. If you have a Summer Sky membership, you can **get a** 5% **discount**.

M: No, thanks.

W: All right. When will you return here?

M: December 30th.

W: I'll **book a seat** for your return. Would 3 p.m. that day be okay?

M: Perfect. Thank you.

W: May I have your name and phone number, please?

M: Scott Hue. 013-4236-9395.

여: 안녕하세요. 무엇을 도와드릴까요?

남: 다음 주 화요일 아침에 파리로 가는 비행기를 예약하고 싶습니다.

여: 왕복 표인가요, 편도 표인가요?

남: 왕복으로 주세요.

여: 잠시만 기다려 주세요. 자리가 있는지 알아보겠습니다. *[잠시 후]* 화요일 오전 10시에 비행기가 있습니다.

남: 좋아요, 그걸로 하죠. 얼마인가요?

여: 어떤 좌석 등급을 원하세요?

남: 일등석으로 해주세요.

여: 200달러입니다. Summer Sky 회원이시면 5% 할인받으실 수 있습니다.

남: 아니요, 괜찮습니다.

여: 알겠습니다. 언제 여기로 돌아오시나요?

남: 12월 30일이요.

여: 돌아오는 좌석도 예약해드렸습니다. 그날 오후 3시 괜찮으신가요?

남: 좋아요. 감사합니다.

여: 귀하의 성함과 전화번호를 알려주시겠어요?

남: Scott Hue입니다. 013-4236-9395.

해설: 떠나는 날은 대화 초반에 다음 주 화요일이라고만 언급했을 뿐 정확한 날짜를 언급하지는 않았다.

Listening Web

Intro: reservation   Web 1: fare

Ending: 30th

True / False

1. F   2. T   3. F   4. F

문항 2 ⑤

Script & Dictation

W: **What a mess**! What are you doing?

M: I tried to make an apricot pie, but I couldn't.

W: Do you want me to help you?

M: Yes, please.

W: Okay, let's get started! First of all, you need to beat the apricot jam, **so that** its texture becomes smooth.

M: I see. Like this?

W: Good. I'll make the dough while you're doing it.

M: Okay. **What's in it**?

W: Butter, sugar, egg, and flour. You need to **beat** them for about 2 to 3 minutes until the dough **becomes smooth enough**.

M: Oh! We forgot to **preheat the oven**!

W: You're right. Preheat it to 180°C. When the dough is ready, put the apricot jam on the dough and bake it for about 20 to 25 minutes until it becomes **golden**. It's quite easy, isn't it?

M: Yes. Thank you. I think you're **an excellent cook**.

여: 웬 난장판이야! 너 뭐 하고 있는 거야?

남: 살구파이 만들려고 했는데, 못하겠어.

여: 내가 도와줄까?

남: 응, 그렇게 해줘.

여: 그래, 시작해 보자! 일단 살구 잼을 휘저어야 해. 그러면 질감이 부드러워져.

남: 알았어. 이렇게?

여: 잘하는데. 네가 그거 하는 동안 내가 반죽을 만들게.

남: 좋아. 거기엔 뭐가 들어가?

여: 버터, 설탕, 달걀, 그리고 밀가루. 이것들도 반죽이 적당히 부드러워질 때까지 한 2-3분 동안 휘저어야 해.

남: 아! 오븐을 예열하는 걸 잊었어!

여: 맞아. 오븐은 섭씨 180도로 예열해. 반죽이 완성되면, 반죽 위에 살구 잼을 바르고 노릇해질 때까지 한 20-25분 동안 구우면 돼. 정말 쉽지?

남: 그래, 고마워. 너 정말 요리를 잘하는구나.

해설: 살구파이가 노릇해질 때까지 구우라고 했지만, 좋은 살구 잼의 색깔에 대해서는 언급되지 않았다.

Listening Web

Intro: apricot   Web 1: texture

Web 2: flour   Ending: golden

True / False

1. F   2. T   3. T   4. T

문항 3 ②

Script & Dictation

M: I'm so glad that you could come to our family feast!

W: Thanks for **inviting me**. I can't wait to try some of the foods you told me about.

M: Right! I'm hungry, too. Let's eat!

W: Great! You've **fixed quite a meal**, so I don't know what to try.

M: Try these shish kebabs. I'm sure you'll love them. My dad cooked them.

W: I've never had it before. What's in it?

M: Meat and vegetables. Grill the meat first, and then just **wrap** the grilled meat and **assorted** vegetables with Turkish bread.

W: It's very easy to make. I'll try to make one at home.

M: You should. And don't forget to invite me then.

W: Sure. What is this **white stuff**?

M: It's the yoghurt sauce. You can **dip** the kebabs in the sauce.

W: Mmm, that's so good!

남: 우리 가족 행사에 와줘서 기뻐!

여: 초대해줘서 고마워. 네가 말했던 음식 먹고 싶어 못 참겠어.

남: 그래! 나도 배고파. 먹자!

여: 좋아! 네가 꽤 많은 음식을 준비해서 뭘 먹어야 할지 모르겠어.

남: 이 시시케밥을 먹어 봐. 네가 분명 좋아할 거야. 우리 아버지께서 만드셨어.

여: 난 이거 한 번도 먹어본 적 없는데. 안에 뭐가 들었어?

남: 고기랑 채소. 고기를 먼저 굽고 이 구운 고기와 여러 가지 채소를 터키 빵으로 감싸.

여: 만들기 무척 쉬운걸. 집에서 하나 만들어봐야겠어.

남: 그래. 그리고 그때 나 초대하는 거 잊지 마.

여: 물론이지. 이 하얀 것은 뭐야?

남: 요거트 소스야. 케밥을 이 소스에 찍어 먹어도 돼.

여: 음, 정말 맛있다!

해설: 시시케밥을 만드는 방법에 관한 언급은 있으나, 먹는 순서에 관한 언급은 없다.

Listening Web

Intro: told   Web 2: them

Web 3: assorted, Turkish   Ending: dip

True / False

1. T   2. F   3. T   4. F

문항 4 ③

Script & Dictation

W: What's this in the pictures? Oh, it's Easter Island!

M: Do you know this island?

W: I've read about this island. It's **full of lots of** mysteries.

M: Right. Look at these statues.

W: So unbelievable, isn't it? Do you know **why it is called** Easter Island?

M: Why?

W: Because it was discovered on Easter Sunday.

M: The discoverer **might have been** a Christian.

W: Maybe. He was a Dutch explorer. It's in the middle of the Pacific Ocean and **the nearest land** is another small island more than 1,000 miles west.

M: It must be **the most remote place** in the world. Look! This island is shaped like a triangle.

W: Yes, and do you see these volcanoes? It has **an extinct volcano** in each corner.

M: Are people living on this island?

W: Sure. They are farming a few crops like bananas or sugar cane.

M: Interesting. I wish I could go there someday.

여: 사진에 뭐 있어? 오, 이스터 아일랜드이구나!

남: 너 이 섬을 알아?

여: 이 섬에 대한 글을 읽은 적이 있어. 미스터리로 가득한 곳이지.

남: 맞아. 이 조각상들 좀 봐.

여: 정말 믿기지 않아, 그렇지? 너 이 섬이 왜 이스터 아일랜드인지 알아?

남: 왜 그런 거야?

여: 이 섬이 부활절에 발견되었거든.

남: 발견한 사람이 기독교인이었을지도 모르겠다.

여: 아마도. 그 사람은 네덜란드 탐험가였어. 이 섬은 태평양 한 가운데 있고, 가장 가까운 땅은 서쪽으로 1,000마일도 더 멀리 떨어진 곳에 있는 작은 섬이야.

남: 세상에서 가장 고립된 곳이겠구나. 봐봐! 섬이 삼각형 모양 이야.

여: 그래, 그리고 이 화산들이 보여? 여기에는 각 모퉁이에 사(死) 화산이 있어.

남: 이 섬에 사람이 살까?

여: 물론이지. 그 사람들은 바나나 사탕수수 같은 작물들을 농사짓고 있어.

남: 흥미로운데. 난 언제 한번 가봤으면 좋겠다.

해설: 서쪽으로 1,000마일 떨어진 곳에 다른 섬이 있다고 했을 뿐, 이스터 아일랜드의 크기에 관한 언급은 없다.

Listening Web

Web 1: on   Web 2: nearest

Web 3: shaped   Ending: cane

True / False

1. F   2. F   3. F   4. T

문항 5 ⑤

Script & Dictation

W: Welcome! How was your flight?

M: It was a long flight. But the weather here in Korea is fantastic, and I'm sure the long and boring **journey is worth it**.

W: Where do you plan to go?

M: First of all, I'll go to Gyongbok Palace and Namsan tomorrow. I heard I can see **the whole of** Seoul from the top of Namsan.

W: You should also go to Changduk Palace. It's **designated as** a UNESCO World Heritage site.

M: Really? I won't miss it. And I'll go to Namdaemun Market.

W: I know some delicious restaurants in Namdaemun Market. I can **guide you** if you want.

M: Thank you very much.

W: Why don't you go to Jeju Island?

M: I've been **thinking of it**, but I'll stay for only three days in Seoul.

W: You don't have enough time. You should go to Jeju another time. Now we've arrived at your hotel.

M: Thanks for **giving me a ride**.

W: My pleasure.

여: 환영합니다! 비행은 어땠나요?

남: 정말 오래 걸렸어요. 하지만 여기 한국 날씨가 정말 멋져서 지루한 비행에 보람이 있습니다.

여: 어디 가실 계획인가요?

남: 우선 내일 경복궁과 남산에 갈 거예요. 남산 꼭대기에서 서울 전체를 내려다볼 수 있다고 들었습니다.

여: 창덕궁에는 꼭 가보셔야 합니다. 유네스코에서 세계문화유산으로 지정된 곳이거든요.

남: 정말이요? 놓치지 말아야겠군요. 그리고 남대문 시장도 가보려고요.

여: 남대문 시장에 맛있는 식당들을 좀 알아요. 원하신다면 안내해드릴게요.

남: 정말 감사합니다.

여: 제주도에 가보시는 건 어때요?

남: 고민을 좀 했는데, 제가 서울에 3일밖에 머무르지 않아서요.

여: 시간이 별로 없으시군요. 다음번에 제주를 꼭 가보세요. 이제 호텔에 다 왔습니다.

남: 태워다 주셔서 감사합니다.

여: 별말씀을요.

해설: 남자는 서울에 3일밖에 머무르지 않을 것이므로, 시간이 부족하여 제주도에는 가지 않을 것이라고 말하고 있다.

Listening Web

Web 2: won't   Ending: stay

True / False

1. T   2. T   3. T   4. F

문항 6 ④

Script & Dictation

M: Wow! Now we're in Namsan Hanok Village.

W: This is authentic Korea! How much is the admission?

M: It's free! Let's go. This is the richest house. This kind of house has a Korean traditional garden. It looks **quite different from** western style houses, doesn't it?

W: Yes, it's very exotic and really beautiful. How many rooms does it have?

M: It is said that the richest house has 99 rooms. And look at this. This is the toilet.

W: It's **outside of the house**. It's separate from the main building.

M: Yes, it reflects that Korean people had **a good sense of** hygiene. And this is the kitchen. That is a kind of heating system. Have you ever heard of "ondol"?

W: Yes, I heard that "ondol" is a scientific **heating system**. I've always wondered how it works.

M: Would you like to **experience it**?

W: Sure. Let's go inside.

남: 와! 드디어 남산 한옥마을에 왔다.

여: 이게 진짜 한국이구나! 입장료가 얼마니?

남: 무료야! 가자. 이게 가장 부자인 집이야. 이런 집은 전통 한국식 정원이 있어. 서양식 집과는 상당히 다르지?

여: 그래, 아주 이국적이고 아름답네. 여기는 방이 몇 개야?

남: 가장 부자인 집은 99개의 방이 있다고 해. 이것 봐. 이건 화장실이야.

여: 화장실이 집 밖에 있네. 집 건물이랑 분리되어 있어.

남: 응. 한국 사람들의 위생관념이 반영된 것이지. 그리고 여기가 주방이야. 저것이 말하자면 난방시설인 것이지. '온돌'에 대해서 들어봤어?

여: 응, '온돌'은 과학적인 난방 시설이라고 들었어. 난 항상 그 원리가 궁금했어.

남: 한번 체험해 볼래?

여: 물론이지. 들어가 보자.

해설: 주방에 있는 난방 시설에 관해 언급하고 있으나, 주방의 위치에 관한 언급은 없다.

Listing Web

Web 1: western
Web 2: 99
Web 3: from
Ending: works

True / False

1. F   2. F   3. F   4. T

Script & Dictation

M: How many stations are left?

W: We still have 19 stations to go. It takes two minutes **on average** to go to the next station,

M: Then 38 minutes exactly for the subway only. Will we **get off at** the Wonderland Park station?

W: That's right. We have to take a bus to **the amusement park**.

M: I see. Have you ever been there?

W: Yes, I have. I think it'll take about an hour **in total from now**.

M: Are there a lot of buses that go to the amusement park at the Wonderland Park station?

W: There are free shuttles to commute from the subway station directly to the amusement park **every 10 minutes** as far as I know.

M: Oh, it's Wonderland Park! Let's get off.

남: 역 몇 개 남았어?

여: 아직 열아홉 개 더 가야 해. 다음 역 가는데 평균적으로 2분 걸려.

남: 그럼 지하철만 정확히 38분 걸리는 거네. 우리 Wonderland Park 역에서 내려?

여: 맞아. 그리고 우리 놀이공원까지 버스 타고 가야 해.

남: 그렇구나. 너 거기 가봤어?

여: 응, 가봤어. 지금부터 적어도 한 시간은 더 걸릴 것 같아.

남: Wonderland Park 역에서 놀이공원까지 가는 버스는 많아?

여: 지하철 역에서 놀이공원으로 바로 가는 무료 셔틀이 10분마다 운행되는 걸로 알고 있어.

남: 오, Wonderland Park 역이다! 내리자.

해설 지금으로부터 지하철을 38분 정도 타야 하지만, 출발지에서부터 목적지까지 지하철 총 탑승 시간에 대한 언급은 없다.

Listening Web

Intro: 19
Web 2: about
Web 3: directly

True / False

1. T   2. F   3. F   4. T

Script & Dictation

M: Hey! I saw **an Indian film**.

W: I've never seen Indian movies before. What was it?

M: The title is "The Robot." It was a **sci-fi movie**, and also it was comic and adventurous.

W: Wow! I heard Indian films are so fascinating.

M: Yeah. Most Indian films are **thrillers** or romantic movies, action-packed, with **extravagant sets** and plenty of singing and dancing.

W: Maybe that's because the film companies want to gather a lot of audience.

M: Yes, and they also make really fantastic posters **to attract people**. The posters are not based on reality. Their colors are manipulated and the eyes are **exaggerated**.

W: Hmm, I'm getting interested in Indian films. I want to see one some time.

M: You should. India makes about 850 films a year. That's 300 more than Hollywood.

W: I've heard of "Bollywood." It means Mumbai has become the center of the film industry, right?

M: You're right.

남: 나 인도 영화 봤다.

여: 난 인도 영화 본 적 없는데. 뭐었어?

남: 제목이 '로봇'이야. 공상과학 영화인데, 웃기기도 하고 모험 스럽기도 해.

여: 와! 인도 영화가 굉장히 재미있다고 들었어.

남: 응. 대부분 인도 영화가 스릴러이거나 로맨틱 영화야. 액션으로 무장하고 화려한 세트장에서 만들어져. 노래나 춤도 많이 나오고.

여: 그건 아마도 영화사가 관람객들을 많이 모으기 위해서 그런 것이겠지.

남: 그렇지. 그리고 사람들의 이목을 끌기 위해서 아주 환상적인 포스터를 만들기도 해. 영화 포스터들은 사실적으로 만들어지지 않아. 색을 보정하고 눈을 과장해서 그려.

여: 음. 인도 영화에 관심이 생기는걸. 언젠가는 인도 영화를 보고 싶어.

남: 꼭 봐. 인도가 일 년에 영화를 850편 정도 만들어. 할리우드보다 300편이나 더 만드는 거야.

여: 난 '발리우드'라고도 들어봤어. 뭄바이가 영화 산업의 중심지가 되었다는 의미이겠지?

남: 네 말이 맞아.

해설 인도 영화 회사가 많은 관객을 모으려 한다고 말했지만, 구체적인 관객 수에 관한 언급은 없다.

Listening Web

Intro: fascinating
Web 1: packed
Web 2: attract
Web 3: exaggerated

True / False

1. T 2. F 3. T 4. F

문항 9 ①

Script & Dictation

W: I went to an **art museum** last weekend.

M: Cool! How was it?

W: Honestly, it was so difficult that I couldn't understand. Superrealism, Conceptual art...

M: Joseph Beuys, the **leading** conceptual artist.

W: Oh, I didn't know that you're well-versed in art!

M: I'm just interested in art. Conceptual artists tried to **convey meaning** by showing something in a new and interesting way, without long explanations. So you need to think about the concept that led the artist to choose and present the works in that way.

W: It's still hard.

M: Yes, it's not easy at all. To show the concept effectively, they used **various kinds of** techniques like performance, video, or installation.

W: Oh, yes. I remember an artist, Nam June Paik. He made a robot with **low-cost materials**. I felt it was like a **humble shelter**.

M: Wow. You're a fast learner. That's the right way to enjoy conceptual art!

여: 나 지난 주말에 미술관에 갔었어.

남: 멋진데! 어땠어?

여: 솔직히 너무 어려워서 이해할 수 없었어. 극사실주의니 개념 미술이니…

남: Joseph Beuys, 개념 미술의 선두 작가.

여: 와, 네가 미술에 조예가 깊은지 몰랐어.

남: 그냥 미술에 관심이 있어. 개념 미술가들은 긴 설명 없이 색다르고 재미있는 방법으로 작품을 주면서 의미를 전달하려고 했던 사람들이야. 그러니까 작가가 왜 그런 식으로 작품을 표현했는지 그 개념을 생각해 봐야 해.

여: 여전히 어려운걸.

남: 그렇지, 쉽지는 않아. 그 사람들은 개념을 효과적으로 보여주기 위해서 행위나 비디오, 설치 같은 다양한 기술을 사용했어.

여: 오, 그래. 예술가 백남준이 기억난다. 싸구려 물건들을 쌓아서 로봇을 만들었어. 초라한 은신처 같은 느낌이었어.

남: 와. 너 빨리 배우는구나. 개념 미술은 바로 그렇게 감상하는 거야.

해설: 대화 초반에 여자는 극사실주의와 개념주의에 대해 감상했다고 말했으나, 개념주의의 등장 배경에 대해서는 언급한 바 없다.

Listening Web

Intro: art   Web 1: leading

Web 2: explanations   Web 3: led

Ending: installation

True / False

1. F 2. T 3. F 4. T

문항 10 ③

Script & Dictation

M: A documentary about Edmund Hillary is on TV. He was the first to get to the top of Mount Everest. **No doubt** he was one of the greatest men in the world.

W: But do you know that Edmund Hillary was **not alone** when he was climbing?

M: What do you mean?

W: The Sherpas **lay the trail** and carry supplies with the climbers. You know Norgay? He was Edmund Hillary's Sherpa when he climbed Mount Everest. He is a very famous Sherpa.

M: By the way, how much are they **paid for** that tough work? I think it should be more than **a million dollars worth** of labor. Think about carrying that heavy stuff up to the mountain.

W: I'm not sure about it. But "Sherpa" itself is not a job, actually. The Sherpas are a group of people **who have always lived** in the Himalayas. It is originally from a Tibetan word which means "East People."

M: That's interesting.

남: Edmund Hillary에 관한 다큐멘터리를 TV에서 하고 있어. 에베레스트 정상에 처음으로 올라간 사람이야. 그는 세상에서 제일 훌륭한 사람 중 하나임이 틀림없어.

여: 하지만 Edmund Hillary도 등반할 때 혼자가 아니었다는 것을 알고 있니?

남: 무슨 뜻이야?

여: 셰르파들은 등산가와 함께 가면서 미리 길을 뚫고 짐을 날라. Norgay 알지? Edmund Hillary가 에베레스트를 오를 때 그의 셰르파였어. 매우 유명한 셰르파지.

남: 그런데 그 사람들은 그렇게 힘들일 하고 얼마 받을까? 100만 달러 이상의 가치가 있는 노동이란 생각이 들어. 그 무거운 짐을 들고 산을 오른다고 생각해 봐.

여: 그건 모르겠어. 하지만 '셰르파' 자체는 사실 직업이 아니야. 셰르파는 히말라야에서 살아오고 있는 사람들이야. 티베트 어로 '동쪽 사람들'이란 뜻의 단어에서 유래됐어.

남: 재미있구나.

해설: 셰르파는 등산가와 함께 가면서 길을 미리 뚫고 짐을 나르는 일을 하고, 유명한 셰르파의 이름으로 Norgay가 언급되었다. 셰르파가 사는 곳은 히말라야이고, 셰르파란 티베트 어로 '동쪽 사람들'이란 뜻이다. 셰르파의 보수에 대해서는 언급되지 않았다.

Listening Web

Intro: documentary   Web 1: trail

Web 2: climbed   Ending: East

True / False

1. F 2. F 3. F 4. T

문항 1 ④

Script & Dictation

W: Excuse me. I'm looking for something for my son.

M: Okay. What kind of thing are you looking for?

W: Well, he's ten years old. What would you recommend for him?

M: How about this jacket? It **comes in several colors**.

W: How much is it?

M: It is $150.

W: It costs more than I thought.

M: **What's your budget?**

W: About $100 or so.

M: Then, what about these shoes? Actually, they cost the same as the jacket, but I can give you **a 50% discount**.

W: They are good, but my son may want clothes more. How much are these jeans?

M: They are $70, but they are **season-off items**. So if you buy one pair, you'll get another **for 50% off**.

W: That's good. I'll take two pairs of jeans.

여: 실례합니다. 저는 아들에게 사줄 것을 찾고 있는데요.

남: 네, 어떤 종류로 찾고 계세요?

여: 음, 아이가 열 살인데요. 어떤 것을 추천해 주실 수 있나요?

남: 이 재킷은 어떠세요? 색상은 여러 가지로 나옵니다.

여: 얼마예요?

남: 150달러입니다.

여: 제가 생각했던 것보다 비싸네요.

남: 가격은 어느 정도 예상하세요?

여: 100달러 정도요.

남: 그럼 이 신발은 어떠세요? 실제로는 재킷과 같은 가격이지만, 50% 할인해 드릴 수 있습니다.

여: 멋지지만, 아들 녀석이 옷을 더 원할지도 모르겠네요. 이 청바지는 얼마죠?

남: 70달러인데, 철이 지난 상품입니다. 그래서 하나 사시면 다른 하나는 50% 할인된 가격으로 사실 수 있어요.

여: 괜찮네요. 청바지 두 벌 사겠습니다.

해설: 청바지는 한 벌에 70달러인데, 한 벌 사면 다른 한 벌은 50% 할인 [35달러] 되므로, 두 벌에 105달러이다.

Listening Web

Web 1: in   Web 3: 50

True / False

1. F   2. T   3. T   4. F

문항 2 ②

Script & Dictation

M: Excuse me. I'd like to send this package to Korea.

W: Do you want to send it by ship or by airmail?

M: By airmail. What's the postage?

W: **The cost depends on** the weight and size. Let me weigh it. *[Pause]* It's $4.

M: And I'd like to **insure this package for** $50.

W: Then you need to fill out this form first. You have to pay $1 for the insurance.

M: How long will it take for the package **to arrive**?

W: Fifteen days.

M: I'm sorry, but how much does it cost to send it by express? I want it to arrive in a week.

W: Three times **as much as regular**. There's no additional charge for the insurance. Would you like to send it by express?

M: Yes, please.

남: 실례합니다. 이 소포를 한국으로 보내고 싶습니다.

여: 배로 보내시겠어요, 항공으로 보내시겠어요?

남: 항공으로요. 우편요금이 얼마인가요?

여: 운임료는 무게와 크기에 따라 다릅니다. 무게를 재어보겠습니다. *[잠시 후]* 4달러입니다.

남: 그리고 이 소포에 50달러의 보험을 들고 싶습니다.

여: 그럼 우선 이 양식을 작성하세요. 보험료로 1달러를 더 내셔야 합니다.

남: 소포가 도착하는데 얼마나 걸릴까요?

여: 15일이요.

남: 죄송하지만 특급으로 보내는데 얼마인가요? 일주일 안으로 도착했으면 하는데요.

여: 일반 운임의 세 배입니다. 보험 인상료는 없습니다. 특급으로 하시겠어요?

남: 네, 그렇게 해주세요.

해설: 특급 운임는 일반 운임 4달러의 세 배이므로, 운임만 12달러이고, 여기에 보험료 1달러를 더하여 남자가 내야 할 총 금액은 13달러이다.

Listening Web

Web 1: weight   Web 3: no, charge

True / False

1. F   2. T   3. F   4. F

문항 3 ③

Script & Dictation

M: Hello. California Tour Company. May I help you?

W: Yes. Do you have **any seats left** on the Dreaming Los Angeles tour tomorrow?

M: Yes, there are several seats left.

W: What is the price of the tour?

M: It's $100 **for an adult**, including lunch.

W: How much is it for a kid?

M: It depends. You'll get 20% off **for under fifteen**, and 30% off for under ten. How old is the child?

W: She's nine. I'll take the tour. Two adults and one child, please.

M: If you are **residents** of California, you can get $10 off for each person.

W: We live **out of the state**.

M: Okay. If you pay $15 more, you'll get 10% off for all our tour packages for the next year. Do you want it?

W: Well, **that's a good deal**. But no, thanks.

남: 여보세요. 캘리포니아 여행사입니다. 무엇을 도와드릴까요?

여: 네, 내일 Dreaming Los Angeles 투어에 남은 자리가 있나요?

남: 네, 몇 자리 남아있습니다.

여: 여행 비용이 얼마인가요?

남: 성인은 100달러입니다. 점심 포함해서요.

여: 어린이는 얼마인가요?

남: 나이에 따라 다릅니다. 15세 이하는 20% 할인되고, 10세 이하는 30% 할인받으실 수 있습니다. 아이가 몇 살이죠?

여: 9살입니다. 그 여행에 신청할게요. 어른 둘, 어린이 한 명 해주세요.

남: 캘리포니아 주민이시면, 개인당 10달러씩 할인받으실 수 있습니다.

여: 저희는 다른 주에 살고 있어요.

남: 알겠습니다. 15달러 더 내시면 앞으로 일 년간 저희 회사 여행 상품을 10% 할인받으실 수 있습니다. 하시겠어요?

여: 음, 좋은 조건이군요. 하지만 안 할게요. 괜찮습니다.

해설: 성인은 한 명당 100달러, 9세 어린이는 한 명당 70달러 (10세 이하는 성인 요금에서 30% 할인되므로)이다. 성인 두 명, 어린이 한 명의 비용은 270달러이다.

Listening Web

Intro: price   Web 1: including
Web 4: 15

True / False

1. T   2. T   3. F   4. F

문항 4 ⑤

Script & Dictation

M: Hi. Do you have **gloves**?

W: Sure. Come in.

M: I was worried I couldn't **get any** because it's summer.

W: **Now is the time** if you want to buy some winter items! All the carry-overs are 50% off.

M: Really? Which ones were the best-seller?

W: These black ones were very popular last winter. They're very light, and the color **looks good on everybody**.

M: How much are they?

W: They were originally $30.

M: What about those brown ones?

W: They were popular, too. And they cost $20 originally. But I recommend the black ones.

M: Hmm. I love this brown color, though. I'll take two pairs.

W: Okay. **Cash or credit**?

M: I'll pay **in cash**. Here's $100.

남: 안녕하세요. 장갑 있나요?

여: 물론이죠. 들어오세요.

남: 여름이라서 구하지 못할까 봐 걱정했어요.

여: 겨울 상품을 사실 거라면 지금이 적기예요! 모든 이월 상품들을 50% 할인하고 있거든요.

남: 정말요? 어떤 것이 가장 잘 팔렸나요?

여: 이 검은색 장갑이 지난겨울에 가장 인기가 좋았어요. 그건 무척 가볍고, 색상도 누구에게나 잘 어울리고요.

남: 얼마죠?

여: 원래는 30달러였어요.

남: 저 갈색은 어때요?

여: 저것도 인기가 많았어요. 원래 20달러였고요. 하지만 저는 검은색을 추천해요.

남: 음. 하지만 전 이 갈색이 정말 마음에 들어요. 두 켤레 사겠어요.

여: 알겠습니다. 현금이세요, 카드세요?

남: 현금으로 낼게요. 여기 100달러요.

해설: 갈색 장갑은 원래 20달러이었으나, 이월 상품으로 50% 할인 중이므로 갈색 장갑 두 켤레의 가격은 20달러이다. 남자는 100달러를 냈으므로, 거스름돈 80달러를 받아야 한다.

Listening Web

Intro: 50   Web 2: 20
Web 3: brown   Ending: in

True / False

1. T   2. F   3. F   4. T

문항 5 ②

Script & Dictation

W: May I help you?

M: I'm looking for a birthday cake for my little daughter.

W: Chocolate cake is popular among kids. Our chocolate is **so** rich **that** kids love it.

M: How much is it?

W: We have three sizes: **regular**, family size, and party size. Which one would you like?

M: Is party size the biggest?

W: That's right. The chocolate cake **in regular size** is $12, and the size bigger costs **two more dollars**.

M: I see. What about the strawberry cake?

W: It's more expensive. The regular one is $13, and the family size is $16. Strawberry cake has only two sizes.

M: Okay. Then I'll take the chocolate cake in family size, please.

W: Do you have a Cake Lovers' membership card? You can get a $1 **discount for each cake** with the membership.

M: Yes, I have the card. Here you are.

W: Thank you very much!

여: 무엇을 도와드릴까요?

남: 제 딸 아이의 생일 케이크를 사려고 합니다.

여: 초콜릿 케이크가 아이들에게 인기가 좋아요. 저희 집 초콜릿은 맛이 진해서 아이들이 매우 좋아한답니다.

남: 얼마죠?

여: 세 가지 크기가 있어요. 중간, 패밀리 사이즈, 파티 사이즈. 어떤 것을 원하세요?

남: 파티 사이즈가 가장 큰 건가요?

여: 맞습니다. 초콜릿 케이크는 중간 사이즈가 12달러이고, 사이즈가 커질 때마다 2달러씩 비싸집니다.

남: 그렇군요. 딸기 케이크는 어때요?

여: 그건 좀 더 가격이 나가요. 중간 것이 13달러, 패밀리 사이즈가 16달러입니다. 딸기 케이크는 두 가지 크기 밖에 없어요.

남: 알겠습니다. 그럼 초콜릿 케이크를 패밀리 사이즈로 사겠습니다.

여: Cake Lovers 회원카드 있으세요? 회원카드 있으시면 케이크 하나 당 1달러씩 할인해 드립니다.

남: 네, 그 카드 있어요. 여기요.

여: 정말 감사합니다!

해설: 초콜릿 케이크는 중간 사이즈가 12달러이고, 사이즈가 커질 때마다 가격이 2달러씩 증가하므로, 패밀리 사이즈가 14달러이다. 회원카드가 있으면 1달러 할인받으므로, 남자가 낼 금액은 13달러이다.

Listening Web

Intro: rich   Web 1: 12

Web 2: family   Web 3: get

True / False

1. T   2. F   3. F   4. F

문항 6 ④

Script & Dictation

M: What are you looking at?

W: **An ad for** a swimming pool. It says they've **renovated** the old swimming pool. I think it's clean and the **facilities** are good. It will open on December 1st.

M: Do you like swimming?

W: Yes. I'm thinking of swimming for exercise. They're **providing discounts** for the renewal event.

M: Let me see. It's $100 a month, and three days of lessons a week. Or $70 a month, and two days of lessons a week. That's quite **reasonable**.

W: You can choose **any 15 days** for a month and it costs only $120. It's not a lesson, but a free swimming class after nine.

M: That's better. You've already learned **how to swim**.

W: Yes, but I haven't learned the butterfly. Shall we go swimming together? I want to take the three days of lessons.

M: I think free swimming is better for me.

W: That's a good idea!

남: 뭐 보고 있어?

여: 수영장 광고. 오래된 수영장을 개조했대. 깨끗하고 시설이 좋은 것 같아. 12월 1일에 문을 연대.

남: 너 수영 좋아해?

여: 응. 운동으로 수영을 할까 생각 중이야. 새단장 이벤트로 할인 해준대.

남: 어디 보자. 일주일에 사흘하고 한 달에 100달러. 또는 일주일에 이틀하고 한 달에 70달러. 꽤 괜찮은 가격인데.

여: 한 달 동안 아무 날이나 15일 고르고 120달러인 것도 있어. 이건 강습받는 게 아니고 9시 이후에 자유 수영을 하는 거야.

남: 그게 더 좋겠다. 넌 이미 수영 배웠잖아.

여: 응, 그런데 접영은 아직 못 배웠어. 우리 같이 수영 다닐까? 나 사흘짜리 강습받고 싶은데.

남: 나한테는 자유 수영이 더 좋을 것 같아.

여: 좋은 생각이야!

해설: 남자는 자유 수영을 원하고 있으므로 120달러를 내야 하며, 여자는 일주일에 사흘 강습받기를 원하고 있으므로 100달러를 내야 한다.

Listening Web

Intro: ad   Web 2: 15, 120

Web 3: three

True / False

1. T   2. T   3. T   4. F

문항 7 ③

Script & Dictation

W: Wow! I'm always excited **when I come to** ski.

M: Did you bring your skis and ski-suit?

W: No. Guess what? I lost my ski-suit, and my skis were broken last winter.

M: Then you need to rent them. How much is the rental fee?

W: It says $15 for the full set, **which includes** the suit and skis.

M: No, that's for snowboards. Look, it costs $20 for the ski full set.

W: You're right. And we need the lift admission. It's $45. It seems more expensive **than last year**.

M: Jessica, it seems you're really excited. Calm down. The $45 is **for adults**. We're under 18.

W: Oops! Sorry. It's $40 for under 18. It's still expensive, though.

M: Yes, I think so. Anyway, we **need to rent** the ski full set for you, and buy the lift admission for us, right?

W: Yes, that's right. Let's go!

여: 와! 난 스키를 타러 오면 항상 신이 나더라.

남: 너 스키랑 스키복 가져왔어?

여: 아니. 무슨 일이 있었는지 아니? 나 작년에 스키복은 잃어버리고, 스키는 망가졌어.

남: 그럼 빌려야겠구나. 대여료가 얼마지?

여: 스키랑 스키복 포함된 풀 세트가 15달러래.

남: 아니야, 그건 스노보드야. 봐봐, 스키 풀 세트는 20달러야.

여: 그렇구나. 그리고 우리 리프트 이용권도 필요해. 45달러네. 작년보다 더 비싼 것 같다.

남: Jessica, 너 정말 흥분했구나. 진정해. 45달러는 어른 요금이야. 우린 18세 이하라고.

여: 어머! 미안. 18세 이하는 40달러네. 그래도 비싸다.

남: 응, 나도 그래. 어쨌든 우리는 네 스키 풀 세트 대여하고, 우리 둘 리프트 이용권을 사면 되는 거지?

여: 그래, 맞아. 가자!

해설: 한 사람의 스키 풀 세트 대여료는 20달러이다. 리프트는 일 인당 40달러이므로, 두 사람 가격은 80달러이다. 따라서 두 사람이 내야 하는 금액은 100달러이다.

Listening Web

Intro: excited   Web 1: rent

Web 2: 20   Web 3: 40

True / False

1. F   2. F   3. T   4. T

문항 8 ③

Script & Dictation

W: What are you doing here?

M: I came here to buy detergent. **I became independent of** my parents last month. Ever since I started **living on my own**, I have so much to do.

W: Now you're grown up. Do you want me to help you?

M: Yes, please. What about the synthetic detergent?

W: It's not **good for the environment**, and it's expensive. Look. It's $40. I think it is better to buy neutral detergent. It's only $32.

M: I need a softener, too. Where is it?

W: Here you are. It's $10.

M: Look, the detergent you told me to get is **for drum washers**.

W: Oh, you don't use a drum washer?

M: No.

W: Then the neutral detergent for general washers is $30.

M: I'll take **two boxes of detergent** and a **softener**.

여: 너 여기에서 뭐해?

남: 세제 사러 왔어. 나 지난달에 부모님으로부터 독립했거든. 혼자 살아보니까 할 게 너무 많아.

여: 이제 어른이 다 되었구나. 내가 도와줄까?

남: 응 도와줘. 합성세제가 어떨까?

여: 그건 환경에 좋지 않고 비싸. 봐. 40달러야. 내 생각엔 중성 세제를 사는 게 더 좋을 것 같아. 32달러밖에 안 해.

남: 섬유유연제도 필요해. 어디에 있지?

여: 여기 있어. 10달러네.

남: 봐, 네가 말했던 세제는 드럼세탁기용이야.

여: 오, 너 드럼세탁기로 안 써?

남: 응.

여: 그럼 일반 세탁기용 중성세제는 30달러야.

남: 난 세제 두 상자하고 섬유유연제를 하나 사야겠다.

해설: 일반 세탁기용 세제는 상자당 30달러이므로, 두 상자에 60달러이다. 섬유유연제는 10달러이므로, 세제 두 상자와 섬유유연제를 합치면 70달러이다.

Listening Web

Intro: independent   Web 1: softener

Web 3: neutral, 30

True / False

1. F   2. T   3. T   4. F

Script & Dictation

W: I'd like to buy a tablet PC.

M: Do you have anything in mind?

W: No, actually I'm **unfamiliar with** IT items.

M: I see. You need to consider the amount of memory available and the **communication method**.

W: What kind of communication methods are there?

M: One is "3G+WiFi," with which you can use the Internet everywhere. And the other is "WiFi," with which you can use the Internet only in a WiFi zone.

W: I'd like to take **the former one**. How much memory is usually good?

M: We have 32GB and 64GB. But "3G+WiFi" allows you to use the Internet everywhere, so you don't need to **store a lot** in the tablet PC.

W: You mean I don't need 64GB? Does the price differ **depending on the manufacturer**?

M: Not very much. But Johnson's design is definitely **superior to** Starworld's.

W: Design is an important factor to me.

여: 태블릿 PC를 사려고 해요.

남: 마음에 두고 계신 물건이 있으십니까?

여: 아니요, 사실 전 IT 제품에 대해 잘 몰라요.

남: 알겠습니다. 메모리 용량과 통신 방식을 고려해 보셔야 합니다.

여: 어떤 종류의 통신 방식이 있죠?

남: 하나는 '3G+WiFi'인데, 어디서나 인터넷 접속이 가능한 것입니다. 다른 하나는 'WiFi'로, WiFi 존 안에서만 인터넷이 가능합니다.

여: 전자가 좋겠어요. 메모리 용량을 대략 어느 정도가 좋은가요?

남: 32GB와 64GB가 있는데요. '3G+WiFi'는 어디에서나 인터넷 사용이 가능하므로 태블릿 PC에 많은 양을 저장해두실 필요가 없습니다.

여: 그럼 64GB는 필요 없다는 말씀이시군요. 제조사에 따라 가격이 다른가요?

남: 큰 차이는 없습니다. 다만 Johnson의 디자인은 Starworld에 비해 단연 우수합니다.

여: 전 디자인이 중요해요.

해설: 여자는 3G+WiFi, 32G를 선택했다. 마지막에 디자인이 중요하다는 말은 Johnson 사의 제품을 살 것이라는 의미이므로, 지불할 금액은 900달러이다.

Listening Web

Web 1: with, with   Web 2: former

Web 3: differ, manufacturer   Web 4: definitely, to

Ending: an

True / False

1. T   2. F   3. T   4. T

Script & Dictation

M: Good morning. May I help you?

W: I'd like to have two cheeseburgers, two bags of potato chips, one iced tea and one Coke.

M: **Why don't you order** a cheeseburger set? It's $8.50. If you order a cheeseburger, potato chips and iced tea **separately**, it costs $10.

W: Okay, then I'll take two cheeseburger sets.

M: Then that would be $17. You have to **choose between** soda **and** iced tea. Or you **can change** a drink to a milkshake for only one more dollar.

W: How much is a milkshake?

M: It's $2, and iced tea is $1.

W: Okay. Then I'll take two cheeseburger sets with one iced tea and one milkshake. Here's $20.

남: 안녕하세요. 무엇을 도와드릴까요?

여: 치즈버거 두 개, 감자 칩 두 봉지, 아이스티 하나하고 콜라 하나 주세요.

남: 치즈버거 세트를 주문하시는 게 어떠시겠어요? 세트는 8.5달러입니다. 치즈버거, 감자 칩, 아이스티를 따로 주문하시면 10달러예요.

여: 알겠어요. 그럼 치즈버거 세트 두 개 주세요.

남: 네. 그렇게 하시면 17달러입니다. 음료는 탄산음료와 아이스티 중에서 고르셔야 해요. 아니면 1달러만 더 내시면 탄산음료 하나는 밀크셰이크로 바꾸실 수 있습니다.

여: 밀크셰이크가 얼마죠?

남: 2달러입니다. 아이스티는 1달러이고요.

여: 알겠어요. 그럼 치즈버거 세트 두 개하고 그 중 음료 하나는 밀크셰이크로 주세요. 여기 20달러 드릴게요.

해설: 여자가 사고자 하는 음식은 치즈버거 세트 (8.5달러) 2개가 17달러이고, 밀크셰이크로 음료 변경에 1달러가 추가되었으므로 총 금액은 18달러이다. 여자는 마지막에 20달러를 냈으므로, 2달러를 거슬러 받아야 한다.

Listening Web

Intro: bags   Web 1: 8.50, separately

True / False

1. F   2. F   3. T   4. T

Unit 10 유형 10 - 일치하지 않는 내용 찾기

문항 1 ⑤

Script & Dictation

W: Mr. Johnson. I'll tell you what you'll do tomorrow. You have to come to the hospital at 7 a.m. Be aware you **must not have breakfast**. When you come to the hospital, you'll **have your blood taken** first. And then you can have breakfast. After breakfast, come back to the hospital by 9:30 a.m. We'll check your blood pressure, and you'll see the doctor. You don't need to pay for the **medical service** tomorrow because everything **is included in** today's bill. Just get the prescription and go to the pharmacy. There are three drug stores across the street. Any questions?

여: Johnson 씨. 내일 할 일에 대해 말씀드리겠습니다. 오전 7시까지 병원에 오셔야 합니다. 아침을 드시면 안 된다는 것을 꼭 알아두세요. 병원에 오시면 제일 먼저 채혈을 할 것입니다. 그런 다음 아침을 드실 수 있습니다. 아침 식사 후에 다시 병원에 오진 9시 30분까지 와주세요. 혈압을 측정한 후 의사 진료가 있을 겁니다. 내일은 진료비를 수납하실 필요가 없습니다. 왜냐하면 모든 것이 오늘 진료비에 포함되어 있으니까요. 바로 처방전 받으셔서 약국으로 가세요. 약국은 길 건너에 세 개가 있습니다. 궁금하신 거 있으세요?

해설: 내일의 진료비가 오늘 진료비에 포함되어 있으므로, 내일 진료비를 별도로 내지 않아도 된다.

Listening Web

Web 1: taken　　　　　Web 3: check
Ending: bill

True / False

1. T　　　　2. T　　　　3. F　　　　4. T

문항 2 ⑤

Script & Dictation

M: In Brazil, most people live in the cities **along the coast**. In the 1960s, the government encouraged people to move **inland** to the Amazon region. The Amazon rain forest was so lush that the soil was very rich. And the people wanted to farm there when **they settled down**, so they started to burn the trees to clear the woods. However, after they **got rid of** the trees, the soil got poor. Any crops could not be grown well there. Moreover, whenever it rained, almost everything **was swept away**. Finally, a lot of people **gave up** living in the Amazon region, and returned to the cities.

남: 브라질에서는 사람들이 대부분 해변을 따라 도시에 살고 있다. 1960년대에 정부는 사람들을 내륙 지역인 아마존 지역으로 이사 가도록 장려했었다. 아마존 열대 우림은 매우 무성하여 토지가 매우 비옥했다. 그리고 사람들은 정착했을 때 그곳에서 농사짓기를 짓고 싶어 했다. 그래서 그들은 숲을 없애기 위해 나무들을 불태웠다. 하지만 그들이 나무를 제거하고 나자, 토양은 척박해졌다. 그곳에서 작물은 자라지 못했다. 더욱이 비가 오기만 하면 모든 것들이 쓸려 내려갔다. 결국 많은 사람들은 아마존 지역에서 살기를 포기하고, 도시로 돌아왔다.

해설: 농사를 지으려고 나무를 모두 불태웠으나, 토양이 척박해져서 작물을 재배할 수 없었다.

Listening Web

Web 1: encouraged, region　　　Web 2: lush
Web 3: burn

True / False

1. T　　　　2. T　　　　3. F　　　　4. F

문항 3 ③

Script & Dictation

W: Attention, please! Our school **will hold** an English Speech Contest on September 1st. Any student who wants to **participate in** this contest should hand in a script to your English teacher by **July 29th**. This contest will be an **individual contest** and groups are not allowed. Twenty speech contest participants will be selected based on the scripts first. And the student who wins the first prize will participate **on behalf of** our school in the High School Student English Speech Contest held by Summerfield City on September 30th. If you have any questions about this contest, please **contact your English teacher**.

여: 주목해주세요! 학교에서 9월 1일에 영어 말하기 대회를 개최하고자 합니다. 영어 말하기 대회에 참가를 원하는 학생은 영어 선생님께 7월 29일까지 대본을 제출해주시기 바랍니다. 이 대회는 개인이 출전하는 대회로 그룹은 참가할 수 없습니다. 우선 대본을 통해 20명의 말하기 대회 참가자를 선발할 것입니다. 그리고 1등을 수상한 학생은 9월 30일 Summerfield 시에서 주최하는 고등학생 영어 말하기 대회에 우리 학교를 대표하여 출전하게 됩니다. 본 말하기 대회와 관련하여 질문이 있으면, 영어 선생님께 문의하세요.

해설: 이 대회는 개인 대회로, 그룹은 참여할 수 없다고 언급하고 있다.

Listening Web

Web 1: hand　　　　　Web 2: allowed
Web 3: selected　　　　Ending: of, held

True / False

1. F   2. T   3. F   4. F

문항 4 ④

Script & Dictation

M: Student President Election time **is nearing**. Anybody who meets the **qualifications** can come forward to be a candidate. Their average grade for the last year should be better than a B⁺. And he or she **should be recommended by** more than three teachers and also more than thirty students. The candidates for the president should be second-year students, and they should choose **two other running mates**. The vice-presidential candidates should be different genders from each other. If you're interested, contact the **current student president** to get the forms you need, or you can download them from our school homepage.

남: 학생회장 선거철이 다가오고 있습니다. 자격 조건을 갖춘 학생은 누구나 후보자가 될 수 있습니다. 작년 한 해 동안 평균 성적이 B⁺ 이상 되어야 합니다. 그리고 세 분 이상의 선생님과 30명 이상의 학생들로부터 추천을 받아야 합니다. 회장 후보는 2학년 학생이어야 하고, 두 명의 부회장 후보를 선정해야 합니다. 부회장 후보들은 서로 다른 성별이어야 합니다. 관심 있는 학생은 현직 학생회장에게 문의하여 필요한 서류를 받아가세요. 또는 우리 학교 홈페이지에서도 내려받을 수 있습니다.

해설: 회장과 부회장 후보자의 성별이 달라야 하는 것이 아니라, 두 부회장 후보자의 성별이 서로 달라야 한다.

Listening Web

Intro: qualifications, forward   Web 1: recommended
Web 3: vice-presidential   Ending: interested

True / False

1. T   2. F   3. F   4. T

문항 5 ②

Script & Dictation

W: Garden Art Museum was originally Mrs. Garden's home. It was built **in the 15th century** Gothic style, and it is famous for being a beautiful building. This museum is full of Mrs. Garden's **personal collection**. When she was alive, she collected drawings, ceramics, and traditional clothing from **all over Europe**. In addition, she had an excellent eye for oriental art, so her collection has virtually **a wide variety**. Since she passed away in 2003, there has been no more new collecting, **in accordance with** her wishes. The admission is $2, and art teachers all over the world can enter for free.

여: 가든 미술관은 원래 Mrs. Garden의 개인 주택입니다. 15세기 고딕 양식으로 지어졌으며, 건물이 아름답기로 유명합니다. 이 미술관은 Mrs. Garden의 개인 소장품으로 가득 차 있습니다. 그녀가 살아있을 때 전 유럽의 그림과 도자기, 전통 의상들을 수집했습니다. 또한 그녀는 동양 예술을 보는 뛰어난 눈을 갖고 있어서, 그녀의 소장품을 사실상 매우 다양합니다. 2003년 그녀가 세상을 떠난 이후 그녀의 유언에 따라 더는 새로운 소장품은 들어오지 않았습니다. 입장료는 2달러이며, 전 세계의 미술 교사들은 무료로 입장할 수 있습니다.

해설: 15세기에 건축된 것이 아니라, 15세기 고딕 양식으로 건축되었다.

Listening Web

Web 1: 15th   Web 2: alive
Web 3: eye, variety   Web 4: passed

True / False

1. T   2. F   3. T   4. F

문항 6 ④

Script & Dictation

M: This Botanic Garden Island consists of a big main island, which you're standing on, and two smaller rocky islands. It has over 800 tropical species and evergreen plants. Because of these **exclusive beautiful** gardens and the ocean **surrounding** this island, this Botanic Garden Island is called "Mini Hawaii." Actually this island is a private island. At first, it was **almost deserted**, but Mr. Green, the owner of this island made **a lot of effort** to make it like this. He was on TV several years ago, and this island became very famous and now is one of the best tourist attractions.

남: 이 Botanic Garden Island은 지금 여러분이 서 계신 한 개의 큰 섬과 두 개의 작은 바위섬으로 이루어져 있습니다. 이 섬에는 800여 개의 열대 품종과 상록수들이 있습니다. 이렇게 독보적으로 아름다운 공원과 섬을 둘러싸고 있는 바다 덕분에 이 Botanic Garden Island는 '작은 하와이'라 불리고 있습니다. 사실 이 섬은 사유지입니다. 처음에 이 섬은 거의 황무지였지만, 이 섬의 소유주이신 Green 씨가 많은 노력을 기울이셔서 이렇게 만들어 주셨습니다. 몇 년 전 그가 TV에 출연하게 되면서 이 섬이 매우 유명해졌고, 지금은 가장 멋진 관광 명소 중 하나가 되었습니다.

해설: 이 섬은 사유지로, 원래는 거의 황무지였지만 주인이 많은 노력을 기울여 지금은 관광 명소가 되었다.

Listening Web

Intro: of   Web 1: species
Web 2: called   Ending: attractions

True / False

1. T   2. F   3. T   4. F

문항7 ⑤

Script & Dictation

W: I'm Jenny Kim, the **supervisor of this workshop**, and I'm so glad to meet you all. I'm here **to introduce** the first lecturer of this workshop. Mr. Lee is a professor in the department of Psychology at Hankuk University. Also, he has worked **as a counselor** for five years. I think all of you've heard of the famous book "Relationship and Leadership." He is the author, and it's been a steady seller for the last three years **since it was published**. Today he's going to give us a good lecture about "Here and Now." This will be useful and helpful to all of you, the would-be counselors. Please give him **a big hand**!

여: 저는 이 워크숍의 관리자 Jenny Kim입니다. 여러분을 만나게 되어 반갑습니다. 저는 이 워크숍의 첫 번째 강사님을 소개하러 이 자리에 나왔습니다. Lee 선생님은 현재 한국대학교 심리학 과 교수이십니다. 또한 5년간 상담가로 활동하셨습니다. 여러 분은 '관계와 리더십'이라는 책을 들어보셨을 겁니다. 선생님 께서는 이 책의 저자이시며, 출간 후 지난 3년간 스테디셀러 였지요. 오늘 선생님께서는 '지금 그리고 여기에'에 관하여 좋 은 강의를 해주시겠습니다. 상담가가 되려는 여러분 모두에 게 유익하고 도움이 되는 시간이 될 것입니다. 큰 박수로 맞아 주시기 바랍니다!

해설: "would-be counselor"란 앞으로 상담가가 되고자 하는 사람들 을 의미한다.

Listening Web

Intro: supervisor   Web 1: department

Web 2: counselor   Web 3: published

True / False

1. F   2. F   3. F   4. T

문항8 ③

Script & Dictation

M: Now we're moving on to go to the Colosseum. The Colosseum was mainly used for gladiatorial combat, but also for circuses or plays. And it was **accessible to** all the people, like the **emperor**, the **nobility**, women, and even **slaves**. It has such wonderful facilities that we cannot believe it was built in the 1st century. It has elevators to move animals, and awnings. It also has 80 arched doors to get all the people out of the stadium within 15 minutes after the show. Unfortunately, today only **one-third of the stadium** remains, so we cannot see the whole Colosseum. We're almost there. You can see the Colosseum on your right side.

남: 이제 우리는 콜로세움으로 이동하겠습니다. 콜로세움은 주로 검투사의 경기장으로 쓰였지만, 서커스나 연극을 위해서도 쓰였습니다. 그리고 황제나 귀족, 여성과 심지어는 노예들까지 모두가 이용할 수 있었습니다. 이것은 매우 놀라운 시설을 갖 추고 있어서 1세기에 지어졌다는 사실을 믿기 어려울 정도입 니다. 동물을 이동시키기 위한 엘리베이터도 있고, 차양도 있 습니다. 또한 쇼가 끝난 후 15분 만에 모든 사람들이 경기장 밖으로 나갈 수 있는 80개의 아치형 문이 있습니다. 애석하게 도 오늘날에는 경기장의 3분의 1만이 남아있어서, 우리는 콜 로세움의 전체 모습을 볼 수가 없습니다. 거의 다 왔습니다. 여러분의 오른편으로 콜로세움을 보실 수 있습니다.

해설: 콜로세움에 설치되어 있는 아치형 문의 개수가 80개이다.

Listening Web

Web 1: accessible   Web 2: awnings

Web 3: arched, 15   Ending: whole

True / False

1. F   2. T   3. F   4. F

문항9 ④

Script & Dictation

W: Sometimes the slaves could sing songs while their masters were listening to them. In fact, a lot of African Americans were **encouraged to take up** Christianity as their religion. And apparently some of the songs were about God or going to heaven. So the masters believed that the slaves were very **happy with the religion** when they were singing. However, some songs were very practical to the slaves as well. For example, the song, "Wade in the Water" let the African Americans remember that they had to stay near water. It was not only **because they needed** water to drink, but also **because** they might be able to catch fish during **their escape**.

여: 때때로 노예들은 주인들이 듣고 있는 앞에서 노래를 할 수 있 었다. 사실 많은 아프리카계 미국인들에게 기독교를 그들의 종교로 받아들이도록 장려했다. 그리고 겉으로 보기에는 이 노래들 중 몇몇은 신이나 천국으로 가는 것에 관한 것들이었 다. 그래서 그 주인들은 노예들이 노래할 때 이들이 종교에 매우 만족한다고 믿었던 것이다. 하지만 어떤 노래들은 노예 들에게 매우 실용적이기도 했었다. 예를 들어, 'Wade in the Water (물속을 거닐며)'라는 노래는 아프리카계 미국인들로 하여금 물 가까이에 머물 것을 기억하도록 한다. 이것은 단지 마실 물이 필요할 뿐만이 아니라 이들이 탈출할 때 물고기를 잡을 수 있기 때문이기도 했다.

해설: 노예들이 부르는 노래 내용이 겉으로는 신이나 천국에 관한 것이었기 때문에, 주인들은 자신의 노예들이 종교에 만족해서 노래한다고 착각했었다.

Listening Web

Web 1: up   Web 3: religion

Ending: because of

True / False

1. F   2. T   3. F   4. T

문항 10 ⑤

Script & Dictation

M: Food means a lot for people. That is, food is not only a way of providing **nutrients**. We eat for pleasure or as a part of **social situations**! So culture has the strongest **influence on** eating habits. There are positive and negative aspects to all kinds of food habits, and any type of diet can be healthy as long as **proper food choices** are made. For example, in Greece or Italy, people enjoy a so-called Mediterranean diet, which includes a lot of olive oil. Studies have shown that a diet rich in olive oil is **associated with** a lower risk of heart disease. It means the Mediterranean diet is considered to be a heart-healthy diet.

남: 음식은 사람들에게 많은 의미가 있습니다. 즉, 음식이 단지 영양분을 공급하는 수단뿐만은 아니라는 겁니다. 우리는 즐거움을 위해 먹기도 하고, 사교 생활의 일부로 먹기도 합니다! 그래서 문화는 식습관에 지대한 영향을 미칩니다. 모든 종류의 식습관에는 긍정적인 측면과 부정적인 측면이 있지만, 적절한 음식이 선택되기만 한다면 어떤 종류의 것이든 건강한 식습관이 될 수 있습니다. 예를 들면, 그리스나 이탈리아에서 사람들은 소위 지중해식을 먹는데, 그것은 올리브유를 많이 함유하고 있습니다. 연구에서 밝힌 바에는 올리브유가 많이 들어간 음식은 심장병에 걸릴 위험을 낮춰주는 것과 관련이 있다고 합니다. 이것은 지중해식이 심장을 건강하게 해주는 음식임을 의미합니다.

해설: 올리브 오일이 들어간 지중해식은 심장병 발병률을 낮춰준다고 말하고 있다.

Listening Web

Intro: pleasure   Web 1: strongest

Web 2: type   Ending: lower

True / False

1. T   2. F   3. T   4. T

문항 1 ④

Script & Dictation

M: When you are pouring tomato ketchup on your burger or potato chips, do you think of Mexico? That's where the tomato **was developed**. When Spanish invaders moved Intro Mexico in 1519, the Aztec people were eating **several kinds of tomatoes**. These early tomatoes looked different. They were not as big, shiny, and red as we eat today. They were smaller and **not as round**. The Spanish took tomato plants back to Europe. But they were **grown as decorative plants**. Because the Europeans had never seen anything like them before, no one knew **how to cook them**. They were also afraid that tomatoes **might be poisonous**.

남: 버거나 감자 칩에 토마토케첩을 부을 때 멕시코가 생각나십니까? 그곳은 토마토가 번성한 곳입니다. 스페인 침입자들이 1519년 멕시코로 옮겨왔을 때, 아즈텍족은 몇 가지 종류의 토마토를 먹고 있었습니다. 이 초기의 토마토들은 다르게 생겼습니다. 지금 우리가 먹는 토마토와 달리 크지도 않고, 윤기도 없고, 붉은색도 아니었습니다. 더 작고 둥글지도 않았습니다. 스페인 사람들은 토마토 나무를 유럽으로 가져갔습니다. 하지만 그들은 관상목으로 키웠습니다. 일찍이 유럽인들은 그런 것을 본 적이 없었기 때문에, 요리법을 몰랐던 것입니다. 그들은 또한 토마토에 독이 있을지도 모른다며 두려워하기도 했습니다.

해설: 스페인 사람들은 토마토를 이전에 본 적이 없어서 요리법을 몰랐기 때문에 관상용으로 키웠다.

Listening Web

Intro: pouring   Web 1: developed

Web 2: smaller   Web 4: decorative

True / False

1. T   2. T   3. T   4. F

문항 2 ①

Script & Dictation

W: This is an announcement for **the immediate opening for** student musicians of our school orchestra. Applicants should **possess strong** communication and interpersonal skills as well as musical skills because you'll be working **in a team environment**. Only string players are wanted at this time: two violinists, one cellist, and one violist, but we don't have an opening for contrabassists. You don't have to have had **a career in** any amateur orchestra, but if you have, it can be beneficial for you **to be chosen**. The audition will be on the 1st of November in the music room. A week later after that we'll announce the applicants **who have passed** the audition on the main bulletin board in front of the cafeteria.

여: 학교 오케스트라의 학생 단원을 급하게 모집하고 있음을 알립니다. 팀으로 연주하기 때문에, 지원할 학생은 연주 실력 못지않게 의사소통 능력과 대인 관계 기술이 뛰어나야 합니다. 이번에는 현악기 연주자만 모집합니다: 바이올린 연주자 2명, 첼로 연주자 1명, 비올라 연주자 1명입니다. 콘트라베이스 연주자는 모집하지 않습니다. 아마추어 오케스트라 경력이 꼭 필요하지는 않지만, 만약 경력이 있다면 선발에 도움이 될 것입니다. 오디션은 11월 1일 음악실에서 열립니다. 합격자 명단은 일주일 뒤에 교내 식당 앞에 있는 메인 게시판에 공지하겠습니다.

해설: 현악기 중 콘트라베이스 연주자는 이번에 선발하지 않는다.

Listening Web

Intro: communication   Web 1: wanted
Web 2: beneficial   Ending: on

True / False

1. T   2. T   3. T   4. T

문항 3 ⑤

Script & Dictation

M: Ladies and Gentlemen, this is your captain speaking. We'll **begin descending for** Incheon International Airport in thirty minutes. Landing is being postponed because it's snowing suddenly. **The current time** is 7:30 a.m. Please **set your watch forward** if you have not done so. The weather in Seoul is cloudy with a strong wind. The temperature is 2 degrees Celsius, which is 35.6 degrees Fahrenheit. And we have an emergency patient **on board**, so after we land, passengers please be seated and wait **so that** the patient can be taken **out of the cabin** first. I hope you enjoyed the flight, and on behalf of the flight deck and cabin crew, I'd like to thank you for choosing Summer Sky Airways today. Welcome to Korea.

남: 신사 숙녀 여러분, 기장입니다. 우리 비행기는 30분 뒤 인천 국제공항에 착륙하기 시작할 것입니다. 갑작스러운 눈으로 착륙이 지연되고 있습니다. 현재 시각은 오전 7시 30분입니다. 아직 시계를 맞추지 않으신 분은 시계를 맞춰 주시기 바랍니다. 서울 날씨는 흐리고 바람이 강하게 불고 있습니다. 기온은 섭씨 2도, 화씨 35.6도입니다. 또한 기내에 응급환자가 있

사오니, 응급환자가 먼저 밖으로 이송될 수 있도록 승객분들께서는 도착 후 잠시 자리에 앉아 대기하여 주시기 바랍니다. 즐거운 비행이 되셨기를 바라며, 조종실과 승무원을 대표하여 저희 Summer Sky 항공을 찾아주신 여러분 감사합니다. 대한민국에 오신 것을 환영합니다.

해설: 기내에 응급환자가 있으므로, 응급환자가 먼저 빠져나갈 수 있도록 자리에 앉아서 기다려 달라고 말하고 있다.

Listening Web

Intro: thirty   Web 3: strong
Ending: taken

True / False

1. T   2. T   3. F   4. T

문항 4 ④

Script & Dictation

W: Look at the picture on the screen. This is the barn owl, a type of **nocturnal bird**. It's smaller than any other type of owl. It is only 30 to 40cm tall and its wings are 116cm at most. And the male barn owl is a little bit smaller than the female. Although its body is small, it has long legs **compared with** the size of body. It hunts small rats, and **builds a nest** in a hollow tree or on the tops of buildings. It lives **everywhere except** the Antarctic. In Korea, one was **first found near** the west coast in 2003. Now it is listed as an endangered species.

여: 화면의 사진을 봐 주십시오. 이것이 가면올빼미로, 야행성 조류 종입니다. 다른 종류의 어떤 올빼미보다도 크기가 작습니다. 키는 30-40센티미터밖에 되지 않고, 날개는 최대 116센티미터입니다. 수컷이 암컷보다 약간 작습니다. 몸집은 작지만, 몸의 크기에 비해 다리가 깁니다. 작은 쥐를 잡아먹고, 속이 빈 나무나 건물 꼭대기에 둥지를 틉니다. 남극을 제외한 모든 곳에서 서식하고 있습니다. 한국에서는 2003년 서해안 부근에서 처음으로 발견되었습니다. 지금은 멸종위기 명단에 올려져 있습니다.

해설: 남극을 제외한 모든 곳에서 서식한다고 했으므로, 남극에서는 살지 않는다.

Listening Web

Web 1: most   Web 2: male
Web 3: hollow   Web 4: except
Ending: found

True / False

1. T   2. T   3. T   4. F

문항5 ②

Script & Dictation

M: **Attention is drawn to** learning a foreign language in a virtual reality space among foreign language learners. A virtual reality space allows a lot of **strangers to meet** each other and communicate in a foreign language. Even though you're a shy or reserved person, you can talk a lot. Because **anonymity is guaranteed** in the virtual reality space, everybody can express their thoughts and emotions freely. So you'll have a lot more chances to practice a foreign language in this space than in reality. In addition, lessons in a virtual reality space are considered a game. That's why it can **attract learners' attention** and few learners will **quit studying** a foreign language.

남: 가상현실 공간에서의 외국어 학습이 외국어 학습자들의 눈길을 끌고 있습니다. 가상현실 공간은 많은 낯선 사람들을 만나 외국어로 의사소통할 수 있도록 해줍니다. 당신이 비록 부끄러움을 많이 타고 소극적인 사람일지라도, 당신은 많은 말을 할 수 있습니다. 가상현실 공간에서는 익명성이 보장되기 때문에, 모두가 자기 생각과 느낌을 자유롭게 표현할 수 있는 것입니다. 그래서 현실보다 가상현실 공간에서 외국어를 연습할 기회가 더 많아지게 됩니다. 또한, 가상현실 공간에서의 수업은 게임처럼 여겨지기도 합니다. 그것이 학습자의 주의를 끌어 학습자가 외국어 학습을 중단하는 일이 거의 없게 되는 이유입니다.

해설: 가상현실 공간에서의 외국어 학습은 익명성이 보장되기 때문에 부끄러움이 많은 학습자도 마음껏 표현할 수 있다.

Listening Web

Intro: drawn   Web 1: reserved
Web 2: guaranteed   Ending: Few

True / False

1. F   2. T   3. F   4. T

문항6 ④

Script & Dictation

W: Are you dreaming of weekend farming? Mr. Kevin's Farm provides **city dwellers** with the whole new experience of growing their own vegetables and fruits **in a rural area**. You can come here once a week or more often and grow carrots, pumpkins or tomatoes in plots for rent. The size of the plot is your choice. The location is so great that it takes only two hours from Mr. Kevin's Farm to the inner city **and back**. We also provide wonderful service such as lending farming tools **for a small charge**. You have to buy seeds yourselves, but if it's a **rare species**, we can buy them for you. And if you have children **under 12**, they can take part in the free farming education program.

여: 주말농장을 꿈꾸십니까? Kevin 아저씨네 농장은 도시인들에게 시골에서 직접 채소와 과일을 재배할 수 있는 새로운 경험을 제공합니다. 일주일에 한 번, 혹은 좀 더 자주 이곳에 와서 임대 구역에 당근, 호박, 토마토를 재배할 수 있습니다. 구역의 크기는 선택하실 수 있습니다. 위치도 아주 좋아 도심에서 Kevin 아저씨네 농장까지 왕복 두 시간밖에 걸리지 않습니다. 또한 소액으로 농기구를 대여해 드리는 멋진 서비스를 제공하고 있습니다. 종자는 직접 구매하셔야 하지만, 희귀 품종일 경우 구매 대행해드립니다. 12살 이하의 자녀는 무료 농장 교육프로그램에 참여할 수 있습니다.

해설: 종자는 직접 구매해야 하지만, 희귀 품종이면 구매 대행을 해주고 있다.

Listening Web

Intro: choice   Web 1: inner
Web 2: lending   Web 3: seeds
Ending: under, part

True / False

1. F   2. F   3. F   4. T

문항7 ③

Script & Dictation

M: East Bike is not a company that sells bicycles. It is a bike rental company. East Bike has hundreds of stations where people rent bicycles and return them near subway stations or at places where a lot of people **pass by**. You can rent a bike in a station and return it to another station which is **near your destination**. So it is very convenient to use. That's why many people use these bicycles when they **commute to work**. In addition, it's **way cheaper** than a taxi, of course - even a bus or subway. An **annual membership** costs only $100, and you can enjoy a one-day free experience before you register. Above all, riding a bike is **eco-friendly**. Why don't you join East Bike?

남: East Bike는 자전거 판매 회사가 아닙니다. 자전거 대여 회사입니다. East Bike는 지하철 역 근처나 사람들의 통행이 잦은 곳에 자전거를 빌리고 반납하는 수백 개의 정류장이 있습니다. 한 정류장에서 자전거를 대여하고, 목적지 근처의 정류장에 반납하실 수 있지요. 따라서 매우 편리합니다. 그것이 많은 사람들이 출퇴근용으로 사용하는 이유입니다. 더욱이 가격이 택시는 물론 버스나 지하철보다도 훨씬 저렴합니다. 연간 회원권은 100달러면 살 수 있고, 등록하기 전에 하루 무료 이용을 해 보실 수 있습니다. 무엇보다도 자전거를 타는 것은 친환경적입니다. East Bike에 가입해 보시는 건 어떠세요?

해설: 사람들의 통행이 잦은 곳에 정류장에 있고, 빌린 곳과 반납하는 곳이 달라도 되기 때문에 출퇴근용으로 많이 쓰이고 있다.

Listening Web

Intro: hundreds

Web 2: commute

Web 1: another

Web 3: free

True / False

1. F   2. T   3. F   4. T

문항 8 ③

Script & Dictation

W: This is called "amber." Actually the English name amber **derives from** an Arabic word. The word originally **refers to** a solid waxy substance. Amber is **fossilized** resin, which is the soft and gummy liquid from pine trees. It has been **appreciated for** its golden brown color and natural beauty since primitive ages. That's why amber has been widely used for decorative objects like jewelry. If it contains animals or plants in it, it **goes up in value**. And it has been used as an ingredient in perfume, and even a healing agent **in folk medicine** as well. These days, scientists use it to study animals and plants that lived in the past. You may remember that this was a motive in a sci-fi movie in the early 1990s.

여: 이것이 '호박(amber)'이라고 불리는 것입니다. 사실 amber라는 영어 이름은 아랍어에서 파생된 것입니다. 이 단어는 원래 딱딱하고 밀랍으로 된 물질을 의미합니다. 호박은 송진이 화석화된 것인데, 송진이란 소나무에서 나오는 부드럽고 점성이 있는 액체입니다. 이것은 원시시대부터 황갈색 색감과 자연적인 아름다움으로 진가를 인정받았습니다. 그래서 호박은 보석과 같은 장신구로 널리 이용되어 왔습니다. 그 안에 동물이나 식물이 들어 있으면 가치는 더욱 상승하는 것이지요. 또한 향수의 원료나 심지어 민간요법에서 치료제로 이용되기도 했습니다. 오늘날에는 과학자들이 과거의 동식물을 연구하기 위해 사용합니다. 이것이 1990년대 초반에 한 공상 과학 영화의 모티브가 되었던 것을 여러분은 기억할 겁니다.

해설: 호박이 아랍에서 제일 먼저 사용된 것이 아니라, 호박이라는 이름이 아랍어에서 파생된 것이다.

Listening Web

Intro: derives, word

Web 3: agent

Web 1: appreciated

True / False

1. T   2. F   3. F   4. T

문항 9 ②

Script & Dictation

M: It was in 1892 when the Great Immigration Hall at Ellis Island first opened. It was in the port of New York. Through the late 1920s, 5,000 people a day were **herded in** and **processed** in Ellis Island's Great Hall. It was at Ellis Island **where it was decided** if you could stay in America. By the end of the 2nd World War in 1945, 17 million people would sail through this New York gateway to America. They came mostly from Europe. They came to escape **oppression and hunger** at home. By the 1950s, the great wave of European immigration to America **had subsided**, and Ellis Island was closed. People were coming here looking for new opportunity, and it's still **the symbol of** new hope today.

남: 1892년, 엘리스 섬의 이민국이 처음 문을 열었습니다. 엘리스 섬은 뉴욕 항구에 있었습니다. 1920년대 후반에는 하루에 5,000명의 사람들이 엘리스 섬으로 밀려 들어와 엘리스 섬 이민국에서 입국 심사를 받았습니다. 미국에 머무를 수 있는지 여부를 가리던 곳이 바로 엘리스 섬이었던 것입니다. 1945년 제2차 세계대전이 끝날 무렵, 1,700만 명의 사람들이 이 뉴욕의 관문을 통해 미국으로 항해해 들어왔습니다. 그들의 대부분은 유럽에서 왔습니다. 그들은 고향에서의 억압과 배고픔으로부터 탈출하기 위해 온 것이었습니다. 1950년대 유럽인들의 미국 이민 열풍이 가라앉았습니다. 그리고 엘리스 섬은 문을 닫게 되었습니다. 사람들은 새로운 기회를 찾아 이곳으로 왔었는데, 이곳은 오늘날에도 여전히 새로운 희망의 상징입니다.

해설: 엘리스 섬은 과거 이민국이 있던 자리이며, 이곳에서 이민 심사가 이루어졌다.

Listening Web

Intro: herded

Web 2: million

Web 1: decided

Web 3: wave

True / False

1. F   2. T   3. T   4. F

문항 10 ②

Script & Dictation

W: The Expo is full of cultural programs with 50 performances and events. They will take place every day for the entire 70 days, that is 3,500 in total. It **features** large-scale events such as the state-of-the-art Multi Media Show, world-class performances, and concerts of popular singers from all around the world. **More frequent** and smaller-scale events such as street performances will also be offered. Today's exposition-goers **are not content with** simply remaining an onlooker. They are **more than willing to** become part of the exposition. So we offer a lot of audience participation programs. The Expo will promote **cultural diversity** and enable visitors to enjoy themselves to the fullest.

여: 박람회는 50개의 공연과 이벤트로 꾸며진 문화 프로그램으로 가득 차 있습니다. 이 공연과 이벤트들은 전체 70일 동안 매일 이루어지며, 전부 3,500개에 이릅니다. 최신식 멀티미디어 쇼나 세계 최상급의 공연, 전 세계에서 온 인기 가수들의 콘서트와 같은 대규모 이벤트가 있는 것이 특징입니다. 또한 길거리 공연과 같은 소규모 공연들은 더욱 자주 있을 예정입니다. 요즘 박람회에 오시는 분들은 구경꾼으로 머무르는 것에 만족하지 않습니다. 그들은 열정적으로 박람회에 참여하고자 합니다. 그래서 저희는 관람객 참여 프로그램을 많이 제공합니다. 이번 박람회는 문화적 다양성을 고취시킬 것이고, 방문객들은 가장 즐거운 시간을 보낼 수 있을 것입니다.

해설: 박람회에서 제공하는 프로그램들은 50개의 공연과 이벤트로 구성되어 있다. 박람회가 70일간 계속되며, 총 3,500개의 공연과 이벤트가 진행된다.

Listening Web

Intro: cultural   Web 1: place

Web 3: frequent   Ending: participation

True / False

1. T   2. T   3. T   4. T

Unit 12 유형 12 - 도표 문제

문항 1 ④

Script & Dictation

W: Wow, it's so cool! Swimming in the sea is fantastic!

M: Yeah, the emerald color also looks cool.

W: I'm kind of thirsty. **Why don't we drink** something?

M: Look! There's a snack bar over there. The snack bar **looks like a lemon**. That's interesting. Let's go.

W: Ade… and frappe… Frappe? What's frappe?

M: Frappe is a drink with fruit pulp and **crushed ice** in it.

W: I see. Then the difference between ade and frappe is the size of the ice seeing that an ade has cubed ice.

M: That's right.

W: I'll have a cherry frappe. I've never had frappe before.

M: Excellent choice! **I'd like mint ade**. Do you want some syrup?

W: No.

M: Me, neither. One lemon frappe and one mint ade.

W: No, cherry frappe for me.

M: Sorry. Wait here. **It's on me**.

W: Thanks.

여: 와, 이거 정말 멋진데! 바다에서 수영하는 거 끝내준다!

남: 그렇지, 에메랄드 빛이 시원해 보여.

여: 난 목마른데. 우리 뭐 좀 마실까?

남: 저기 봐! 저쪽에 매점이 있다. 매점이 레몬 모양이야. 재미있네. 가보자.

여: 에이드… 그리고 프라페… 프라페? 프라페가 뭐야?

남: 프라페는 과육과 잘게 부순 얼음이 들어간 음료수야.

여: 알았어. 그럼 에이드에는 각얼음이 들어가니까, 에이드와 프라페의 차이점은 얼음의 크기인 거구나.

남: 그렇지.

여: 난 체리 프라페 먹어 볼래. 프라페 처음 먹어 봐.

남: 좋았어! 난 민트 에이드 먹을래. 시럽 넣을래?

여: 아니.

남: 나도 안 넣어. 레몬 프라페 하나, 민트 에이드 하나.

여: 아니야. 난 체리 프라페.

남: 미안. 여기에서 기다려. 내가 살게.

여: 고마워.

해설: 프라페에는 잘게 부순 얼음이 들어가고 에이드에는 각얼음이 들어간다. 남자는 민트 에이드를 원하고 있고, 시럽을 넣지 않는다고 했다.

Listening Web

Intro: thirsty   Web 1: crushed

Web 2: cubed   Ending: neither

True / False

1. F   2. T   3. T   4. T

문항 2 ③

Script & Dictation

M: Mom, my leg hurts.

W: What happened?

M: I think **I hurt my leg** while I was playing football with my friends hours ago. I could stand it, but the pain is getting worse.

W: **You should've been careful**. Always remember that you were treated for the disk problem in your neck.

M: It seems it **has nothing to do** with it. My right leg is swollen and hurts badly.

W: Isn't it the knee? Show me your leg.

M: The calf under the knee is swollen.

W: Let's go to the hospital right now.

M: Do you think I'll have to **wear a cast**?

W: I'm not sure.

M: Oh, no. I have an appointment tomorrow. I want to go to the hospital the day after tomorrow.

W: The doctor's office will be closed because **the day after tomorrow** is the weekend. Hurry up!

남: 엄마, 다리가 아파요.

여: 무슨 일이니?

남: 친구들이랑 아까 축구 경기를 하다가 다리를 다친 것 같아요. 참을 만했는데, 통증이 점점 심해져요.

여: 조심했어야지. 너 목 디스크로 치료받았다는 걸 항상 기억하렴.

남: 그것과는 상관없는 것 같아요. 오른쪽 다리가 붓고 너무 아파요.

여: 무릎이 아니고? 다리 좀 보여줘 봐.

남: 무릎 아래 종아리가 부었어요.

여: 당장 병원에 가자.

남: 엄마 생각엔 제가 깁스를 할 거 같아요?

여: 글쎄다.

남: 오, 안 돼요. 내일 약속 있단 말이에요. 병원에는 모레 갈래요.

여: 모레는 주말이라 진료가 없어. 서둘러!

해설: 무릎 아래 종아리 부었으므로 "leg"를 담당하는 의사에게 가야 한다. 모레는 주말이라 진료가 없다고 했으므로 오늘은 목요일임을 알 수 있다.

Listening Web

Intro: hurts   Web 1: should've been

Web 2: badly   Web 3: calf

Ending: closed

True / False

1. T   2. T   3. F   4. F

문항 3 ②

Script & Dictation

W: Let's have lunch here.

M: Yes, sandwiches are good because we don't have enough time.

W: It seems we have to check the menu on this sheet. **What would you like** to have?

M: A club sandwich and diet coke.

W: What else? **Salad or potatoes?**

M: Hmm. Mango salad.

W: Okay. Then I'll have a turkey sandwich, and I'll have diet coke, too.

M: Wait. They sell a ham and egg sandwich **for half price.** I'll have it.

W: Do we need to buy Victoria lunch? She is in the office alone and I think she is too busy to **take a break** for lunch.

M: I think so. Let's order another ham and egg sandwich and diet coke. And Caesar salad, too. She loves it.

W: Oh, look! A green salad **is included for free** with sandwiches at lunch. We don't need to order it.

M: That's nice!

여: 여기에서 점심을 먹자.

남: 그래, 우린 시간이 많지 않으니까 샌드위치가 좋겠어.

여: 이 종이에 우리 메뉴를 표시해야 하는 것 같아. 뭐 먹을래?

남: 클럽 샌드위치하고 다이어트 콜라.

여: 다른 거는? 샐러드나 감자는?

남: 음. 망고 샐러드 먹을래.

여: 그래. 그럼 난 터키 샌드위치하고, 나도 다이어트 콜라 마실래.

남: 잠깐만. 햄앤에그 샌드위치를 반값에 팔고 있어. 난 그거 먹을래.

여: 우리가 Victoria에게 점심도 사줘야 할까? 그녀는 사무실에 혼자 있는데, 너무 바빠서 점심 먹으러 짬을 내기도 어려운 것 같아.

남: 그런 것 같아. 햄앤에그 샌드위치랑 다이어트 콜라 하나 주문 더 하자. 시저 샐러드도. 그녀가 이거 좋아해.

여: 봐봐! 점심에는 그린 샐러드가 샌드위치에 무료로 포함된대. 샐러드는 주문할 필요 없겠는걸.

남: 좋았어!

해설: 남자는 사무실에 남아있는 동료(Victoria) 것과 함께 햄앤에그 샌드위치와 다이어트 콜라를 주문했고, 여자는 터키 샌드위치와 다이어트 콜라를 주문했다. 점심에는 샌드위치에 샐러드가 포함되어 다시 주문하지 않아도 된다고 했으므로, 최종 주문 메뉴는 햄앤에그 샌드위치 두 개, 터키 샌드위치 한 개, 다이어트 콜라 세 잔이 된다.

Listening Web

Web 2: sell   Web 3: another

Ending: included

True / False

1. F   2. F   3. T   4. T

문항 4 ④

Script & Dictation

M: How about going to a movie?

W: Cool. **What is on** now?

M: "Finding Sora" will **be released** tomorrow. The actors will come to the theater at 5:30 p.m. Maybe Jennifer Bake will come.

W: That's awesome. But **come to think of it**, I have a dinner appointment at 6 p.m. It's my grandmother's birthday tomorrow. I have to go home by 5 p.m.

M: Then what about "Who's There"? It starts at 2 p.m.

W: I don't like scary movies.

M: But you'll **never regret it**. It's had the top spot at the box office since last week.

W: What about "Don't Touch"?

M: My brother saw it yesterday, and he told me **never to see** the movie.

W: Really? Then let's see the scary movie you said. See you tomorrow in front of the theater 30 minutes before the movie starts. Don't be late! And don't forget that I have to go home by 5 p.m.

남: 영화 보러 갈래?

여: 좋아. 지금 뭐가 상영 중이지?

남: 'Finding Sora'가 내일 개봉해. 배우들이 오후 5시 반에 극장에 올 거야. 아마 Jennifer Bake도 올걸.

여: 멋진걸. 그런데 생각해 보니 내일 오후 6시에 저녁 약속이 있어. 내일 우리 할머니 생신이야. 오후 5시까지는 집에 가야 해.

남: 그럼 'Who's There'는 어때? 그건 오후 2시에 시작해.

여: 난 무서운 영화 안 좋아해.

남: 그렇지만 절대 후회하지 않을 거야. 지난주부터 박스오피스 1위였어.

여: 'Don't Touch'는 어때?

남: 우리 형이 어제 보고 왔는데, 나보고 그거 절대 보지 말래.

여: 정말? 그럼 네가 말한 그 무서운 영화 보자. 내일 영화관 앞에서 영화 시작하기 30분 전에 보자. 늦지 마! 그리고 나 오후 5시까지 집에 가야 하는 거 잊지 마.

해설: 두 사람이 보기로 한 영화 "Who's There"는 두 번째에 언급되었다. 여자는 영화 시작 30분 전인 1시 30분에 만나자고 했지만 영화를 보는 시간을 묻고 있으므로 헷갈리지 않도록 유의한다.

Listening Web

Web 1: at

Web 2: scary

Web 3: see

Ending: starts

True / False

1. F

2. T

3. F

4. F

문항 5 ②

Script & Dictation

M: Have you reserved a hotel?

W: Not yet. I'm looking at a hotel site now, and it looks clean and pretty. Will you come and see it?

M: Sure. Which one would you like?

W: I'd like **an ocean view**. How about you?

M: **The cheaper, the better**. You know, the hotel charge **makes up** the largest part of our travel expenses.

W: Paul, it's **our 10th anniversary**. I don't think it should be luxurious, but I want it to be beautiful and comfortable.

M: I agree. But the mountain view is not bad. And I don't like the hotel breakfast buffet because I can't usually eat much in the morning. I don't think it's **worth the additional charge**.

W: I see, Paul. But I can't give up the ocean view.

M: You won't regret that you chose the mountain view.

W: Paul, please.

M: Okay, okay, then we'll **pay over** $100 **a night**.

W: Paul, we can save money in other areas. Don't worry.

남: 당신 호텔 예약했어요?

여: 아니 아직 이요. 지금 호텔 사이트 보고 있는데, 여기가 깨끗하고 예쁜 것 같아요. 와서 볼래요?

남: 그럼요. 어떤 게 마음에 들어요?

여: 바다 전망이면 좋겠어요. 당신은요?

남: 저렴할수록 좋아요. 당신도 알다시피, 우리 여행 비용 중에서 호텔 비용이 제일 많은 부분을 차지하잖아요.

여: Paul, 우리 10주년이잖아요. 호텔이 호화로워야 하는 건 아니지만, 예쁘고 편안했으면 좋겠어요.

남: 나도 그래요. 하지만 산 전망도 나쁘지 않아요. 그리고 난 보통 아침에 많이 못 먹어서 아침 조식 뷔페도 별로 원하지 않고요. 추가 비용만큼의 가치가 없는 것 같아요.

여: 알겠어요, Paul. 하지만 바다 전망은 포기할 수 없어요.

남: 산 전망을 선택해도 후회하지 않을 기예요.

여: Paul, 제발요.

남: 알았어요, 알았어요. 그럼 우린 하룻밤에 100달러가 넘게 써야 하는 거네요.

여: Paul, 다른 부분에서 절약할 수 있어요. 걱정하지 마요.

해설: 여자는 조식 뷔페는 안 해도 되지만, 바다 전망은 포기할 수 없다고 했다. 마지막에 남자가 하룻밤에 100달러가 넘는다고 했으므로, 두 사람이 머물 방은 ②번이 된다.

Listening Web

Intro: reserved

Web 2: don't

Ending: in other

True / False

1. T

2. T

3. F

4. T

문항 6 ②

Script & Dictation

M: What's the matter?

W: I need your help. I'm planning to go to Australia this winter. It's not easy to **plan the itinerary**. I heard you've traveled in Australia.

M: Yes. First of all, where do you want to go?

W: Brisbane, Sydney, Melbourne, Uluru. Uluru is **far away from** the rest, so I'm thinking of Uluru as the first destination.

M: But there's no **international flight** that goes directly to Uluru. You have to drop by another city and transfer through a **domestic airline**.

W: I see. Then I'll go to Melbourne first, and then Brisbane, and then Uluru, and the last stop will be Sydney.

M: That's not bad. But traveling to Uluru is not easy. It's a desert. But Brisbane is near the beautiful beach. So I think Uluru **followed by** Brisbane is better.

W: Then is it better to **switch them** with each other?

M: I think so.

W: Thanks a lot. Now I have outlined my travel.

남: 무슨 일이야?

여: 너의 도움이 필요해. 이번 겨울에 호주에 가려고 계획 중인데. 일정을 잡기가 쉽지 않아. 네가 호주 여행을 가본 적이 있다고 들었어.

남: 응. 우선 어디 가보고 싶어?

여: 브리즈번, 시드니, 멜버른, 울룰루. 울룰루는 나머지 장소들과 멀리 떨어져 있어. 그러니까 울룰루를 첫 번째 도착지로 하면 될 거 같아.

남: 하지만, 울룰루로 바로 가는 국제 항공이 없어. 다른 도시에 들러서 국내선으로 환승해야 돼.

여: 그렇구나. 그럼 멜버른을 먼저 가고, 그 다음 브리즈번, 그 다음 울룰루, 마지막을 시드니로 하지.

남: 나쁘진 않은데. 울룰루를 여행하는 건 쉽지 않아. 사막이거든. 브리즈번은 아름다운 해변 가까이 있어. 그러니까 울룰루 다음 브리즈번이 더 좋을 것 같아.

여: 그럼 두 개를 서로 바꾸면 좋겠네?

남: 그럴 것 같아.

여: 정말 고마워. 이제야 여행의 윤곽이 잡힌다.

해설: 여자는 첫 여행지로 멜버른을, 마지막 여행지로 시드니를 선택했다. 울룰루는 바로 가는 국제 항공이 없어서 멜버른 다음으로 가고, 울룰루를 여행한 뒤 해변이 가까운 브리즈번으로 가기로 했다.

Listening Web

Intro: Australia   Web 2: directly

Ending: followed

True / False

1. F   2. F   3. T   4. T

문항 7 ②

Script & Dictation

M: It's summer, Eunice! We need a break. Let's go to a beach next week.

W: I have a commitment next Tuesday. Where do you want to go?

M: What about L.A. or San Diego?

W: But it **depends on** the weather.

M: Let's check the weather forecast.

W: Wow! Monday and Tuesday both in L.A. and San Diego are **sunny and clear**, but we cannot go anywhere because I have a commitment. It'll be rainy **all weekend**; we have to go **during the weekdays**.

M: What about going to San Diego on Wednesday?

W: It's cloudy. I cannot imagine the San Diego beach without the sun.

M: Then what about Thursday?

W: Brian, it says it'll be raining.

M: No, I mean L.A. **It says** it's not sunny, but Wednesday is sunny and Friday is sunny. I think it can be sunny on Thursday.

W: Brian, come on. Why don't we go to L.A. on Wednesday or Friday?

남: Eunice, 여름이야! 우린 휴식이 필요해. 다음 주에 해변에 가자.

여: 나 다음 주 화요일에는 약속 있어. 넌 어디로 가고 싶은데?

남: 로스앤젤레스나 샌디에이고가 어때?

여: 하지만 날씨에 달려있어.

남: 일기예보를 확인해 보자.

여: 와! 월요일과 화요일은 로스앤젤레스와 샌디에이고 모두 맑고 화창한걸. 하지만 우린 아무 데도 갈 수 없어. 왜냐하면 내가 약속이 있으니까. 주말엔 내내 비가 오니, 주중에 가야겠다.

남: 수요일에 샌디에이고는 어때?

여: 그날은 흐린데. 태양 없는 샌디에이고는 상상할 수 없어.

남: 그럼 목요일은?

여: Brian, 비 온다고 쓰여있잖아.

남: 아니, 내 말은 로스앤젤레스 말이야. 맑다고 되어 있진 않지만, 수요일도 맑고, 금요일도 맑으니까, 목요일 날씨도 맑을지도 모르잖아.

여: 아, Brian. 수요일이나 금요일에 로스앤젤레스 가는 게 어때?

해설: 수요일과 금요일 로스앤젤레스 날씨가 맑음인 것을 보고 남자가 목요일 로스앤젤레스 날씨가 맑을 수도 있다고 말하고 있지만, 남자의 예상일 뿐 일기예보 상 그렇게 나온 것은 아니다.

Listening Web

Intro: clear   Web 1: all

Ending: not

True / False

1. F   2. T   3. F   4. T

문항 8 ③

Script & Dictation

M: Rachel, what are we going to do when we go to Canada? You wanted to go to Banff National Park.

W: Yes. Look at this travel agency website. They provide **various kinds of** activities. Everything looks fantastic. What do you want to do there?

M: Above all, we need to **climb up** the beautiful mountain and see the emerald lake. What was the name?

W: Lake Louise. I'd like to go hiking, too.

M: And I want to ride an MTB. It's thrilling.

W: Yes, it's **a real thrill**. But I'm afraid of riding a mountain bike. I've **fallen off a bike** when I was younger. I'll never do it again.

M: Then would you like to go paragliding? You've always been dreaming about it.

W: Yeah... but is it safe?

M: Yes, maybe. You need to wear the suit **with the equipment**, and you'll paraglide with a professional pilot.

W: With a professional pilot? **That's a relief**. I'll try it.

M: Okay, then I'll click this one.

남: Rachel, 캐나다 가서 뭐 할 거야? 벤프 국립 공원에 가고 싶어 했잖아.

여: 응. 이 여행사 사이트 좀 봐. 많은 활동들을 제공하고 있어. 전부 멋져 보인다. 넌 뭐하고 싶어?

남: 무엇보다도 아름다운 산에 올라가 봐야겠지. 그리고 에메랄드 호수를 봐야지. 이름이 뭐였더라?

여: 루이스 호수. 나도 등산하고 싶어.

남: 그리고 산악자전거도 타고 싶어. 짜릿하잖아.

여: 그래, 정말 끝내주게 짜릿하지. 그런데 난 산악자전거 무서워. 나 어렸을 때 자전거에서 떨어졌어. 다시는 안 탈 거야.

남: 그럼 패러글라이딩 타러 갈래? 너 항상 패러글라이딩하는 거 꿈꿔왔잖아.

여: 응… 그런데 안전할까?

남: 아마도 그렇겠지. 장비가 갖춰진 옷을 입어야 해. 그리고 전문 조종사와 같이 패러글라이딩하는 거야.

여: 전문 조종사하고 같이? 다행이다. 해 볼래.

남: 그래, 그럼 이거 클릭한다.

해설: 두 사람 다 등산을 원했고, 산악자전거는 여자가 무서워하여 선택하지 않았으며 전문 조종사와 함께 하는 패러글라이딩을 선택했다.

Listening Web

Web 1: climb

Web 2: riding a

Web 3: paragliding

Ending: relief

True / False

1. F   2. F   3. F   4. F

문항 9 ④

Script & Dictation

W: I'm so excited! It's the first time **for me to go** to America. Will we go to Niagara Falls?

M: Sure. We're going to stay there for two days. I can't believe I'll be there again!

W: What are we going to do there?

M: I think we have to go up **to the observatory** and look down at the huge Niagara Falls.

W: Wow! It must be amazing. And **what else**? Just looking at the falls is all that we can do?

M: There are balloons and cruises.

W: Cruises? Can we go down to the water and **get on board** a cruise? I'd love to do it.

M: Me, too. And you can also look down Niagara Falls from a balloon.

W: That'll be fantastic, too. But getting on a balloon and going up to the observatory are almost the same thing.

M: Hmm... I think you're right.

W: Then **let's just pick one**. We don't need to spend money doing the same thing twice.

M: Then I'd like the balloon. It can be kind of scary, but I want to try it.

W: Okay.

여: 정말 짜릿한데! 나 미국 처음 가는 거야. 우리 나이아가라 폭포도 갈 거지?

남: 물론이지. 우리 거기에서 이틀 동안 머무를 거야. 내가 거길 다시 가게 되다니 믿기지 않아!

여: 우리 거기에서 뭐할 건데?

남: 전망대에 올라가서 나이아가라 폭포를 내려다보는 걸 꼭 해야 할 것 같아.

여: 와! 정말 멋질 거야. 그리고 다른 건? 우리가 그냥 폭포를 볼 수 있는 게 다야?

남: 열기구도 있고 유람선도 있어.

여: 유람선? 물에 내려가서 유람선을 탈 수 있어? 정말 해 보고 싶다.

남: 나도. 그리고 열기구 타고 나이아가라 폭포를 내려다볼 수도 있어.

여: 그것도 멋지겠는걸. 하지만 열기구 타는 거랑 전망대 올라가는 거랑 거의 똑같은 거잖아.

남: 음… 네 말이 맞는 것 같다

여: 그럼 하나만 고르자. 똑같은 걸 두 번 하는데 돈 쓰고 싶지 않아.

남: 그럼 난 열기구가 좋은데. 무서울 것 같기도 하지만, 한번 타 보고 싶어.

여: 그래.

해설: 처음에 남자와 여자는 모두 전망대와 유람선에 동의했고, 열기구와 전망대는 비슷한 것이므로 전망대를 포기하기로 했다.

Listening Web

Web 1: observatory

Web 2: on board

Web 3: balloon

True / False

1. T   2. F   3. T   4. T

문항 10 ⑤

Script & Dictation

M: Hey, what's up?

W: Hi. **I'll work out** during the vacation. I have to lose weight. Do you go to this gym?

M: I'm new, like you. **I registered yesterday**. What are you going to do?

W: Well, I've never worked out regularly before. I don't know what to do. Can you help me?

M: Sure. **Take the registration form** and check which classes you want to join. How about yoga? It's a kind of stretching, so it's not that hard, but you'll **sweat**.

W: Oh! That's exactly my style. But yoga class is **every other day**. I need to choose a Monday, Wednesday, and Friday class or a Tuesday, Thursday, and Saturday class.

M: Then you can do some other things when you don't have a yoga class, like swimming or squash...

W: I've wanted to try squash. But squash class is only on Friday.

M: That's **the intermediate class**. Have you ever learned squash?

W: No. A-ha, the beginner class is on Monday and Wednesday.

M: Then you can do both yoga and squash.

W: All right. Thank you.

남: 어이, 어쩐 일이야?

여: 안녕. 나 방학 동안 운동하려고 해. 살 빼야 하거든. 너 이 체육관 다니니?

남: 나도 너처럼 처음 왔어. 어제 등록했어. 넌 뭐 할 거야?

여: 글쎄, 난 규칙적으로 운동해 본 적이 없어. 뭘 해야 할지 모르겠어. 나 좀 도와줄래?

남: 그래. 신청서에 네가 어떤 반에 등록할 건지 표시하면 돼. 요가는 어때? 스트레칭 같은 건데, 격하지 않지만 땀이 날 거야.

여: 오! 딱 내 스타일이야. 하지만 요가반은 격일로 있어. 월수금 반이랑 화목토 반 중에 선택해야 하네.

남: 그럼 요가반이 없는 날엔 다른 걸 해, 수영이나 스쿼시 같은…

여: 나 스쿼시 해 보고 싶었어. 그런데 스쿼시는 금요일밖에 없어.

남: 그건 중급반이잖아. 너 스쿼시 배워 본 적 있어?

여: 아니. 아하, 초급반은 월요일 수요일에 있구나.

남: 그럼 요가랑 스쿼시 둘 다 할 수 있겠다.

여: 좋아어. 고마워.

해설: 요가는 월수금 반과 화목토 반 중에 선택해야 하는데, 스쿼시 초급반이 월요일과 수요일에 있으므로, 요가와 스쿼시를 모두 하기 위해서는 요가를 화요일, 목요일, 토요일에 해야 한다.

Listening Web

Intro: work   Web 1: other

Web 2: some other   Ending: both

True / False

1. F   2. F   3. T   4. F

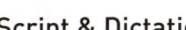

Unit 13 유형 13 - 적절한 응답 찾기

문항 1 ③

Script & Dictation

M: Excuse me. I cannot find the book **I'm looking for**. Can you help me to find it?

W: Why don't you check on the computer?

M: I tried to, but there are too many books whose titles **are similar to** each other.

W: What's the title?

M: "Language and Culture." The author is Amy Baker.

W: Is it about **the African tribes**?

M: Yes, that's right.

W: It's been **checked out**. It's **due** on December 28th. Do you want us to reserve the book for you?

M: Yes, please.

W: Can I see **your student ID**? [Pause] Thank you. And give me your phone number, please.

M: 013-4236-9395.

W: We'll let you know as soon as the book is returned.

남: 실례합니다. 제가 찾고 있는 책을 찾을 수가 없네요. 책 찾는 것 좀 도와주시겠습니까?

여: 컴퓨터로 찾아보시는 건 어떠세요?

남: 해 봤는데, 제목이 비슷한 책들이 너무 많습니다.

여: 제목이 무엇인가요?

남: '언어와 문화'입니다. 저자는 Amy Baker입니다.

여: 아프리카 부족에 관한 것인가요?

남: 네, 맞습니다.

여: 대출 중이네요. 12월 28일까지인데요. 예약해 드릴까요?

남: 네, 그렇게 해주십시오.

여: 학생증 좀 보여주시겠어요? [잠시 후] 감사합니다. 그리고 전화번호 알려주세요.

남: 013-4236-9395.

여: 저희가 책을 반납 받는 대로 알려드릴게요.

해설: 남자는 이미 대출 중인 책의 대출을 예약했다. 이어질 여자의 마지막 말은 책이 반납되는 대로 알려주겠다고 하는 것이 가장 자연스럽다.

Listening Web

Intro: find it   Web 2: out

Web 3: reserve

True / False

1. T   2. F   3. T   4. F

문항 2 ⑤

Script & Dictation

M: Wow, almost all the theaters show only Hollywood blockbusters.

W: Is that a problem?

M: Minor films cannot have opportunities **to be released**.

W: Theaters don't work as a **charity**. They want to **make profits**.

M: But some people want to see other films. Think about this situation: you went to the theaters, and all of them showed only Spiderman. You cannot **make a choice**.

W: You're right. But the theaters have rights to show any profitable films.

M: That would be **short-sighted**.

W: What do you mean?

M: Money is not everything. We have to think of the future of the film industry.

W: So you mean experimental movies need to have chances to be shown to people, right?

남: 와, 대부분 영화관에서 할리우드 흥행작밖에 상영을 안 해.

여: 그게 무슨 문제 있어?

남: 비주류 영화들은 상영할 기회조차 없게 되잖아.

여: 영화관이 자선사업 하는 건 아니잖아. 영화관도 돈 벌어야지.

남: 그렇지만 어떤 사람들은 다른 영화를 보고 싶어하기도 해. 이런 상황을 생각해봐. 네가 영화관에 갔는데, 전부 스파이더맨만 상영하는 거야. 넌 고를 수도 없어.

여: 맞아. 하지만 영화관도 수익성 있는 영화를 상영할 권리가 있는 거지.

남: 그건 근시안적인 생각이야.

여: 무슨 뜻이야?

남: 돈이 전부가 아니라고. 우린 영화 산업의 미래를 생각해야 해.

여: 그러니까 네 말은 실험 영화가 사람들에게 선보일 기회가 있어야 한다는 거야, 그렇지?

해설: 남자는 수익성만을 따지며 할리우드 흥행작만을 상영하는 영화관의 태도가 옳지 않음을 지적하고 있다.

Listening Web

Web 1: opportunities, released   Web 2: rights

Web 3: sighted   Ending: film

True / False

1. F   2. F   3. T   4. T

문항 3 ④

Script & Dictation

W: Hmm. We have to clean the house today.

M: Sarah, I've just come back from London. I'm so tired. Can we just **wipe the floor** with a cloth today?

W: There is a lot of dust so it's better to **vacuum**.

M: Okay. The house will be clean because of my neat sister.

W: If the house is clean, we'll feel better and you can **focus more on** your studying.

M: What about listening to music while cleaning?

W: That's nice!

M: Now, **what should I do** first?

W: Put the newspapers and empty bottles Intro the **recycling bin**. We need to get them out tomorrow morning.

M: I'll **throw them away** now. Why do we have to wait until tomorrow?

W: Recyclable trash is collected every Tuesday.

여: 음. 우리 오늘 청소해야겠어.

남: Sarah, 나 런던에서 방금 돌아왔어. 나 정말 피곤해. 오늘은 그냥 걸레로 바닥만 닦으면 안 될까?

여: 먼지가 너무 많아서 진공청소기를 돌려야 해.

남: 알았어. 깔끔한 우리 누나 덕분에 집이 깨끗해지겠다.

여: 집이 깨끗하면 기분도 더 좋아질 거고, 공부도 더 잘 될 거야.

남: 우리 청소하면서 음악 들을까?

여: 좋아!

남: 자, 내가 뭐부터 하면 되지?

여: 신문이랑 빈 병들을 재활용함에 넣어. 우리가 내일 아침에 내놓아야 해.

남: 내가 지금 갖다 버릴게. 왜 내일까지 기다려?

여: 재활용 쓰레기는 매주 화요일에 수거돼.

해설: 재활용 쓰레기를 당장 버리면 안 되는 이유에 대한 설명이 와야 한다.

Listening Web

Intro: clean   Web 1: wipe

Web 3: bin

True / False

1. T   2. F   3. T   4. F

문항 4 ②

Script & Dictation

M: Hey, why aren't you ready?

W: I am ready.

M: I don't think so. First of all, where is your helmet?

W: It **messes up my hair**.

M: If you fall without it, you'll have a messed-up head.

W: Oh, be serious.

M: I am serious. And what is up with those bell-bottom pants?

W: Don't you like them?

M: Sure. But **not on a bike**. What do you think will happen when those bell-bottoms **flap Intro** your bike chain?

W: They won't.

M: You cannot say **for sure**. Go inside and change.

W: Okay. But I can't take off my lovely pink sandals.

M: Come on. Put on some real shoes. You can't **wear sandals** on a bike.

W: Helmet, sneakers... I don't like them.

M: <u>Safety is more important than fashion.</u>

남: 야, 너 왜 준비 안 해?

여: 준비 다 했어.

남: 아닌 것 같은데. 우선 네 헬멧 어디 있어?

여: 머리카락이 헝클어져.

남: 헬멧 없이 넘어지면 네 머리가 망가질 거야.

여: 오, 장난하지 마.

남: 진심이야. 그 나팔바지는 뭐야?

여: 이거 안 예뻐?

남: 예쁘지. 하지만 자전거 탈 때는 아니야. 그 나팔바지 펄럭이다 자전거 체인에 말려들어 가면 어떻게 되겠어?

여: 그렇지 않아.

남: 장담할 수 없는 거야. 들어가서 갈아입어.

여: 알았어. 하지만 분홍색 샌들은 꼭 신을 거야.

남: 제발 좀. 제대로 생긴 신발을 신도록 해. 자전거 탈 때 샌들을 신으면 안 돼.

여: 헬멧에, 운동화에… 난 이런 거 안 좋아해.

남: <u>안전이 패션보다 더 중요해.</u>

해설: 남자와 여자가 자전거를 타러 나가면서 나누는 대화이다. 여자는 예쁘게 보이는 것에 더 집중하지만, 남자는 안전이 더 중요하다고 말하고 있다.

Listening Web

Intro: aren't   Web 1: messed

Web 2: flap

True / False

1. T   2. T   3. F   4. T

문항 5 ④

Script & Dictation

M: Hey, what's up? You haven't **turned up** for a while.

W: I was in Spain last week.

M: A business trip?

W: No, I **took a week off** and traveled to Spain by myself.

M: That's cool. How was the weather? I heard it's rainy during winter in Europe.

W: Yeah, but it was quite good. It wasn't raining a lot. Do you want to see the pictures?

M: Of course. Let me see.

W: Look. This is my first day in Spain.

M: Beautiful. By the way, do you **store** all your pictures as image files?

W: Yes, does it matter?

M: Actually I **used to store** all my pictures as image files, but one day my computer was broken, and all my picture files **had gone**.

W: I am sorry to hear that. Then what am I **supposed to do**?

M: <u>Make hard copies of the image files.</u>

남: 야, 웬일이야? 한동안 안 보이더니.

여: 나 지난주에 스페인에 있었어.

남: 출장?

여: 아니, 한 주 휴가 내고 혼자 스페인에 다녀왔어.

남: 멋지다. 날씨는 어땠어? 유럽은 겨울에 비 온다고 하던데.

여: 응, 그런데 날씨는 꽤 좋았어. 비도 많이 안 오고. 사진 볼래?

남: 물론이지. 보여줘.

여: 봐봐. 이게 스페인에서의 첫날이야.

남: 멋지구나. 그런데 사진들을 전부 이미지 파일로 보관해?

여: 음, 그게 문제가 되니?

남: 사실 나도 사진들을 이미지 파일로 보관했었는데, 어느 날 컴퓨터가 고장 났거든. 그랬더니 내 사진들이 다 없어졌어.

여: 그랬다니 유감이네. 그럼 난 어떻게 해야 하지?

남: <u>이미지 파일을 출력해 둬.</u>

해설: 사진을 이미지 파일이 아닌 보다 안전한 방법으로 보관하는 방법을 제안하는 것으로 대화가 마무리되는 것이 가장 자연스럽다.

Listening Web

Intro: off   Web 1: raining

Web 3: store, broken, files

True / False

1. F   2. T   3. T   4. T

문항 6 ②

Script & Dictation

M: May I help you? Do you have a reservation?

W: Yes, I have a **reservation for** Lisa Smith.

M: I'm sorry, but we don't have your name **on the list**. Did you happen to make a reservation on the Internet?

W: Yes, I did it three days ago.

M: I'm really sorry. Sometimes the on-line reservation service doesn't work. We've been **working on it** since last week.

W: But there was nothing to warn against.

M: We put the notice not to use the on-line reservation service on the top of the website with blinking letters. You may have missed it.

W: Really? Do you have a **table for five** available now?

M: We don't have one right away, but one should be **available soon**. Do you want to leave your name on the list?

W: Yes. My name is Lisa Smith. **Someplace quiet**, please.

M: Please have a seat while you wait.

남: 무엇을 도와드릴까요? 예약은 하셨나요?

여: 네, Lisa Smith라는 이름으로 예약했어요.

남: 죄송합니다만 명단에 없는데요. 혹시 인터넷으로 예약하셨습니까?

여: 네, 사흘 전에요.

남: 정말 죄송합니다. 종종 온라인 예약이 되지 않습니다. 저희가 지난주부터 작업 중이에요.

여: 하지만 온라인으로 예약하지 말라는 이야기가 없었어요.

남: 웹사이트 상단에 온라인 예약은 사용하지 말라고 반짝이는 글씨로 올려놓았습니다. 아마 못 보신 것 같네요.

여: 정말이요? 지금 5명 자리가 있나요?

남: 지금 당장은 없지만 곧 생길 겁니다. 성함을 명단에 올려드릴까요?

여: 네. 제 이름은 Lisa Smith입니다. 조용한 자리로 부탁해요.

남: 기다리시는 동안 앉아계세요.

해설: 온라인 예약에 문제가 생겨서 여자는 식당에 자리가 날 때까지 일단 기다려야 하는 상황이다.

Listening Web

Intro: for	Web 1: on
Web 2: on	Web 3: for
Ending: leave	

True / False

1. T	2. F	3. F	4. F

문항 7 ①

Script & Dictation

M: Hey, what's up? You don't look good.

W: I **stayed up** all night studying, but I screwed up the science exam.

M: I'm sorry to hear that.

W: It was **incredibly difficult**. I spent too much time on the first question, so I just marked the answer sheet randomly after number 20.

M: Don't worry. The other students are in the same situation, aren't they?

W: The problem was that **I should have skipped** the difficult question during the exam.

M: You might have been able to save some time.

W: I can't **concentrate on** preparing for the next exam.

M: Just forget it. It's already over. Get a **sound sleep** tonight. It'll help you to concentrate on the exam tomorrow.

W: Thank you for your advice. I'll **review it quickly** and go to bed early tonight.

M: I'm sure it will work out all right tomorrow.

남: 안녕? 안색이 안 좋아 보인다.

여: 밤새도록 공부했는데, 과학 시험을 망쳤어.

남: 유감이네.

여: 엄청나게 어려웠어. 1번 문제를 푸는데 시간을 너무 많이 써서, 20번 뒤로는 찍었어.

남: 걱정하지 마. 다른 아이들도 너와 같은 상황일 거야, 그렇지 않니?

여: 문제는 내가 시험 볼 때 어려운 문제는 그냥 건너뛰어야 했었다는 거야.

남: 그럼 시간이 좀 절약됐겠지.

여: 다음 시험 준비에 집중이 안 돼.

남: 그냥 잊어버려. 이미 끝난 거잖아. 오늘은 잠을 푹 자도록 해. 내일 시험에 집중하는 데 도움이 될 거야.

여: 충고해줘서 고마워. 빨리 훑어보고 오늘은 일찍 자야겠어.

남: 그러면 내일은 분명히 잘 볼 거야.

해설: 시험을 망친 여자에게 내일은 잘 될 것이라고 용기를 북돋아 주는 것이 가장 자연스럽다.

Listening Web

Intro: up	Web 1: on, randomly
Web 2: skipped	Web 3: on

True / False

1. F	2. F	3. F	4. T

문항 8 ④

Script & Dictation

W: That's my favorite program. I like **the host**.

M: I think almost all women like her.

W: Yes. When I watch her talk show, I feel like I'm talking with a friend.

M: You mean she makes people very comfortable.

W: That's right. Sometimes she cries and **spreads her arms** for a hug when the guest's story moves her.

M: I heard her childhood was very tough, though.

W: Yeah. I've read an article on her. She was **raised by** her grandmother, and then **handed over to** her mother, and then over to her father.

M: But do you know that she won a beauty contest?

W: Really? I didn't know that!

M: She was invited to a local radio program after she won at the contest, and she got a chance to work for **a broadcasting studio**.

W: That's interesting. Now she is a famous show host, and also a **millionaire**.

M: <u>Life is full of ups and downs.</u>

여: 저건 내가 제일 좋아하는 프로그램이야. 난 그 진행자가 좋더라.

남: 여자들은 대부분 저 사람을 좋아하는 것 같아.

여: 응, 저 사람 토크쇼를 보고 있으면, 친구랑 이야기하는 것 같은 느낌이야.

남: 저 사람이 사람들을 편안하게 해 준단 말이지.

여: 맞아. 출연자의 이야기가 감동적일 때는 울기도 하고, 출연자를 안아주기도 해.

남: 그렇지만 저 사람 유년시절은 아주 힘들었다고 들었어.

여: 응. 나도 저 사람에 관한 기사 읽은 적 있어. 할머니 손에 자라다가 엄마한테 넘겨지고, 다시 아빠한테 넘겨졌대.

남: 그런데 너 저 사람 미인대회 출신인 거 알아?

여: 정말? 몰랐어!

남: 미인대회에서 상 타고 나서 라디오 지역방송에 초대받았다가, 방송국에서 일하게 된 거래.

여: 흥미롭네. 이제 그녀는 유명한 토크쇼 진행자에 돈도 많잖아.

남: 인생은 좋을 때도 있고 나쁠 때도 있는 거지.

해설: 인생의 역경을 딛고 일어나 크게 성공한 쇼 진행자에 관한 대화이다. 인생에는 나쁜 일과 좋은 일이 모두 같이 있다는 말로 마무리되는 것이 가장 자연스럽다.

Listening Web

Intro: host	Web 1: talking
Web 2: tough	Web 3: handed
Web 4: invited, won at	

True / False

1. T	2. F	3. F	4. T

문항 9 ①

Script & Dictation

W: It's **freezing** out here. I don't like winter.

M: Me, neither.

W: It's too cold. I feel like my ears are frozen.

M: Yeah. No matter how many clothes I wear, I still feel cold. Winter in Korea is really long and cold.

W: Right. I love summer. We can have **lots of delicious fruit**, and imagine lying down on the beach and enjoying the sun.

M: I love fruit, too. My favorite fruit is pineapple. It doesn't look good, and it's a little hard to cut it, but it's really sweet.

W: Oh, no. Now I'm **in the mood** for pineapple.

M: You know they're really expensive in winter **even though** they're imported.

W: I'll get some **dried fruit instead**.

M: Well, you don't like winter, and neither do I. You like fruit, and so do I. It's interesting, isn't it?

W: <u>We have a lot in common.</u>

여: 여기는 밖이 너무 추워. 난 겨울이 싫어.

남: 나도 싫어.

여: 너무 추워. 귀가 얼어붙는 느낌이야.

남: 그래. 옷을 아무리 많이 입어도 여전히 추워. 한국의 겨울은 정말 길고 추워.

여: 맞아. 난 여름이 좋은데. 맛있는 과일도 많이 먹을 수 있고, 해변에 누워서 태양을 즐기는 상상을 해 봐.

남: 나도 과일 좋아해. 내가 제일 좋아하는 과일은 파인애플이야. 못생겼고 자르기 어렵지만 정말 달콤해.

여: 오, 이런. 파인애플을 지금 먹고 싶어.

남: 겨울에 파인애플 정말 비싼 거 알지. 수입품이라도 말이야.

여: 대신 말린 과일이나 먹어야겠다.

남: 너도 겨울 싫어하고, 나도 싫어하고. 너도 과일 좋아하고 나도 과일 좋아하고. 재미있지 않아?

여: <u>우리 공통점이 많은걸.</u>

해설: 겨울을 싫어하고 과일을 좋아하는 공통점에 관해 이야기하고 있다.

Listening Web

Intro: freezing	Web 1: neither
Web 2: lying, enjoying	Ending: do

True / False

1. T	2. F	3. T	4. T

문항 10 ④

Script & Dictation

M: Where are you going?

W: I'm going to the library **to return these books**.

M: Wow, I didn't know that you're interested in handicrafts.

W: No, **I'm all thumbs**. Erin asked me to return them.

M: Erin is really good at art. By the way, it's so hot and humid. Shall we drop by the store and have some ice cream?

W: No, I have to return them quickly and go to swimming class. **It's already started**. I'll be late today.

M: Then why did you do her a favor? I think you should've **refused it**.

W: Erin said she had a project to do with her friends, and these books are due today.

M: No, you should've said that you had a class. You went to the library to check out a book for David the other day.

W: I can't refuse somebody a favor. I think I have a **hole in my head**.

M: <u>Just say no when you don't want to do something.</u>

남: 어디가?

여: 이 책들 반납하러 도서관에 가는 길이야.

남: 와, 네가 수공예에 관심 있는 줄 몰랐어.

여: 아니야, 난 재주 없어. Erin이 반납해 달라고 부탁한 거야.

남: Erin은 미술을 잘하지. 그런데 너무 덥고 습하다. 우리 가게에 들러서 아이스크림 좀 먹을까?

여: 아니, 나 이거 빨리 반납하고 수영 강습 가야 해. 수업이 이미 시작했어. 나 오늘 지각이야.

남: 그런데 Erin의 부탁은 왜 들어줘? 거절했어야지.

여: Erin은 친구들과 함께 해야 하는 프로젝트가 있대. 이 책들은 오늘까지 반납해야 하고.

남: 아니지, 너 수업 있다고 말을 했어야지. 너 지난번에도 David 대신 도서관 가서 책 빌려 왔잖아.

여: 다른 사람 부탁을 거절 못 하겠어. 나 바보인가 봐.

남: _네가 하기 싫은 일은 그냥 싫다고 말해._

해설: 여자는 자기 일을 희생하면서까지 남의 부탁을 거절하지 못하고 있다. 원치 않은 때에는 싫다고 말하라고 충고해주는 것이 가장 자연스럽다.

Listening Web

Web 1: started   Web 2: should've

Web 3: class   Ending: favor

True / False

1. F   2. T   3. F   4. F

Unit 14 유형 14 - 설명을 듣고 상대방에게 할 말 찾기

문항 1 ②

Script & Dictation

W: This morning, Jessica got up a little bit **later than usual**. She took a **quick shower** and got dressed, and ran out of the house to catch the school bus. When she ran around the corner, she saw the bus still waiting for her. But when she almost got there, the bus left. After the morning classes, while she was talking with her friend Lucy about **what happened to her** that morning, she realized that she didn't bring her science homework. It was **due** today, so she tried to call her mom to bring the homework, but **the battery was out**. She forgot **to recharge it** last night. In this situation, what would Lucy most likely say to Jessica?

* _Lucy: Jessica, when it rains, it pours._

여: 오늘 아침 Jessica는 평소보다 늦게 일어났다. 빨리 샤워를 하고 옷을 입고, 학교 버스를 놓치지 않기 위해 집에서 뛰어나 갔다. 모퉁이를 돌았을 때, 버스가 아직 그녀를 기다리고 있는 것을 보았다. 하지만 거의 다 왔을 때, 버스는 떠나버렸다. 오전 수업이 끝나고 그녀의 친구 Lucy와 오늘 아침에 있었던 일을 이야기하던 중, 과학 숙제를 가져오지 않은 것을 깨달았다. 오늘이 마감일이어서, 그녀는 엄마에게 숙제를 갖다 달라고 전화하려고 했다. 하지만 배터리가 없었다. 어젯밤에 배터리를 충전하는 것을 잊었던 것이다. 이런 상황에서, Lucy는 Jessica에게 무슨 말을 해줄까?

* _Lucy: Jessica, 안 좋은 일은 겹쳐 일어나기 마련이야._

해설: 종일 일이 풀리지 않는 Jessica의 상황을 묘사하는 말이 와야 한다.

Listening Web

Intro: usual   Web 1: around

Web 2: there   Ending: tried

True / False

1. F   2. F   3. F   4. T

문항 2 ④

Script & Dictation

M: Sarah is a **movie director**. Actually she is a **rookie**. She has completed her first film after working on it for six years. On the day on which **her film was released**, she invited her best friend Eunice to the theater. Eunice was willing to go to the theater with Sarah. Both of them were so excited. However, when they got there, they were surprised because **there was nobody but** them. It was only **five minutes to go** before the movie started. Eunice looked at Sarah. She looked so **disappointed**. In the end, no more people came Intro the theater until the movie was over. In this situation, what would Eunice most likely say to Sarah?

* _Eunice: Sarah, it is only beginning. You've worked very hard._

남: Sarah는 영화감독이다. 사실 그녀는 신인이다. 그녀는 자신의 첫 번째 영화를 촬영한 지 6년 만에 완성했다. 영화가 개봉하던 날, 그녀는 자신의 가장 친한 친구인 Eunice를 극장으로 초대했다. Eunice는 기꺼이 Sarah와 함께 극장으로 갔다. 둘 다 매우 흥분되어 있었다. 하지만 영화관에 도착했을 때, 영화관에 그들 둘뿐이어서 깜짝 놀랐다. 영화 시작 5분 전이었다. Eunice가 Sarah를 보았다. 매우 실망한 모습이었다. 결국 영화가 끝날 때까지 사람들이 더는 들어오지 않았다. 이런 상황에서, Eunice는 Sarah에게 무슨 말을 해줄까?

* _Eunice: Sarah, 이제 시작이야. 너 정말 열심히 해오고 있어._

해설: 오랫동안 고생해서 만든 영화가 개봉했는데, 관객이 하나도 없어서 실망하는 친구에게 용기를 북돋아 주는 말을 해주어야 한다.

Listening Web

Intro: completed	Web 1: on
Web 2: surprised	Web 3: disappointed
Ending: no	

True / False

1. T   2. F   3. F   4. T

문항 3 ③

Script & Dictation

W: Liz **is dissatisfied with** a skirt. Three days ago, she bought a skirt on an online shopping mall that a **famous singer runs**. It doesn't have an off-line mall, so she depended on the pictures and the comments that the customers wrote on the items **after purchase**. She trusted everything about the shopping mall because a celebrity **runs the business**. But the skirt she received today **looks totally different from** what she saw online. The color is different, the quality is different, and the size is different. In this situation, what would her mom most likely say to Liz?

* *Mom: Liz, fame doesn't always guarantee the reliability of a business.*

여: Liz는 치마에 실망했다. 3일 전, 유명 가수가 운영하는 온라인 쇼핑몰에서 치마를 샀다. 오프라인 매장이 없어서 그녀는 온전히 사진과 구매자들의 후기에 의존했었다. 유명인사가 운영하는 것이었기 때문에 그녀는 그 쇼핑몰의 모든 것을 신뢰했다. 하지만 오늘 그녀가 받은 치마는 온라인에서 본 것과 매우 달랐다. 색상도 다르고, 질도 다르고, 치수도 달랐다. 이러한 상황에서 그녀의 엄마는 Liz에게 무슨 말을 했을까?

* *Mom: Liz, 명성이 사업의 신뢰도를 항상 보장해주지는 못한단다.*

해설: 유명 가수가 운영하는 온라인 쇼핑몰에서 물건을 샀다가 실망한 딸에게 명성이 모든 것을 보장해줄 수는 없다는 충고를 해주는 것이 가장 자연스럽다.

Listening Web

Intro: dissatisfied	Web 1: runs
Web 2: items	Web 3: because
Ending: received	

True / False

1. T   2. T   3. F   4. F

문항 4 ③

Script & Dictation

M: The winter vacation has started. When **the alarm went off** at 6 a.m., Christine recognized that she didn't need to get up early, so she turned it off and went back to sleep. Around 10 a.m. she got up, but didn't **have an appetite**. She skipped breakfast and surfed the Internet, **reading articles** on pop singers or movie stars. At 1 p.m. her mom told Christine **to eat lunch**, but she felt her back hurt and it was hard to digest. Her mom thought Christine **should have gotten up** earlier and exercised more. In this situation, what would her mom most likely say to Christine?

* *Mom: Christine, lead yourself a regular life.*

남: 겨울 방학이 시작되었다. Christine은 6시에 알람이 울렸을 때 일찍 일어날 필요가 없다는 것을 깨달았다. 그래서 알람을 끄고 다시 잠이 들었다. 10시 즈음 일어났지만, 입맛이 없었다. 아침 식사를 거른 채 인터넷 서핑을 하며 가수와 영화배우들에 관한 기사들을 읽었다. 오후 1시에 그녀의 엄마는 점심을 먹으라고 말씀하셨다. 하지만 허리가 아픈 것을 느꼈고 소화가 잘되지 않았다. 그녀의 엄마는 Christine이 좀 더 일찍 일어나서 운동을 더 했어야 한다고 생각했다. 이러한 상황에서 그녀의 엄마는 Christine에게 무슨 말을 해주실까?

* *Mom: Christine, 스스로 규칙적인 생활을 하렴.*

해설: 방학이 되어 게으름을 피우는 딸에게 규칙적인 생활을 하라고 충고해주는 것이 가장 자연스럽다.

Listening Web

Intro: has	Web 1: off
Web 2: appetite	Web 3: hurt
Ending: exercised	

True / False

1. F   2. T   3. F   4. F

문항 5 ②

Script & Dictation

W: Julie is Erin's roommate. They had **gotten along with** each other before they came to live together. At first, they decided who would do what so as not to get themselves **Intro trouble**. For example, Julie would make breakfast every morning, and Erin would clean the house twice a week. Julie didn't break her promise, but very often she **got on** Erin's **nerves**. Julie made breakfast every morning, but didn't wash the dishes. And she never answered the phone when Erin was home. Finally, Erin was very **upset with** Julie, but she wanted to **keep their friendship**. In this situation, what would Erin most likely say to Julie?

* *Erin: Julie, I want you to be more considerate of me.*

여: Julie는 Erin의 룸메이트이다. 그들은 함께 살기 전에는 서로 잘 지냈었다. 처음에 그들은 곤란한 상황이 생기지 않도록 누가 무엇을 할지를 정해두었다. 예를 들어, Julie는 매일 아침마다 아침 식사를 준비해야 했고, Erin은 일주일에 두 번씩 청소를 해야 했다. Julie는 약속을 어기지는 않았지만, 매우 자주 Erin의 신경을 건드렸다. Julie는 매일 아침마다 아침 식사를 만들었지만, 설거지를 하지 않았다. 그리고 Erin이 집에 있을 때에는 절대로 전화를 받지 않았다. 결국 Erin은 Julie에게 매우 화가 났지만 두 사람 사이의 우정을 지키고 싶었다. 이러한 상황에서 Erin은 Julie에게 무슨 말을 할까?

* *Erin: Julie, 난 네가 나를 좀더 배려해줬으면 좋겠어.*

해설: 식사 준비만 하고 설거지를 하지 않고, 절대 전화를 받지 않는 룸메이트에게 상대방을 배려해 달라고 부탁하는 것이 가장 자연스럽다.

Listening Web

Web 1: along   Web 2: themselves
Web 3: on, nerves   Ending: keep

True / False

1. F   2. F   3. F   4. T

문항 6 ③

Script & Dictation

M: Chloe decided to write about **the relations between** breakfast and grades. She thought that students who eat breakfast every day would **get a good grade** on a test. First, she needed to **do a survey targeting** more than three hundred high school seniors. So she went to the high school she **graduated from**, and met with her teacher. She asked if he could do a survey for her paper instead of her. But he **had already been asked** to do two other surveys on different topics, and he was too busy to do another survey. In this situation, what would the teacher most likely say to Chloe?

* *Teacher: Chloe, I'm sorry, but what about asking to some other teachers?.*

남: Chloe는 아침 식사와 학업 성적과의 관계에 대해 쓰기로 했다. 그녀는 아침 식사를 매일 하는 학생이 시험에서 좋은 결과를 얻을 것이라고 생각했다. 우선 300명 이상의 고등학교 3학년 학생들을 대상으로 한 설문조사가 필요했다. 그래서 그녀는 모교에 가서 그녀의 선생님을 찾아갔다. 그녀는 선생님이 설문조사를 대신 해주실 수 있는지 여쭈어보았다. 하지만 선생님은 이미 두 개의 다른 주제로 설문조사를 부탁받은 상황이었고, 너무 바빠서 또 하나를 더 할 수 없는 상황이었다. 이러한 상황에서 선생님은 Chloe에게 무슨 말을 할까?

* *Teacher: Chloe, 미안하지만 다른 선생님께 여쭤보면 어떻겠니?*

해설: Chloe의 선생님은 지금 그녀의 청을 들어주기가 어려운 상황이므로, 다른 선생님에게 요청해 볼 것을 권하는 것이 가장 자연스럽다.

Listening Web

Intro: relations   Web 1: do a
Web 2: met with   Ending: another

True / False

1. F   2. T   3. T   4. F

문항 7 ③

W: Susie got a **disappointing** grade on the final exam again. No matter how hard she thought about it, she couldn't **come up with** a reason. Finally she decided to go see a counselor and discuss this problem. The counselor asked her **how she had studied**. She thought for a while, and then said that she didn't sleep a lot and didn't hang out with friends, either. The counselor said that **wasn't the point**. Come to think of it, she just sat at the desk for a long time, **not focusing on studying**. And she thought she had studied a lot. In this situation, what would the counselor most likely say to Susie?

* *Counselor: Susie, the quality is more important than the quantity.*

여: Susie는 기말고사에서 또 실망스러운 점수를 받았다. 아무리 열심히 생각해 보아도 이유가 뭔지 알 수 없었다. 결국 상담 선생님을 찾아가 고민을 이야기하기로 결심했다. 상담 선생님은 그녀가 어떻게 공부했는지 물으셨다. 그녀는 잠시 생각하다가, 잠도 많이 자지 않았고, 친구들과 돌아다니지도 않았다고 대답했다. 상담 선생님은 그게 요점이 아니라고 말씀하셨다. 생각해보니, 공부에 집중하지 못한 채 그냥 책상에 오랫동안 앉아있었고, 자기가 매우 열심히 공부했다고 생각했던 것이다. 이러한 상황에서 상담 선생님은 Susie에게 무슨 말을 하실까?

* *Counselor: Susie, 질이 양보다 더 중요하단다.*

해설: Susie는 그냥 책상 앞에 앉아 있었던 시간을 모두 자신이 공부한 시간이라고 착각했다. 이러한 상황에서 상담 선생님은 Susie에게 공부에 투자한 시간의 양보다 질이 더 중요하다는 말을 해줄 필요가 있다.

Listening Web

Intro: disappointing   Web 1: discuss
Web 3: at   Ending: had studied

True / False

1. F   2. T   3. F   4. T

문항 8 ⑤

M: The report is **due today**, but Cindy is still working on it. Actually she already finished the report a week ago, and **was proofreading it**. Two days ago, she **dropped** her USB **Intro water** by mistake. She quickly took it out and checked if there was any problem. Unfortunately, the computer couldn't read any files on the USB. She tried to rewrite everything again in time, but two days were not enough. Moreover, the teacher is well-known for not **collecting late homework**. But Cindy couldn't hand in the homework without a conclusion. In this situation, what would Cindy most likely say to the teacher?

* _Cindy: Could you please give me two more days to finish the report?_

남: 보고서가 오늘까지 마감이다. 하지만 Cindy는 아직도 작업 중이다. 사실 일주일 전에 보고서를 모두 마치고 검토 중이 었다. 이틀 전에 실수로 USB를 물에 빠뜨렸다. 얼른 건져서 문제가 없는지 확인했다. 안타깝게도 컴퓨터가 USB 안에 있 는 파일들을 전혀 읽지 못하였다. 제시간 안에 다시 작성하 려고 노력했지만, 이틀은 충분하지 못했다. 게다가 선생님은 늦게 제출하는 숙제는 절대 받아주지 않는 것으로 유명했다. 하지만 Cindy는 결론을 맺지 못한 채 보고서를 제출할 수 없 다고 생각했다. 이런 상황에서 Cindy는 선생님께 무슨 말을 할까?

* _Cindy: 제가 레포트 끝낼 수 있게 이틀을 더 주시면 안 될 까요?_

해설: Cindy는 마감일을 넘긴 숙제를 절대 안 받아 주시는 선생님이라도 미완성 상태로 숙제를 제출할 수 없었다. 피치 못할 사정이 있었던 만큼 선생님께 시간을 좀 더 달라고 요청하는 것이 가장 자연스럽다.

Listening Web

Intro: due, working on   Web 1: she
Web 3: in   Web 4: not
Ending: without

True / False

1. F   2. F   3. T   4. T

문항 9 ④

W: Kelly is **throwing a party** this evening. She was going to cook a special dinner. In the meantime, she found an online market. The website said that everything could be **ordered online** and would be **delivered in thirty minutes**. So she ordered online what she needed, but it never came. She called the online market, and they said everything would be **there in a minute**. Fifteen minutes later, she finally got the food items. However, they were not **what she ordered**. She was upset and decided to complain to the manager about it. In this situation, what would Kelly most likely say to the manager?

* _Kelly: I got different things than what I ordered._

여: Kelly는 오늘 저녁 파티를 열 것이다. 그녀는 특별한 저녁을 준비하려고 했다. 그러던 중 온라인 마트를 발견했다. 모든 것을 온라인으로 주문할 수 있고, 30분 안에 배달해 준다는 것이었다. 그래서 온라인으로 필요한 것을 주문했지만, 물건 이 오지 않았다. 온라인 마트에 전화해 보니 곧 물건이 도착 할 것이라고 했다. 15분이 지나서야 그녀는 주문한 물건들을 받아보았다. 그런데 그것은 그녀가 주문한 것들이 아니었다. 그녀는 화가 나서 매니저에게 항의해야겠다고 생각했다. 이 런 상황에서 Kelly는 매니저에게 무슨 말을 할까?

* _Kelly: 저는 제가 주문한 게 아닌 물건을 받았어요._

해설: 주문한 물건과 다른 것들이 배달되었음을 매니저에게 알려야 한다.

Listening Web

Intro: throwing   Web 1: ordered, delivered
Web 2: online   Web 3: ordered
Ending: complain

True / False

1. F   2. T   3. F   4. T

문항 10 ②

Script & Dictation

M: Amy went on a picnic to an amusement park with her family. It was Sunday and the weather was fine, so it was **crowded with people**. As soon as she arrived at the amusement park, she **rushed to** "Jungle Adventure." She had seen it on a TV commercial. It was a brand new ride, and she had been **looking forward to** it. She was **standing in line** with her family. At that time, several boys were going to go through in front of Amy. She **stepped aside** for them to pass by, but she was embarrassed because they stopped in front of her. In this situation, what would Amy most likely say to the boys?

* _Amy: Excuse me, I'm in line._

남: Amy는 가족과 함께 놀이공원으로 놀러 갔다. 일요일이었고, 날씨도 좋아서 사람들로 붐볐다. 놀이공원에 도착하자마자, 그녀는 'Jungle Adventure'로 달려갔다. 그녀는 그것을 TV 광 고에서 봤다. 최신형 놀이기구였고, 이것을 타기를 학수고 대하고 있었다. 그녀는 가족과 함께 줄을 섰다. 그때 몇 명의

소년들이 Amy 앞으로 지나가려고 했다. 그녀는 아이들이 지나갈 수 있도록 옆으로 비켜섰다. 그런데 그들이 그녀 앞에 멈춰서 버려서 당황스러웠다. 이런 상황에서 Amy는 소년들에게 무슨 말을 할까?

* *Amy: 실례합니다만, 제가 줄을 서고 있어요.*

해설: 새치기당한 상황이므로 Amy는 자신이 줄을 서 있던 것임을 소년들에게 알려야 한다.

Listening Web

Web 1: rushed   Web 2: in
Web 3: through   Ending: aside

True / False

1. T   2. F   3. F   4. T

Unit 15 유형 15 - 세트형 문제

문항 1-1 ⑤
문항 1-2 ⑤

Script & Dictation

M: Wolves are mammals. A mammal is an animal that has hair, gives birth to live young, and **feeds them milk**. You are a mammal, too. So are mice, cats, and dogs. In fact, dogs and wolves are **closely related**. Thousands of years ago, humans came Intro **contact with** wolves and tamed some of them, just like what we do with dogs these days. They may also have taken in lost wolf pups. If it happened, wolves became **domesticated**. Humans were able to use them to help with work. Over time, dog species were developed from the wolves. Siberian huskies and German shepherds are dog species that look and act a lot like wolves. Wolves and dogs are both carnivores. Carnivores are animals that eat meat. That's why they have sharp teeth. The biggest difference between dogs and wolves, though, is that wolves are wild. They don't depend on humans for **any of their needs**. Wolves will become unhappy if they cannot roam free. They live in their own group and hunt together. When they chase a large animal, they cooperate with each other. One wolf starts the chase first. Then as it gets tired, another wolf **takes its place**.

남: 늘대는 포유류입니다. 포유류는 털이 있고 새끼를 출산하며 새끼에게 젖을 먹이는 동물입니다. 여러분도 역시 포유류입니다. 쥐도 그렇고, 고양이도, 개도 그렇습니다. 사실, 개와 늑대는 밀접하게 관련이 있습니다. 수천 년 전, 인간은 늑대와 가깝게 지냈고, 일부는 길들이기도 했습니다. 마치 우리가 오늘날 개를 대하듯 말입니다. 또한 길 잃은 새끼 늑대를 데려다 키우기도 했을지 모릅니다. 만약 그런 일이 있었다면, 늑대는 사람과 함께 가정에서 사는 동물이 되었을 것입니다. 사람은 일손을 돕기 위해 늑대를 이용할 수 있었습니다. 시간이 흐르면서, 늑대로부터 개의 종이 진화하였습니다. 시베리안 허스키와 독일 셰퍼드는 늑대와 같은 외모에 늑대처럼 행동하는 개의 종입니다. 늑대와 개는 모두 육식동물입니다. 육식동물이란 육류를 먹는 동물입니다. 그래서 둘 다 날카로운 이빨을 갖고 있습니다. 그러나 개와 늑대의 가장 큰 차이점은 늑대는 야생동물이라는 점입니다. 이들은 자신들의 그 어떤 욕구도 인간에게 의존하지 않습니다. 만약 늑대가 자유롭게 돌아다니지 못한다면 행복을 잃어갈 것입니다. 이들은 자신들의 무리 안에서 함께 사냥하며 살아갑니다. 큰 동물을 쫓을 때는 서로 협력합니다. 늑대 한 마리가 먼저 쫓기 시작합니다. 그러다 지치면, 다른 늑대가 대신 나섭니다.

해설: 1-1. 늑대와 개의 공통점과 차이점에 대해 이야기 하고 있다.
1-2. 늑대는 독립적으로 생활하지 않고 무리지어 생활한다.

Listening Web

Intro: live   Web 1: related
Web 2: Thousands   Web 3: carnivores
Web 4: biggest   Ending: own

True / False

1. T   2. F   3. F   4. F

문항 2-1 ③
문항 2-2 ⑤

Script & Dictation

W: Good evening, I'm Irene Taylor from Gloria University. I'm so pleased to have a chance to introduce you to Gloria. I understand it's not easy for you to choose a university. There are hundreds of universities, and every university insists that they have a special program and **promises a bright future**. But Gloria is different. We provide the unique Personal Guide program. Every individual student has his or her own personal advisor who will take care of you from entrance to graduation. When you choose your major, you can **consult** with your advisor, and when you're a senior, you can **conduct a mock interview** to get a job. Gloria University has had the largest number of applicants for the last six years, and last year it was listed at the top of **the most satisfying**

universities by the national survey. Now all you have to do is to choose Gloria. If you have any questions about Gloria, you can email us at the address below the bulletin, or call the admission department. It's open for 24 hours this month to help you **as much as possible**. Thank you very much.

여: 안녕하세요, 저는 Gloria 대학교에서 나온 Irene Taylor입니다. 여러분에게 Gloria 대학교를 소개할 기회를 갖게 되어 매우 기쁘게 생각합니다. 저도 대학을 선택하는 것이 쉽지 않다는 것을 잘 알고 있습니다. 수백 개의 대학교가 있는 데다가, 제각각 특별한 프로그램을 제공하고 있다고 주장하며 밝은 미래를 약속하죠. 하지만 Gloria는 다릅니다. 저희는 독특한 Personal Guide 프로그램을 제공하고 있습니다. 학생 개개인에게 입학부터 졸업까지 신경 써주는 개인 지도 교수를 배정합니다. 전공을 선택할 때, 지도 교수와 상의할 수 있고, 4학년 때는 취업을 위해 모의 면접을 할 수도 있습니다. Gloria 대학교는 지난 6년간 가장 많은 학생들이 지원했고, 작년 국가 설문에 의하면 가장 만족스러운 대학 1위에 뽑혔습니다. 이제 여러분이 할 일은 Gloria를 선택하는 것입니다. Gloria에 대하여 질문이 있으시면, 게시물 하단에 있는 주소로 이메일을 보내거나 입학처로 전화해 주시기 바랍니다. 여러분에게 가능한 많은 노력을 드리고자 이번 달에는 24시간 열려 있습니다. 감사합니다.

해설: 2-1. 여자는 지원자를 받기 위해 학교를 소개하고 있다.
2-2. 이번 한 달 동안 지원자의 편의를 위해 전화 문의를 24시간 개방한다고 말하고 있다. 언제까지 지원해야 한다는 언급은 없다.

Listening Web

Intro: pleased   Web 2: choose
Web 3: largest   Web 4: admission
Ending: open

True / False

1. T   2. T   3. T   4. F

문항 3-1 ③
문항 3-2 ②

Script & Dictation

M: English proficiency is a **critical quality** these days. In order to get a job, or enter a university or a graduate school, you need not only an excellent grade on an English proficiency test, but also ability in speaking and listening **at a significant level**. A lot of college students tend to think that it is **mandatory** to take an English language training course in the U.S. or England. But you don't need to go to English speaking countries. You have

many chances to study English in Korea. There are some TV cable channels with which you can practice listening to English. **Chatting online with** foreign friends helps you to improve colloquial English. It is a good idea to **participate in** a language exchange program if your school provides one. You can teach Korean to somebody who wants to learn Korean, and you can be taught English by them. The last tip to improve your English is to memorize a large amount of vocabulary. Vocabulary is not everything in studying English, but if you have a wide range of vocabulary, **you'll be confident** when you encounter English at an unexpected moment.

남: 영어 능력은 오늘날 매우 중요한 자질입니다. 직장을 구하고, 대학이나 대학원에 들어가기 위해서는 영어 능력 시험에서 우수한 점수를 받아야 할 뿐만 아니라, 말하기와 듣기 능력이 상당한 수준에 이르러야 합니다. 많은 대학생들은 미국이나 영국으로 어학연수 가는 것을 필수라고 여기는 경향이 있습니다. 하지만 꼭 영어권 국가에 가야만 하는 것은 아닙니다. 한국에서도 영어를 공부할 기회가 많이 있습니다. 영어 듣기를 연습할 수 있는 TV 케이블 채널들이 있습니다. 외국인 친구들과 채팅을 함으로써 구어체 영어 능력을 향상시킬 수 있습니다. 여러분의 학교에서 언어 교환 프로그램을 제공한다면 여기에 참여하는 것도 좋은 생각입니다. 한국어를 배우고 싶어하는 사람에게 한국어를 가르쳐주고, 그 사람으로부터 영어를 배울 수 있습니다. 영어 실력 향상을 위한 마지막 조언은 많은 양의 어휘를 암기하라는 것입니다. 어휘가 영어 공부의 모든 것은 아닙니다. 하지만 다양한 어휘를 알고 있다면, 예기치 못한 순간 영어와 마주쳤을 때 자신감을 가질 수 있습니다.

해설: 3-1. 한국에서 영어 공부를 효과적으로 할 수 있는 다양한 방법을 소개하고 있다.
3-2. 많은 대학생들이 영어권 국가에 가서 어학연수를 받는 것을 필수로 여기는 경향이 있으나, 꼭 영어권 국가에 가야만 하는 것은 아니라고 주장하고 있다.

Listening Web

Intro: critical   Web 1: mandatory
Web 3: exchange   Ending: amount

True / False

1. T   2. F   3. F   4. T

문항 4-1 ④
문항 4-2 ①

Script & Dictation

W: These days you can see many people in the park. Some of them are **walking a pet**; some jogging or exercising; some others sitting and chatting with friends. Everybody looks happy and peaceful. However, very often **our attitude towards** public toilets goes against proper etiquette. **Needless to say**, that the smell is often too bad to even enter the toilet. The walls are covered with a mass of scribbles, the light bulbs and sink are broken. So the lights flicker or have gone out. There's no water in the sink, and sometimes cigarettes have been thrown away in the sink. A lot of people want to **avoid using public toilets** when they are out of their house. This is not a situation of a particular area. It reflects our attitude toward public facilities that we don't think of them **as valuable as** our own stuff. If we keep using the public toilet the way that we used to do, we'll be the victims of a dirty atmosphere in the end. You may use a toilet in a clean and pleasant atmosphere, or in a dirty and smelly atmosphere. It depends on you.

여: 요즘에는 공원에서 많은 사람들을 볼 수 있습니다. 어떤 사람들은 애완동물을 산책시키고, 어떤 사람들은 조깅을 하거나 운동을 합니다. 또 어떤 사람들은 앉아서 친구들과 이야기를 나눕니다. 사람들이 행복하고 평화로워 보입니다. 그러나 공중화장실에 대한 우리의 태도는 예절에서 심심치 않게 벗어납니다. 악취가 너무 심해서 들어갈 수 없는 것은 말할 것도 없습니다. 낙서들이 벽을 가득 메우고 있고, 전구와 세면대가 부서져있습니다. 그래서 전등은 깜빡거리거나 아예 나가버리기도 했습니다. 세면대에는 물이 나오지 않고 때때로 담배꽁초가 버려져 있기도 합니다. 많은 사람들이 집 밖에 나오면 공중화장실을 이용하기를 꺼립니다. 이것은 특정 지역만의 문제는 아닙니다. 이는 공공시설을 내 것처럼 소중히 여기지 않는 공공시설에 대한 우리의 자세를 반영하는 것입니다. 만약 지금처럼 계속해서 공중화장실을 이용한다면, 결국 그 지저분한 환경의 희생자는 우리 자신이 될 것입니다. 당신은 화장실을 깨끗하고 쾌적한 환경에서 이용할 수도 있고, 더럽고 냄새나는 환경에서 이용하게 될 수도 있습니다. 그것은 여러분에게 달려있습니다.

해설: 4-1. 공중화장실을 지저분하게 사용하는 것에 대해 경고하고, 깨끗한 공중화장실을 사용하는 것과 더러운 공중화장실을 사용하는 것은 바로 우리의 자세에 달려있다고 말하고 있다.

4-2. 요즘 사람들이 공원에서 애완동물을 산책시킨다고 언급했을 뿐, 그들이 애완동물의 배설물을 제대로 처리하지 않는다는 언급은 없다.

Listening Web

Web 1: towards　　　　　　Web 2: using

Web 3: facilities, stuff　　　Ending: atmosphere

True / False

1. T　　　　2. F　　　　3. T　　　　4. F

문항 5-1 ③
문항 5-2 ①

Script & Dictation

M: Last class, we talked about the roles of producers and consumers. Today we're going to talk about this issue **in another aspect**. I told you to read Alvin Toffler's "The Third Wave." You might have found a very interesting word, "prosumer." It is a **combination of producer and** consumer. It means consumers who take part in producing goods or services. It means consumers no longer just consume what the producers **have already produced**. After you purchase a shirt or a printer at an online shopping mall, some of you may write what you think of it on the Internet. What do you think will happen next? The producers will accept your idea, and it'll **be reflected** in the next items. You are indirectly taking part in producing the items. Several years ago, businesses started to give **potential consumers** chances to use their brand new items, and get very practical feedback. In addition, in the field of education, students and parents are not passive any more. They often ask for the educational services they want. The writers of Wikipedia are also prosumers because they directly take part in producing and sharing information.

남: 지난 시간에는 생산자와 소비자의 역할에 대해 알아보았습니다. 오늘은 다른 시각에서 이 문제를 논의해 보도록 하겠습니다. 여러분에게 앨빈 토플러의 '제3의 물결'을 읽어보라고 이야기했었습니다. 아마 '프로슈머'라는 재미있는 용어를 발견했을 겁니다. 그것은 생산자(producer)와 소비자(consumer)의 합성어입니다. 이는 재화나 서비스 생산에 참여하는 소비자를 의미합니다. 이는 소비자가 이제는 생산자가 이미 만들어 놓은 것을 소비만 하는 것이 아니라는 뜻입니다. 온라인 쇼핑몰에서 티셔츠나 프린터나 혹은 다른 물건을 구매하고 나서 여러분 중 몇몇은 제품에 대한 여러분의 생각을 인터넷에 남길 겁니다. 그다음에는 무슨 일이 일어날까요? 생산자들은 여러분의 생각을 받아들여, 다음 제품에 여러분의 의견을 반영할 것입니다. 여러분은 제품 생산에 간접적으로 참여하고 있는 것입니다. 몇 해 전 기업들은 구매력 있는 소비자들에게 신제품을 사용해 볼 기회를 주고 실질적인 피드백을 받기 시작했습니다. 더욱이 교육 분야에서도 학생과 학부모는 이제는 수동적이지 않습니다. 자신들이 원하는 교육 서비스를 종종 요구합니다. 위키피디아를 집필하는 사람들 또한 직접 정보를 생산하고 공유하고 있으므로 프로슈머인 것입니다.

해설: 5-1. 소비자가 소비하는 역할에만 머무르지 않고 생산에도 참여한다는 이야기를 하고 있다.

5-2. DIY는 프로슈머의 대표적인 예시이나, 이 담화에는 언급되어 있지 않다.

Listening Web

Intro: another
Web 2: part, goods
Ending: indirectly, part

Web 1: combination
Web 3: purchase

True / False

1. T 2. T 3. T 4. F

문항 6-1 ①
문항 6-2 ②

Script & Dictation

W: This is a game that was **originally invented** by Native Americans. But its name, lacrosse was given by a French missionary. When the French arrived in North America, they saw the Native Americans playing this game. They **put together** their own team, and wanted to play each other. Later in the late 1800s, lacrosse had become the national sport of Canada, and now a lot of people throughout the world play lacrosse. Lacrosse looks **similar to** ice hockey in many ways. It's a very speedy game like ice hockey. You need to **hit the ball** Intro the goal as many times as possible. And **the number of goal-ins** will be your score. It's quite simple, isn't it? But it is different, too. It is played on grass, not ice, as you see. And the players use a ball instead of a puck. These are lacrosse sticks. They are shaped differently. This shape allows the player to **scoop up the ball** and throw it, like this. See it? That's all I can tell you about lacrosse. Now, it's your turn to enjoy lacrosse yourself. Have fun!

여: 이것은 원래 미대륙 원주민들에 의해 만들어진 게임입니다. 하지만 lacrosse 라는 이름은 프랑스 선교사에 의해 붙여졌습니다. 프랑스인들이 북미에 도착했을 때, 원주민들이 이 게임을 하고 있는 것을 보았습니다. 그들은 자신들의 팀을 조직하여 함께 경기하기를 원했습니다. 나중에 1800년대 후반에는 lacrosse가 캐나다의 국민 스포츠가 되었고, 현재에는 전 세계적으로 많은 사람들이 lacrosse를 즐기고 있습니다. lacrosse는 많은 면에서 아이스하키와 비슷하게 보입니다. 아이스하키처럼 매우 빠르게 진행되는 게임입니다. 여러분은 공을 쳐서 골대 안으로 최대한 많이 넣어야 합니다. 그리고 골인의 개수가 여러분의 점수가 되는 것입니다. 정말 간단하죠? 하지만 다른 점도 있습니다. 보시다시피 얼음이 아니라 풀밭에서 경기가 진행됩니다. 그리고 선수들은 퍽 대신 공을 사용합니다. 이것은 lacrosse의 스틱입니다. 모양이 다르게 생겼죠. 이런 모양이 선수들이 공을 떠서 이렇게 던질 수 있게 합니다. 보셨죠? lacrosse에 대해서 제가 말씀드릴 수 있는 것은 이것이 전부입니다. 이제 여러분이 직접 해 보실 차례예요. 즐거운 경기가 되시길 바랍니다!

해설: 6-1. Lacrosse의 역사와 특징, 경기 방법을 소개하고 있다.
6-2. Lacrosse는 아이스하키와 매우 비슷하지만, 얼음이 아니라 풀밭에서 진행된다고 설명하고 있다.

Listening Web

Intro: originally
Web 2: to

Web 1: become
Ending: turn

True / False

1. F 2. F 3. T 4. F

문항 7-1 ⑤
문항 7-2 ②

Script & Dictation

M: Have you ever heard about Machu Picchu? It is believed that people lived in Machu Picchu until the early 1500s. The Spanish **invaded and conquered** the Incas in the middle of the 1500s. But Machu Picchu was already **deserted** at that time. Nobody knows why this city was built or why it was deserted. Some people say the reason is that its **geographical conditions** were not very good. It was located too high between two mountain peaks. It may have been too hard for it to thrive. Some scientists think **the water ran out**. The springs from underground were the main source of water, but they dried up. Whatever the reason, the most interesting thing is that this desertion saved the city in the long run. The Spanish army destroyed everything in the Inca Empire. They killed many people and took away many valuable things. However, they never found this **lost but wonderful city**, Machu Picchu, because it was **hidden** high in the Andes Mountains. That's why now we can enjoy the beautiful buildings and culture of Machu Picchu.

남: Machu Picchu에 대해서 들어본 적이 있습니까? 1500년대 초반까지 Machu Picchu에 사람이 살았던 것으로 여겨집니다. 스페인 사람들이 1500년대 중반에 잉카를 침략하여 정복하였습니다. 하지만 그 당시 Machu Picchu는 이미 폐허 상태였습니다. 이 도시가 왜 만들어졌는지, 왜 멸망했는지 아무도 알지 못합니다. 몇몇 사람들은 지리적 조건이 좋지 않았기 때문이라고 합니다. 그것은 두 산맥 정상 사이 높은 곳에 있었습니다. 번성하기에는 너무 어려웠을지도 모릅니다. 어떤 과학자들은 물이 없었기 때문이라고 생각합니다. 지하에서 나오는 샘물이 주요 수원이었는데, 이것이 말라버렸다는 것입니다. 이유가 무엇이었든, 가장 흥미로운 사실은 이 도시의 멸망이 결국 이 도시를 지켜냈다는 것입니다. 스페인 군대는 잉카제국을 완전히 파괴했습니다. 많은 사람들을 죽였고, 값진 것들을 앗아갔습니다. 하지만 그들은 버려졌지만 아름다운 도시 Machu Picchu를 결코 발견하지 못했습니다.

왜냐하면 안데스 산맥 높은 곳에 숨어 있었기 때문입니다. 덕분에 지금 우리는 Machu Picchu의 아름다운 건물과 문화를 감상할 수 있습니다.

> **해설:** 7-1. Machu Picchu의 멸망이 역설적으로 이 도시를 영원히 보존되도록 했다는 이야기를 하고 있다.
> 7-2. 주요 수원이었던 지하 샘물이 말라서 Machu Picchu가 멸망했다는 설에 대한 언급이 있다.

Listening Web

Intro: Spanish   Web 1: geographical
Web 2: ran   Web 3: desertion

True / False

1. T   2. F   3. T   4. F

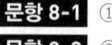 **문항 8-1** ①
문항 8-2 ③

Script & Dictation

W: Archaeologists don't just go around digging things up. Like other scientists, they have a lot of work to do. They start with a problem or idea, and **come up with** a hypothesis. Then they go about trying to prove their hypothesis. They do surveys and study old maps to find good places to dig. They look in riverbeds, in deserts, in the jungle. They also dig in mountains and under the ocean. They are in search of data to collect, **looking for artifacts**. Then they use a grid to **divide** the site **Intro** small areas. That way, they can record where they found a bit of pottery, an old tool, or a piece of bone. Archaeologists dig very carefully, using tiny shovels. Then they use toothbrushes to brush away dirt. They **figure out** how old the objects are and they date them. Archaeologists must complete one more step. They **draw conclusions**. They decided whether their findings prove that their **hypothesis is correct**. Many times, what they dig up makes them ask even more questions. And they get to have a lot to study and examine.

여: 고고학자들은 그냥 발굴하며 돌아다니는 것이 아닙니다. 다른 과학자들처럼 이들도 할 일이 많이 있습니다. 고고학자들의 일은 문제나 생각에서 출발하여 가설을 도출해냅니다. 그리고 나서 가설을 증명하기 위해 돌아다닙니다. 그들은 발굴하기 좋은 장소를 찾기 위해 옛 지도를 조사하고 연구합니다. 그들은 강바닥이나 사막, 정글을 들여다봅니다. 또한 산이나 바다 밑을 발굴하기도 합니다. 인공 유물을 찾아다니며 수집할 정보를 찾습니다. 그리고 나면 격자판을 이용하여 발굴 장소를 작은 영역들로 나눕니다. 그런 식으로 이들은 도자기 파편이나 오래된 도구, 뼛조각을 찾아낸 장소를 기록합니다. 고고학자들은 작은 삽을 이용하여 매우

조심스럽게 발굴합니다. 먼지를 털어내기 위해 칫솔을 사용합니다. 그들은 그 물건이 얼마나 오래된 것인지 계산하고 연대를 추정합니다. 고고학자들은 한 가지 과정을 더 완수해야 합니다. 결론을 내리는 것입니다. 그들은 자신들이 발견한 것이 그들의 가정을 옳게 증명해냈는지 그 여부를 결정합니다. 많은 경우 자신들이 발굴한 것이 더 많은 의문점을 만들어 내기도 합니다. 그리고 그들은 더 많은 연구와 조사를 하게 되는 것입니다.

> **해설:** 8-1. 고고학자들이 일하는 방법 알려주기 위한 담화이다.
> 8-2. 격자판을 이용하여 유물을 찾아낸 위치를 기록한다 (record)고 하였다. record라는 단어만 듣고 녹음기로 착각하지 않도록 한다.

Listening Web

Intro: around   Web 1: prove
Web 2: search   Web 3: correct

True / False

1. F   2. T   3. F   4. F

문항 9-1 ②
문항 9-2 ③

Script & Dictation

M: People have many theories about **what happened to** the dinosaurs. The most popular theory is that an asteroid struck the earth about 65 million years ago. When a **huge asteroid hit**, it threw up a huge cloud of dust. The dust was so thick that it blocked the sunlight. The cloud might have stayed in the sky for months or years. It caused the longest night ever. At that time, it **might have killed** a few dinosaurs, but not many. However, the plants on the earth could not survive without sunlight. In time, many or most of the plants died. By the way, how did the dinosaurs die? The dinosaurs that ate plants no longer had **anything to eat**. They starved. Then the dinosaurs that ate other dinosaurs starved and died at last. An asteroid hit is one theory that might explain why the dinosaurs died. How can anyone be sure the **reason of the death** of dinosaurs? Scientists will keep researching this question. Someday, we will know the answer for sure.

남: 공룡에게 무슨 일이 일어난 것인가에 관한 이론들이 많이 있습니다. 가장 널리 알려진 이론은 6천5백만 년 전 소행성이 충돌했다는 것입니다. 커다란 소행성이 충돌했을 때, 그것은 큰 먼지 구름을 일으켰습니다. 그 먼지가 너무나 자욱하게 깔려서 햇빛을 차단했습니다. 먼지 구름은 하늘에 수개월 혹은 수년간 머물렀을지도 모릅니다. 그것은 사상 최고로 긴 밤을 야기시킨 것입니다. 그 당시 몇몇 공룡이 죽었을지도

모르지만, 많은 수는 아니었습니다. 그러나 지구 상에서 햇빛 없이 식물들을 살 수 없었습니다. 이윽고 많은 식물들이 거의 다 죽어버렸습니다. 그런데 어떻게 공룡이 사라졌을까요? 초식 공룡은 더는 먹을 것이 없었습니다. 초식동물들이 굶어 죽은 것입니다. 그리고 나서 다른 공룡들을 잡아먹던 공룡들이 결국 굶어 죽은 것입니다. 소행성 충돌은 공룡의 죽음을 설명하는 하나의 이론일 뿐입니다. 누가 공룡 멸망의 원인을 확신할 수 있겠습니까? 과학자들은 계속해서 이 질문에 대한 해답을 찾아갈 것입니다. 언젠가 우리는 그 답을 확실하게 알게 될 것입니다.

해설: 9-1. 공룡이 멸종한 이유에 관한 이론들을 언급하면서 공룡 멸종의 원인에 대해 이야기 하고 있다.

9-2. 새로운 별의 생성에 관한 이야기는 언급된 바 없다.

Listening Web

Web 1: threw, thick   Web 2: survive

Web 3: starved   Web 4: ate

Ending: one

True / False

1. F   2. T   3. F   4. T

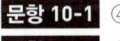 **문항 10-1** ④

문항 10-2 ②

Script & Dictation

W: In the 1800s, most people living on the west coast went there hoping to find gold. But they still wanted to **stay in touch with** their families back east. The only way to send messages long distances was in Morse code. If they sent letters by ship, it took six months. Sending mail overland seemed like a better idea. So, in 1860, William Russell started a new company, "Pony Express," whose riders on speedy horses would **carry mail** and **news overland**. Russell promised that the riders could deliver mail in ten days even though the route would be tough especially in winter. The "Pony Express Company" had 500 horses and 120 stations **along the route**. When it was time for a rider to come by, the station man got a **fresh horse ready**. Often they were attacked or chased by robbers. They knew the mail might contain gold or money. On October 24, 1861, the first telegram was sent from San Francisco to Washington D.C. And two days later, "Pony Express" closed. There was **no longer a need** for it.

여: 1800년대, 서부 해변에 살던 사람들 대부분은 금을 찾기 바라는 마음으로 그곳으로 간 것이었습니다. 하지만 그들은 여전히 동부에 남아 있는 가족들과 연락하고 싶어했습니다. 먼 곳으로 메시지를 보낼 수 있는 유일한 방법은 모스 부호뿐이었습니다. 만약 배로 편지를 보낸다면, 6개월이 걸렸습니다.

육로로 편지를 보내는 것은 매우 좋은 생각인 것 같았습니다. 그래서 1860년, William Russell은 'Pony Express'라고 하는 새로운 회사를 창립했는데, 그곳의 빠른 말을 탄 기수들이 육로로 편지나 소식을 전달하였습니다. Russell은 겨울에 특히 길이 좋지 않음에도 불구하고 기수들이 10일 안에 편지를 배달할 것을 약속했습니다. 'Pony Company'에는 500마리의 말이 있었고, 120개의 정거장이 길을 따라 있었습니다. 한 기수가 (정거장에) 들를 때가 되면 정거장 직원이 새 말을 대기시켜 놓았습니다. 이들은 자주 강도들에게 공격당하거나 추격을 당했습니다. 그들은 편지 안에 금이나 돈이 있을지도 모른다는 사실을 알았던 것입니다. 1861년 10월 24일 최초의 전보가 샌프란시스코에서 워싱턴 D.C.로 보내졌습니다. 그리고 이틀 뒤 'Pony Express'는 문을 닫았습니다. 더는 이 회사의 수요가 없었기 때문입니다.

해설: 10-1. 우편배달 회사인 Pony Express의 역사에 대해 설명하고 있다.

10-2. 금을 찾아 서부로 떠난 사람들이 동부에 남아있는 가족들과 연락하고 싶어 했던 것이 이 회사의 창립 계기가 되었지만, 회사의 위치에 대한 언급은 없다.

Listening Web

Intro. living, coast   Web 1: with

Web 2: speedy   Web 3: fresh

Ending: closed

True / False

1. T   2. T   3. F   4. F

Unit 16 유형 16 - 장문을 듣고 요약하기

문항 1 ⑤

Script & Dictation

W: Learning history is very important because it teaches us the **wisdom of life**. Literally, history is **a record of** all the facts from the past to the present. Carr, a historian, has said that history is an endless conversation between the past and the present. In order to study history, you should **make sure about** the chronology. For example, when you study European history, you need to set the timeline, such as the birth of ancient civilization, the Middle Ages, the fall of the Western Roman Empire, the Early Modern Period, the civil revolution, the Modern Era, and then the era after World War I and so on. In addition, you have to check what happened **in other places** in the world over the same period. For example, the ancient Chosun Dynasty was **in the same era** as the ancient Egyptian Empire.

여: 역사를 배우는 것은 우리에게 삶의 지혜를 가르쳐주기 때문에 매우 중요하다. 문자 그대로 역사란 과거부터 현재까지의 사실들을 기록한 것이다. 역사학자인 Carr는 역사란 과거와 현재의 끊임없는 대화라고 말한 바 있다. 역사를 공부하기 위해서는 연대기를 확실히 해야 한다. 예를 들어, 유럽의 역사를 공부한다면, 고대 문명의 출현, 중세, 서로마제국의 함락, 근세, 시민 혁명, 현대 사회, 그리고 제1차 세계대전 이후 시대 등과 같은 연대기를 정리해야 한다. 아울러, 같은 시대에 세상의 다른 곳에서는 무슨 일이 일어났는지를 정리해야 한다. 가령 고조선은 고대 이집트 왕국과 같은 시대에 있었다.

해설: 역사 공부를 할 때에는 연대기별로 일어난 일들을 정리하는 것과, 동시대 다른 지역에서 일어난 일들을 함께 정리해 두는 것이 필요하다. 즉 시간적, 공간적 정보를 모두 공부해야 한다는 것이다.

Listening Web

Intro: life   Web 1: chronology

Web 2: European   Web 3: happened

Ending: Egyptian

True / False

1. T   2. T   3. F   4. T

문항 2 ②

Script & Dictation

M: What makes an effective leader? To be sure, only one characteristic does not **define** an effective leader. However, it is true that the most effective leader holds the group members to very **high standards of performance**. Setting such standards increases productivity because they try to live up to the expectation which has already been set for them by the leader. In other words, the leader's expectation of success or failure becomes a self-fulfilling prophecy. We call this phenomenon Pygmalion effect, and it works in a subtle and almost **unconscious way**. For example, when the leader believes that the group members will succeed, the leader communicates with them positively with that **firm belief**. Conversely, if the leader thinks the group members will fail, the leader expresses disappointment without realizing he or she is doing so. And the leader's attitude **contributes to** the failure in reality in the end.

남: 무엇이 효과적인 지도자를 만드는가? 분명한 사실은 단 한 가지 특징이나 자질이 효과적인 지도자를 결정짓지는 않는다는 것이다. 그러나 효과적인 지도자는 구성원들의 활동을 최고 기준치로 끌어 올린다. 그렇게 (높은) 기준을 설정하면, 사람들이 지도자에 의해 설정된 기대에 부응하기 위해 노력하기 때문에 생산성이 높아진다. 다시 말해서, 성공이나 실

패에 대한 지도자의 기대가 자기충족적 예언이 되는 것이다. 우리는 이것을 피그말리온 효과라고 부른다. 그리고 이것은 감지하기 어렵게 거의 무의식적으로 작용한다. 예를 들어, 지도자가 구성원들이 성공할 것이라고 믿는다면, 지도자는 굳은 신념을 갖고 구성원들과 긍정적으로 의사소통할 것이다. 그러나 구성원들이 실패할 것으로 생각한다면, 지도자는 자신이 그렇게 하고 있다는 것을 깨닫지 못한 채 실망을 드러낼 것이다. 그리고 지도자의 이러한 태도는 결국 진짜 실패를 낳는다.

해설: 효과적인 지도자는 성공에 대한 기대를 구성원들에게 심어주어, 구성원들로 하여금 스스로 그 기대에 부응하도록 한다. [*피그말리온: 자기가 만든 상아상을 연모한 조각가, 선입관에 의한 기대가 학습자에게 주는 효과를 '피그말리온 효과'라고 함]

Listening Web

Intro: an effective, leader   Web 1: holds

Web 2: prophecy   Web 3: disappointment

Ending: contributes

True / False

1. F   2. T   3. T   4. T

문항 3 ④

Script & Dictation

W: Shakespeare has strongly influenced the English language. He has no rivals **in regard to** the extent and the depth of his influence on the English language. He created a lot of new English words, so he **extended the volume** of English vocabulary. In addition, he put a large number of sophisticated expressions in his writings. Some of them have become **literary terms**, and some others have entered Intro our daily conversation nowadays. For example, 'lonely,' 'gloomy' or 'eyeball' are words Shakespeare created. Interestingly, a woman's name, Jessica, **first appeared** in "The Merchant of Venice." There had been no Jessica before "The Merchant of Venice" was published. All of you may have heard or read the famous phrase 'to be, or not to be, that is the question,' which comes from Hamlet. It poetically represents that Hamlet was **burning with revenge** and full of doubts about life.

여: 셰익스피어는 영어에 큰 영향을 끼쳤다. 그가 영어에 끼친 영향의 범위와 깊이에 대해서 그와 필적할만한 사람이 없다. 그는 많은 영어 단어를 만들어내서 영어 어휘를 확장시켰다. 또한 그의 작품 속에서 많은 세련된 표현들을 써넣었다. 그 중 몇몇은 문학 용어가 되었고, 또 어떤 것들은 오늘날 우리가 일상 대화 속에서 사용하고 있다. 예를 들어 '외로운', '우울한', '눈알'과 같은 단어들은 셰익스피어가 만들어낸 단어

들이다. 흥미롭게도, 여자 이름 제시카는 '베니스의 상인'에 처음으로 등장한다. '베니스의 상인'이 출판되기 전에 제시카라는 이름은 없었다. 여러분은 아마 '죽느냐 사느냐, 그것이 문제로다'라는 유명한 구절을 들어봤거나 읽어 보았을 것이다. 이것은 햄릿에 나오는 것이다. 이 구절은 복수심에 불타오르고 인생에 대한 회의로 가득 차있는 햄릿의 모습을 시적으로 표현하고 있다.

해설: 셰익스피어는 영어 어휘를 수적으로 확장시켰을 뿐만 아니라, 세련된 표현들도 만들어 냈다.

Listening Web

Intro: influenced   Web 1: extent

Web 2: extended   Ending: number

True / False

1. T   2. T   3. F   4. F

문항 4 ③

Script & Dictation

M: Sometimes the Internet takes a **crucial role in** finding people. Very often, we find childhood friends on the Internet. By the way, some victims use the Internet to find the suspect. The Internet has the advantage of making it possible to **capture the suspect** in a short time. If you had an accident and the police said it would be difficult to catch the suspect, how would you feel? Maybe you'd want to find the suspect **with the help of** the Internet. But the problem is that the identity of the suspect can be released on the Internet, so everybody can see it. It could be a violation of **human personal rights**. The suspect is not the criminal yet. At worst, **a hasty judgment** can hurt an innocent person irrevocably. And it really happens. When the police openly search on the Internet for the wanted person, there should be **strict regulations**.

남: 때때로 인터넷은 사람을 찾는 데 중요한 역할을 한다. 우리는 매우 자주 인터넷을 통해 어릴 적 친구를 찾아낸다. 그런데 어떤 사람들은 인터넷을 용의자를 찾는 데 사용하기도 한다. 인터넷은 용의자를 짧은 시간 내에 찾아낼 수 있다는 장점을 갖고 있다. 만약 당신이 사고를 당했는데, 경찰에서는 범인을 잡기 어렵다고 한다면 기분이 어떻겠는가? 아마 인터넷의 도움을 빌어서라도 범인을 잡고 싶을 것이다. 하지만 문제는 용의자의 신상이 인터넷에 공개되어 모두가 볼 수 있게 된다는 것이다. 이것은 개인 인권 침해가 될 수도 있다. 용의자는 아직 범죄자가 아니다. 최악에는 성급한 판단이 무고한 사람에게 돌이킬 수 없는 상처를 줄 수도 있다. 그리고 그런 일은 실제로 일어난다. 경찰도 인터넷으로 공개수배를 할 때에는 엄격한 규칙을 적용한다.

해설: 인터넷은 사람을 빨리 찾을 수 있다는 장점을 갖고 있지만, 아울러 개인의 인권이 침해될 우려도 있다.

Listening Web

Intro: crucial   Web 1: capture

Web 2: identity   Web 3: violation

Ending: wanted

True / False

1. T   2. T   3. F   4. T

문항 5 ④

Script & Dictation

W: A survey shows that even more Australians feel happy than Koreans. But it's strange. Korea is a powerful country in the IT industry, and Korean people have a **strong desire** for education. But they feel they are not as happy as they are expected to be. The reason is simple. There's no **absolute standard** of happiness. The people who are rich or in a high social position are expected to be happy. However, they **suffer from** stress because they cannot avoid competition. Moreover, to **win the competition**, they should invest more time and effort Intro work, and they cannot spend a lot of time with their loving family or friends. That's why they feel lonely and unhappy. Children may not feel happy if their parents don't have time enough to play with them. Parents' love **cannot be replaced** by expensive toys. Nobody thinks children will be happy as long as they are put Intro a toy factory.

여: 설문조사에 따르면 더 많은 호주 사람들이 한국인들보다 자신이 스스로 행복하다고 여기는 것으로 나타났다. 하지만 이것은 이상한 일이다. 한국은 IT 강국인데다 한국인들은 교육에 대한 열망이 매우 높다. 하지만 그들은 자신들이 그만큼 행복하지 못하다고 느끼는 것이다. 이유는 간단하다. 행복에 대한 절대적인 기준이 없기 때문이다. 돈이 많거나 사회적 지위가 높은 사람들은 행복할 것이라고 생각된다. 하지만 그들은 경쟁을 피할 수 없기 때문에 스트레스에 시달린다. 게다가 경쟁에서 살아남기 위해 그들은 일에 더 많은 시간과 노력을 투자해야 하고, 사랑하는 가족이나 친구들과 많은 시간을 보내지 못하는 것이다. 그래서 그들은 자신들이 외롭고 불행하다고 느낀다. 만약 부모가 함께 놀아줄 시간이 없다면 아이는 행복하지 못할 것이다. 부모의 사랑을 비싼 장난감으로 대신할 수는 없다. 아이들을 장난감 공장에 데려다 놓기만 하면 행복해 할 것이라고 생각하는 사람은 아무도 없다.

해설: 돈이 많거나 사회적 지위가 높은 사람들이 행복하지 않다고 느끼는 것은 행복에 절대적인 기준이 없기 때문 (there's no absolute standard of happiness)이라고 말하고 있다.

Listening Web

Intro: survey	Web 1: expected
Web 2: competition	Web 3: invest
Ending: replaced	

True / False

1. T	2. F	3. T	4. F

문항 6 ②

Script & Dictation

M: We've suffered from **a lack of** drinking water for decades. Research has shown that the amount of drinking water has decreased since the 1970s, and that slightly less than 3 billion people on earth suffer from a lack of drinking water for more than a month a year. What is the reason for it? First, it's because of population growth. As the population grows, a large amount of water is in demand, and the supply cannot **meet the demand**. Another reason is a lack of infrastructure. For example, some developing countries have no facilities **to purify polluted water**. Or some underdeveloped countries have water, but do not have facilities to carry water. That is, they don't have **access to** a water supply. Water is essential to every living thing and there's no substitute. So we need to **take swift action** to stabilize the water supply.

남: 우리는 수십 년 동안 식수의 부족에 시달리고 있다. 한 연구에 따르면 1970년대 이래로 식수의 양이 줄어들어 3억 명이 약간 안 되는 사람들이 일 년에 한 달 이상 식수 부족으로 고통받는다고 한다. 그 이유가 뭘까? 우선 인구 증가에 원인이 있다. 인구가 증가함에 따라 많은 양의 물이 필요하게 된다. 그리고 공급이 수요를 따라가지 못하는 것이다. 또 다른 이유는 사회 기반 시설의 부족이다. 예를 들어 어떤 개발도상국에는 오염된 물을 정화시키는 시설이 없다. 또 어떤 저개발 국가에는 물을 운반하는 시설이 없다. 즉, 물 공급이 원활하지 않은 것이다. 물은 모든 생명체에게 필수적이며, 대체물이 없다. 따라서 우리는 안정적인 물 공급을 위해 즉각적인 조치를 취해야 한다.

해설: 식수 부족의 원인은 인구 증가에 따른 수요 증가와 사회 기반 시설 부족으로 말미암은 정화 시설 미비 및 식수 운반 시설 부족이다.

Listening Web

Intro: decades	Web 1: growth
Web 2: Another	Web 3: essential
Ending: stabilize	

True / False

1. F	2. T	3. T	4. T

문항 7 ③

Script & Dictation

W: Mass media including the Internet **provides us with** a wide variety of information. However, it is not always beneficial to us. People tend to select only the information or ideas they would like to read or listen to. Of course, it is a great ability to select only what they need in the ocean of information. But just as eating only what they want is not good, selecting only the information that they want is not good, either. This kind of **partial attitude** towards information interrupts us from taking the world **as it is**. That is, we look at the world through the newspaper, TV or Internet, which decide what we should **believe in**. Therefore we should remember that there could be **more than one argument** about an issue.

여: 인터넷을 포함한 대중매체는 우리에게 다양한 정보를 제공해 준다. 하지만 그것이 우리에게 언제나 유익한 것은 아니다. 사람들은 자신들이 읽고 싶거나 듣고 싶은 정보만을 선택하려는 경향이 있다. 물론 정보의 바닷속에서 필요한 정보를 선택하는 것은 매우 훌륭한 능력이다. 하지만 먹고 싶은 음식만 먹는 것이 좋은 것이 아니듯 원하는 정보만을 취하는 것 또한 옳은 일이 아니다. 이런 식의 편향된 태도는 우리가 세상을 있는 그대로 바라보지 못하도록 한다. 즉 우리는 우리가 무엇을 믿어야 하는지 결정해주는 신문이나 TV, 또는 인터넷을 통해 세상을 보는 것이다. 그러므로 우리는 하나의 문제에 대해 하나 이상의 논점이 있을 수 있음을 기억해야 한다.

해설: 화자는 편향된 정보 선택을 비판하고 있고, 다양한 관점에서 문제를 바라보는 것이 중요하다고 주장하고 있다.

Listening Web

Intro: would	Web 1: ocean
Web 2: selecting	Web 3: from
Ending: argument	

True / False

1. F	2. F	3. T	4. T

문항 8 ③

Script & Dictation

M: You may have heard that you're **legally responsible for** your spouse's debts, if any. Likewise, the same rules should apply in society. I don't think we can avoid our collective responsibility for the **crimes committed** in our community. If a person is starving to death, who can blame a person for stealing some food? If somebody cannot get proper educational opportunities in time, he will try to improve his social status **by all means** available. Even though he behaves against common sense at the time, we cannot **punish** him **for his ignorance**. In addition, if a person grows up in an environment without refined manners or moral guidance, he never knows what standards are expected in society. Now we're supposed to **take measures** to lessen the economic gap and get rid of ignorance. It is the welfare state that many countries pursue these days.

남: 여러분은 자기 배우자의 빚에 대해 자신도 법적인 책임이 있다는 것을 들어보았을 것이다. 마찬가지로 같은 규칙이 사회에 적용되어야 한다. 우리는 우리 사회 안에서 일어나는 범죄에 대한 연대 책임을 피할 수 없을 것이다. 만약 어떤 사람이 굶주려서 죽어간다면, 그 사람이 음식을 훔친 것을 누가 탓할 수 있겠는가? 만약 어떤 사람이 제때에 교육받을 기회를 잡지 못했다면, 그는 가능한 모든 수단을 동원하여 사회적 지위를 상승시키려고 노력할 것이다. 그러던 중 그가 상식에 어긋나는 행동을 한다고 해서, 그의 무지를 벌할 수 없다. 또한 만약 세련된 예의나 도덕적인 가르침이 없는 환경에서 성장한 사람이 있다면, 그는 사회가 어떤 규범을 기대하는지 알 턱이 없다. 이제 우리는 경제적인 격차를 줄이고 무지를 없애기 위한 조치를 취해야 한다. 이것이 오늘날 많은 국가들이 추구하는 복지 국가인 것이다.

해설: 가난이나 무지로 말미암은 범죄에 대한 책임을 온전히 개인에게 묻는 것은 무리가 있으며, 사회가 이 문제에 대해 연대 책임을 져야 한다고 주장하고 있다.

Listening Web

Intro: collective, committed   Web 1: status

Web 2: punish   Web 3: refined, expected

Ending: economic

True / False

1. T   2. F   3. T   4. T

문항 9 ⑤

Script & Dictation

W: The Greeks **used to be** able to recite all of Homer, because they had learned his works **by heart**. Printing techniques had not been developed yet, so there wasn't a large volume of books. Reciting the whole book or story was the only way to share knowledge. Now we can't even remember the names of our classmates only a few years after graduation. We think we can look up the old buddy's name in the album any time. The printing press has destroyed our memory. I don't think many of you remember your close friend's phone number. We **store all the numbers** in a tiny and handy cell phone, and

manage to remember the fact that we have the number in the phone. Navigation systems tell us the smartest route in traffic, but thanks to them, we don't need to remember the map. Smart people have created **great inventions**, but people seem to be **losing their memory**.

여: 그리스인들은 호머의 시집 전체를 외울 수 있었다. 왜냐하면 그들은 그것을 암기하는 방식으로 배웠기 때문이다. 인쇄술이 아직 발달하지 않아서 대량의 서적들이 없었다. 책이나 이야기 전체를 암기하는 것이 지식을 공유할 수 있는 유일한 방법이었다. 지금 우리는 졸업을 하고 몇 년 후면 학급 친구의 이름조차 기억하지 못한다. 우리는 언제든지 동창의 이름을 앨범에서 찾아보면 된다고 생각한다. 인쇄기가 우리의 기억을 망쳐놓았다. 여러분 가운데 친한 친구의 전화번호를 기억하고 있는 사람은 많지 않을 것이라고 생각한다. 우리는 모든 전화번호를 작고 유용한 휴대폰에 저장해 두고, 휴대폰에 번호를 저장해 두었다는 사실만을 가까스로 기억하고 있다. 네비게이션은 교통 체증 속에서 우리에게 빠른 길을 안내해 주지만, 네비게이션 덕분에 우리는 지도를 기억할 필요가 없다. 똑똑한 사람들이 위대한 발명을 해냈지만, 사람들은 기억을 잃어가고 있는 것 같다.

해설: 기술이 발달한 현대 사회를 살아가는 우리는 무언가를 암기할 필요가 없어지고 있다.

Listening Web

Intro: had   Web 2: close

Web 3: map   Ending: losing

True / False

1. F   2. T   3. T   4. F

문항 10 ④

Script & Dictation

M: Why are some people **willing to take risks** whereas others want to be safe? Although the risk of danger may be real, **perception** of the risk can **vary** from person to person, or from time to time. How many among you would walk on a line strung ten meters above the ground? But some people do it on an almost daily basis and **think nothing of it**. Most people won't take the same risks at fifty as they did at twenty. Age tends to convince us that death is a reality while the young people think it will happen to somebody else. Sometimes the **vision** of future rewards can **cloud our assessment** of danger. Some people are willing to work in very dangerous environments for a high salary. They think money is worth taking risks. And some young adults drive a car very fast with a desire for social admiration.

남: 왜 어떤 사람들은 안전하기를 바라는 반면, 어떤 사람들은 기꺼이 위험을 감수할까? 비록 그 위험이 현실이라 해도, 사람마다 또는 시기마다 위험을 감지하는 것이 다양하기 때문이다. 땅으로부터 10미터 위에 매달려 있는 줄 위를 걸을 사람이 여러분들 중 몇 명이나 될까? 하지만 어떤 사람들은 매일 그 일을 하고 아무렇지도 않게 생각한다. 대부분 사람들은 50세에는 20세 때 했던 것처럼 위험을 감수하지는 않는다. 나이는 죽음을 현실로 인식하게 하는 경향이 있는 반면 젊은 사람들은 죽음이란 내가 아닌 다른 누군가에게 일어나는 일이라고 생각한다. 때때로 미래의 보상에 대한 기대가 우리가 위험을 평가하는데 판단력을 흐리게 할 수도 있다. 어떤 사람들은 높은 봉급 때문에 매우 위험한 환경에서 기꺼이 일한다. 그들은 돈이 위험을 감수할 가치가 있다고 생각하는 것이다. 또 젊은이들은 사람들의 감탄에 대한 열망으로 엄청나게 빠른 속도로 차를 몰기도 한다.

해설: 사람마다 위험을 다르게 감지하며, 차후의 보상이 위험에 대한 판단을 흐리게 하기 때문이다.

Listening Web

Intro: whereas

Web 1: perception

Web 2: convince

Web 3: vision of

Web 4: worth

Ending: desire

True / False

1. T   2. F   3. T   4. T